13.15

`D1200260`

Fatherland
or
Promised Land

Fatherland
or
Promised Land

The Dilemma of the German Jew, 1893–1914

by
Jehuda Reinharz

Ann Arbor   The University of Michigan Press

To the memory of my grandfather

HERMAN HERZL WEIGLER

(October 12, 1883 — February 10, 1963)

whose classic journey from Galicia to Germany to Israel culminated in three decades of selfless devotion to those who made the journey after him.

Preface

The dilemma of the Jews in Germany reflects the struggle of all Western European Jewries in the postemancipation period. To understand its complexity, the dilemma must be seen as a coalescence of three paradoxes. The first was the emergence of vituperative German political and radical anti-Semitism that flew in the face of the simultaneously espoused idealistic principle of emancipation. In the presence of this contradiction, each German Jew sought to resolve his own inner conflict between the equally compelling ideological concepts of *Deutschtum* and *Judentum;* accordingly, each was forced to examine his loyalties to German nationality and culture on the one hand and to Jewishness on the other. Among the questions that had to be answered by the postemancipation Jew were: Which was the real Germany, the Germany of emancipation or the Germany of the anti-Semites? and If *Deutschtum* is inherently anti-Semitic, could a Jew participate in it?

Since this conflict affected all segments of German Jewry, a variety of organizations emerged, each adopting a different stance along the ideological continuum of *Deutschtum* and *Judentum*. Within this range of German Jewish organizations, a second paradox appeared. The ideological spokesmen for these organizations felt constrained to represent the positions of their members accurately without endangering the security of the German Jews by the very pronouncement of their ideology.

The third paradox was that, since each organization defined the convictions of a discrete sector of German Jewry vis-à-vis *Deutschtum* and *Judentum* and thus dealt with the anti-Semites in its own individual way, each one felt threatened by the differing positions adopted by every other German Jewish organization.

This book focuses on the emergence of two such organizations—the *Centralverein deutscher Staatsbuerger juedischen Glaubens* and the *Zionistische Vereinigung fuer Deutschland,* and on the ideological conflict between them. The organizations were, from their beginnings at the turn of the century until their dissolution under the Nazis in the 1930s, the most dynamic forces in German Jewry. The conflict between them had quickened the crystallization of their respective ideologies even before 1914. It is, therefore, useful and logical to confine this examination to the period between the inception of the organizations and the first rumblings of World War I.

To understand the dilemmas that surfaced during the two decades from 1893 to 1914 necessitates a thorough comprehension of the period immediately preceding. The introductory chapter, therefore, is an attempt to adumbrate (for the first time in English) the major features of this period without pretending to be an exhaustive treatment. This important lacuna awaits a future historian. In addition to the need for a sketch of the period before 1893, it is occasionally important to indicate developments after 1914 so that the analysis may not be cut short in an artificial or arbitrary manner. In any study periodization is a mixed blessing; while it helps the historian to focus on his topic, it can also unduly restrict his vision should he hesitate to transcend his self-imposed boundaries.

For encouragement and guidance during all phases of this manuscript I would like to thank the following people: Professor Walter Z. Laqueur originally suggested that I study German anti-Zionism, and Dr. Robert Weltsch provided useful comments in formulating the problem. For their continuous concern and interest I am grateful to Professors Alexander Altmann, Nahum N. Glatzer, and Ben Halpern. I was most fortunate to have the advice of Professor Ben Halpern, whose insight and constructive criticism are present in every stage of the book.

During my research visits in Israel in 1970–71 and 1973, I benefited from conversations with Dr. Shalom Adler-Rudel, Dr. Siegfried Moses, Dr. Pinhas Rosen, and Professor Gershom Scholem. Professor Jacob Toury of Tel Aviv University made useful comments on the entire manuscript. Dr. Michael Heymann, director of the Central Zionist Archives in Jerusalem, made suggestions concerning my treatment of German Zionism, while Dr. Arnold Paucker, director of the Leo Baeck Institute in London, carefully examined my analysis of the *Centralverein deutscher Staatsbuerger juedischen Glaubens.* Dr. Abraham Margaliot of the Hebrew University in Jerusalem read my manuscript with extraordinary thoroughness and was a most exacting critic, much to my benefit. Dr. Jochanan Ginat, director of the Leo Baeck Institute in Jerusalem, drew my attention to the need for a more exact formulation of general theories. Professor Ismar Schorsch of the Jewish Theological Seminary in New York City shared with me his knowledge of the period and commented on all sections of the manuscript. Thanks are also due to Professor Uriel Tal of Tel Aviv University for elucidating certain historiographical problems. Needless to say, despite the assistance of these scholars, I alone assume responsibility for every aspect of this book.

The following archives made their holdings available to me: the Central Archives for the History of the Jewish People (Jerusalem); Yad Vashem Archives (Jerusalem); Oral History Division of the Institute of Contemporary Jewry (Hebrew University, Jerusalem); the Buber Archives (Jerusalem); the Schwadron Archives (Jerusalem); the Schocken Archives (Jerusalem); the Weizmann Archives (Rechovot); and the Leo Baeck Institute Archives (New York).

Financial support for this project was granted at various stages by the Woodrow Wilson National Fellowship Foundation, the American Friends of the Hebrew University, and the Memorial Foundation for Jewish Culture. The National Foundation for Jewish Culture made special efforts to assist me financially and showed interest in the progress of the manuscript from its beginning until its completion. I am grateful to the Horace H. Rackham School of Graduate Studies of the University of Michigan for its generous support.

I would also like to acknowledge with thanks the permission of the Conference on Jewish Social Studies to include in this book a modified version of my article, *"Deutschtum* and *Judentum* in the Ideology of the 'Centralverein deutscher Staatsbuerger juedischen Glaubens,' 1893–1914," which appeared in *Jewish Social Studies* 36 (January, 1974). I am grateful to Professor Michael A. Fishbane and Dr. Paul R. Flohr, editors of *Texts and Responses: Studies Presented to Nahum N. Glatzer* (1975), and to the publisher, E. J. Brill, for permission to incorporate a revised version of "Consensus and Conflict between Zionists and Liberals in Germany before World War I."

Thanks are due to Mrs. Esther Rentschler for typing the final manuscript and to Sister Claudia Carlen, I.H.M., librarian of St. John's Provincial Seminary, for preparing the index. Mrs. Alice Gibson scrutinized the manuscript with her superb editorial skill; her care and concern for every detail are sincerely appreciated.

Finally my gratitude to my wife cannot be sufficiently expressed within the context of these acknowledgments. Her intellectual partnership made the writing of this book a rewarding experience for both of us.

Contents

I

German Jewry's Reactions
to Anti-Semitism: 1848–93

The years 1848 and 1869 loom as landmarks in the history of
the emancipation of German Jews. German Jewry in general
believed that legal emancipation would destroy the last vestiges of the discrimination and isolation that separated them
from their Christian fellow citizens. Reality proved to be
quite different. The legal bulwark of emancipation provided a
very shaky protection. Reaction against emancipation developed in 1848 and again with greater force in 1869. The
German Jews, having fought hard to gain the rights of citizenship and having witnessed the actual fulfillment of their
highest hopes, were surprised and confused in the face of this
hostility. Emancipation led to a gradual dissolution of the
German Jewish community[1] to the extent that not one
Jewish organization nor congregation (*Gemeinde*) and not a
single leader of the Jewish community considered formulating a unified Jewish response to the anti-Jewish attacks.
Organization implied a distinct and common identity; precisely that which the Jewish community wanted to avoid.

No significant replies were made to anti-Semitism by
large segments of the German Jewish community until the
1890s when two organizations were created: the *Centralverein deutscher Staatsbuerger juedischen Glaubens* (here-

after referred to as C.V.) and the *Zionistische Vereinigung fuer Deutschland* (hereafter referred to as ZVfD). The striking difference between their responses to anti-Semitism was that the C.V. formed an organized Jewish defense, whereas the Zionists turned their attention almost exclusively to internal Jewish affairs. The reactions of the two organizations can be understood only in the light of German Jewish history between 1848 and 1893.

Emancipation and Reaction: 1848–69

From its very beginning, the German revolution of 1848 was coupled with violence against the Jews. The peasant revolts which erupted in the early months of 1848 were most serious in the Odenwald and Black Forest regions. The revolts began with anti-Jewish manifestations in Neckar-bischofsheim, Breisgau, and Muehlheim. One peasant leaflet proclaimed that the goal of the revolution was, among other things, "the banishment of all Jews from Germany."[2] The Jewish community, however, dismissed the outbreaks as incidental, momentary aberrations on the part of excited crowds.[3] There was a tendency to ignore the outbreaks altogether. Leopold Zunz (1794–1886) believed that the violence would present no obstacle to Jewish emancipation.[4] Martin Philippson (1846–1916), despite his historical perspective on the events around 1848, minimized as much as possible the import of the anti-Semitic outbreaks that accompanied the revolution. Anti-Semitic manifestations did not deter the Jews from participating enthusiastically in the revolutionary skirmishes. At least 130 Jews took part in the armed battles in Berlin and Frankfurt, in the uprisings in Baden, Sachsen, and the Pfalz, in the fighting at Posen and Schleswig Holstein, as well as in many other smaller conflicts.[5] It was even claimed that the revolution in Berlin had been instigated by "Frenchmen, Poles, and Jews"; the proof advanced for this claim was that among the 230 revolutionaries who were killed, at least 21 were Jews.[6]

The outbreak of the revolution had been hailed by almost all German Jews as the harbinger of complete emancipation. Ludwig Philippson (1811–89) called 1848 the "year of freedom; a year in which general equality and personal freedom were to be realized as the fundamental truths of society."[7] Leopold Zunz's literally messianic fervor was an extreme example of the excitement and enthusiasm that gripped the entire German Jewish community:

> He [Leopold Zunz] expected the revolution to bring Messianic fulfillment. He hoped for a development that would "soon, in our time," or, at least, in a foreseeable future, lead to a complete termination of what he termed a "medieval" system and to the rise of democracy, an essentially new era of the freedom of man and the union of nations.[8]

For a while it seemed that these expectations would be fulfilled. Germany incorporated the idea of emancipation[9] into programmatic form and actually attempted to implement it. The revolution was accompanied by a flood of petitions from non-Jews who demanded freedom of religion for themselves and their Jewish fellow citizens. When such stipulations were not made, they were clearly implied by the context. In spite of the violence, the dominant spirit of the German people was idealistic and the primary motif, brotherhood. Public opinion was in favor of granting all political rights to the Jews who had demonstrated their willingness to die for the ideals of the revolution.[10]

On May 18, 1848, the National Assembly convened in St. Paul's Church in Frankfurt am Main, and in Berlin the Prussian Assembly met to discuss and draw up new constitutions.[11] Election to the assemblies was based on the equal voting rights of all German citizens, regardless of religion. [12] Jews were also elected as deputies: the Prussian Assembly included such influential Jewish politicians as the physicians Johann Jacoby (1805–77) and Raphael Kosch (1803–72); the assembly in Frankfurt included Gabriel Riesser (1806–63) (Hamburg), and Moritz Veit (1808–64) of Berlin, as well as the Austrians Moritz Hartmann (1821–72) and Ignaz Kuranda (1812–84).[13] Gabriel Riesser, for many years the leading protagonist in the struggle for Jewish emancipation, was elected second vice-president of the assembly in October, 1848.[14]

In the assembly at Frankfurt Riesser succeeded in defeating a proposal by Moritz Mohl that Jews be excluded from the application of paragraph 13 of the proposed constitution, which stated that the rights of every citizen were in no way to be limited by race.[15] On December 21, 1848, the "Declaration of Fundamental Rights" was passed.[16] Paragraph 16 of the Declaration stated: "The enjoyment of civil [*buergerlich*] and political [*Staats-buergerlich*] rights should not be limited or conditioned by religious belief." Paragraph 17 granted religious communities freedom in the administration of their affairs. Paragraph 20 instituted civil marriage and declared that religion should not constitute a deterrent in any matters concerning marriage.[17] The Declaration also provided for freedom of movement for everyone within the German Reich, for the freedom of person, speech, assembly, and press,[18] a guarantee upheld by the revised constitution of January 31, 1850. The other northern and southern German states soon followed suit and incorporated these fundamental rights into their constitutions.[19]

In Prussia two additional articles to the "Declaration" were of great importance to the Jews. Article 4 provided for the equality of the rights of citizens in general. Article 12 stipulated that all citizens were to have equal access to public office and to enjoy civil and political rights without fear of discrimination on the grounds of religious belief.[20]

Soon after the revolution, a reaction developed and became manifest in legal setbacks for German Jewry.[21] In Prussia, article 12 was declared inapplicable to Jews who sought admission to the judiciary or to a teaching faculty. The government invoked article 14 which based those institutions of the state relating to the exercise of religious conviction upon the Christian religion, notwithstanding the freedom of religion guaranteed by article 12.[22] Other German states soon followed, proclaiming in the spirit of Friedrich Julius Stahl that the Christian nature of the state should not be violated.[23] As a consequence most German states withdrew some of the privileges granted to Jews in 1848.[24]

In Prussia the editor of the conservative *Kreuzzeitung* suggested in 1856, that article 12 be stricken from the constitution, but his motion was defeated under protest of the Jewish community. This, however, was a Pyrrhic victory. The minister of the interior declared no need to amend the constitution since it provided that in all religious matters Christianity should be regarded as fundamental, a sufficient grounds for excluding non-Christians from judicial, administrative, and other state offices.[25]

Seemingly, the Italian liberation and unification movement that began in 1859 changed the political climate in Germany to one of greater tolerance.[26] The new liberalism first appeared in legislative action; in 1861, restrictions on the Jews' political rights were removed in Wuerttemberg and the Electorate of Hesse. Between 1861 and 1864, Jews were granted full civil rights in Bavaria, Wuerttemberg, and Baden. At the convening of the North German Diet in 1867, a petition was presented from 371 Jewish communities requesting the removal of all religious restrictions on civil and political rights. Moritz Wiggers, a member of the Diet and a veteran of the revolution of 1848, introduced a bill encompassing the main demands of the petition that was adopted by an overwhelming majority.[27] Only on July 3, 1869, however, did the Federal Council representing the "Allied Governments" of northern Germany accept the text of the resolution:

> All restrictions on civil and political rights are hereby abolished. In particular, the ability to participate in communal and state affairs and to become public representatives should be independent of religious belief.[28]

With the unification of Germany, this law was incorporated in the German constitution of January 11, 1871.[29] In Bavaria the final emancipation of the Jews was accomplished by the adoption of the constitution of the Reich in 1872.[30]

The struggle for emancipation then, which had begun at the turn of the nineteenth century, had made considerable progress by 1848, and it was successfully completed in the years between 1869 and 1872. Those Jews who had witnessed and participated in the events of 1848 recognized the culmination as a crucial turning point in their history. Their belief in progress and liberalism, strengthened in 1848, was reconfirmed in 1869 when their demands were coupled with the cause of universal freedom and emancipation. The importance of Jewish freedom for the general welfare of the fatherland was indeed a theme often repeated by German Jews. Riesser had always emphasized that the Germans who supported Jewish demands for equality and justice were, in fact, supporting the very essence of liberalism. By the same token he stressed that Jews who fought for their own freedom were fighting at the same time for a free and enlightened Germany.[31] To German Jewry it seemed that with the unification of the Reich, Riesser's words had come true. The Jews who remembered the revolution of 1848, the wars of the 1860s, and the struggle for unification, had a sense of unity and brotherhood with their Christian fellows. In 1871 their dream seemed to have been fulfilled; their demands were in fact accepted as an integral part of the new German constitution. They now shared with all other Germans "one Kaiser, one Reich and one nation."[32]

The Socioeconomic Impact of Emancipation

The events of 1848 and 1869 had a positive effect on the German Jewish community's economic and social status. Germany was beginning its transformation from an agrarian to an industrialized state. Migration flowed from the countryside to the cities, from eastern Germany to the central and western sections. Large urban centers arose and with them new living conditions, an urban proletariat, and new political trends.

The internal migration of the German Jewish population more than kept pace with the popular movement to the cities. In Berlin the growth in the Jewish community between 1840 and 1871 was from 6,456 to 30,015 or from 2 percent to 3.3 percent of the population; in Cologne from 615 to 3,172 or from .89 percent to 2.45 percent. In Breslau the Jewish population of 6,000 in 1840 had tripled by 1880. Between

1814 and 1866, Frankfurt increased its Jewish population from 5,007 to 8,000 and Hamburg from 7,000 Jews to 12,550. A rate of extremely rapid growth was also registered in Dresden and Hannover,[33] whereas the reverse was true in the eastern sections of Germany, a fact partly due to Jewish emigration to the United States.[34] The Jewish communities of Mecklenburg, Pommern, and West Prussia declined rapidly. Posen, which in 1843 still had 79,575 Jews, had 61,982 in 1871, and only 56,609 in 1880, a reduction of about 34 percent. Whereas the Jewish migration paralleled and even exceeded the prevailing pattern, their percentage within the general population gradually declined. In 1871 their total number was 512,153, by 1890, 567,884.[35] Although these figures show an increase in the absolute numbers, they do represent a decline in their ratio to the total population from 1.33 to 1.14 percent. Their birthrate declined from 37 per thousand to 22, whereas the birthrate of the Christian population remained constant at 38 per thousand.[36]

With their concentration in the large urban centers, Jewish economic opportunities widened. Bankers and businessmen (such as Rathenau, Reichenheim, Bleichroeder) were active in the development of German industry, banking, and commerce,[37] although Jews almost totally disappeared from agriculture.[38] In accordance with the new socioeconomic stratification, the percentage of Jewish high school and university students increased markedly. By 1860, for example, Jews comprised nearly 6 percent of all students in secondary schools, a trend matched in the higher institutions of learning.[39]

Jews were making modest gains in public service and politics as well. Eduard Lasker (1829–84) and Ludwig Bamberger (1823–99), leaders of the National Liberal party, and Bismarck's allies during his political maneuvers against other parties wielded considerable power. Even after Bismarck threw his support to the Conservatives, they remained Liberal leaders. Still, Jews in high public office were rare; Moritz Ellstaetter (1827–1905), the Minister of Finance in Baden, was the only Jew to hold so exalted a rank before 1918. At a lower level, however, Jews had gained access to the teaching professions and by 1880 one hundred Jewish judges sat in the lower courts.[40] The only profession systematically closed to Jews until 1914 was the army's officer corps.[41]

The Dissolution of Jewish Communal Life

The rapid integration of the Jews into the German state was coupled with a simultaneous disintegration of the Jewish community and its major institutions. This dissolution was largely the result of a new Weltanschauung developed by the Jewish community after the revolution of 1848. The Jews had believed that a new era was beginning in which they would be accepted by their peers simply as human beings.[42] In 1848 the ideology expressed during the French Revolution and the French-Jewish Sanhedrin finally triumphed: there was no longer a Jewish nationality, but instead only German Jews of the Mosaic faith. For many Jews the revolution of 1848 and the final emancipation act of 1869 had replaced their religion by the secular belief in progress. Liberal ideologies took the place of theology, although Jews claimed that their political activities reflected the "true spirit" of Judaism.[43]

The Jewish community was further weakened by numerous conversions to Christianity. Between 1822 and 1840, 2,200 Jews converted to Christianity in Prussia alone. Between 1841 and 1880, the number of converts increased to 7,000;[44] taking into account their slow increase in absolute numbers and the decline of the Jewish birthrate during the same period, these figures represent a substantial increase. Those who converted removed themselves from everything that could identify them as Jews and eschewed involvement in Jewish affairs.

Even those who retained their identification with the Jewish tradition lost their cohesiveness and were religiously divided into four distinct groups: the *Reformgemeinde* in Berlin, liberals, conservatives (community orthodox), and the neo-orthodox.[45] Each group established its own newspapers, rabbinical seminaries, synagogues, and even welfare institutions. Only rarely could these groups agree on united action; each sought to defend its vested interests against encroachment by the others. Their antipathies persisted even in the face of the intolerance directed toward them all. During the riots that accompanied the revolution of 1848, the various religious leaders made no effort to cooperate in helping Jews who had been injured physically or economically. Instead, the anti-Jewish outbreaks seemed only to increase intra-Jewish tensions, and both the orthodox and liberal groups expended their energies throughout the disturbances in continual depreciation of the other.[46]

The internal divisions of German Jewry were further intensified by the abyss that separated the lay leadership from the religious groups. A large percentage of the generation of German Jewish politicians that followed Riesser either converted to Christianity or did their utmost to conceal their Jewish heritage. These parliamentarians who had committed themselves to the political parties were understandably anxious to suppress any impression of Jewish cohesion that might damage their careers. It was only on rare occasions that politicians, such as Heinrich Bernhard Oppenheim (1819–80), Levin Goldschmidt (1829–97), Ludwig Bamberger, or Eduard Lasker, pressed by particularly offensive anti-Semitic charges, defended the loyalty of the German Jews to their fatherland, and even then their statements were apologetic and replete with patriotic phraseology. Eduard Lasker, for example, who spoke for Jewish emancipation in 1869, hastened to add that his action was "out of the ordinary, since I am not usually in the habit of defending my coreligionists . . . because after all, it might seem as if I were speaking for my own person."[47] It was clear that the posture of the Jewish parliamentarians was not conducive to Jewish unity under their leadership.

Other factors contributed to the dissolution. Each German state made its own laws in respect to the Jewish communities within its jurisdiction. The southwest German states encouraged close bonds between individual Jewish communities, whereas the northern states discouraged such tendencies. The Prussian situation was more complicated. According to the Law of 1847, the areas that fell to Prussia retained their ancient Jewish rights, and thus twelve different definitions of the position of the Jewish communities there existed side by side. The confusion was reflected in the legal names of the communities. In Bavaria they were called *Kultusgemeinden,* in Prussia *Synagogengemeinden,* in Baden and Wuerttemberg *Kirchen* and later *Religionsgemeinden*, in Saxony and Hessen they were called *Religionsgemeinden.* [48]

From the middle of the nineteenth century all Jewish communities were recognized as "public bodies," in the technical term used by the state, and compulsory membership was accepted by all German states until 1876. [49] All communities were entitled to levy taxes on their members. Beyond these basic requirements, rules and regulations for the communities and their members varied widely. [50] The communities had been created to serve as an encompassing structure for the individual Jew, but as these structures were breached by emancipation and equal citizenship, the communities turned their attention almost exclusively to social welfare, philanthropy, and synagogue organization.

The legal position of the Jews in the German states added to the organizational difficulties. The legislators of 1848 hoped to grant the individual Jew legal and even political rights and to integrate him into the state, but they were not anxious to help German Jewry organize into a coherent whole. By isolating Jewish communities, they were preventing the formation of effective national organizations. [51] In 1869–72 the communities organized a philanthropic national group called the *Deutsch-Israelitischer Gemeindebund* only under great difficulties, and even then it was not recognized as an official spokesman for these communities. The internal divisions within the Jewish communities meant that the state could deal with them as it wished, and the state in fact often denied them state subsidies. Although the Jewish community was legally on an equal basis with the Christian community, it was treated significantly worse. [52] In sharp contrast, the state placed no obstacles in the way of groups like the *Trennungsorthodoxie,* which further divided the community. When Rabbi Samson Raphael Hirsch (1808–88), with the help of Esriel Hildesheimer (1820–99) and Eduard Lasker, asked to secede from the Jewish community on the grounds

of conscience, the state gave ready permission, and the Seces-
sion Law was passed on July 28, 1876.[53]

Attempts at Organization: The Deutsch-Israelitischer
Gemeindebund

Leaders of the Jewish community had long been aware of its
anomalous position. Ludwig Philippson, the publisher of the
Allgemeine Zeitung des Judentums, suggested in 1848 that a
Synod be formed to unify German Jewry on a religious basis
and to propose guidelines for religious reform. In 1850 the
Berlin community proposed the establishment of a central
authority for the Prussian Jewish community along the lines
of the Central Consistory in Paris, but both proposals failed
for lack of concerted agreement.[54] Some influential individuals, such as Leopold Zunz and Abraham Geiger (1810–74),
unequivocally opposed a central organization lest it impinge
on the freedom of the communities.[55] In Leipzig, on June
29, 1869, a Synod, made up of eighty-three leaders and
rabbis from Germany and abroad, was finally convened under
the chairmanship of Moritz Lazarus (1824–1903). Although
its members heard impassioned speeches about the compatibility of Judaism with the basic concepts of the new
Prussian state, the Synod took no organized action, and no
permanent central institution emerged.[56]

Additionally, a few Jewish communities formed a voluntary association, the *Deutsch-Israelitischer Gemeindebund*
(hereafter referred to as D.I.G.B.) on June 29, 1869. The
association became a permanent organization only after it
had acquired the necessary one hundred *Gemeinden* on April
14, 1872, and had established its seat in Leipzig.[57] When the
German Reich was created in 1871 the D.I.G.B. continued,
but without official recognition by the state. In 1882 the
D.I.G.B. moved to Berlin, where it became the largest Jewish
organization in Germany and at its height served 1,200 communities.[58]

The D.I.G.B. attempted to represent the *Gemeinden* under its jurisdiction before the state authorities in all matters
concerning social welfare and communal administration. Its
activities touched many areas: it founded a "Historical Com-

mission for the History of the Jews in Germany" which published important studies,[59] subsidized Jewish education and community religious instruction, and made significant strides in social welfare.[60] The D.I.G.B.'s primary objective was "the exchange of experiences in matters of administration and especially in the promotion of the common interests of German Jews."[61] These interests were interpreted as economic and educational; interference in political activity or in matters related to ritual observance was excluded.[62]

The D.I.G.B. also excluded the contest against anti-Semitism from its sphere of numerous activities. Its constitution, reprinted in its official organ in 1898, enumerated those matters in which it was permitted to take part, but defense against anti-Semitism was a striking omission. The reasons behind this lack of interest in one of the most pressing concerns of German Jewry was never made clear, except for a vague statement by the leadership that to undertake such action would overextend the resources and capabilities of the organization.[63] This was clearly a poor excuse from an organization that supported numerous funds and institutions and boasted an administrative and bureaucratic machinery extending throughout Germany.[64]

The real reasons for the D.I.G.B.'s inertia probably lay in its structure and the nature of its leadership. As in most other German organizations and community boards, the leadership of the D.I.G.B. was not democratically elected by the entire membership, but rather came from a small and powerful circle of Jewish notables. Its first presidents—Moritz Kohner (1818–77), Jacob Nachod (1814–82), and Samuel Kristeller (1820–1900)—were highly acculturated, upper-class Jews, disinclined to radical reform and unwilling to disturb the status quo lest it unsettle their own base of power as well. Under their influence, the D.I.G.B. reacted to anti-Semitism by adopting the proven and traditional medieval role of intercessor (*Shtadlanut* in Hebrew; *Fuerbitte/Fuersprache* in German). The D.I.G.B. relied on the justice and authority of the state in the belief that, when called upon, the proper authorities would protect the physical and legal rights of the German Jews. Therefore the leaders of the D.I.G.B., while issuing leaflets and brochures in defense of German Jewry, turned to the state in times of emergency. After the founding of the *Centralverein deutscher Staatsbuerger juedishen Glaubens* in 1893, the D.I.G.B. abandoned even these activities and turned all its energies to philanthropic and welfare causes.

Anti-Semitism after 1871: Reactions of the Jewish Establishment

The German Reich was founded on January 18, 1871. Many expected the long-awaited unification to usher in an era of constructive cooperation among all the former German states, as well as among all religious and political parties. The German Jews welcomed the change as an indication of stability and a promise of new freedom.[65] The constitution of Bismarck, however, was not to eliminate the social and political problems of the new state. Tensions continued between Prussia and the other German states, between the new industrial and commercial classes and the old feudal agrarian classes. The newly annexed territories of the Reich added to its heterogeneity. In June, 1871, Bismarck, supported by the National Liberals and Progressives, began his Kulturkampf against the Catholics, a program that continued with great intensity throughout the 1870s.[66] In addition, economic depressions in 1873 and 1877 ruined hundreds of industries and caused great hardship to large segments of the population.[67]

The political, social, religious, and economic troubles of the Reich set the stage for the anti-Semitic attacks that set in soon after unification and came from all quarters. Pope Pius IX was one of the first to blame the Jews for the discrimination against German Catholics, and his arguments were eagerly embraced by the German Catholic Center party.[68] Another early assault came at the beginning of the depression from Wilhelm Marr (1818–1904), who is credited with coining the term "anti-Semitism."[69] In his *Der Sieg des Judentums ueber das Germanentum,* Marr warned that the Jews had become the dominant power in the West and were destroying the Teutonic nature of the German state. He urged the German people to resist this Jewish conquest with all the means at their disposal.[70] A series of articles labeling the Jews as "swindlers and financial racketeers" came from Otto Glagau (1834–92), who published the magazine *Die Gartenlaube* between 1874 and 1875. In 1877 he expanded his articles into a book, *Der Boersen und Gruendungs-schwindel in Deutschland.*[71] Among the conservatives who were at odds with the liberal policies of the Second Reich and blamed the Jews for its misfortunes were: Konstantin Frantz (1817–91),[72] Rudolf Meyer,[73] and Paul de Lagarde (Boettlicher) (1827–91).[74] Discontented elements, who saw Bismarck as dominated by Jews, were determined to eradicate the influence of the Jewish minority.[75]

In the midst of the Reich's turmoil and anti-Semitism, Bismarck changed his political orientation. In the early years after unification, he had relied on the support of the liberal parties, which included many Jews in their ranks and advocated full political and civic emancipation for the Jews. In the 1874 elections, the National Liberals won by an overwhelming majority; for a time they proved to be the strongest party in Germany.[76] In the mid-1870s, however, the Social Democratic party was coming to power, and it joined the left wing of the National Liberals in support of a parliamentary government. Bismarck, in defense of his authoritarian state, instituted social legislation and economic protectionism designed to appeal to the Conservatives and Catholics. Bismarck's alignment with the reactionary and anti-Jewish forces thus left the Jews without a patron in the political arena.[77]

The climate of opinion in Germany was favorable enough to the spread of anti-Semitism that the literary attacks of the early 1870s soon swelled into a mass movement popular among all strata of society. The first to capitalize on the unrest was Adolf Stoecker (1835–1909). Stoecker, whose patriotic fervor had caught the attention of the Imperial Court, was called to Berlin in 1874 as court preacher in the Domkirche. In this position Stoecker's word had the sanction of the state, a factor that he exploited in his political maneuvers. Stoecker imparted to anti-Semitism the respectability of his high office of court chaplain. Those middle-class groups who had felt a certain reluctance to endorse the anti-Jewish sentiments of the lower classes were now encouraged by one of Wilhelm I's most trusted servants to embrace anti-Semitism.

Stoecker's political career began on January 3, 1878, when he founded the *Christlich-soziale Arbeiterpartei* (Christian Social Workers' party).[78] An avowed opponent of Marxist philosophy, he hoped to unseat the Social Democrats by attracting the proletariat to a platform supporting church and state. When his party suffered a crushing defeat in 1878, Stoecker changed his tactics and turned to anti-Semitism as a more effective propagandistic approach to the middle classes. In 1879 he founded the "Berlin Movement," a cover organization that included Christian missionaries and Conservatives, united under the banner of anti-Semitism.

On September 19, 1879, Stoecker delivered the first in his series of lectures on Jews, entitled "Our demands to modern Judaism."[79] Stoecker firmly believed that the German state could exist only as a Christian state. He detested the new materialism that was so pervasive in Germany—an outgrowth of industrialization—and he held the Jews responsible for the capitalistic orientation that was drawing people away from the churches. He urged a Christian renaissance and a resurgence of devotion to the "crown and the church." He regarded the Jews as a hindrance to universal Christianization, accusing them of forming a state within a state. By proposing social, economic, and administrative measures prohibiting the employment of Jews in public institutions, he sought to reduce their influence.[80]

Like Stoecker, Wilhelm Marr too turned in 1878 from literary polemics to political and social attack. Marr's opposition to the Jews was not on religious, but on historical-racist grounds. His pamphlet, *Der Sieg des Judentums ueber das Germanentum*, first printed in the early 1870s, now received renewed publicity and popularity. In October, 1879, Marr founded the *Antisemiten Liga* (anti-Semitic league) whose declared aim was to "save the fatherland from complete Judaization." In 1880, he began the publication of his *Antisemitische Hefte* (anti-Semitic notebook).[81]

The Jewish community remained unmoved by the hostility of Stoecker and Marr. There were a few isolated replies by individuals, unsupported by the Jewish establishment. The *Frankfurter Zeitung* reported in October, 1879, that Stoecker's and Marr's theories were gaining wide acceptance; nevertheless, the paper advised its readers to refrain from appealing to the government lest such action spur the anti-Semites to more emphatic action. The editorial board of the *Allgemeine Zeitung des Judentums* supported this point of view:

> In our opinion, it would be very unfortunate to complain to the government about a few insults [*Schimpferein*] of religious fanatics. . . . This would only give members of these [anti-Semitic] circles . . . the chance to spread their accusations against us within the lawful legislating bodies of the government. Beware of such foolishness.[82]

The German branch of the *"Alliance Israélite Universelle"* at its meeting of December 8, 1879, in Erfurt discussed the course of events. The following resolution was adopted:

> We must maintain contemptuous silence toward the degrading assaults against Jews and Judaism. Slanders cast in a pseudo-scientific garment should be countered with the strictest scientific defense.[83]

Adolf Stoecker's stance signaled encouragement and support from the highest quarters of German society for all anti-Semites. Until its adoption by Stoecker, the supporters of anti-Semitism had been more or less obscure journalists and politicians whose ideology had been considered "eccentric and demagogic."[84] Under the patronage of Stoecker anti-Semitism became a force capable of unifying many small and insignificant groups into a political movement. The only class to remain unimpressed by Stoecker's religious office was the intellectual elite. Heinrich von Treitschke (1834–96), professor of history at the University of Berlin, was soon to provide the link to the German academic circles. "While the pastor had shaped an anti-Semitic movement of the lower middle classes in Germany, Treitschke's classroom became

created wide-ranging interest and controversy.[94] He was immediately labeled "anti-Semite" by Jews and Christians alike; though his remarks were more moderate than those of Stoecker or Marr and purported to be factual and unemotional, they were recognized everywhere as support and encouragement for anti-Semitism. Nevertheless, Treitschke, who repeated in his essay the most common and popular of the anti-Semitic charges, was not just another anti-Semite; he was a respected intellectual guardian of the honor and authority of the German state. By virtue of his position as professor of German history at one of the most prestigious universities of the Reich, Treitschke's pamphlet opened the academic circles of Germany to anti-Semitism. Both his students and colleagues were swayed by his lectures on the "Jewish Problem," and the topic became one of frequent discussion in the academic establishment. In view of his stature and importance, it is not surprising that many prominent Jews were determined to refute his allegations of their disloyalty to the Reich; they included rabbis, professors, and even one Jewish politician.[95] The replies remained, however, on a literary level, and no political action was taken by any organization within the Jewish community.

The most vigorous reply to Treitschke's article of November, 1879, came from Heinrich Graetz (1817–91), the only Jew who had been singled out by Treitschke as an advocate of a separate Jewish nationality. In an open letter, "Erwiderung an Herrn von Treitschke" published on December 7, 1879, in the *Schlesische Presse*,[96] Graetz took issue with Treitschke in vehement and uncompromising language. He interpreted Treitschke's statement that the Jewish historian was pompous and self-satisfied, despising German culture in favor of a Jewish national spirit, as an attack not only against himself, but against all German Jewry. As a consequence Graetz defended not only his *History*, but he also totally rejected the idea that the Jews were a harmful and foreign element within the state.[97] Graetz repeated, however, the charge he had made in his *History:* that medieval Christianity, in contrast to the early Christianity of love and truth toward all mankind, had become hypocritical, and he em-

phasized the church's harsh treatment of the Jews throughout the centuries.

On December 15, 1879, Treitschke responded with a
lengthy piece published in the *Preussische Jahrbuecher,* [98]
directed almost exclusively against Graetz. [99] Treitschke presented statistics to bolster his objections to the overwhelming
immigration of East European Jews into Germany. He repeated his demand that the Jews become a part of German
culture, a goal he conceded was not likely to be achieved.
Much of the article was devoted to an attack on Graetz's
History; Graetz was characterized as "a stranger on German
soil," a man who repudiated the great cultural traditions of
the German nation. [100]

Graetz responded immediately with a diatribe against
Treitschke's ignorance and willful misrepresentation of the
facts, and he justified the opinions expressed in his *History* as
those of a loyal German patriot. [101] As for the lack of
German partisanship in the eleventh volume of his *History*,
he had written that volume before the "glorious victory of
Germany" in 1871, and uncomplimentary passages were being revised for the English translation. [102] In addition, Graetz
held that Judaism was independent of Jewish nationalism,
and he implied, perhaps in order to appease his critics, that
he was not a Jewish nationalist. [103] This defensive response
was something of a misrepresentation, since Graetz's sympathies for Jewish nationalism were known—never in the past
had he seen a contradiction between Jewish nationalism and
German patriotism. [104]

Graetz's essay concluded with some modification of his
initially strong attack, perhaps because not a single important
Jewish leader nor politician had publicly sided with him. [105]
Even those Jews who had defended German Jewry against
Treitschke's charges of disloyalty hastened to register their
dissociation from Graetz. The historian Harry Bresslau
(1848–1926), a colleague of Treitschke's at the University of
Berlin, declared that German Jewry was not responsible for
the actions and opinions of Graetz. [106] Hermann Cohen
(1842–1918), a former student of Graetz, wrote in reference
to Graetz's support in his *History* of a separate Jewish culture
and identity:

Many will think that I have accorded the Palestinians among us too much consideration, because in reality they have no foothold within the German culture and as a party they are able to maintain a propagandistic sort of existence only because of the sick, untrue, and mindless religious currents of our times. But this touches upon a related mood that during quieter times would be distinctly separate from that of Mr. Graetz and would even oppose him. It is a pity that a Jewish historian, who after all has achieved a certain measure of fame, though to a limited degree, could have arrived at such a perverse emotional judgment.[107]

Attacks on Graetz came from other prominent Jews. Ludwig Bamberger called him "a Stoecker of the synagogue, a zealot and a fanatic."[108] H. B. Oppenheim and Manuel Joel (1826–90) also hastened to dissociate themselves from him.[109]

All the important Jewish personalities repudiated Graetz's arguments against Christianity and condemned his Jewish-national sympathies. Graetz was able to find support only among a few conservative rabbis, and from Moritz Guedemann of Vienna. Most Jewish intellectuals were apologetic and self-effacing in their replies to Treitschke. Manuel Joel, the Rabbi of the Breslau community, disputed Treitschke's theme of Jewish disloyalty to Germany only very superficially.[110] Moritz Lazarus spoke at the convocation of the *Hochschule fuer die Wissenschaft des Judentums* on December 2, 1879, on the theme "What Is the Meaning of National?"[111] Here he defined nationality as a subjective matter and claimed, therefore, that the Jews were loyal German citizens. True, they had to uphold their Jewish religion and heritage, but this did not make them foreigners. On the contrary, their heritage and values contributed and enriched German culture.[112] Hermann Cohen, the eminent Marburg philosopher, came closest to meeting Treitschke's demand that the Jews become assimilated in return for emancipation; he even urged them to strive for spiritual connections between Judaism and Christianity.[113]

The most apologetic and obsequious reply came from

Harry Bresslau. Bresslau defended neither Judaism nor German Jewry and sympathized with Treitschke's demand that the Jews be completely integrated within the German state, asking Treitschke for guidelines and suggestions to this end.[114]

It is significant that between 1879 and 1882, the period during which the debate around Treitschke's essay took place, there were twenty-six Jewish politicians in active service in the Reich.[115] Of these, only one, Ludwig Bamberger, entered the arena by presenting his point of view in an essay, *Deutschtum und Judentum*. Unlike Bresslau, Bamberger maintained that the Jewish "spirit" contributed constructively to the synthesis of *Deutschtum* and *Judentum* since the two cultures had much in common and were in no way antagonistic. Yet Bamberger's effort was marked by a spirit of apologetic argument and appeasement.[116]

Rebuttals by Jewish intellectuals such as Bamberger, Lazarus, and Cohen were at best shocked and confused responses to the sudden upsurge of anti-Semitism, which was especially disconcerting because German Jewry had assumed that final emancipation had been achieved in 1869. The defensive rejoinders had no expectations of establishing an independent Jewish position within Germany. With the exception of Heinrich Graetz, who implied repeatedly in his *History* that he hoped for a Jewish national renaissance, the intellectuals agreed that Judaism was a religion that did not interfere with complete loyalty to the state, and they denied loyalty to any international Jewish organization. They pointed out that fanatic Germanophile anti-Semites were in the minority, while stressing the German majority's support of Jewish emancipation, an assessment shared by all German Jewish organizations. When seventy-five prominent Germans, among them Theodor Mommsen and Johann Gustav Droysen, published a declaration against the anti-Semites, the Jewish community was vastly relieved; they interpreted this action as indicative of German support.[117]

The anti-Semitic movement that emerged between 1875 and 1880 provoked a mixed reaction from the general Jewish community. Some Jews wanted to leave the charges unanswered for fear of provoking further outbursts of hostile propaganda.[118] The exclusively Jewish newspapers, such as the *Allgemeine Zeitung des Judentums* and *Jeschurun* as well as the Jewish-owned *Berliner Tageblatt* and *Frankfurter Zeitung,* although aware of the mounting intensity of anti-Semitism throughout the Reich, were reluctant to acknowledge that a turning point had been reached in relations between Jews and Christians, and they therefore dismissed the hate propaganda as a temporary aberration. When it persisted, the official news media of the Jewish community identified the financial crisis and the struggle between the Catholic church and the state as the roots of this hatred. Thus the German Jewish community remained content and optimistic until Treitschke joined the anti-Semites. The respected scholar's opposition represented a decisive turn for the worse.[119]

German Jewry was shocked by the intensity of the assaults: "at first they were paralyzed . . . they had done their best to become assimilated and to make their Judaism as inobtrusive as possible . . . and now they found that all their efforts did not suffice, that their very being was a disturbing element . . . they could not grasp the idea that the era of liberalism had ended; they were totally disoriented." [120] They were in a paradoxical position: their efforts to eradicate distinctions between themselves and their Christian fellow citizens had reduced the Jewish community to a religious and social welfare institution. Driven by fear of condemnation for separatism, they had been reluctant to organize for any but philanthropic purposes,[121] and as a result they had no effective organization of defense against the anti-Semites.

Other factors contributed to the paucity of their political defense. The Jewish communities and organizations were led by men who had traditionally cooperated with the civil authorities. Their position was wholeheartedly supported by the Jewish liberal politicians, who although not involved in the internal affairs of the communities, discouraged any independent political action. From the point of view of their leaders and politicians, independent Jewish action was illegal, dangerous, and unnecessary since the state was responsible for the protection of their interests. The laws of 1869 had declared Jews to be full-fledged citizens; to doubt these laws was to question the authority of the state. Again, tensions within the Jewish communities mitigated against collective action. Finally, their enthusiastic embrace of the Reich's liberal constitution left the Jews ill-prepared psychologically and emotionally either for anti-Semitic outbreaks or for organized defense. Rather, their first reaction was to pray in the synagogues and listen to their rabbis' sermons refuting Treitschke and enumerating Jewish contributions to the German fatherland.[122]

Despite these barriers to unified action, a few bids were made to defend Jewish honor against the increasingly violent anti-Semitic attacks;[123] for the most part, they were as ineffectual as the apologetic replies to Treitschke. The first to take action was the single large Jewish organization in Germany, the D.I.G.B. As early as 1879 the D.I.G.B. had decided to take legal measures against the anti-Semites and, if possible, to bring them to court. In line with its policy of acting only as intercessor for the community, the D.I.G.B. did not undertake independent action but turned to the authorities for help. When Marr's pamphlet received widespread publicity at the end of the 1870s, the D.I.G.B. asked the Ministry of Justice of Saxony to prohibit its accusations against the Jews as "oppressive capitalists"—a phrase that could be applied to all propertied groups including the government. Their request was ignored.[124]   A similar appeal to Bismarck urging him to use his moral authority against anti-Semitic slander went unheeded. On November 18, 1879, the D.I.G.B. asked the public prosecutor of Berlin to bring Marr to trial for inciting racial hatred; the plea was unsuccessful.[125]   An attempt at court action by the D.I.G.B. against the anti-Semitic publisher Otto Hentze in February, 1881, also failed.

The notables of the Berlin community followed the example of the D.I.G.B. in turning to the authorities. Their determination to act solely as intercessors for the community and for German Jewry, no matter what the circumstances, is evidenced by their repeated application to the government.

On October 29, 1879, the community registered with the Minister of the Interior, Count Eulenburg, the first of three appeals to contain the wild agitation against its members; none of them received a reply. When the chairman of the board of the Berlin Jewish community, Meyer Magnus, tried to secure an audience with the minister, he was curtly told that the ministry had no time for the requests of individuals. When the board of the community once more sought an interview, Eulenburg delivered the opinion, in 1880, that the Berlin community could not speak for all Prussian Jewry and that the activities of the Christian Socialist party were not illegal.[126]

The communities and organizations of German Jewry did their utmost to avoid direct confrontation. Their leaders were unwilling to form separate political parties or even temporary organizations to combat the anti-Semites. Their reluctance to engage publicly with the opposing forces restrained them even from initiating legal action; they felt it was the place of the state to protect their legal rights. An unusual departure from this Weltanschauung, however, occurred on December 1, 1880, when Moritz Lazarus convened a meeting of two hundred Jewish notables in Berlin to discuss defensive measures. They elected the "Jewish Committee of December 1st" with Lazarus as chairman,[127] and a membership that included Berthold Auerbach (1812–82), Julius Bleichroeder, Ludwig Loewe (1839–86), and Harry Bresslau.[128] On December 16, a larger group of six or seven hundred people met in Berlin. The distinguished audience listened to Lazarus as he urged defense by the Jewish community, Jewish self-improvement, and the enhancement of Jewish values and morals. He admonished them to remain loyal to Judaism despite any detachment they might feel from religion.[129] The meeting adopted the following resolution:

> The meeting approves the train of thought developed by the chairman. It strongly protests: (1) the agitation of the so-called anti-Semites who try time and again to hold the entire German Jewish community responsible for the misdeeds and tactlessness of individuals; (2) the undigni-

fied attempt to portray the German Jews as a national entity which stands apart from the entity of the German nation. Moreover it [the meeting] declares that they [German Jews] will continue steadfastly to serve the fatherland loyally and that they consider it an unchangeable goal, in fulfilling their civil obligations, to work for the welfare of the fatherland with all their might.[130]

This resolution ended the brief history of the "December Committee" because its members, not personally affected by anti-Semitism, were too entrenched in Prussian politics and finance to act unilaterally. The resolution was more an expression of their loyalty to Germany than a proclamation that the time for independent action had arrived.[131]

The attempts by the D.I.G.B., the Berlin Jewish community, and the Assembly of Notables to organize for protest were half-hearted and feeble; their attitudes, thereafter, remained apologetic and self-effacing, and no further attempts were made to initiate defensive proposals. In December, 1880, the D.I.G.B. published a pamphlet that accurately expressed the reaction of the community. The pamphlet implied that certain assessments of Jewish shortcomings might be valid and that these should be recognized and corrected. Entitled "How the Jew Should Conduct Himself Toward the Anti-Semitic Movement,"[132] it made the following suggestions:

1. Even in the light of the recent excesses against Jews, do not hate your fellow Christian citizens.
2. Love work and hate the lust for power.
3. Conduct yourselves in an ethical and moral way.
4. Try to cultivate friendships with Christians; do not be too sensitive to expressions of dislike by Christians toward Jews or Judaism . . . avoid every conflict with Christians and shy away from arguments about the nature of Judaism. Only in cases where such a discussion is unavoidable should we try to reply in a scientific and serious manner to malicious opponents; but here too we ought to be careful to avoid insults, action, or force.

Duels are the remnant of the Middle Ages . . . they are forbidden both by law and religious morality. Whoever avoids them is not a coward.

5. Above all, you journalists [*Schriftkundigen*] , be careful with your words. Omit every unwise, useless discussion; above all every mocking expression about non-Jews.

6. Let us remain true Germans, happy to sacrifice ourselves for the welfare of the fatherland.

7. Let us concentrate our energies on welfare and social work with an unselfish and total devotion. . . .

8. Let us develop and cultivate the science [*Wissenschaft*] and the history of Judaism and let us support those who have dedicated their lives in the service of these disciplines.

9. Let us consider the current painful events as a hint from Providence to pay attention to our own self-examination even more than hitherto. The stricter the criticism which we direct at ourselves, the more the malicious and therefore painful criticism of our opponents will come to naught. This criticism will benefit not only ourselves, but all those who serve truth and who disdain religious or racial hate.[133]

This pamphlet had a dual purpose. By emphasizing that there was room for Jewish self-improvement, it was clearly intended to appease the anti-Semites. At the same time, and of even greater importance to the leaders of the D.I.G.B., it was intended as a gesture to the government which had rejected intervention and maintained that anti-Semitic activities were legal. The D.I.G.B. was implying, then, that the Jews had accepted the judgment of the authorities; that the charges, however violent and painful, were based on a measure of truth, and that Jews would share the blame for the current deplorable situation. It is not surprising, therefore, that this publication was successful; it found wide acceptance in Jewish circles, and the Christians applauded it as a sincere expression of Jewish desire for self-improvement.[134]

A similar response came from the German branch of the Bnei Brith organization. The *Bnei Briss* in Germany was founded by Julius Fenchel, Moritz Jablonski, and David Wolff, Free Masons who left their lodge when anti-Semitism became rampant. On March 20, 1882, they founded the *Deutsche Reichs-Loge* in Berlin.[135] The German *Grossloge (Der Orden Bnei Briss in Deutschland U.O.B.B.)* was formed in 1885 to unite the twelve existing lodges.[136] Despite the impetus behind the formation of the Bnei Brith, its program did not include defense against anti-Semitism. The major aim of the organization was akin to that of other Masonic orders: "to unite the Israelites in order to promote the highest and most idealistic interests of humanity." [137] This goal was to be realized through a three-fold program: (1) ethical educational work, (2) social and humanitarian actions, (3) progress toward brotherhood by strengthening of common solidarity.[138]

The German Jewish communities did not recognize the *Bnei Briss,* at least in its early years, as a spokesman for their cause, but saw it merely as a private group pursuing its own interests. For its part, the *Bnei Briss* refrained from interference in communal affairs, including elections, and it devoted its time and energy to social problems and welfare causes. [139] Its presidents: Julius Fenchel (term, 1885–87), Louis Maretzki (term, 1887–97), and Berthold Timendorfer (term, 1898–1924), were acculturated, well-to-do Jews who emphasized cooperation with the communities and Jewish organizations in all philanthropic causes, but deprecated political action lest they be accused of serving the interests of world Jewry—a charge to which they were especially sensitive. Under these circumstances, it was clear from its inception that the *Bnei Briss* would lead no crusade against the anti-Semites.

In the face of Jewish inaction, the opposition continued its offensive. In the fall of 1880, Bernhard Foerster, Max Liebermann von Sonnenberg, Ernst Henrici, and other anti-Semitic leaders of the "Berlin Movement" collected signatures for a petition. [140] The signers demanded: restriction of Jewish immigration; exclusion of Jews from all government positions including the judiciary and teaching professions; and the reestablishment of a special census of the Jewish population. In April, 1881, this petition, signed by 250,000 people, was presented to Bismarck.[141]   Anti-Semitic agitation grew so heated that mob riots broke out in Berlin. Another ominous sign was the election of Adolf Stoecker to the Reichstag in 1881 as representative from Siegen. Between the years 1881 and 1884 Stoecker achieved his greatest triumphs. In the spring of 1882, the Kaiser paid a special tribute to the "Berlin Movement" by inviting Stoecker and some of his lieutenants to his chambers on the eve of his birthday. Stoecker was granted the special honor of delivering a speech and the Kaiser's response seemed to indicate that he supported Stoecker's political activities.[142]

During the same period anti-Semitism found a growing number of new adherents among German students. Treitschke's position had made anti-Semitism acceptable *(Gesellschaftsfaehig)* in academic circles. The petition of 1881 included 4,000 student signatures, ten times the ratio of signers in the total population.[143]   On December 16, 1880, the Association of German Students *(Verein deutscher Studenten)* was formed in Berlin, and it soon included groups in Breslau and other universities.[144] The statutes declared:

> The Association will form clubs that will accept full-time Christian students who attend higher institutions of learning in Germany.

Paragraph 5 added:

> It is forbidden to demand or accept satisfaction with a weapon from members of the Jewish race.[145]

Other student organizations *(Burschenschaften)* carefully scrutinized those Jews who wished to be admitted. Finally in 1886 the organizations decreed that "Jewish subjects of the Reich" were not Germans and, therefore, could not be admitted to the fraternities.[146]   The *Verein deutscher Studenten* found wide response in Germany and abroad. In 1882, the *Verein deutscher Studenten in Wien* was founded, adopting a program identical to its German parent organization.[147]

Reactions of Jewish Students

Jewish students were doubly stigmatized as a foreign element within the German people and as cowards unworthy of a duel; although they were an integral part of the culture, they were excluded from the crucial social functions of the German students. They had espoused the ideals of honor and courage that characterized every self-respecting German, but their exclusion made it impossible for them to testify to these admirable qualities. Their first reaction was to form their own organizations. By 1883 the Jewish students of the University of Berlin had formed the *Akademische Verein fuer juedische Geschichte und Literatur,* [148] professional enclaves such as the *Akademisch-medizinische Vereinigung* and the *Juristische Verein.* [149] These organizations, unlike the *Akademische Verein,* had planned originally to include Christians as members, but they became, in fact, exclusively Jewish.

Intellectually oriented organizations, however, failed to satisfy the psychological needs of those Jewish students who longed to demonstrate their courage and excellent German character. A decisive turn of events in the history of student associations and of Jewish organizations in general occurred in 1886. At the end of the summer semester, a group of Jewish students met in Breslau and on October 28, 1886, founded the *Freie Verbindung Viadrina.* [150] The new fraternity published a "word to our co-religionists" explaining the necessity for its existence in terms of the depth and pervasiveness of anti-Semitism in all strata of society, the unlikelihood that this agitation would be quelled in the foreseeable future, and the strong probability that the growing social, racial, and religious hatred would become part of the German tradition. They saw their dilemma as a poignant one:

> In the face of such overwhelming odds the Jewish undergraduate is bound to lose self-confidence and it is easy to understand that he will lose heart and give up the fight. But there is more to it. Jewish depravity is put forth in anti-Semitic propaganda with such conviction and zeal, that the young Jew himself begins to doubt the righteousness of his cause and the right of Jewry to exist at all. . . .

Thus they [the Jewish undergraduates] get used to the idea that their being of Jewish descent is a misfortune which cannot be changed and has to be endured with patience. . . . They lose hope and do not try to improve their situation. . . . Even those among us who have retained a sense of independence and personal dignity retire from communal life at the university, depressed by these circumstances, embittered by the fanatical hatred of our opponents as well as by the lack of principle in our Jewish fellow-students.[151]

This analysis suggested one possible way in which their condition might be alleviated: the formation of an independent organization that would revive among those of Jewish consciousness a love for their own history and civilization. Its program would stress equal loyalty to *Judentum* and to the German fatherland. The organization was not designed to segregate Jews culturally or nationally from Christian society, yet would unite them against those Christians who threatened their future welfare. The practical aims were closely linked to defense:

We think, first of all, of physical training as a means of achieving our purpose. . . . Our association is to be, first of all, a place for physical training of every kind: gymnastics, fencing, rowing, swimming. We have to fight with all our energy against the odium of cowardice and weakness which is cast upon us. We want to show that every member of our association is equal to every Christian fellow student in physical exercise and chivalry. Physical strength and agility will increase self-confidence and self-respect, and in future nobody will be ashamed of being a Jew. All those who bitterly suffered insults to the Jews as insults to themselves, all those whose sense of justice was hurt by the abominable misdeeds of the anti-Semitic movement, whose blood boiled when they heard the defamations with which we were slandered and felt the hatred with which we were opposed, should see the prospect of a brighter future. Let them not withhold their interest from those who are resolved to use all their youthful energy to carry these plans to success.[152]

The *Viadrina's* stand met favorable response among Jewish students in other German universities. A second fraternity, the *Badenia*, was founded in October, 1890, in Heidelberg. In October, 1894, the *Sprevia* was founded in Berlin and the *Licaria* in Munich. These fraternities united in 1896 to form the *Kartell Convent deutscher Studenten juedischen Glaubens.*[153]   The goals of the new association were stated:

> The K.C. stands firmly on the foundation of patriotic German ideology; its aim is to combat anti-Semitism among German students. The goal of the K.C. is to educate its members to become self-confident Jews who will know that through their historical, cultural, and legal bonds they are inseparably united with the German fatherland. Its members will always be ready and able to defend the political and legal rights of the Jews.[154]

The appearance of these fraternities, and especially of the *Viadrina*, introduced a radically new approach to anti-Semitism. Only a few years earlier the largest Jewish organization, the D.I.G.B., had warned emphatically against the use of force and condemned duels as immoral, and the Jewish communities and organizations had been reluctant to move against anti-Semites for fear of feeding their anger and hateful propaganda. They failed to perceive that the temporary lull in political anti-Semitism, which was a movement of German adults, was not accurately reflected in the widespread anti-Semitism among German students. "It was therefore something of a shock to a large part of middle-class Jewish society, when a body of Jewish students decided in 1886 to establish an exclusively Jewish students' association."[155]   The Jewish community of Breslau thoroughly disapproved of the *Viadrina*, on the grounds that a Jewish fraternity would only serve to compound anti-Semitism. The only community members to support it were Rabbi Joel and Heinrich Graetz.[156]

The community's attitude was understandable enough in the light of their past experiences. The leaders of the German Jewish communities and organizations—Moritz Kohner (1818—77), Moritz Lazarus (1824—1903), Emil Lehmann (1829—98), Samuel Kristeller (1820—1900), Leven Gold-schmidt (1829—97), Leopold Auerbach (1828—97), Ludwig Philippson (1811—89), and others—were at least one genera-tion older than the young founders of the *Viadrina*. Born at the beginning of the nineteenth century, they had seen the slow but steady progress of Jewish emancipation. Many of them had fought in the revolution of 1848, and with the Prussian and German armies in the wars of 1864, 1866, and 1870—71. They had reaped the rewards of their involvement: the revolution of 1848 had given them civil rights; the Nord-deutsche Reichstag had abolished all remaining professional and political restrictions. They remembered that a temporary reaction, which threatened to abolish their rights, had occur-red after 1848 and were, therefore, inclined to consider the racial currents of the 1870s and 1880s as similar passing phenomena. Their successful careers reassured them. Many of them had attained a comfortable and even wealthy life style and were confident of enjoying permanent social, economic, political, and religious equality. From this vantage point they were unprepared for resistance to anti-Semitism but felt obliged to condemn a militant Jewish fraternity that might endanger their welfare and that of the entire community.[157] Jewish members of the general political parties supported the communities' rejection of the fraternities. Even Bamberger, who in 1880 was willing to engage in a public debate with Treitschke, was not in sympathy with the "radical" Jewish groups; the most any politician would do on behalf of the community was to testify to its German loyalty.

The students who were founding the independent Jewish *Burschenschaften* had had a different generational experi-ence. They were born in the late 1860s or early 1870s, too late to have witnessed the events of the 1869 *Bundesgesetz*. From their parents they had acquired a belief in progress, emancipation, and the value of being a part of German culture. Their adolescent experiences brought only disillusionment in respect to progress, and a mounting pessimism. At the gymnasium and the university they encountered insults and indignities. Their fathers were typically former members of the German *Burschenschaften* and, as "alte Herren," continued to take an active interest.[158]   Like their fathers, "the young Jewish students were influenced by the Teutonic ideals of virile virtues."[159]   They eagerly awaited their turn to take part in the cultural and social activities of the universities, but, once there, anti-Semitism barred their way.[160]   Those students who retained a sense of Jewish pride did not feel limited by the experiences and expectations of their parents. Their reaction was twofold: those who were members of anti-Semitic fraternities resigned, like Herzl who resigned from the *Albia;*[161]   others joined Jewish fraternities where they would have a chance to defend their honor.

Honor and courage were indeed the most important elements in the founding of the *Viadrina*. These concepts were the cornerstone of the Christian *Burschenschaften* and corps, and they were readily adopted by the Jewish fraternities. The anti-Semitic organizations had stigmatized the Jews as cowardly, unworthy opponents in a duel. Now the Jewish students had the chance to prove that they were as qualified and competent as the Christians in using weapons. They had become aware of their status, and they longed to command respect as Jews. By proving their prowess in physical strength, discipline, and courage, they hoped to honor Judaism and the German fatherland as well. The Jewish fraternities tried to combine these two elements of *Deutschtum* and *Judentum*. They upheld their Jewish heritage, expelling anyone who converted to Christianity, but, at the same time, they stood as models of German patriotism and loyalty.[162]

Despite the K.C.'s pride in Jewish heritage, however, its substantive Jewish identification was very vague. The K.C.'s adherence to *Judentum* was more an adherence out of spite against the anti-Semites (*Trutzjudentum*) than out of a deep conviction of the value of the Jewish tradition. On the other hand, the K.C.'s attitude toward *Deutschtum* was clearly defined; it stipulated that German Jews should seek complete acculturation into the German *volk*. It was simply adhering to the ideology professed by most German Jews.

Almost ten years after the founding of the *Viadrina,* another Jewish student organization, the *Verein juedischer Studenten* (V.J.St.), was formed at the University of Berlin in reaction to anti-Semitism there. Opposing the assimilationist tendencies of the K.C.,[163] the V.J.St. of Berlin united with other organizations in sympathy with the Zionist cause to form the *Bund juedischer Corporationen* (B.J.C.) in 1902.[164] Like the K.C., the B.J.C. was made up of academic fraternities of the general pattern of "drinking and fighting fraternities" (*schlagende Verbindungen*), but at the same time it sought to develop and defend a sense of Jewish consciousness.

Despite ideological differences between the K.C. and the B.J.C., both groups hoped to inculcate the basic values of honor and courage in their membership. Members were instructed to develop their knowledge of Judaism and to fight for their rights as German citizens. Both organizations followed the teachings of Gabriel Riesser. A whole younger generation thus adopted a radically different attitude toward anti-Semitism that was to alter their identity as Germans and as Jews and to govern their behavior during the years before World War I as well as during the Weimar Republic. The founders of the K.C. and the B.J.C. were later to become important members of the *Centralverein deutscher Staatsbuerger juedischen Glaubens* (C.V.) and the *Zionistische Vereinigung fuer Deutschland* (ZVfD): Ludwig Hollaender, Felix Goldmann, Ludwig Haas, and Benno Jacob, who had been members of the K.C., became the most influential members of the C.V.[165] Erich Rosenkranz, Isaak Zwirn, Max Jungmann (all of the V.J.St. Berlin), Richard Lichtheim (*Kartell Zionistische Verbindungen, Ivria*), and Felix Rosenblueth (V.J.St. Freiburg) became influential in the ZVfD.[166]

The 1890s saw a mushrooming of defense organizations in the wake of renewed political anti-Semitism. In 1891, the *Verein zur Abwehr des Antisemitismus* was formed by liberal politicians and professors, both Jews and non-Jews. Begun under the leadership of Eugen Richter, Heinrich Rickert, Rudolf von Gneist, Theodor Mommsen, and other prominent figures in German society, the *Verein's* founding declaration was signed by 535 prominent Christians, and after one year the organization claimed more than 13,000 members. The propaganda of the *Verein* was published in popular literature, leaflets, and pamphlets; the Berlin chapter published the *Antisemitenspiegel,* and after October 21, 1891, the weekly *Mitteilungen aus dem Verein zur Abwehr des Antisemitismus.* [167] From time to time the organization appealed directly to the authorities. [168]

In 1892, a group of leading Jews founded the *Komitee zur Abwehr antisemitischer Angriffe.* The committee, organized by Julius Isaac, included men who were later to play a major role in German Jewish history. Among them were Alfred Friedemann, Paul Nathan (1857–1927), James Simon (1851–1932), and Adolf Ginsberg. Upon the founding of the C.V. in 1893, the committee lost its *raison d'être* and the membership joined the ranks of the C.V. [169]

During the latter part of the nineteenth century, therefore, a major shift in German Jewish self-consciousness and sensitivity toward the "Jewish Question" occurred. The idealism and enthusiasm that had followed the revolution of 1848 and the unification of 1871 was giving way to a more realistic assessment of the predicament of German Jewry. Jews were still in the process of assimilation and were unquestionably loyal to Germany, but the anti-Semitic movements of the 1870s and 1880s made them aware of their own heritage and retarded that process. It was this new consciousness that was most pervasive in the German Jewish organizations founded in the 1890s. The two most significant ones were the *Centralverein deutscher Staatsbuerger juedischen Glaubens* and the *Zionistische Vereinigung fuer Deutschland.*

II

The Centralverein deutscher Staatsbuerger juedischen Glaubens *before World War I*

The first organization within the German Jewish establishment to emphasize the integrity and respectability of the Jew as a human being and his honorable and equal status as a German citizen was the *Centralverein deutscher Staatsbuerger juedischen Glaubens*, which was founded in 1893.[1] For the next forty-five years, until the seizure of complete power by the Nazis, the C.V. was the largest Jewish organization in Germany, and it shaped and expressed the attitudes and beliefs of most German Jews. A study that seeks to explore the identity of the mainstream of German Jewry and its attitude toward Zionism before World War I must concentrate on the development of the C.V. as the most representative and lucid expression of that identity.[2]

The appearance of the C.V. was due to the coalescence of several factors: the continued incursions of the German anti-Semitic movement in the 1880s and 1890s; the publication by two outspoken Jews of a call to action; the inadequacy of existing Jewish and Christian organizations to deal with anti-Semitism; the gradual disappearance of Jews from seats of public power; and the rise of a successful model, the Catholic Center party. Underlying all these factors was the new demand, which first emerged among the K.C., that Jews defend their rights and honor as a matter of public service to their own communities and to the German fatherland.

The Founding of the C. V.

Shortly before the founding of the C.V. the anti-Semitic movement reached a climax of intensity. In March, 1890, Bismarck resigned as chancellor of the Reich and was succeeded by General Leo von Caprivi, who served as chancellor until 1894.[3] Caprivi proved unable to unify and lead the government in the authoritarian Bismarck manner. Soon after he took office a constellation of forces united against him; their common denominator was an anti-Semitic thrust. In December, 1892, the convention of the Conservative party met at the Tivoli hall in Berlin.[4] Their revised program adopted on December 8, 1892, contained paragraphs of direct concern to German Jewry:

> State and church are institutions decreed by God; their cooperation is a necessary prerequisite to our people's moral health.
> We consider the denominational Christian grammar school the basis of public education and the most important safeguard against the growing brutalization of the masses and the advancing disintegration of all social ties. We oppose the multifarious and obtrusive Jewish influence that disrupts our people's lives.
> We demand Christian authority and Christian teachers for Christian pupils.[5]

The program demanded that the monarchy be left unhampered by "parliamentary restrictions" and that every effort be made to combat the segment of the press which "was undermining the state and the church."[6]

Thus, the Conservatives became the first major political party formally to declare themselves anti-Semitic. The Agrarian League (*Bund der Landwirte*) under the leadership of Bismarck's son, Herbert, became the strongest ally of the Conservatives.[7] The combined forces of the Agrarian League, the Conservatives, and other anti-Semitic groups, proved very powerful in the Reichstag elections of June, 1893. The success of the anti-Semites was spectacular. The anti-Semitic vote jumped from 47,000 in 1890 to 263,000 in 1893, raising the number of anti-Semitic representatives from five to sixteen.[8] On the other hand, the Progressive parties (*Freisinnige Vereinigung* and *Freisinnige Volkspartei*), traditional supporters of Jewish demands, suffered a serious defeat; their combined seats in the Reichstag declined from sixty-seven in 1890 to thirty-seven.[9]

To these tangible political gains by the anti-Semites, one must add Herman Ahlwardt's (1846–1914) success in arousing public opinion against the Jews in the period immediately before the founding of the C.V. In 1890 Ahlwardt entered German politics with the publication of his book, *The Aryan Peoples' Battle of Despair Against Jewry.* "The German public had by then become accustomed to anti-Jewish writings but nothing had yet been printed to match Ahlwardt's attack in vituperation, irresponsibility, and sheer madness." As soon as the excitement generated by the book had subsided, he published a pamphlet, *Judenflinten* (1892), in which he accused a certain Jewish firm of supplying the army with faulty rifles. A great scandal erupted, and twenty editions of the pamphlet were sold within a few weeks. Even though he was later proved a liar and a vicious slanderer, Ahlwardt was elected to the Reichstag and his popularity skyrocketed. German public opinion was obviously on his side.[10]

In response to these social and political events the German Jewish community felt threatened and helpless.[11] The board of the Berlin *Gemeinde* considered a plan to dispatch a delegation to the Kaiser asking for his moral and legal support.[12] The immediate reaction to this plan was a pamphlet written anonymously in 1893 by Raphael Loewenfeld (1854–1910), entitled *Protected Jews or Citizens of the State?*[13] In it, Loewenfeld beseeched his fellow Jews not to rely on the Kaiser's intervention. He claimed that their legal rights were sufficient protection and that these were incapable of being destroyed by the anti-Semites. He condemned the plan of the Berlin notables as cowardly, and as projecting an image of *Schutzjuden* or medieval Jewish serfs.[14] Loewenfeld argued persuasively that Jews should use and defend their equality as loyal, equal *Staatsbuerger.*

Loewenfeld's disapproval of an appeal to the Kaiser can best be understood in the framework of his ethics. Born into an orthodox Jewish family in Posen, Loewenfeld studied Slavic languages and literature in the Polish gymnasium in Posen, then traveled to Russia to further his studies in the field. There he became a close associate of Count Tolstoi, and he translated a few of Tolstoi's works into German upon his return to Germany.[15] Loewenfeld's socialist convictions were in all probability a reflection of his Russian visit. He believed that the working people deserved educational opportunities that would enable them to appreciate and contribute to their culture. On this premise he founded the Schiller Theater, the first "people's theater" of Germany in Berlin, soon to be followed by a second, the Lessing Theater. Both theaters operated on strict socialist principles; the administration, actors, attendants, and the director (Loewenfeld) received equal shares of the profits.

Loewenfeld's socialism was coupled with a fervent commitment to ethical standards and justice. At an early age he had abandoned the orthodox observances of his home and joined the Foerster Ethical Society. His humanism impelled him to repudiate those national tendencies that set ethnic and religious groups apart from the rest of society. Although neither he nor his children converted to Christianity, he hoped that Jews would in time merge culturally with their Christian neighbors. Loewenfeld believed in an ethical supreme God, but he opposed the religious ritual that he held responsible for strife and division throughout the world. In ethical convictions and moral conduct he found forces that transcended ritual observance. Within the political sphere, Loewenfeld considered a common love for their fatherland the sole basis for Christian and Jewish harmony.[16]

Loewenfeld's strong feeling that the Jews should not turn to the Kaiser reflects his opposition as a socialist to the authority of Kaiser Wilhelm and to monarchical intervention in the political and religious affairs of any group within the German state.[17] A firm believer in humanity and in freedom of choice for all people, Loewenfeld protested encroachment on Jewish rights. So far as he was concerned, Jews, like all human beings, had inalienable rights not dependent on the Kaiser or on any interest group. He urged German Jews not to separate themselves from their Christian fellow citizens. He did not counsel conversion, condemning outside interference with those Jews who wanted to maintain their religion. Nevertheless Loewenfeld urged them to prove that their loyalty to "the dear fatherland" was even stronger than their loyalty to Judaism.[18]

In his pamphlet Loewenfeld formulated six tenets later adopted with but slight change by the C.V.:

1. We are not German Jews, but German citizens of the Jewish faith [*Deutsche Staatsbuerger juedischen Glaubens*].
2. As citizens we neither need nor demand any protection beyond our legal rights.
3. As Jews we do not belong to any one political party. Political views, like religious ones, are matters of individual choice.
4. We stand firmly on the foundation of German nationality. We have no special ties with the Jews of other lands, except in the sense that German Catholics and Protestants have ties with Catholics and Protestants of other countries.
5. Our moral standards do not differ from those of other German citizens.
6. We condemn the unethical behavior of the individual, whatever his religion: we reject on the other hand any responsibility for the individual Jew and we reject the generalizations that malicious observers transpose from the individual Jew to the entire Jewish community.[19]

Loewenfeld's repugnance of religious particularism made him label the Jewish orthodox community, and especially S. R. Hirsch's *Austrittsgemeinde,* as a narrow-minded, bigoted group, concerned with promoting its own interests. The Jewish community supported Loewenfeld's fourth point; Jews were citizens of Germany only, without ties to Jews in other countries.[20] His tenets in fact were generally accepted, although some members of the C.V. criticized his attacks on orthodox Jews as unwarranted. When Loewenfeld's six theses subsequently became part of the C.V. program, his condemnation of the orthodox sector was omitted.

Almost simultaneously with the publication of Loewenfeld's brochure, a pamphlet by F. Simon, *Defend Yourselves, an Admonition to the Jews,* appeared in Berlin in January, 1893. In passionate terms the author demanded that the Jews organize with all means at their disposal. With the help of Bertha von Suttner, a foremost crusader of the time for human equality, Simon's pamphlet received wide circulation. In a lengthy article in the public press, von Suttner commended Simon's proposals. She pointed out that few Christians would be willing to help the Jews if they were meekly to accept the insults of the anti-Semites; such an attitude would be, in her opinion, tantamount to collaboration with the anti-Semites. She encouraged German Jewry to heed Simon's words and to organize for effective countermeasures.[21]

Unlike Loewenfeld who from a universal and humanitarian perspective was imbued with a sense of moral outrage at the prevailing injustice, Simon strongly identified with the Jewish community. He believed that a thorough knowledge of Judaism and the Jewish heritage was the first element in unification and strength:

> Whoever knows the history of the Jews will be protected against all attacks against Judaism. Whoever does not know this history, will be like a reed shaking in the wind.[22]

Above all Simon warned the Jews to retain their personal dignity and to repulse any encroachment upon their honor; to consider themselves obligated to take swift and decisive action in accord with the maxim: "We will no longer tolerate insults" (*sich nichts gefallen lassen*):

Whoever permits an anti-Semite to insult his person as a Jew, without immediately punishing the anti-Semite, commits a grave injustice to his own personal honor and to the honor of all Jewry . . . therefore defend yourselves with all the means available to you. . . . Defend yourselves! The Jews are no longer protected servants of the Middle Ages [*Schutz und Kammerknechte*], they are citizens.[23]

Finally, Simon offered a detailed plan for a defense organization, recommending the establishment of a local agency in each German province under a central office in Berlin. The local agencies would send delegates periodically to national conferences to rule on major legal problems that had risen. Simon suggested that the Berlin office dispatch eloquent speakers throughout Germany to discuss the Jewish Problem in public meetings. In addition literature would be disseminated countering anti-Semitic charges. He suggested that the organization adopt the motto: "We want to be Germans, yet remain Jews; true and loyal citizens of the Reich, but at the same time unflinching believers in Judaism."[24]

Simon's pamphlet supported and complemented Loewenfeld's theses, and it also contributed to the founding of the C.V. The significant difference between Loewenfeld's and Simon's proposals was that the latter advocated defense as Jews, not merely as citizens who had suffered legal setbacks. The ideals of honor and courage are the underpinning of all his recommendations. The messages of these two men made a significant impact on the German Jewish community. Both pamphlets were welcomed by many who disregarded their variations in perspective but paid close attention to the common theme—the call for self-defense. Loewenfeld, a well-known personality in Berlin, received the wider publicity. By January 9, 1893, his pamphlet had appeared in a third edition.[25] The general press was discussing it at great length, and the Jewish middle class in Berlin were sending him letters of gratitude.[26] His most important supporters were Eugen Fuchs (1856–1923), Martin Mendelssohn (1860–1920), and

Hugo Preuss (1860–1925), who began to formulate a plan for a defense organization on the model suggested by Simon and Loewenfeld.

It is reasonable to conjecture that another factor that influenced the founders of the C.V. was that in 1893 the Jews suddenly found themselves without a fellow Jew to represent their interests in parliament. Shortly before this date, Ludwig Bamberger had been the sole remaining Jewish parliamentarian in Germany. He was revered by the Jewish community as the only politician who had dared to defend German Jewry against Treitschke's attacks. In 1893, Bamberger retired after twenty-five years of active service, giving as the reason for his retirement the increasing and virulent anti-Semitism that seemed not to disturb "three-fourths of my colleagues."[27] Without Bamberger, German Jews felt more vulnerable than ever. The founders of the C.V. considered this state of affairs altogether dangerous and, in their opinion, immediate action was needed to correct it.

Bamberger's departure from active political life contrasted sharply with the Catholics' method of dealing with discrimination against them. Although there is no direct evidence that the leaders who were eventually to form the C.V. imitated the German Catholics, there is an undoubted resemblance between the Catholic Center party and the Jewish *Centralverein*.[28] In both cases ethnic groups united against hostile forces that were unchecked and occasionally even upheld by the state. The founders of the C.V. were of course aware of the recent Kulturkampf in which the Catholics had thwarted Bismarck's attempt to crush them by uniting their forces into a political party. Probably the most important idea extracted from the Catholic example was that strength could best be acquired by forming an organization in which all Jews would be united. A major difference between the two organizations remained—the Catholics tried to achieve their goals through political means, whereas the C.V. preferred legal methods.

On February 5, 1893, some two hundred Jewish notables met in the house of Julius Isaac, a member of the *Comité zur*

Abwehr antisemitischer Angriffe,[29] to discuss the information of a defense organization that would have the support of the entire Jewish community.[30] They spoke of the format and purpose of the new organization and the possible problems they would face. The most important and immediate question was whether or not the new organization should merge with the *Comité* and/or with the *Verein zur Abwehr des Antisemitismus* to prevent the splintering of existing pro-Jewish forces. The decision was to create an independent organization. The meeting decided that the future organization's functions would not coincide with those of the *Comité*: the *Comité's* task would be quiet lobbying behind the scenes; the new organization would be directed to public and dramatic fighting for self-defense. Similarly the founders of the C.V. decided not to merge with the *Verein zur Abwehr des Antisemitismus* because its leadership and most of its membership was composed of Christians. The fledgling organization did not need the protection of a Christian organization; furthermore, Christians could not be true representatives of German Jews. Martin Mendelssohn, who was to become the first president of the C.V., explained the position in these words:

> We do not have to emphasize the fact that we do not stand in opposition to the *Verein zur Abwehr des Antisemitismus*; we are different from each other—not opposed to each other—through the principle of self-help; it is the duty of every decent human being to defend himself through his own efforts.[31]

In order not to offend the leaders of the *Verein,* who had done their utmost to help German Jews gain equal rights, the C.V. was to make regular financial contributions to various projects and funds sponsored by the *Verein.*[32]

During a second meeting, on March 26, 1893, the C.V. was officially constituted. The participants included professors Julius Wolff (1836–1902) and Hermann Senator (1834–1911), members of the "December Committee," as well as

Martin Mendelssohn, Eugen Fuchs, and Hermann Stern. [33] These founding members made a public declaration, circulated in May, 1893:

> For almost two decades our fatherland has been disturbed by a movement whose final aim is to destroy our social and political condition. We had hoped that the sense of justice which fills the majority of our fellow citizens, and our common culture would prove to be sufficient protection against the machinations and intrigues of a minority which stands ready to blame its Jewish fellow citizens for every evil of our society. . . .
>
> Ever since we have been fortunate enough to be a part of the life of the German nation, we Jews have given all our energy to the fatherland with a willing heart and a great enthusiasm. . . . And now an organization has arisen which seeks to destroy the newly found harmony [of the Reich]. Through its unscrupulous agitation and unfounded teachings this organization has reached an increasingly larger public. . . . While we find it necessary today to organize, nothing is further from our mind than the spirit of isolation. . . . We follow only the duty to defend our position within the fatherland through our own efforts, and we are convinced that this attitude will gain for us the respect of our fellow citizens. Our relationship to our fatherland is in no way different from that of Protestants or Catholics . . . we are all united through our national thinking and stand together when the welfare of the Reich is at stake. [34]

The last paragraph was clearly interpolated to justify the creation of the C.V. as an exclusively Jewish organization. The implication was that if Protestants and Catholics could organize to defend themselves, Jews were entitled to form similar organizations.

On November 19, 1893, the C.V. issued a second leaflet that elaborated the aims set forth in May. Of particular interest for its future development is the acceptance here of Simon's admonition that Jews should become better acquainted with their heritage as a means for successful defense. At the same time the C.V. outlined a facet of its work that was to become of first importance—the enlightenment of Gentiles about the nature of Judaism. The leaflet read:

> The *Centralverein* . . . has set itself the following goals: to defend the rights of Germans of the Jewish faith against attack and to implant in the Jews themselves the feeling of belonging collectively to the German people. Through word of mouth and publications, through public meetings and lectures, the *Centralverein* wants to arm the individual Jew with ammunition that will enable him to withstand the daily struggle in the light of truth; it wants to enlighten the public, both friends and enemies, through all available public media, about the nature of Judaism, about the thinking and feeling of Jews who live in the German Reich. The organization will maintain an office which will become the center for all defense activities. . . .
>
> We invite all citizens to enlist in our endeavors. . . . Through defense of our equality we fight for the highest ideals of humanity, for the holiest interests of our German fatherland.[35]

The first public proclamations by the C.V. were acknowledged by the German Jewish public, but they were granted a cool reception. The major Jewish organizations (*Bnei Briss,* D.I.G.B.) ignored the C.V. completely for several months. One Jewish paper warned against "the new organization that intends to make a lot of noise which will finally reveal its ineffectiveness."[36] Many Jews feared that the new organization would only irritate the anti-Semites and increase their venom.[37] Others claimed that the anti-Semitic movement, having reached its maximum strength, would shortly recede, rendering unnecessary and even counter-productive a Jewish defense organization that could only provide the anti-Semites with a new focus against which to direct their attacks.[38] Objections, however, did not deter the initiators of the C.V. from proceeding with the founding of their organization.

The German Jewish community's response can be seen as an unwillingness to disturb the status quo, a consequence of their history of reliance on the state and the authorities to institute changes for their benefit. They considered it improper and futile to assume responsibility for their own future. Their sense of powerlessness sprang not only from their fear in the face of anti-Semitism, but also from their lack of organizational experience on a national level. Intimidation and lack of self-confidence thus combined to produce a conservative and skeptical appraisal of the "radical" C.V.

The newly founded organization adopted the name, *Centralverein deutscher Staatsbuerger juedischen Glaubens* ("Central Union of German Citizens of the Jewish Faith"), popularly known as the C.V. The name was carefully chosen to express the avowed purpose: the centralizing of the legal defense work of all Jewish political and religious parties. The order of the words in the title deliberately indicated that its members were first and foremost German citizens, and only secondarily members of the Jewish faith. The Jewish aspect, a sub-category of the political and legal status of the membership, referred merely to a set of religious beliefs. This order of priorities in its title had practical implications for the daily work of the C.V., which tended to emphasize German ideology (*Gesinnung*) to the neglect of Jewish substantive issues.

On April 4, 1893, a third and larger meeting of the C.V. membership took place to discuss the drafting of statutes. Paragraph one states that the C.V. aimed:

> ... to unite all German citizens of the Jewish faith, regardless of religious and political orientation, in order to help them maintain their civil and social equality as well as to help them to cultivate their German-mindedness [*deutsche Gesinnung*].[39]

This first paragraph became the most important statement of C.V. ideology, often reiterated as an example and guideline for future conduct. It contained the essential justification for the organization: that "all German citizens of the Jewish faith" should be united in an effort to guard their position in Germany as it was then defined and to foster their German loyalty.

Five years later, Maximilian Horwitz (term, 1894–1917), the second president of the C.V., elaborated on the ideas expressed in this first paragraph. Horwitz's reasoning was that since all German Jews were subjected to the attacks of the anti-Semites, all German Jews needed protection. Individually they could achieve very little; their only hope was to unite. A powerful central organization could not easily be ignored by the Christian majority:

> We will have real and lasting success only when all our coreligionists join our organization. When our Christian fellow citizens realize that when we appear before them we represent 500,000 Jews, they will no longer be able to shut their ears and pretend they do not hear our demands; nor will they be able to dismiss our demands in the same cavalier fashion as heretofore. It is therefore of the utmost importance that *all* our coreligionists join our ranks. . . . It is a matter of honor to every German Jew to promote our cause as his own.[40]

The first paragraph of the statutes makes it clear that the C.V. saw self-defense and loyalty to Germany as of equal importance. All its members endorsed Horwitz's point of view that the defense of their rights should not be left to the state and could not be accomplished without total and unconditional loyalty to Germany.[41]

Simon's admonition that Jewish education should be a prerequisite for self-defense was disregarded. The absence of any reference to Judaism or Jewish education in this first most important paragraph of the statutes and in the remainder of the official program of the C.V. was no mistake. It was an accurate reflection of the early attitude of the C.V.: that its sole task was to organize for Jewish defense.[42] Although there is no record of a debate on the subject among the C.V. leaders, the statutes do express their rejection of Simon's stance. Additionally, the C.V. refused to devote itself to Jewish education lest involvement in the teaching of Judaism require a clearly defined religious position. The C.V. could not possibly have devised a religious formula that would have satisfied both the liberal and orthodox sectors. By sedulously avoiding the issue, therefore, the C.V. hoped to extend its influence throughout the diverse segments of the community. One vague statement, that Judaism was mainly a "religious confession," seemed to suffice for the members of the C.V., and this attitude toward Judaism solely as a religion existed, with some exceptions, until shortly before World War I.[43]

The philosophy of the C.V. closely resembles that in the third paragraph of the K.C. statutes:

> The fraternities of the K.C. stand firmly on the foundation of patriotic German loyalty [*Gesinnung*]. Their aim is to fight anti-Semitism among the German students as well as to educate their members to become self-confident Jews who will be conscious of the fact that through their history, culture, and legal ties they are inseparably bound to the German fatherland and therefore constitute an integral part of the German nation.[44]

The similarity is not coincidental. From its inception the C.V. was closely allied with the K.C. both in membership and ideology. The first generation of the C.V.—Eugen Fuchs, Maximilian Horwitz, Hugo Preuss (1860–1925), and others—did not belong to the K.C., having graduated from the universities long before the fraternities were formed. Those individuals who became influential in the C.V. after the retirement of the founders were, however, former K.C. members. They were the so-called *alte Herren* of the K.C. who had joined the C.V. immediately after graduation.

For the most part this second generation continued to take an active interest in the K.C.: Ludwig Hollaender (1877–1936, a former member of the *Licaria*) who became the director of the C.V. continued to hold his position as chairman of the K.C. board of directors; Felix Goldmann (1882–1934, former member of the *Thuringia*), an important member of the C.V. governing board, concurrently held the position of editor of the *Kartell-Convent-Blaetter;* Bruno

Weil (1883–1961, *Licaria*) and Ludwig Haas (1875–1930, *Badenia*) held positions on the boards of both the K.C. and the C.V. The powerful and influential C.V. became the parent organization of the K.C. and supported it with funds and various other services. After 1919 both organizations were, for all practical purposes, united and shared the same staff and offices in Berlin.[45] The K.C. continued to function as an active student fraternity, while the C.V. carried out its program among the Jewish middle class.

The similarity of the ideologies of the K.C. and the C.V. is remarkable. Both shared the same attitudes toward the problematic relationship of the concepts of *Deutschtum* and *Judentum*. The ideological basis for them both was the philosophy of Gabriel Riesser. Riesser's definition of honor as reliance on one's own power of forthright and honorable self-defense was seized upon as a leitmotif by both the K.C. and C.V. Indeed, the exaltation of honor was the principal impetus for the founding of the C.V.

At the 1898 annual convention of the C.V. in Berlin, Maximilian Horwitz spoke on "Duties of Honor" (*Ehrenpflichten*). Throughout he addressed the assembled delegates as "men of honor, fulfilling honorable duties."[46] These duties included defense of their dignity as Germans and Jews, closely connected with defense of *Deutschtum*. It was the contention of the C.V. that defense of Jewish rights was defense of all honorable German values; to leave such defense to Christians was tantamount to the abrogation of one's duty as a loyal German citizen.

Although Horwitz acknowledged the help of the Christians Gneist and Rickert, who, at a time when most Jews lacked the courage to defend themselves, had created the Christian *Verein zur Abwehr des Antisemitismus* to defend the Jewish cause, he claimed that the anti-Semites could be thwarted only if the Jews upheld their dignity as men. In addition Horwitz emphasized that public attacks against Jews could be countered only by Jews, who alone could and should sacrifice everything to the battle:

Assuming that the objection that our efforts will be

unsuccessful were true, could we permit our honor to be bespoiled? . . .

Even if our battle is doomed to failure from the start, it is our duty to fight and if in the end the opposition overpowers us . . . we will at least die fighting.[47]

Although both the K.C. and the C.V. emphasized the safeguarding of Jewish rights and professed loyalty to the German fatherland, the significant difference between the two was the C.V.'s aim "to unite *all* German citizens of the Jewish faith *regardless* of their religious and political orientations." The K.C. did not make any special effort to unite all the students and always remained a relatively small organization. The C.V.'s reference here was intended to serve notice to the orthodox community that the C.V. did not accept Loewenfeld's diatribe against religious Judaism, that it was inviting the orthodox to join and informing them that the C.V. intended to represent the orthodox as well as all other segments of the Jewish community. The phrase "regardless of political orientations" was essentially an empty proforma clause, and not directed toward a particular group, since it was well known that German Jews, with few exceptions, supported the liberal and left-liberal parties.

What then unified the membership of the C.V., if not common religious observances or political loyalties? The C.V. stated that it had a sufficiently strong and binding foundation for its membership in their common loyalty as German citizens of the Jewish faith. This statement appealed to the broadest cross-section of German Jews; it was in keeping with the C.V.'s policy of marshaling as many Jews behind its organization as possible.

Membership

Membership in the C.V. was voluntary and required only German citizenship and the payment of a fee.[48] A common practice in Germany was that the head of a family would register, and his entire family would thereby be included in the membership. Besides memberships by heads of families, the C.V. accepted entire organizations, clubs, and synagogues as members. On January 20, 1896, for example, the C.V. appealed to all *Gemeinden* in the Reich to support its work through active membership. On February 24, during a special meeting organized for delegates of these *Gemeinden,* the C.V. announced with pride that most of the German Jewish *Gemeinden* had joined the C.V. and had promised to make financial contributions.[49]

The available data clearly indicate that from its inception the C.V. rapidly increased in both individual and corporate membership. In its first year the C.V. registered 1,420 members;[50] in 1902, there were 10,000 individual members and 90,000 members registered through their synagogues and other organizations.[51] In 1916, the C.V. declared that it had 40,000 individual and 200,000 corporate members.[52] From the end of World War I until 1933, the individual membership of the C.V. flucuated between 45,000 and 72,000.[53] During the same period the total number of German Jews throughout the Reich fluctuated between 500,000 and 600,000.[54] The assertion then that the C.V. represented the majority of German Jews seems to be justified. It has been estimated that the C.V. represented between 300,000 and 400,000 Jews. Alfred Wiener, a member of the C.V. governing body during the Weimar Republic, claimed that one-third of all German Jews were individual members, while another third belonged to the C.V. through corporate membership.[55] Bruno Weil estimated that the C.V. had 300,000 members,[56] and another C.V. official went so far as to claim in 1924, the peak year of C.V. individual membership, that the C.V.

Table 1
C.V. Individual Membership from 1894–1933[57]

Year	Membership	Year	Membership	Year	Membership
1894	2,000	1918	38,260	1926	70,000
1903	16,000	1919	45,024	1927	70,104
1913	35,248	1920	54,714	1929	60,000
1914	37,875	1922	62,995	1930	60,000
1915	36,027	1923	68,203	1932	60,000
1916	35,597	1924	72,450	1933	64,000
1917	36,255	1925	70,134		

represented 85 to 90 percent of all German Jews.[58] By comparison one should note that the number of Zionists in Germany never rose above 20,000 individual members.[59] Table 1 (on page 53) gives an indication of the C.V. individual membership from 1894 to 1933.[60]

The influence of the C.V. extended beyond its official membership. It was a common phenomenon in Germany that the leading Jewish citizens of the community headed a number of organizations, and through their personal control assured a unanimity of ideology and philosophy in the community. The C.V. leaders themselves frequently occupied positions of leadership in other important Jewish organizations, thereby assuring the C.V. of a broad mass support. Eugen Fuchs and Maximilian Horwitz, foremost leaders of the C.V. in its early years, were also cofounders of the *Verband der deutschen Juden.* Similarly, Paul Nathan, [61] an important member of the executive board of the C.V. and a frequent contributor to its official publications, was the most influential leader of the *Hilfsverein der deutschen Juden* and a member of the executive board of the *Verband der deutschen Juden.*[62]

Few lists of C.V. membership and leadership are extant, and these are patently incomplete. On the basis of available information, however, it is clear that the C.V. leadership as well as the rank-and-file membership represented the German Jewish middle and upper-middle classes.[63] Most of the leadership comprised well-to-do individuals in business or the professions.[64] A list of the top leadership of the C.V. in 1918 reveals that more than one-third of the 250 men were members of the legal profession, the remainder in the academic profession, medicine, banking, and the rabbinate (liberal and reform rather than orthodox).[65] In 1929, one-half of the 150 leading members practiced law.[66] This socioeconomic composition of the C.V. leadership remained unchanged through the last stage of the organization's existence.[67] The great influx of Eastern European Jews into Germany during World War I did not alter the composition of the leadership of the C.V. A list of the members of its governing body during the last days of Weimar includes only middle-class Jews: five scientists, seven rabbis, eight bankers, industrialists, and merchants, ten civil servants, editors, and politicians, and eight lawyers.[68]

There are no available data on the members' social and economic positions. The only clue is a survey of K.C. members and *alte Herren* that was conducted in 1913. Since most members of the K.C. joined the ranks of the C.V. upon graduation from the university, this survey is a relatively accurate social indicator for the C.V. members.[69] The survey of 824 members of the K.C. provides the following socio-economic data:[70]

Table 2
Survey of Kartell Convent, 1913

Profession		Number	Percent of K.C. Members
Law (lawyers, notary publics, judges)		365	44.5
Medicine (physicians, dentists, veterinarians)		338	41.3
Engineers, chemists, technologists		70	8.6
Other		51	5.6
pharmacists	17		
salesmen, landlords	17		
philologists, theologians	10		
farmers	2		
artists (singer, painter)	2		
editors	2		
theatrical producer	1		
Total		824	100.0

This information suggests that the membership of the K.C. and C.V. reflected the middle-class professional composition of their leadership.

In contrast, two groups within German Jewry were poorly represented or not represented at all within the C.V. membership: recent Jewish immigrants from Eastern Europe who belonged to the lower socioeconomic classes, and orthodox German Jews. The absence of Eastern European Jews did not escape the attention of the C.V. members who frequently discussed the *Ostjudenfrage*. Since the C.V. leaders assumed that all *Ostjuden* were members of the Zionist organization, no efforts were made to recruit them.[71] German orthodox Jews' reluctance to join the C.V. stemmed from the ill-feeling aroused by Loewenfeld; they were by no means convinced that the C.V. had repudiated Loewenfeld's position.[72] The C.V.'s attitude toward religion was similarly significant for the orthodox.[73] When the C.V. officially changed its position to a more neutral one toward religion, some orthodox Jews responded to the efforts of Rabbi Hirsch Hildesheimer (1855–1910) and began to join the organization.[74] Nevertheless their ratio to the total membership remained very small.

Organization

In the statutes formulated in 1893, the first paragraph had defined the purpose of the C.V. while the remainder outlined the organizational elements necessary for the realization of its goals.

During its forty-five year existence the C.V. had four different constitutions; the 1893 statutes were revised in 1909 and 1928, and again in 1935.[75] The statutes of 1909 allowed for some decentralization of the C.V. through the formation of local chapters and regional associations, while those of 1928 were primarily concerned with the C.V.'s significantly enlarged membership, new public organs, and the internal relationships between the central office in Berlin, the state-based districts (*Landesverbaende*), and the local groups (*Ortsgruppen*).[76] The changes of 1935 came as a response to the seizure of power by the Nazis.

The C.V. bureaucracy was organized from the bottom up according to the following categories: representatives from the provinces (*Vertauensmaenner*), local chapters or groups (*Ortsgruppen*), federations of *Ortsgruppen* (*Landesverbaende*), the general assembly (*Hauptversammlung*), a smaller group of representatives elected by the *Hauptversammlung* (*Hauptvorstand*), and the executive committee (*Arbeitsausschuss*). The last three were the major administrative bodies.

In small cities and in rural districts with a small Jewish population, the C.V. was represented by so-called persons of confidence (*Vertrauensmaenner*) who were appointed by the director of the C.V. with the approval of the *Arbeits-ausschuss*. These representatives were men who could be trusted to uphold the honor and ideology of the C.V. and to protect its interests within their communities. Periodically they were requested to submit reports to the *Hauptvorstand* in Berlin, and these were used as guidelines for further action by the C.V. Before undertaking any initiative in the communities of the *Vertrauensmaenner,* the *Hauptvorstand* sought the approval of these representatives, a measure that in turn assured the success of the C.V. programs.[77]

In larger centers "city organizations" (*Ortsgruppen*) existed as local chapters of the C.V. and were composed of at least twenty-five members. Each city organization belonged, in turn, to a larger federation of *Ortsgruppen (Landesverbaende)*. In 1911 the C.V. had six *Landesverbaende,*[78] in 1918 there were thirteen *Landesverbaende* and 174 *Ortsgruppen;*[79] five years later there were twenty-one *Landesverbaende* and 550 *Ortsgruppen.*[80] In 1932 the 60,000 members of the C.V. were organized in twenty-three *Landesverbaende* and 634 *Ortsgruppen.*[81] Each *Landesverband* had an executive, a lawyer, and two or three employees in its office;[82] the principal offices were in Berlin, Breslau, Essen, Frankfurt am Main, Hamburg, Stettin, and Stuttgart.[83]

The *Hauptversammlung* was the largest body of the C.V. and was composed of individual *Vertrauensmaenner,* delegates from the *Ortsgruppen* and *Landesverbaende* plus all members of the *Hauptvorstand.* At least 50 percent of the *Hauptversammlung* (as well as the *Hauptvorstand*) were delegates of the Berlin community of 170,000 Jews.[84] This fact led to the accusation that "Berlin ruled the C.V.," a charge implying that the Berlin delegates did not respond to the needs of the entire membership. The complaint that Berlin was over-represented was in fact unfounded. The K.C. survey of 1913 shows that 76 percent of the members of the K.C., and by inference those of the C.V., lived in Prussia. It is, therefore, not surprising that Berlin was indeed the power center of the C.V.[85]

The *Hauptvorstand* was composed of eighteen members

before 1914, then of twenty-five members, of whom at least ten had to be residents of Berlin. Of these twenty-five, the *Hauptversammlung* elected eight members; the seventeen remaining positions were filled by delegates elected directly by the *Landesverbaende* in proportion to their numerical representation in the C.V. In addition to its twenty-five members, the *Hauptvorstand* was entitled to add twenty individuals from organizations with ideologies similar to that of the C.V. (such as the *Reichsbund juedischer Frontsoldaten, Hilfsverein der deutschen Juden* and *Verband der deutschen Juden*), plus honorary members and public personalities in the sciences, art, and politics.[86] The tasks of the *Hauptvorstand* were to formulate policies for the organization and to elect the president, his deputy, and the director of the C.V.

This small body of top C.V. officials was called the executive branch (*Engerer Vorstand* or *Arbeitsausschuss*) and was responsible for supervising the execution of C.V. policies. They carried on the daily business and had full authority. In 1924 a business office was created (*Verwaltungskommission*) to conduct all monetary transactions.[87] The C.V.'s main office was in Berlin where approximately sixty officials, headed by the director and two executive secretaries (*Syndici*) worked.[88]

The director of the C.V. often enlisted the help of a small group of intellectuals to advise him in an unofficial capacity. Ludwig Hollaender made extensive use of the resources of this group. The members of this "brain trust" were often the leading exponents of the C.V. ideologies; their ideas and arguments were publicized through the official organs of the C.V. and were thus assured of wide circulation and influence.

During the years from 1893 to 1938, the C.V. had five presidents who strongly influenced the ideas and practices of the C.V.: Martin Mendelssohn (term, 1893–94),[89] along with Loewenfeld and Simon, was instrumental in founding and organizing the C.V. Maximilian Horwitz (term, 1894–1917) is credited with an unusual organizational talent; it was through his relentless energy and personal drive that the enormously complex bureaucracy of the C.V. functioned smoothly and effectively. Eugen Fuchs (term, 1917–20) laid the cornerstone of the ideology of the C.V.; he was known as the founder of the C.V.'s philosophical synthesis of *Deutschtum* and *Judentum*.[90] Julius Brodnitz (term, 1920–36) had the organizational talents of Horwitz; and he managed to strengthen the C.V.'s membership and eminence within the German Jewish community during a difficult period when the basic ideologies of the C.V. were being questioned by its own membership. Ernst Herzfeld (term, 1936–38), the youngest of the C.V. leaders, had the task of trying to maintain an organization which was by then virtually powerless. Most of his efforts were devoted to cooperating with the *Reichsvertretung der deutschen Juden,* which tried to pool the resources of the entire German Jewish community in the face of the Nazi threat.

C.V. Press and Official Publications

An important aid to the administrative hierarchy of the C.V. were its official publications. The first issue of the organization's monthly, *Im Deutschen Reich (IDR),* appeared on July 1, 1895. The paper was not intended as a polemical mouthpiece to counteract the "lies of the anti-Semites," but as a "respectable" paper devoted to "scientific" and objective examination of daily events and to the reporting of them in a style in keeping with the ideologies of the C.V.[91] Most of the space in the *IDR*'s pages was used to convey news about the C.V.'s activities throughout Germany, but it also published feuilletons, editorials, eulogies, memoirs, occasional historical essays, and replies to anti-Semitic charges.

The *IDR* was intended also for leading German Gentile readers. The goal was to provide a public forum in which the problems of German Jews could be discussed freely. To realize this aim the *IDR* was sent free of charge to many Christians who occupied responsible government and military positions in German public life.[92] There are no indications that these goals were achieved. The number of Christians who contributed articles to the periodical was very small; discussions between Christians and Jews were almost nonexistent. In addition the paper, published monthly, necessarily presented an analysis of events that was out of date. In 1922, the *Im Deutschen Reich* ceased publication, since its format had become inadequate for the needs of the C.V. membership, which had increased greatly after the war. Additionally, the swelling number of anti-Semitic attacks and daily abuses made prompt communication and defense even more pressing than before. The C.V. could not afford delayed reactions to daily events if it was to be effective.[93]

Anti-Semitism and Jewish Identity

As we have seen, the statutes and organization of the C.V. and the main thrust of its publications and ideology were geared, at least in the early years, to helping German Jews realize full integration and emancipation in Germany.[94] Since anti-Semitism was seen as the chief obstacle to the achievement of these goals, the C.V. considered its major task the battle against anti-Semitism in Germany. The creation of a Jewish organization, which for the first time in the history of German Jewry was not devoted to religious or scholarly matters, did not take place without elaborate justification by its founders. The leaders were faced with two questions: what was the impetus for founding such an organization if similar ones already existed; and why was the newly founded organization determined to be identified as specifically Jewish? Both questions of course implied that a Jewish organization founded solely for Jewish purposes was of little benefit to the German Jewish community and that it might in fact retard the process of Jewish acculturation into the German nation.

The C.V. leaders believed that defense of Jewish rights had to be carried out by Jews rather than by Gentiles who had no direct personal interest in the matter; and that Jews alone were willing and able to make meaningful sacrifices for the sake of preserving their personal and collective honor. At the same time these leaders made every effort to dispel the notion that their organization sought to segregate Jews from the main body of the German people. Ideologically the C.V. faced a three-way dilemma in respect to its identity: it was distinct from non-Jewish organizations such as the *Verein zur*

Abwehr des Antisemitismus in its exclusively Jewish emphasis; its primary goal was to fight anti-Semitism in its role as a Jewish organization, yet it was at the same time unable to clarify its own concept of Jewishness.

According to the C.V., the Jews were citizens who had to fulfill their obligations to the state, while at the same time demanding that their own rights be preserved. Since they did not want to burden the state with their defense they took the initiative themselves and carried out their goals, but within the limits of the law and for the general welfare of the German nation: "only if we ward off every encroachment upon our emancipation may we claim that we are worthy of our equality."[95] In other words, the dilemma was avoided by ignoring ideology in favor of engaging in the contest against anti-Semitism. Other organizations shared the same goals but the C.V. differed from them in the nature of its methods, the number of its activities, and the ethnic homogeneity of its membership. The C.V. concentrated on two practical areas: daily refutation of anti-Semitic attacks on Jewish rights; and the inculcation among its members of German sentiments, values, and Weltanschauung (*deutsche Gesinnung*). The C.V.'s stand against anti-Semitism was grounded less on the defense of Jewish values and Judaism than on the rights of Jews as German citizens. To friends and foes alike the C.V. proclaimed that civil and moral responsibilities justified the establishment of an exclusively Jewish defense organization.

For many Jews who hesitated to press a specific charge against the anti-Semites for fear of reprisals or for lack of funds, the C.V. served as a convenient instrument for dealing with the case in return for a moderate membership fee. The C.V.'s legal offices throughout Germany were headed by lawyers whose function was to protect individuals and communities from the insults and physical abuses of anti-Semitism, and they would press charges against anyone who infringed upon Jewish civil and political rights. For many German Jews the C.V. was the only road to Jewish identification. The organization bound them with other individuals who had at least a vague knowledge of Judaism combined

with a strong feeling of German *Gesinnung*.[96] Ismar Freund,
one of the most active members of the C.V. in the 1920s and
a member of the *Hauptvorstand,* wrote:

> The battle against anti-Semitism in Germany was one of
> the clearest paths to Jewish identity for a large part of
> the assimilated Jewish community. For the most part
> [these assimilated Jews] had emancipated themselves
> from the hampering ties of Jewish ritual observance. On
> the other hand they had rejected the national traits of
> Judaism. The will to Judaism, the feeling of Jewishness,
> was present, however, and demanded some activation. It
> needed some content. They found both in the political
> struggle conducted by the C.V. Some found in the work
> of the C.V. an added attraction, since there they could
> give vent to political ambitions which could not be satis-
> fied in the general political life of Germany; the fight
> against anti-Semitism was a substitute for other political
> activity.[97]

The decision of the C.V. leaders (with few exceptions) to
ignore questions of Jewish identity is closely tied to their
personal backgrounds. Most of the C.V. membership and
leadership were religiously liberal Jews, and some were even
members of the *Juedische Reformgemeinde zu Berlin,* an
extreme reformist and assimilationist congregation whose
membership came from the upper middle class.[98] The members and rabbis of this congregation were reluctant to press
for specifically Jewish demands; by the 1920s they were to
become the strongest supporters of the highly assimilationist
Verband Nationaldeutscher Juden founded by Max Nau-
mann. Those members and leaders of the C.V. who did not
belong to the *Reformgemeinde* were by and large affiliated
with liberal congregations that did not stress Jewish group
identity or national traits. Such affiliations were not conducive to identification with traditional Jewish values, and it is
not surprising that the Jewish content of the organization
remained ill-defined. For many Jews, membership in a Jewish
organization was the only expression of their Jewish identi-

ty.[99] Ernst Feder analyzed the attitude of Paul Nathan, one
of the foremost leaders of the C.V., thus:

> Jewish questions and problems which were raised in Ger-
> man public life . . . appeared to him to be no more impor-
> tant and of no more interest than they would have been
> to any liberal politician of the time. This meant in prac-
> tice that equality of rights for the Jews . . . should be put
> into effect and safeguarded, not for the sake of the Jews,
> but in the interest of the modern state which is founded
> on equality of rights for all its citizens. Paul Nathan was
> not naive enough to believe that the Jewish question
> would be "solved" by a liberal victory. Rather, it ap-
> peared to him that the fight against anti-Semitism was
> one facet of the general struggle for law and justice.
> Other solutions to the Jewish question, which were al-
> ready being explored at the time, did not concern
> him.[100]

Within the framework of a united battle against anti-
Semitism and the nonspecificity of the definition of "Jew,"
the C.V. attempted to attract all Jews regardless of their
religious attitudes. It consistently stated that its primary
purpose was defense, that it had no cause to exclude the
orthodox from this endeavor, nor did it wish to be a party to
the religious controversies which erupted regularly in Berlin
between the liberal and orthodox parties. The C.V. did declare itself, however, categorically opposed to conversion to
Christianity. Eugen Fuchs was unconcerned about the liberals' disdain of religious ritual, but viewed conversion as
treachery; after all, the C.V. had intimated that leaving one's
religion simply because of anti-Semitic attacks was the merest
cowardice. It was of no significance to the C.V. whether
orthodox or liberals were elected to head the *Gemeinden,* so
long as the general defense work of the C.V. moved
ahead.[101]

It is ironic that the C.V., which advocated complete
acculturation, was organized by Jews who *ipso facto* formed
a special interest group. The very constitution of the C.V. is

in plain contradiction to its aims. The C.V. minimized the contradiction by omitting all reference to distinctions between its members and the surrounding culture, claiming rather that it intended merely to serve as an aid to the individual who wanted to achieve full integration in Germany. Despite Friedrich Brodnitz's solemn declaration that the C.V. had no intention to create a group identity (*Unser Zusammenschluss zur Organisation war nicht Zusammenschluss zur Gruppe*), in the long run the creation of the C.V. did exactly that.[102]

The generational experience of the founders of the C.V. shaped their attitudes toward defense against anti-Semitism. The founding members had witnessed two waves of political anti-Semitism in Germany: one that surfaced in the 1870s and lasted until approximately 1883; and a second from about 1889 to 1893. Although the C.V. came into being in response to the second wave, its founders had also witnessed the ebb of the organized anti-Semitic campaigns of the middle nineties.[103]   Hence, they considered political anti-Semitism a phenomenon that could once more be routed. "The C.V. fathers were strong believers in the enlightened liberal era and were inclined to see in anti-Semitic barbarity nothing more than the ephemeral residue of an unintelligent past which they considered doomed and practically gone."[104]   For them anti-Jewish discrimination was an evil that could be fought by education and by legislation. They felt the duties of the C.V. should include: dissemination of information, refutation of anti-Jewish slander by publicly branding the offenders in the courts, lobbying in favor of legislative reforms, and above all the securing of legal protection and advice for victims of discrimination.[105]

At this time the anti-Semites had long since ceased to persecute Jews solely because they had rejected Christianity. Although religion continued to play a substantial role in political and racial anti-Semitism, it was clear that the Jews were now being condemned as members of another, inferior race. The C.V., however, insisted until just prior to World War I that Jews were distinguished from other Germans by their religion alone, and in no way by their loyalty to Germany. It was a point of view that adhered to the century-

old German Jewish tradition, one that rejected Jewish nationalism in favor of assimilation into the German culture in
accordance with liberal ideology and presumably with the
wishes of the Prussian emancipators. Not by coincidence did
the process toward the "confessionalization" of the Jewish
religion find its zenith with the liberalism of the year 1848.
The majority of German Jews continued to see Judaism as
nothing more than a confession of faith. Later, toward the
turn of the century, when relations between Jews and non-
Jews had begun to be explained in terms of race, German
Jewry still insisted that it was unique only by virtue of its
religious faith. The continued adherence of the C.V. to its
liberal ideology is apparent from its "Guidelines for German
Jews" published at the turn of the century:

1. Justice is the foundation of our state and society.
2. To combat a religious minority which is recognized
   by the state contradicts the judicial ethics of the
   nation.
3. The practice of the Jewish religion and its ethical
   teachings does not contradict in any way the ethical
   foundations of the modern state . . . it is therefore in
   accordance with the justice of the state to give Jews
   full equality.
4. Anti-Semitism violates the basic command which
   teaches both Jews and Christians to love their neighbors. . . .
5. Only the united effort of all the ethical and intellectual forces has helped to unite and glorify Germany. It
   is the duty of every patriot to safeguard these values.
6. No one who has given to the fatherland his fortune
   and blood, or his intellectual resources, be he Aryan
   or Semite, Jew or Christian, may be turned away from
   Germany. The well-being of the fatherland depends on
   justice.[106]

The Ties of the C.V. with German Political Parties

Throughout its history the C.V. retained an ambivalent attitude toward politics. The C.V.'s faith in the impartial justice
of the state had had a major impact on the original statutes

of 1893, which declared that the C.V. would not intervene directly in politics. In this regard the C.V. deliberately dissociated itself from its counterpart, the Catholic Center party, which established a source of power to protect its own interests against an unjust state. The C.V. premise, however, was that since the state was just, political intervention was unnecessary and possibly harmful. "We are," declared Eugen Fuchs,

> a *Centralverein*, a central organization which encompasses all Jews regardless of their modes of worship. The Jews as a religious community do not belong to any one political party. Political ideologies, like religious ones, are the business of the individual. The experience of the past has proven that the ties of Jews with political parties, such as the Progressive party, have not benefited either partner. Even if the Jews as a whole tend to favor the liberal parties there are many questions which could be solved only from a Jewish point of view and not by any one political party.[107]

The C.V.'s insistence on complete political neutrality was compelling enough to warrant incorporation into its statutes.

An additional motive for abstaining from politics was the fear that such activities would place the Jews in the limelight and exaggerate the importance and problematic nature of the "Jewish Question." Leaders of the C.V. noted that the Jews in Germany were not the major concern of the German state, and therefore it behooved them not to press for special demands. For this reason the C.V.'s position that all political questions, even those concerning the Jews directly, should be judged solely with respect to the interests of the German nation, remained entrenched through the late twenties.

The C.V.'s occasional participation in German politics was carried out with extreme reluctance and for limited periods of time. "Jewish" policies and politics were categorically rejected, even though other interest groups were using political means to achieve their goals. The paradox of the C.V. position was that despite its public insistence that the

Jews deserved an equal position in German society, its members privately agreed that no special effort should be exerted to qualify for such a position. Maximilian Horwitz, a president of the C.V., often said: "Stepchildren must behave themselves" (*Stiefkinder muessen artig sein*).[108]

Despite the early and repeated assurances by the C.V. of its political neutrality it quickly had to come to terms with the fact that the German political parties were divided into anti-Semitic and philo-Semitic groups, a fact that made political impartiality untenable. Two other factors played a role in the C.V.'s eventual decision to engage in political activities: the anti-Semites had begun to form political parties and actively to participate in the affairs of already existing parties. If the anti-Semites were not to attain complete control of German politics, opposition had to be created in the equivalent arena of party politics. Early in its history the C.V. conceded that even the finest slogans, based on noble moral and ethical principles, were not a sufficient practical defense against anti-Semitism. In addition, the C.V. recognized that protection of German Jewish rights demanded confrontation with anti-Semitic parliamentarians. The reevaluation of its stance resulted in the C.V.'s practical alliance with the left liberal parties (*Freisinnige*), the bastions against anti-Semitism. The *Sozialdemokratische Partei Deutschlands* (SPD) also gained Jewish support as an outgrowth of the same reconsideration.[109]

As early as 1894, a year after its foundation, the C.V. supported pro-Jewish candidates in the Berlin elections. Not until 1898, however, did the C.V. participate in nation-wide campaigns by actively opposing anti-Semitic candidates, as they did in Posen, and thus publicly acknowledge a departure from neutrality.[110] The C.V. leaders themselves, however, maintained that this new orientation was not a breach of neutrality, since the C.V. had not formed an independent party (like the Catholic Center party), nor was it indefinitely allied with any one political party.[111] But the practical result of the 1898 elections was the formation of a close tie between the C.V. and the *Freisinn* parties, a bond that lasted until World War I.[112] The C.V.'s activities included the support of candidates who were well disposed toward Jewish rights. It even considered proposing Jewish candidates to represent Jewish rights and demands directly, on behalf of organizations that shared the C.V.'s Weltanschauung, although this idea never advanced beyond the planning stage.[113] Although the C.V. would have been happy to see a Jewish politician reoccupy Bamberger's position in Parliament, it was reluctant to press for Jewish candidates for fear of being accused of supporting "confessional candidates."[114]

Of the two *Freisinn* parties, the *Freisinnige Volkspartei* and the *Freisinnige Vereinigung,* the C.V. maintained a stronger union with the former, especially in Berlin and Posen.[115]   Both splinter groups occasionally placed Jews, sometimes baptized Jews, on their lists, and some of them were even elected to Parliament. Because of the strong pressure of anti-Semites, the *Freisinn* parties were not always consistent in their philo-Semitic policies, and in 1903 they openly supported anti-Semitic candidates.[116]   To a large extent the C.V.'s association with the liberal parties was a matter of default. After the "Tivoli Program" was announced, the C.V. could not ally with the conservatives. Nor could it form close ties with the Center party with its strong Catholic identification. Consequently, the C.V. leaders supported the liberal parties whose ideological and philosophical viewpoints they shared and with whose members they enjoyed personal and professional ties.

The C.V. was often criticized by friends and enemies alike for contradicting its avowed apolitical posture. The C.V.'s reply was that legal action against libelous statements and aggressive behavior was inadequate self-defense. Its leaders also justified political activity on the programmatic basis that Parliament was the arena of state policy-making and the setting for attacks on Jews. In Parliament alone would the Jews' fate be decided. [117] The moral and practical obligation of the C.V. was therefore to influence local and national elections. Fuchs echoed the admonition of Bertha von Suttner:

The fruits of success do not fall into people's laps effortlessly; the battle is of the utmost importance especially in political matters. We do not have the patience nor the aptitude to wait . . . for the dawn of a future day that will bring us equality and brotherhood. We want to determine our own fate through our own strength.[118]

Against the charges that the C.V. had betrayed liberalism by supporting "confessional candidates" constrained to function in terms of narrow Jewish interests, the organization replied that it was a greater infringement of liberalism to have a Parliament comprising 430 Christian delegates who took offense at the prospect of having among them one Jewish member.[119] "A confessional candidate in the true sense of the expression is a Jew who is elected by Jews not for his parliamentary skills, but because of his faith."[120] The C.V. asserted that the Jews who had been elected to Parliament were well-qualified politicians, who had been active before the existence of the C.V. As a comprehensive rejoinder to criticism, the C.V. assured the public that even if Jewish officials were elected by Jewish support, it would always vote in terms of the general welfare of the German state which was synonymous with its own.[121]

In addition to supporting the liberal pro-Jewish parties with funds and votes, the C.V. acted as their legal adviser in matters pertaining to the Jews in Germany. The C.V. lawyers were consulted on all matters concerning suits against anti-Semites as well as on any legislation that could affect the Jewish position. In this area of jurisprudence the C.V. was highly competent, its leadership consisting primarily of men trained in the legal profession, and these lawyers contributed significantly to the C.V.'s involvement in politics. For them the best means of achieving legal demands lay in legal measures enacted by the proper authorities. As a consequence, a pro-Semitic party, supported by the C.V., had the tools to press for legislation to check anti-Semitism.

In keeping with the commonly held view in Germany, the C.V. leaders saw the state as a *Rechtsstaat,* a legal entity which could function properly only within the boundaries of the law. For them the Jewish question was not political, but legal, and the C.V.'s involvement in politics was therefore a necessary measure rather than an ideal situation. Ultimately, the C.V., whose faith in the justice of the German state never wavered, came to believe that a legal confrontation, supported by the occasional political pressure of friendly parties, would overcome the anti-Semitic movement and grant to the Jews the place due them within the German state.

Ideology of the C.V.

It has been pointed out that the C.V. was both a defense organization (*Abwehrverein*) and a proponent of a specific ideology (*Gesinnungsverein*). These dual functions were intimately related in the organization's basic platform, which consistently stated that anti-Semitism could be defeated by those who professed utter loyalty to *deutsche Gesinnung*. Despite consistency on this point, the C.V.'s ideological position was in a continual process of modification in response to the external and internal events between 1893 and 1938. [122] World War I, the Balfour Declaration, the influx of *Ostjuden* into Germany, and the demands of the younger C.V. generation during the late 1920s were, among other factors, instrumental in these changes. An analysis of the C.V.'s attitude toward *Deutschtum* and *Judentum* before World War I is, therefore, crucial to a proper understanding of the evolution of its ideology up to 1938.

In its early years the C.V. emphatically declared that it was *solely* a defense organization which aimed to protect the honor of the German Jews in the face of anti-Semitic insults. [123] This statement plainly contradicts the first paragraph of the C.V. statutes which demanded "German-mindedness" from its members. This demand meant that membership in the C.V. was conditional on loyalty to *Deutschtum* above all other loyalties, including loyalty to *Judentum,* and this was the overriding position of the C.V. before World War I. [124] Despite its stress on patriotism and love of everything German, the C.V. did not completely neglect to define its stand toward *Judentum*. A major task of the C.V. before World War I was therefore to make both *Judentum* and *Deutschtum* components of the Weltanschauung of the German Jew, but with *Judentum* relegated to a place of secondary importance.

Before the founding of the C.V. in 1893, there had been many attempts to define the place of the Jew within the German state. These definitions, philosophical, historical, and polemical, were painstakingly constructed to prove the same thesis—that the Jews were solely a religious body, analogous to the Catholics and Protestants, completely integrated within the state. This definition is the essence of the liberal assimilationist ideology developed and refined from the eighteenth century on. Foremost among the men who shaped this ideology were Gabriel Riesser, Moritz Lazarus, Hermann Cohen, and Eugen Fuchs. Riesser, Lazarus, and Cohen were influential in formulating the theoretical ideology of the general German Jewish community while Fuchs, the acknowledged ideologue of the C.V., related their theories to the specific needs of the C.V. The names of these four exponents of the synthesis of *Deutschtum* and *Judentum* appear continuously in the C.V. publications, especially in *Im Deutschen Reich* and *Central-Verein Zeitung*. The philosophy of the C.V. was derived wholly from one or all of these men.[125]

In the early years of its existence the *IDR* referred most frequently to Riesser, to whose personality and achievements it devoted many essays and in whom it saw its most important spiritual progenitor. Like many of his contemporaries, Riesser was concerned with the "Jewish national problem." Supporters of Germany's national revival claimed that the Jews were a nation and should therefore not have equal rights. Riesser, a foremost champion in the fight for equality, expressed his views frequently and with great passion. His most complete exposition on the subject is "Ueber die Verteidigung der buergerlichen Gleichstellung der Juden,"[126] in which he concludes that the Jewish nation no longer exists and that all that remains is the "fable of Jewish nationality."[127] Although Jews comprised a separate nation two thousand years ago, this fact from the past has ceased to have any relevance.

Riesser asserted that Jews born in Germany could have no other fatherland. He tried to prove that the Jewish Question was also regarded by the Gentiles as a purely religious one without national implications. As proof, Riesser pointed out that every Jew could free himself from the restrictions to which he was subjected by converting to Christianity; conversion guaranteed automatic admission to German society and opened all avenues hitherto closed.[128] The Jewish nation no longer existed, since the basic requirement, a territory, did not exist. The Jews constituted a religion only and, as a consequence, were full members of any nation in whose midst they happened to reside.[129]

When the question arose in Prussia as to whether the Jewish religion should be recognized by law as a separate nationality, Riesser was vehemently opposed and claimed that the persistence of Judaism is based on an idea, not a nationality. The distinguishing marks of a nation were for Riesser "land, language, a constitution, political power, and independence; or the struggle for these requirements. These elements are the preconditions of a nation; where all of them were lacking, as in the case of the Jews, the foundation for a nation was nonexistent."[130] Thus for Riesser, Jews were *ipso facto* only a religious community. Their belief in a Messiah was a religious tenet, not based on a hope for an actual national revival.

Despite this point of view, Riesser was the example *par excellence* of a proud Jew who valued the ethical and moral teachings of his religion very highly. He considered himself as good a German citizen as any of his Christian neighbors and was prepared to resist any infringement of his rights as a citizen. The determination to wage his own battles, added to his complete loyalty to German culture and national values, made him a favorite and almost heroic figure in the C.V.'s ideology. Riesser despised the idea of turning to baptism as a solution either for anti-Semitism or private difficulties. He wanted to solve the problems of the Jews in Germany as a Jew. Even in his first article, "Ueber die Stellung der Bekenner des mosaischen Glaubens," he urged the Jews to fight for emancipation rather than to convert. He continued this strug-

gle all his life, particularly as a deputy in the National
Assembly in Frankfurt. He made practical suggestions for the
establishment of a defense organization that would include
all Jews. This proposed organization would need a public
organ, so in 1832 Riesser founded *Der Jude* to be its mouthpiece.[131]

Riesser's call for organized Jewish defense, his conception
of Judaism as a religion like all others within the framework
of the *Rechtsstaat,* and his desire for an open and public
organization to include all Jews in the struggle against anti-
Semitism were clearly forerunners of similar programs put
forth by the C.V. The C.V. often acknowledged its intellectual and even organizational debt to Riesser. His famous
characterization of Germany as the "motherland" of German
Jews, "Einen Vater in den Hoehen, eine Mutter haben wir,
Gott ihn aller Wesen Vater, Deutschland unsere Mutter hier,"
was often used by the C.V. as an accurate expression of its
early ideology.[132]

Unlike Riesser, Moritz Lazarus was not actively political;
his contributions to German political thought were primarily
scientific and scholarly.[133] In 1880 Lazarus, the cofounder
of the *Voelkerpsychologie* and of the *Hochschule fuer die
Wissenschaft des Judentums,* published the pamphlet *Was
Heisst National?* as a reply to Treitschke. It identified him at
once as a German of the Jewish faith who was not ashamed
to profess publicly his loyalty to both *Deutschtum* and
Judentum.[134]

In this pamphlet Lazarus discussed the opinions of experts as to the characteristics that make up a nation, and he
came to the conclusion that no definition of nationality, thus
far given, is complete.[135] A nation, according to Lazarus,
cannot be described solely in objective terms but is dependent on subjective factors as well, particularly on the emotional response of an individual or a collective group toward
its nation: "My people are those whom I recognize as my
people, those whom I call mine, those to whom I am tied
forever."[136] Lazarus claimed that the attachment of the
Jews to their fatherland was unquestionable; he answered the
question of the nationality of Jews in no uncertain terms:

"We are Germans, nothing but Germans, when we talk about the concept of nationality we belong to only one nation, the German one."[137]

He saw the Jews as ideally suited to be good German citizens because they shared with non-Jewish Germans the language, birthplace and residence, devotion to the state, obedience to the law, education, and culture; the latter two deeply steeped in *Deutschtum*. Admittedly, they were of Semitic descent, but many of their fellow citizens were of non-Germanic origin. In any case ancestry was not the crucial factor, as the case of Immanuel Kant should demonstrate: "Would it not be considered heresy of the first order to say that Kant was not a good German because his ancestors came from Scotland?"[138]

The Jews, according to Lazarus, had the admirable capability of being totally assimilated into other cultures precisely because they were unhampered by national barriers and a separate culture. Therefore, they were able to absorb other cultures and to make lasting contributions to their host countries.[139]

The great Kantian philosopher of Marburg, Hermann Cohen, who was also concerned with national self-consciousness, stressed, as did Lazarus, the subjective-voluntary elements that make a nation. Cohen rejected Lazarus's denial of the cosmopolitan nature of religion, believing that such a notion made religion a subjective individual criterion in the national definition, rather than an objective one.[140] Cohen, who identified Judaism with religion, considered religion the ethical force on which all cultural values were based. He devoted himself to furthering respect for and knowledge of the Jewish religion while at the same time fostering the "ethical idealism of *Deutschtum*." A contemporary of the C.V. founders, Cohen was the most respected member of the German Jewish community at that time. His interpretations were readily accepted by all the publications of the C.V.[141]

Cohen examined the relationship of Judaism and Christianity in detail and concluded that the two religions were not only based on the same biblical foundations, but that in the historical process they had become so similar that all distinctions between them were merely the product of illusion and prejudice.[142]   Cohen claimed that differences between the two faiths were confined to variations in modes of worship within a common religious community. This historical-cultural link (*Kulturgeschichtliche Verbindung*) was "the strongest, most potent tie for an internal national fusion."[143]   He praised those faithful Jews who loved their fatherland as deeply as their religion, and who wanted to be good German Jews as well as good Jewish Germans.[144]

In his various expositions, Cohen emphasized that the Jews in Germany, totally immersed in the surrounding Christian religion, completely accepted this cultural phenomenon. German Jews loved their fatherland not because it was "worthy of their love," but because it was their fatherland. In fact, this was unconditional love: "we all have our fatherland, because it is our 'mother-earth,' because we love our homeland, because we view Palestine as nothing more than a place to which we occasionally travel." To the charge that the Jews were of a different race and, therefore, could not possibly be good Germans, Cohen answered: "We all wish we had a Germanic appearance . . . in this question we simply have to say: Have patience!"[145]

Cohen criticized his former teacher, Heinrich Graetz, for having emphasized the national traits of the Jews in his historical writings. He condemned dual nationalism as senseless and claimed that the Jews should act in unison only when defending their honor as Jews.[146]   In his opinion, "to belong fully to a nation is not a light matter easily to be acquired; one has to devote all his energies and aspirations to this goal. . . . Serving the German state should be considered a holy privilege, like an important religious service."[147]

In another important essay Cohen summarized his convictions:

We German Jews are in a particularly favorable position since we were able to influence the rest of world Jewry in the spirit of our German culture, through the *Wissenschaft des Judentums* and our religious reforms. Our own

intellectuals have expressed the synthesis of Jewish mes-
sianism and German humanism, and we are trying to
impart these values to our brethren outside Germany.
The basis for our German national feeling is securely
rooted, religiously and culturally. Our soul swings symet-
rically and harmoniously between our German patriotism
and our religious consciousness, which find their apex in
the one and only God of mankind. We breathe, think and
compose, work and create, under the protection and
guidance of the German spirit. To honor it . . . is the goal
of our work.[148]

Although the theories of Riesser, Lazarus, and Cohen
provided the foundation for the Weltanschauung of the C.V.,
they had many other less important spiritual predecessors.
One such precursor was Emil Lehmann (1829–98), who in
1880 wrote that "Judaism is a religion that teaches its members to fulfill their duties. . . . The true Jew is a good man
and loyal patriot."[149]   When the C.V. was created in 1893,
and proceeded to espouse beliefs that he had long held,
Lehmann hailed it as a great moral achievement on the part
of German Jewry and an enormous step forward toward the
realization of full emancipation. Lehmann's description of
the German Jews as "German national representatives of the
Jewish faith" (*deutsche Volksvertreter juedischen Bekenntnisses*)[150]   which he later modified to "Germans of the
Jewish faith" (*Deutsche juedischen Bekenntniss*)[151]   was
nearly identical with ideas later held by the C.V. In a speech
delivered in 1869, Emil Lehmann responded to the accusations that Jews constituted a separate nationality by saying
that "the Jewish kingdom was only a faint fantasy in the
heads of a few Jews." In this connection he coined the
famous phrase, "I desire a Jewish kingdom only if I could be
its ambassador in the court of the king of Prussia."[152]   To
show that the German Jews loved their homeland unconditionally, Lehmann employed Goethe's verse, "If I love you,
what concern is it of yours?"[153]
The individual and collective loyalty of the German Jew
to his homeland was accepted by the C.V. in its synthesis of

Deutschtum and *Judentum*. It was not coincidental, however, that the C.V. statutes clearly gave precedence to *Deutschtum*.[154] As we have seen, every member of the C.V. believed that the most important precondition for self-defense was the demonstration of loyalty to Germany, even in the face of the most malicious anti-Semitic attacks.[155] This precondition changed the nature of the C.V. almost from the beginning from a defense organization to one with a specific ideology.[156] The motto of the C.V. was always that "Jews should know that they stand for the honor of being German-Jewish human beings. They have the right to be accepted as full-fledged citizens, members of the German culture."[157]

Members of the C.V. liked to believe that they were but "one color within the multicolored kaleidoscope of the German nation" (*Eine Farbe im vielfaeltigen Gemaelde des deutschen Volkes*). This politically liberal point of view persisted throughout the C.V.'s history and is best illustrated in a speech given by Eugen Fuchs in the general meeting of the C.V. (*Hauptversammlung*) in 1913:

For me the synthesis of *Deutschtum* and *Judentum* lies in the following: By virtue of my nationality I am a German; a Jew, by virtue of religion and heritage. My Silesian homeland, the business of my parents, and my academic-legal profession have left a certain imprint on my character, so has my Jewish home. The Jewish environment in which I was raised and continue to live left as strong a mark on my personality as my belonging to Prussia. But this Jewish heritage does not separate me in the national sense from German Christians, does not influence my belonging to the genus *"volk,"* and it estranges me from *Deutschtum* as little as the heritage of a Friesian farmer estranges him in the national sense from a proletarian on the Rhine or one in Berlin. As a lawyer I feel socially and intellectually closer to the Christian lawyer than to a Jewish businessman or worker. . . . I am deeply convinced that were I banished with other people to a desert, I would first try to establish contact with a German, be he

Jew or Christian, and that I would not be drawn first to someone who is not German but a Jew.[158]

The C.V. considered the Jews to be fully integrated in German society on the basis of three factors: (*a*) historical—Jews had lived on German soil for many centuries; (*b*) cultural—the intimate relationship with and the numerous contributions of the Jews to German culture in all its manifestations; (*c*) volitional—the Jews' acceptance of Germany as their only possible homeland and their collective desire to live as loyal citizens.[159]   Other thinkers ascribed the integrated position of the Jews in Germany to deeper emotional and psychological phenomena; the Jews were not Germans by choice, but by emotional and intellectual necessity. [160] The C.V. passionately claimed that the existence of German Jews on German soil rested not on artificial foundations but on "the holiest feelings of *Deutschtum* and *Judentum;* should this foundation be attacked it would shake the C.V., the most powerful organization of German Jewry, to its very foundation."[161]   Those members of the C.V. who argued for a synthesis of *Deutschtum* and *Judentum* claimed that they could be loyal to both. The intellectual and theoretical formulation of the synthesis was more problematical, however. Most arguments for synthesis started from the negative premise that the two components contained no contradictions. The second, or positive, argument stated that the two elements were inseparable and that it was in combination that they enriched German culture.

Despite all arguments it was obvious that this synthesis was necessary only for "German citizens of the *Jewish* faith"; it was tantamount to a proclamation that loyalty to *Judentum* did not interfere with the obligations of a German citizen. Moreover, within the framework of a nationalist state, the C.V. found it imperative to stress *Deutschtum* over *Judentum* lest it be charged with being more Jewish than German. From a practical point of view, *Deutschtum* as patriotism and *Gesinnung* could be demonstrated daily in civic activities, army service, and financial contributions to patriotic causes; it was, then, the more necessary component, and the easier to express.

As for *Judentum,* the C.V. was faced with the problem of presenting Judaism to the Gentile public in a manner that would not compromise German patriotism, while still leaving room for a stance acceptable to its membership. The first solution to this delicate balance was to avoid it altogether; the C.V. proposed no definitions of Judaism. This position could not be maintained, however, by men who claimed to be the heirs of Riesser and were proud of their heritage. The C.V. was simultaneously under pressure from German anti-Semites and German Zionists to define its position toward *Judentum.* [162] Initially the C.V. definition stemmed from an emphasis on the honor and dignity of the German Jew who, despite pressure from anti-Semites, would not be baptized. This point of view, held by the members of the K.C. and soon adopted by the C.V., clung to Judaism out of "defiance of the anti-Semites" (*Trutzjudentum*).[163] From a positive perspective, the C.V. declared:

> Loyalty to Judaism serves the cause of the fatherland; when we work together to uplift our moral and ethical community, we are in fact working in the interest of the fatherland. The great forces in Judaism—the ideas of unity, tradition, and optimism serve us well. . . . Because we are loyal [to Judaism] we are also loyal to the fatherland.[164]

The C.V. defined *Judentum* essentially as a religion (*Konfession, Glaubensgemeinschaft,* or *Religion*) that could not interfere in any way with the state.[165] Felix Goldmann, a rabbi in Oppeln and later in Leipzig and one of the most respected and lucid proponents of the C.V. ideology, asserted that the religious contents of Judaism were identical with the ethical values which had produced the foundation for the modern state.[166] The idea closely resembles Fuchs's "mission theory," common among Western European Jews who hoped to strengthen their claims to a secure haven by offering in return religious and ethical eternal truths. This theory of spiritual mission was upheld by the C.V. until the final days of Weimar.[167]   Goldmann elucidated it further:

> Only a few examples should suffice to prove that our community has an ingenious aptitude for religion. Ethical monotheism, the belief in a good and just God, was created in Israel. . . . Within the framework of its religion Israel has produced a social legislation whose heights other nations have begun to reach only in our own time.[168]

Most scholars conclude that, until well into the time of the Weimar Republic, the C.V. consistently maintained that Judaism was strictly a religion. According to this theory the C.V. added in the 1920s the elements of descent (*Abstammung*) and common fate (*Schicksalsgemeinschaft*) to the original definition of Judaism as a *Konfessionsgemeinschaft*.[169]   This analysis is based on the C.V.'s official revision in 1928 of its self-image from an *Abwehrverein* to a *Gesinnungsverein*.[170]   Much evidence, however, indicates that the C.V.'s trend toward a more positive definition of Judaism began even before World War I. Ludwig Hollaender, for example, declared that Eugen Fuchs had always maintained that Judaism was much more than a religious "confession," and quoted a 1913 speech by Fuchs:

> It would be unethical to deny that I have a special peculiarity by virtue of my being a Jew, that my Jewish descent (*Abstammung*), my Jewish home has imprinted upon me special intellectual as well as physical traits. I can say about myself what Achad Ha'am says about himself: "I think German and feel Jewish." I am a man whose special Jewish traits and peculiarities are the product of thousands of years of tradition. I do not find it necessary to segregate myself from the society around me in order to continue functioning as a Jew and I do not have to argue myself out of my Jewishness in order to continue living as a man among other men.[171]

Fuchs, who deeply believed in the compatibility of *Deutschtum* and *Judentum,* recognized that Judaism also implied descent (*Stamm* or *Abstammung*).[172] For Fuchs *Stamm* was not the same as nationality nor did it have racial connotations. *Stamm* was rather a common tribal descent, a shared Jewish background and inheritance,[173] and was in essence equivalent to all other German *Staemme,* which together formed the ultimate unity of the German *Volk.*[174] In 1919 Fuchs reiterated his pre-World War I synthesis:

> We want . . . to revive *Judentum* on the soil of the German fatherland and with the aid of the other faiths to merge into a higher type of humanity. We have found our synthesis in that we are Germans of the Jewish faith and Jewish *Stamm,* in that *Deutschtum* for us means nation and *volk* whereas *Judentum* is faith and *Stamm.* . . . We reiterate, however, that our religion and *Stamm* do not separate us in the *voelkish* sense from other Germans.[175]

Almost fifteen years before Hollaender's formal revision of the C.V. position toward *Judentum,* Fuchs had publicly declared that between 1893 and 1913 the C.V. had become increasingly concerned with the question of *Judentum.*[176] Two reasons can account for this change: (*a*) soon after its founding the C.V. learned that the constant battle against the anti-Semites necessitated a reexamination of the values being defended; the C.V. leaders recognized that knowledge of the Jewish heritage was essential for an efficient battle against the anti-Semites and (*b*) the rise of the Zionist movement in Germany forced the C.V. to redefine its position in the face of an organization which challenged its basic beliefs.[177] The C.V. was torn between the extremes of German nationalism and Jewish nationalism. Every possible means of expressing its loyalty to *Deutschtum* was exhausted; the anti-Semitic movements rendered further efforts in this direction futile. The only avenue open to the C.V. was the expansion of its Jewish identity through increased awareness of and adherence to Jewish values. Because of outside pressures, the two components in the C.V.'s synthesis of *Deutschtum* and

Judentum were moving toward an equal significance immediately prior to World War I.[178]

Implementation of Ideology

The C.V.'s efforts to prove the validity of the synthesis of
Deutschtum and *Judentum* were supplemented by daily hard
work which required a tremendous expansion of energy and
funds. C.V. propaganda tried to present the Jews to the
German public as an unjustifiably persecuted minority denied
of basic rights through no fault of its own.

One assumption of the C.V. was that by means of "scientific" proofs the organization would be able to convince the
general public of the eternal values of Judaism and the
loyalty of the German Jews to their country. For this purpose a "literary-apologetic committee" (*Literarisch-Apolo-
getische Kommission*) was formed, which after 1904 was also
supported by the *Verband der deutschen Juden.* The
committee was established on December 30, 1896, under the
chairmanship of Professor Ignaz Maybaum. Its goals were: (*a*)
to influence public opinion in a manner favorable to the Jews
and (*b*) to become a center for all efforts at Jewish justification in Germany and to share in various tasks of other
existing Jewish organizations.[179] The realm of "scientific"
propaganda for the C.V. included: Jewish crimes, refutation
of charges by Gentiles against Jewish morals and ethics especially with respect to business, race problems, and the battle
against religious and blood libels.[180]

To bring its arguments to the general Christian public, the
C.V. sent its monthly (after 1922, weekly) official paper to
thousands of Germans known to have moral or political
influence. Most of the Christians who received the paper had
not requested it, and both the *IDR* and *CVZ* note that some
of these people asked to have the mailing stopped or sent in
closed envelopes. It is almost impossible in retrospect to
gauge the influence these official papers may have had on the
Christian public.

The educational work of the C.V. within the Jewish
community was aimed at preventing both conversion and the
development among Jews of anti-German sentiments that

could issue from the unceasing flood of anti-Semitic harass-
ment. Baptism had already become a major threat, and the
C.V. attempted to counteract it by constantly emphasizing
the great values inherent in Judaism and the importance of
the Jews as the bearers of this religion.[181]   The aim of these
statements was to foster pride and self-respect among the
Jews, but a complementary tactic used by the C.V. was to
demonstrate that the Jews would gain very little by conversion to Christianity.[182]

The C.V.'s resistance to conversion clearly points to the
fact that its support of assimilation was cultural, that it was
not predicated on the physical disappearance of Judaism. The
Zionists often called the C.V. an "assimilationist organization" in the worst sense of the word, which for the Zionists
meant that the C.V. had betrayed the Jews and all Jewish
values and was willing to submerge itself totally in the German culture.[183]   All evidence points to the fact, however,
that the C.V., without concerning itself too much with Jewish tradition and beliefs, still saw a positive value in the
ethical teachings of Judaism and was proud to identify with
them. The C.V. position was succinctly summarized by Felix
Goldmann:

> The main criterion [for remaining a Jew] is, and shall
> remain, religion. Whoever abandons our religion is an
> assimilationist, whoever remains true to this religion with
> all his heart, may, without fear of damaging the Jewish
> tradition, assimilate himself culturally to his heart's con-
> tent.[184]

Goldmann's definition of the limits of assimilation, then,
indicates that by the word "assimilation" he actually meant
acculturation, that is, the adoption of all German values and
customs without giving up the most important element of
Jewish identity—religion.

The second educational task of the C.V. was to teach the
German Jews to view anti-Semitism as a perverse aberration
rather than an honest expression of German civilization. As
early as 1895, the C.V. had declared that, no matter what the

attacks upon the Jews might bring, they would always remain loyal Germans.[185]   This solemn task, which tried to absolve the German nation of "the aberration of the few," clearly shows that the C.V. was committed to a liberal and enlightened position; its view of anti-Semitism remained primarily intellectual:

> Those who hated the Jews did not know them or, at best, did not want to know the whole good truth about them. Conflicts in society were essentially conflicts between inadequately enlightened individuals, not social groups.[186]

It has already been pointed out that Hermann Cohen's search for a synthesis between the German and Jewish "spirits" (*Seelen*) was used by the C.V. as a basis for its own ideology.[187]   In evolving a rationale for this synthesis he felt that history reveals a gradual merging of Christianity and Judaism; he predicted that Judaism and Protestantism would eventually become almost identical. In his lecture "Jewish Postulates" Cohen asserted that until that time, the German Jews shall serve the messianic ideal of the perpetuation and development of morals within the German nation and thereby make a significant contribution to German culture.[188]

With some reservations the C.V. adopted all of Cohen's ideas. [189]   The C.V.'s continuing attempts to find a common denominator between Jewish ethics and German idealism reflect his influence. Both Jews and Germans are portrayed here as peoples who detest materialism and constantly strive for eternal values and truths.[190]   Another essay in the *IDR* finds in the Jewish faith the precursors of Kantian transcendental concepts such as God immortality, and freedom.[191] The Jewish religion is described as the first religion of reason, the most enlightened of all faiths.[192]

A major theme of the apologetic literature was the glorification of contributions by individual Jews to German culture.[193]   The enumeration usually started with Mendelssohn and his enrichment of the German language and included a long list of scientists, artists, and politicians. The emphasis on innovations in the German language stemmed from the widely accepted theory, developed and elaborated by Lazarus, that language was the decisive factor in determining nationality. In this connection the C.V. frequently mentioned that German Jewish emigrants usually continued to cherish the German language and culture wherever they settled, a decisive proof of attachment. The argument went so far as to point out the importance of the Yiddish language as the link between Jews and the German language.[194]

Jewish contributions to German culture, however, went beyond those of language. Many essays referred to Jewish achievements in other fields, especially in literature and philosophy. To give these arguments added validity, the C.V. often invited Christian scholars to write articles on the accomplishments of Jews.[195] The usual conclusion was that Jews had contributed to German culture long before German unification, in fact that these contributions had provided the structure and support for German civilization. Finally, they served as a living proof that the Jews had a strong determination to belong to the German nation.[196] It should be pointed out that this whole question was especially important in a country with so high a regard for "*Kultur*," in which culture was a vital factor in assessing one's real bond with German nationality.

The most frequent apologetic discussion dealt with the question: Are the Jews a separate nation with loyalties outside the boundaries of the German Reich? On the basis of earnest philosophical and theological arguments, the C.V. went to great lengths to prove that the German Jews were solely a religious community, that the very concept of Jewish nationality was alien to Jewish religion and ethics.[197] Until the end of World War I, the C.V. was careful never to use the words "*Nation*" or "*Volk*" except to repudiate their applicability. In 1893, it had made only a very general statement about the nature of nationality without any attempt to apply the concept to Jews. The C.V. clearly pointed out the basis for regarding Jews as good German citizens:

The nature of nationality depends on the unison of thinking and feeling; its outward, but most decisive, feature is the common mother tongue. People of the most diverse heritage and religious beliefs forge a nation together through their common history. The unity of the German nation was built upon the most diverse heritage and religions.[198]

Again the C.V. is expressing the liberal enlightened opinion that because they shared a common culture, the Jews would be accepted into the "pluralistic" society around them to become an integral part of that society's nationality.

At one point the *IDR* went so far as to take Martin Philippson to task for having chosen as the title of his book *The History of the Jewish Nation*, instead of the less offensive and more appropriate "History of Judaism and Its Adherents." Nevertheless, he was commended for the true German spirit evident in his historical work.[199]

In defining nationality, the C.V. emphasized that even though the formal citizenship (*Staatsbuergerschaft*) of an individual within a state is a sufficient determination of his nationality for all practical purposes, subjective factors, such as the will of the individual to belong to the nation, also play a part. Riesser's famous words, "whoever denies me my right to my German homeland, denies my rights to have free thoughts, feelings, the language I speak, the air I breathe—and therefore I must defend myself from him as from a murderer," were often quoted and wholeheartedly accepted by the C.V.[200]   The *IDR* obviously grounded its propositions in many instances on Lazarus's statement that "nationality" is a concept tied not to territory or tradition, but to language and desire.[201] To clinch the proof, the C.V. presented historical evidence that the Jews had been assimilated into German culture as early as the Reformation, underlining the closeness between the spirits of *Deutschtum* and *Judentum*.[202]

The C.V. asserted that by being loyal citizens of Germany, the Jews were expressing their satisfaction with the existing order and their rejection of revolutionary activities or ideologies. Martin Philippson noted that there were very few Jews among the socialists and that in every country which ensured equal rights, e.g., Germany, Jews did not belong to left-wing or radical enclaves. As for conservatism and constancy, he pointed to the Jews whose religion and commandments had endured for three thousand years. [203] The C.V. denounced the theories of Karl Marx, emphatically denying that his Jewish background made him representative of Jewish political attitudes.[204] With an air of triumph and satisfaction the C.V. paper described anti-Semitic socialists, in order to discredit talk of an alignment between socialists and Jews.

Good citizenship and loyalty to the state include rights as well as obligations. The C.V. presented detailed accounts of Jewish contributions to the German wars, both monetary and in active service, of the sacrifices of Jewish soldiers, Jewish valor, and excellence in fulfilling their duties. The popular slogan of the pre-war days, "With God for Kaiser and the fatherland" (*mit Gott fuer Kaiser und Vaterland*) was frequently espoused by the C.V. and was an oft-repeated theme in their meetings and conventions before 1918.[205] The sacrifices of the Jews on behalf of their country were encapsulated in the expression that the Jews had given all they could "in property and blood" (*an Gut und Blut*), and the C.V. published long lists of the Jewish soldiers who had fallen in all the German wars, beginning with the battles against Napoleon. [206] These lists included not only names and places of birth but enumerated the decorations, medals, and citations awarded to the soldiers, in addition to their rank and the circumstances of their death.[207] The full participation of the Jews in the German army was deemed to have special significance in a society so heavily steeped in military traditions.

The C.V. was very sensitive to the problem of the Jews in the eastern parts of the Reich, notably in Posen, where there were a large number of *Ostjuden*, immigrants from Eastern Europe. These Jews were often torn between the conflicting national ambitions of the Poles and the Germans. The C.V. contended that they were helping to spread German civilization and culture, were true ambassadors of the German spirit, and were transforming these territories into virtual fortresses of *Deutschtum*. Whereas the Christian German emigrants completely assimilated into the Polish culture, not one Jew abandoned his loyalty to Germany.[208] The C.V. supported German ambitions in Eastern Europe and declared that the *Ostjuden* and the entire membership of the C.V. were always in favor of the Germanization of the *"Ostmark."*[209]

Although we are not dealing here with the C.V.–Zionist controversy, some remarks should be added to fill out the presentation of C.V. ideology. Within the framework of the C.V. positions, it was logical for it to attack the ideology of the Zionists. Whereas the C.V. considered the Jews to be a religious community, integrated in German culture and society, the Zionists were adamantly opposed to this fundamental definition. Their first postulate was that the Jews constituted a separate people which was also a nationality, and this was a point of view that the C.V. found so intolerable that it saw no possibility of compromise. The *Centralverein* and most other religiously liberal German Jews conceded that a Jewish nation was necessary in Eastern Europe, but that in Germany religion was the only factor which separated Jews from their Christian neighbors.[210]   As late as 1919, Ludwig Hollaender denied any solidarity of German Jews with Jews elsewhere unless on a religious basis.[211]

From its beginning the Zionist movement was attacked by the C.V. One of the C.V.'s first reactions to Zionism, issued a year before the Basel congress, is implicit in an article by Karl Gustav, in which he compared Zionism with anti-Semitism.[212]   He dismissed Herzl's *Judenstaat* with the following *ad hominem* argument: "Let's not forget that Herzl is after all not a German citizen but an Austrian," implying thereby that Herzl did not reflect the opinions or feelings of the German Jews.[213]

There was a difference, however, between the C.V.'s attacks on Zionism before and after 1912. Until about 1912, criticism was directed against Zionist ideology, often without even mentioning "Zionism," "Jewish nationality," or the name of the "Zionist organization of Germany" (ZVfD). These were primarily abstract ideological statements and referred only indirectly to the Zionist movement. After 1912, the C.V. directly attacked Zionism, the various manifestations of Jewish nationality, and the institutions of the Zionist organization in Germany.[214] The C.V., for example, did not directly support the *Protestrabbiner* nor did it make any other comments concerning the intention to have a congress convene in Munich; one can observe, however, the abundant denials of separate Jewish nationality throughout the heated debate that took place. The emotional involvement of the C.V. membership with the issue of Zionism did not finally crystallize until 1913. Before that date the C.V., as an organization, took no official stand, but in March, 1913, the C.V. finally announced that from then on it would have to "part ways with those who deny German national feelings and who feel like strangers in a host country" and "have only Jewish national feelings."[215]

The resolution of 1913 was maintained with only slight changes until 1933. Whatever form the C.V.'s attitude toward Zionism took in later years, especially after World War I, the basic position remained intact. The deep differences of Weltanschauung between the Zionists and the C.V. were rooted in their diametrically opposed assessments of the relationships between Jews and non-Jews, which were seen in disparate historical perspectives. The C.V. tried to explain the Jew to the non-Jewish world, whereas the Zionists were precisely addressing themselves to Jews and expounding the relevance of Jewish values to Zionism. The C.V. saw the Jewish Problem as the attempt by anti-Semites to prevent the Jews from assuming their lawful place in society. The Zionists identified the problem of the Jews as their anomalous position in Gentile society. Although they were themselves the product of emancipation and of liberal ideology, the Zionists challenged, on a theoretical plane, the myth that emancipation and liberalism, and the assimilation and acculturation which followed in their wake, would solve the Jewish Problem in the Diaspora. By so doing, they challenged the very foundations of the C.V.; a clash was inevitable.

III

The Zionistische Vereinigung
fuer Deutschland: *1897–1914*

The German Jews who founded the *Zionistische Vereinigung fuer Deutschland* (ZVfD) were the first to challenge the C.V.'s basic ideological and philosophical premises.[1] At the outset, however, one must distinguish between the intellectual and cultural backgrounds that shaped their respective thinking, and between their differing ideologies, in many cases the consequence of reassessments of the "Jewish Question" in the light of new social and political phenomena.

It is certain that the Zionists in Germany saw in political emancipation a necessary and welcomed stage in the development of Jewish history. No Zionist would have thought of speaking against emancipation and the civic and political rights it promised. Wherever the question had arisen, in Germany and elsewhere, Zionists had always spoken and fought for civil rights. What is more important, German Zionists not only viewed emancipation from a historical perspective; they recognized the fact that Zionism, as a national and political movement, was itself a product of emancipation. Kurt Blumenfeld, an important ideologue of the ZVfD, often said that "Zionism was Europe's present to the Jews," by which he meant that Zionism had become possible only through emancipation and equal civil rights.

It is in the light of these facts that one must try to understand the ideology of the German Zionists. They had declared in their earliest pamphlets that they rejected emancipation and assimilation as the preferred modes of Jewish existence and that they rejected the legal process as the solution to the problem posed by the anti-Semites. But, in fact, the Zionists did not reject emancipation. They had put emancipation and assimilation into a single category because they believed that assimilation, which they deprecated, was a necessary corollary of emancipation; thus their negative evaluation of assimilation was extended to emancipation.[2] In addition, the German Zionists claimed that the formal recognition of Jewish civil rights and the entrance of the Jews into Gentile society would never solve the Jewish Question in Germany. In sum, neither emancipation nor—even less—assimilation had alleviated the multitude of problems that faced the German Jew at the turn of the century.

The Zionist solution stood in opposition to the assimilationist preference of the C.V.; it saw Zionism as the means of strengthening Jewish identity and national pride. As an argument against assimilation, the Zionists pointed to the anti-Semites' dissatisfaction with it as a solution to the Jewish Problem. As the Zionists began to recognize the failure of emancipation and assimilation, they developed an alternative program to revitalize Jewish social and cultural life.[3] Nationalism urged the commitment of Jews to values based on "belief in the existence of a common past and common future for the Jewish people."[4] In their eyes this was a "modern" solution to the Jewish Problem.[5] Seen as a problem of historical dialectics, one might say somewhat simplistically that for the German Zionists emancipation was the thesis, assimilation and anti-Semitism the antithesis, and Zionism the synthesis.

Ostjuden *and German Jewry*

Both the C.V. and the ZVfD were organized responses to anti-Semitism, but each organization conceptualized the antagonist in its own way. The C.V. was concerned primarily with anti-Semitism in Germany and with the safeguarding of

German Jewry's civil and political rights. The founders of the ZVfD, on the other hand, were disturbed by the appearance of a Jewish Problem in Eastern Europe, which required the emigration of *Ostjuden* to safe lands. These men were especially aroused by the anti-Semitic outbreaks against Russian Jewry during the 1880s and 1890s.

After the murder of Alexander II on March 1, 1881, a reactionary government under Alexander III had come to power in Russia. Shortly after the new Czar's accession to the throne, a wave of pogroms spread throughout southern Russia during the summer months, disrupting more than a hundred Jewish communities.[6] The official reactionary policy of the new regime condoned the pogroms and instituted the "May Laws" of 1882, limiting Russian Jews to the "Pale of Settlement." In July, 1887, the minister of public instruction announced a *numerus clausus*, restricting the number of Jews admitted to the universities and secondary schools. In the Pale of Settlement the number of Jews could reach 10 percent of the Christian school population; outside the Pale the ceiling was fixed at 5 percent; in St. Petersburg and Moscow at 3 percent.[7] The persecution of Jews continued into the 1890s with the expulsion of Jews from Moscow in 1891. Under the reign of Nikolai II (term 1895–1900), ruthless pogroms and explusions persisted with government approval.[8]

The pogroms in Russia set in motion a mass migration of Jews, whose search for safety took them primarily to the United States. This large-scale movement also affected Germany and German Jewry. From the turn of the century until World War I, Germany shared a border with Russia. Because of its geographical proximity and access to the sea, Germany became the transit country for Eastern European Jews traveling to the United States. Not all of them who passed through Germany reached their overseas destination; under some circumstances, or for a variety of personal reasons, many chose to settle in Germany.[9] During these years, therefore, the number of Eastern European Jews in Germany increased dramatically. Available statistics indicate that the countries of origin of "foreign" Jews in Germany included Russia, the

Austro-Hungarian Empire, Rumania, and Poland. In 1900 there were 41,113 *Ostjuden* in Germany of whom 14,810 had been born in Austria, 12,752 in Russia and Finland. Prussia had the largest concentration; in 1905, there were 38,844 foreign Jews of whom 16,665 were Austrian, 13,185 Russian, and 3,386 Hungarian. The number of foreign Jews loomed large among the total foreign population of the Reich; on December 1, 1900, Berlin alone had 11,651 foreign Jews in a total foreign population of 35,142.[10] By 1910, out of a total Jewish population of 137,043 in Berlin and its suburbs, 21,683 (15.82 percent) were from Eastern Europe.[11]

The pogroms in Eastern Europe and the massive emigration of the *Ostjuden* to the West were significant factors in the history of German Zionism. The *numerus clausus* forced many young Jews in search of higher education to turn to the universities of the West, particularly to the University of Berlin which had no special requirements for foreign students. Consequently, "after 1887 . . . the University of Berlin was flooded with Jewish students who had gone through high school at home and had been stopped at the threshold of the Russian universities by the new decrees."[12] The number of foreign Jewish students there increased steadily as conditions in Russia deteriorated: in 1886–87 there were 129 foreign Jewish students in Prussia out of a total of 13,658 Jewish and non-Jewish students (less than one percent). By 1905–6 there were 483 Jewish students in a student population of 18,667 (2.6 percent).[13] The percentage of foreign Jewish students among the total Jewish student population of the entire Reich was much higher. In 1886–87 the foreign Jewish students, who numbered 129, comprised 9.8 percent of the 1,313 Jewish students in the German Reich.[14]

Despite their comparatively large numbers, the students from Russia were isolated from both the Christian and Jewish German students. The contact between the "foreigners" and the Germans was confined to the lecture halls; no political or social contacts took place. As a result the Russian Jewish students formed their own societies. Most of them were socialists who belonged to the *Russischer Studentenverein* which, despite its overwhelmingly Jewish membership, refused to be recognized as a Jewish club.[15] In 1889, a few Russians who had nationalist Jewish sentiments formed another group, the *Russisch-Juedisch Wissenschaftlicher Verein*, under the leadership of Leo Motzkin (1867–1933). Other members included Shmarya Levin (1867–1935), Yosef Luria (1871–1937), Nachmann Syrkin (1868–1924), Avigdor Jacobsohn (1869–1934), Selig Soskin (1873–1959), and Chaim Weizmann (1873–1952).[16] The only German Jewish student in the *Verein* was Heinrich Loewe (1869–1951), who had been invited to join by Levin Lurje and Nachmann Syrkin.[17]

The aim of the *Verein* was to explain nationalist ideas to the Jewish students in Berlin. After the 1891 expulsion of Jews from Moscow and the worsening economic and physical conditions that brought so many of them into Germany, the members of the *Verein* were able to help the newly arriving *Ostjuden* by serving as interpreters for them in the German Jewish community.[18]

The *Verein* was able to influence a few German Jewish students, and in 1891, Heinrich Loewe founded the student club, *Jung Israel*, to unite German Jews with German-speaking Jews from Eastern Europe, particularly from Galicia. Among its members were Mordechai Broida (1870–1952), Yehoshua Thon (1870–1936), David Neumark (1866–1924), and Mordechai Ehrenpreis (1869–1951), as well as the German-born Willy Bambus (1863–1904).[19] In cooperation with the Russian *Verein*, *Jung Israel* developed elaborate plans for the spread of Jewish-national ideals throughout Europe. In 1893 the two groups collaborated on the organization of an international congress, with delegates from all the national-Jewish groups. The plans for the congress were not carried out, however, until 1896–97 when the two organizations joined Theodor Herzl in his plans for a congress.[20]

The *Verein* and *Jung Israel* in Berlin kept in close contact with the Viennese *Kadimah*, the first Zionist student organization to be formed in the West. It was founded in 1882 in Vienna by Nathan Birnbaum (1864–1937) and the Russian

Jewish students Reuben Bierer (1845–1930), Oser Kokesch (1860–1904), Peretz Smolenskin (1842–1885), and Moritz Tobias Schnirer (1861–1941). The purpose of *Kadimah* was to combat assimilation, to increase Jewish self-awareness, and to settle Jews in Palestine.[21] In 1888 it became a fighting organization (*schlagende Verbindung*), better to defend the honor of those who were targets of the anti-Semites. In 1885, Birnbaum instituted the paper *Selbst-Emancipation* as mouthpiece for the *Kadimah.* It spoke not only for Austrian Jews, but for all German-speaking Jews, and for a while Vienna became the center for nationalist groups in the West. When the Zionist student circles of Vienna and Berlin were hoping to convene a congress in 1893, Nathan Birnbaum was an active planner.[22] In 1894, the center of Zionist activities in the West moved from Vienna to Berlin; *Jung Israel* began at that time to support the publication of the *Juedische Volkszeitung* under the nominal editorship of Nathan Birnbaum. This paper served as a substitute for his previous paper, *Selbst-Emancipation,* which had closed for lack of funds.[23]

Despite untiring efforts and enthusiasm, the *Verein* and *Jung Israel* gained few adherents among the German-born Jews. Those few who did join *Jung Israel*—such as Albert Goldberg (1847–1905), Max Jungmann (1875–1970), and Theodor Zlocisti (1874–1943)—were sons of former Russian immigrants.[24] Max Oppenheimer, who had recently espoused the idea of Jewish nationalism, realized that both organizations, whose membership consisted mostly of Russian and Galician students with a temperament and outlook different from their colleagues, would not be able to attract the German Jewish students. In 1893 he founded, therefore, the *Juedische Humanitaetsgesellschaft* which was in sympathy with the ideas of the *Verein* and *Jung Israel.* Its members, Adolf Friedemann (1871–1933), Arthur Hantke (1874–1955), and Walter Munk, all German-born, became the future leaders of the ZVfD. These intellectuals created among the Jewish students a new sense of self-awareness; they adopted slogans that expressed pride in the past of the Jewish people and concern for their needy brothers in Eastern Europe.[25]

The Russian and German Jewish student groups, active in Germany in the 1880s and the 1890s, were not the only groups to concern themselves with the plight of Eastern Jewry. A number of other organizations were founded at the same time to help Russian Jews emigrate to safe havens. Although initially influenced by the Russian Lovers of Zion (*Hovevei Zion*) groups, they did not espouse a nationalist ideology.[26] In 1884 a small group of orthodox *Hovevei Zion* formed the *Esra* society (*Esra, Sammelbuechse fuer Palaestina*), which proposed the settlement of Eastern European Jews in Palestine. In 1886 Willy Bambus joined the *Esra* and became its most active member. Under his guidance the organization became the counterpart of the Russian *Hovevei Zion*, and starting in 1886, it published a nationalist and Palestine-oriented monthly, *Serubabel*. Another organization, *Lemaan Zion*, founded under the guidance of Esriel Hildesheimer, devoted its energies to the settling of Jews in Palestine especially after 1891 when the Russian Jewish immigrants arrived there.[27] Because of general apathy and the outright opposition of the liberal establishment, the activities of these and many smaller organizations remained limited. Despite its twenty-five-year existence, for example, *Esra*, the largest of the German *Hovevei Zion* groups, was able to collect only 115,000 marks.[28]

Very few German Jews believed that the Jewish Problem in the East could be solved by sending Russian Jews to Palestine. The abject condition of the refugees, however, aroused discussion in Germany as to what ought to be done with them. In the spring of 1891, sixty-four Russian students submitted a petition to the Central Committee to Aid Russian Jewry, which had been founded in May of that year in Berlin. Their petition, published in Birnbaum's *Selbst-Emancipation*, urged the transfer of Russian Jews to Palestine.[29] This committee did not act on the proposal, but in October a smaller subcommittee met in Berlin under the chairmanship of Karl Emil Franzos (1848–1904) to discuss solutions to the refugee problem.[30]

The decisions of the subcommittee were based on the attitudes of the Jewish community; it affirmed the duty of

German Jews to aid their coreligionists in the East, but it
tried to avoid "commitments that implied an ethnic ideological view of the problem."[31] For political and practical reasons, the committee concluded that Jewish refugees should
be settled neither in Western European countries nor in
Palestine. The implicit objection to settlement in Europe was
the fear of increased anti-Semitic reaction; Palestine was
rejected because the committee repudiated Jewish national
bonds with Palestine. Another criterion for resettlement lay
not in the interests of the refugees themselves, but in the
ultimate welfare of the German state. The committee, therefore, expressed the hope that:

> no other, similar group of French, British, or American
> Jews should be in a better position, because of geography
> or the political influence of their own government in the
> territory in question, to act as the sponsor of the
> colony.[32]

The decisions of the subcommittee clearly indicate that,
when dealing with the problem of the Russian refugees, the
majority of German Jewry was concerned more with its own
parochial interests than with those of the people they proposed to aid. German Jews had no wish to be identified with
the masses of Eastern European Jews. Their denial of ethnic
bonds with Jews in foreign countries precluded any program
that might have affected the welfare of the German government or the interests of the German Jewish community.

The Founding of the ZVfD

In 1891, the year in which Franzos's committee met in
Berlin, Max Bodenheimer (1865–1940), a young lawyer
from Cologne, proposed a different solution to the problem
of the *Ostjuden*. Born in Stuttgart into a highly assimilated
family, Bodenheimer's early life and student years were typical of young middle-class German Jews and of most of the
members of the K.C. Like many Jewish students of his time,
Bodenheimer encountered occasional anti-Semitism in the
fraternity to which he belonged. In 1885, he challenged an

anti-Semitic fraternity brother to a duel and, having won, resigned from the fraternity.[33]   In 1889, he also challenged an officer who had made anti-Semitic remarks to him. This time the duel was not carried out; the officer apologized instead. Except for these isolated incidents, Bodenheimer paid little attention to Jewish traditional values, and until 1890 he considered himself successfully assimilated.[34]   His sole involvement with Jewish affairs was his membership in the German branch of the *Alliance Israèlite Universelle* and in the *Verein zur Abwehr des Antisemitismus,* and until the middle of the nineties he was the official representative of both organizations in Cologne.[35]   In essence then, Bodenheimer's university days closely resembled those of the K.C. members who at that time were organizing to defend their honor as Jews.

Bodenheimer's first recognition of the Jewish Problem in Germany and in Eastern Europe came when he read the anti-Semitic propaganda of Avé Lallemant, which forced on him the conclusion that Palestine must again become the national center of the Jewish people and a haven from persecution.[36]   His desire to reawaken Jewish consciousness led him to establish in 1890 a *Verein fuer Juedische Geschichte und Literatur* with the help of Rabbi Frank of Cologne.

Bodenheimer's public efforts to settle Jews in Palestine began in 1891, when he published a widely circulated pamphlet, *Wohin mit den russischen Juden?* In this he advocated the settlement of the Eastern European Jews in Syria and Palestine, both to protect them and to rehabilitate them socially in occupations such as farming and crafts.[37]   During the same year Bodenheimer sent a circular to all the Zionist clubs and organizations calling on all the *Hovevei Zion* clubs to unite (*Zionisten aller Laender vereinigt Euch*). Through his writings Bodenheimer encountered *Jung Israel* and Nathan Birnbaum; he received encouragement from Leo Pinsker (1821–91) just before Pinsker's death. On the other hand he was discouraged by Karl Emil Franzos and the leaders of the *Alliance,* who considered Bodenheimer's plans for settling Jews in Palestine "unrealistic."[38]

Franzos's reaction was typical of the entire German Jewish establishment with which Bodenheimer was dissatisfied,
and it led him to form his own organization. In 1894, after
having passed his bar examinations and with the help of
David Wolffsohn (1856–1914), an Eastern European mer-
chant who had made his fortune in Cologne, Bodenheimer
founded the *Verein behufs Foerderung der juedischen Acker-
baukolonien in Syrien und Palaestina* for the purpose of collecting funds to settle Jews as farmers in the Near East.[39] Also
in 1894 he became president of the philanthropic *Kolonial-
ausschuss der Freien Israelitischen Vereinigung* of Hamburg,
which gave financial assistance to Russian Jews who wanted
to emigrate to Palestine.[40]

In 1895 Bodenheimer wrote to Colonel Goldsmid
(1846–1904), a member of a *Hovevei Zion* group in England, who drew Bodenheimer's attention to Theodor Herzl
(1860–1904).[41] On May 20, 1896, Bodenheimer wrote to
Herzl and invited him to come to Berlin to deliver a lecture at
the convention of the *Freie Israelitische Vereinigung*.[42] In
his letter Bodenheimer mentioned with pride that "he had
been in the movement [*Hovevei Zion*] for six years," and
was greatly interested in Herzl's recently published *Judenstaat*. Herzl responded that previous commitments prevented
his acceptance, but he praised Bodenheimer's efforts and
invited him to join him in the diplomatic campaign to secure
Palestine for the Jews.[43]

In their memoirs of the period immediately preceding the
establishment of the ZVfD, members of both the Russian and
German *Hovevei Zion* groups in Germany describe their
excitement on first reading Herzl's *Judenstaat*.[44] Even so,
Herzl's political plans for the attainment of Palestine were
not favorably received by all of them. For Herzl the pro-
jected Zionist movement was to symbolize the "embodiment
of the sovereign will of the Jews, as a kind of provisional
'government in exile,' "[45] and he called for Jewish settlement in Palestine under international guarantees. Many German *Hovevei Zion* groups, who in the past had worked to the
same end, now rejected Herzl's political approach because
they considered it impossible of realization and a threat to

their own civic and political positions within Germany.[46] Herzl's *Judenstaat* served to divide these groups; some of them joined his movement of political Zionism and some, such as Willy Bambus and Esriel Hildesheimer, preferred practical settlement over political solutions.

Herzl's political aspirations aroused a new problem among Western Jews, especially those of the German *Hovevei Zion;* many of them refused to cooperate with him for fear of being accused of divided loyalties. Herzl tended to dismiss this problem. He did not consider his policies inimical to the emancipation of the Jews in the West. He saw his plan as no threat to those Jews who formed an integral part of their host nations; it would merely serve those Jews who would not and could not assimilate. German Zionists like Bodenheimer who supported Herzl's basic position became political Zionists, but with certain modifications. Bodenheimer's discussions with another *Hovevei Zion* leader, Hermann Schapira (1840–98), a professor of mathematics in Heidelberg, indicate that Bodenheimer recognized that he would have to deal with the German Jewish community's sensitivity to a dual loyalty.[47] Although Bodenheimer emphatically discounted Schapira's fears of destroying the unity of the Jewish community by political Zionism, he was practical enough to know that local German Jewish sentiments had to be considered if he wanted his organization to succeed.

Bodenheimer's care not to disrupt the civil and political status of German Zionists and the community in general is evident in all the declarations of the German Zionist organization. In early 1897, Max Bodenheimer, David Wolffsohn, and Fabius Schach (1868–1930), who had previously been employed by Bodenheimer as a secretary for the *Verein zur Abwehr des Antisemitismus,* founded the *National-Juedische Vereinigung Koeln.* The statutes confirmed the ethnic bonds of the German Zionists to the Jewish people, but they also emphasized patriotism toward Germany:

Bound together by common descent and history, the Jews of all countries constitute a national community. This conviction in no way infringes upon the active patriotic sentiments and fulfillment of the duties of citizenship on the part of the Jews, and in particular of the German Jews toward their German fatherland.[48]

Other tenets foreshadow the Basel Program promulgated in 1897 by the first Zionist Congress:

Emancipation of Jews in other nations has not sufficed to ensure the social and cultural future of the Jewish race; the final solution of the Jewish problem can therefore be attained only through the building of a Jewish state, because only this [state] will be in a position to represent those Jews who cannot and will not remain in the countries of their birth. The natural location for this state, which is to be founded legally, is on the historically consecrated land of Palestine. This final goal is to be attained through the raising of Jewish self-awareness as well as by practical work. The ways to attain this goal are:

1. promotion of Jewish colonies in Syria and Palestine,
2. cultivation of Jewish knowledge and morals,
3. improvement of the social and cultural position of the Jews.[49]

Soon after, Herzl issued the call for the first Zionist Congress in Munich, whereupon there arose a chorus of protest from the Munich Jewish community and the Association of German Rabbis, who denounced Herzl's plan on religious, political, and practical grounds. The effect of these reactions became apparent at the first delegates' conference of German Zionists, which took place in Bingen on July 11, 1897.[50] The first order of the day was the formulation of a response to the *Protest-Rabbis*. Paragraph 2 of the Zionist declaration, published in the *Koelnische Zeitung*, reaffirmed loyalty to Germany:

We strongly reject as groundless the accusation . . . of the Rabbis concerning loyalty to the fatherland. . . . Our Zionist beliefs do not prevent us from fulfilling our obligations to the fatherland, nor from fulfilling our civic obligations to the state.[51]

At this conference the *National-Juedische Vereinigung Koeln* changed its name to *Nationaljuedische Vereinigung fuer Deutschland.* The organizational procedures were completed during two later meetings which took place the same year: in Basel on August 28 and in Frankfurt am Main on October 31 where the final name of the organization was adopted: Zionist Organization of Germany (*Zionistische Vereinigung fuer Deutschland*).

Despite repeated reassurances by the Zionists of their loyalty to Germany, strong anti-Zionist reactions persisted within the Jewish community. In Frankfurt the opposition was led by Charles Hallgarten, a philanthropist connected with the *Alliance,* and by Dr. Vogelstein of Stettin, one of the signers of the *Protest,* as well as by the editors of the *Allgemeine Zeitung des Judentums.*[52] Opposition to the Zionists during the early years of their organization came largely from the individual Jewish communities and the rabbis: in Austria, an early opponent to Zionism was Rabbi Moritz Guedemann; in Germany, the Association of German Rabbis issued a formal declaration against Zionist aims. On the other hand, the liberal newspapers owned by Jews, such as the *Neue Freie Presse* and *Berliner Tageblatt,* and major German Jewish organizations like the D.I.G.B. and the C.V. ignored Zionism altogether, at least in public statements. This policy, called *Totschweigen* by Zionists and anti-Zionists alike, was founded on the assumption that to deny publicity to the Zionists would undermine their organization and purpose.

Organization and Press

Bodenheimer and Wolffsohn were responsible for the transformation of the Zionist ideas in Germany into a formal organization that could stand behind Herzl. They were also instrumental in the transformation of Zionism from a philanthropic venture into an organized political movement that became an integral part of the World Zionist Organization

(WZO). Since both men came from Cologne, the ZVfD concentrated its activities at first in their home city. A second center of Zionist activity was Berlin, where power struggles ensued between the leaders of those groups who identified with Herzl's political Zionism and those who favored practical settlement projects. The disagreement between Heinrich Loewe and his *Jung Israel* group who supported Herzl, and Willy Bambus of the *Esra,* made it impossible for Loewe to unite all the former *Hovevei Zion* behind Herzl. Consequently he formed a new organization, the *Berliner Zionistische Vereinigung* (B.Z.V.) of which he became chairman. Bambus continued to oppose Herzlian Zionism until the second Zionist congress in 1898; after that date he severed all contact with the ZVfD and resumed his independent philanthropic endeavors.[53]

After the differences between the conflicting interests and personalities in Berlin had been resolved and the B.Z.V. had acquired more members, the German Zionist *Delegiertentag* of 1904 decided to establish a central office in Berlin under the supervision of two law partners and *alte Herren* of the *Kartell Zionistische Verbindungen,* Arthur Hantke and Eduard Leszinsky (1884–1967), in collaboration with Emil Simonsohn.[54] Despite the move from Cologne to Berlin, Bodenheimer remained the president of the ZVfD until 1910. In 1910 he was replaced by Arthur Hantke, who remained as president until he moved to London in 1920 to take up his duties as a member of the World Zionist Executive. From 1920 until 1923, Felix Rosenblueth (b. 1887) was president (*Vorsitzender*) of the organization;[55] from 1923 to 1924 Alfred Landsberg, and from 1924 until 1933 the office was filled by Kurt Blumenfeld (1884–1963). Apart from Rosenblueth, a religious orthodox Jew, most of the leaders of the ZVfD were assimilated Jews with backgrounds similar to Bodenheimer's. These men, however, represented the younger, more aggressive generation who were later radically to alter the whole Zionist orientation of the ZVfD.

Until 1914 the Zionist movement in Germany was the strongest and most influential branch of the World Zionist Organization. The strength of the German Zionists lay in the personal qualities of some of their leaders and in the fact that the offices of the World Zionist Organization were in Berlin from 1905 to 1920. German influence was greater than the actual membership figures of the ZVfD, in comparison with other national Zionist organizations, would suggest. Before 1914, the highest estimate of Zionist members in Germany was ten thousand, yet the ZVfD was more vital and active than many larger branches in other countries.[56] To a great extent the leadership of the German and the World Zionist Organization was identical. This ever-present support of the WZO gave the German group the stamina to withstand the *Totschweigen* policy of the C.V. and of other German Jewish organizations, as well as the open hostility of the *Gemeinden* and rabbis.

At the central offices of the World Zionist Organization, the members of the ZVfD constituted most of the staff and heads of departments. While the central office of the WZO was located in Cologne (1905–11), David Wolffsohn and Otto Warburg (1859–1938) were members of the *Engere Aktionskomitee* (EAC) of the WZO. During the years in which the central office was located in Berlin (1911–20), Otto Warburg and Arthur Hantke were members of the EAC. From 1905 to 1911 David Wolffsohn, one of the ZVfD cofounders, was president of the EAC; and Otto Warburg was president of the WZO until Weizmann took office in 1920 with the transfer of the central office to London.[57] Before 1920, therefore, the leadership of the WZO and that of the ZVfD overlapped; the most striking example is Arthur Hantke, who from 1911 until 1920 served simultaneously as president of the ZVfD and as a member of the EAC.

Many of the men who led the ZVfD in the 1920s acquired their initial training and experience in the offices of the WZO in Berlin; among them were Kurt Blumenfeld, Julius Berger (1884–1948), and Richard Lichtheim (1885–1963), all assimilated Jews who had belonged to Zionist fraternities; and Martin Rosenblueth (1886–1963), who came from an orthodox home.[58] All the important publications and offices of the WZO were located in Germany and to a considerable extent were staffed by

German Zionists. The official organ of the WZO, *Die Welt,* was edited by Richard Lichtheim, assisted by Moritz Zobel, later by Julius Becker, a Jewish journalist from Silesia,[59] and by Kurt Blumenfeld from 1913 until mid-1914. The Jewish National Fund and the *Palaestina Ressort* were also located in Germany. The establishment of the *Palaestina Amt* under the supervision of Arthur Ruppin (1876–1943) was a joint enterprise of the two organizations. Full cooperation between the ZVfD and the WZO was symbolized by the fact that both organizations were located in the same building in Berlin, at Saechsische Strasse 8.[60]

The ZVfD was run on strictly democratic principles.[61] Any German Jew who paid a *shekel* automatically became a member, with all implied rights and obligations.[62] The structure of the organization rested on *Ortsgruppen* (local groups) and *Landesverbaende* (federal organizations that supervised the *Ortsgruppen*), as was the case with the C.V. All *Ortsgruppen* were entitled to send one member to the *Delegiertentage* (national conventions which usually met every two years), but *Ortsgruppen* with more than fifty members sent a correspondingly larger delegation. The *Delegiertentag* examined, approved, or rejected the program and budget of the central committee of the ZVfD; it also elected the party leadership, whose highest executive was the president of the ZVfD.[63] Other organizational similarities with the C.V. included the creation of district bureaus to disseminate information and propaganda materials within the various *Landesverbaende*. Like the C.V., the ZVfD supported *Vertrauensmaenner* in localities too small to constitute *Ortsgruppen* or too distant to be under the supervision of the district bureaus.[64]

Although their organizational structures were remarkably similar, the C.V. and the ZVfD differed in the use they made of their bureaucracies. Unlike the C.V., the ZVfD had neither corporate membership nor affiliation with any other large German Jewish organization. Zionist *Vertrauensmaenner* were usually men who did not command great power or resources as leaders in the community or in philanthropic organizations; whereas in the C.V. these individuals had the

freedom to initiate policies and programs within their communities.[65] Zionist *Vertrauensmaenner* frequently suffered
indignities to the point of social ostracism because of their
beliefs; their activities were limited to filing reports on local
anti-Zionist activities.

The first public organ to serve the national interests of
German Jews was the *Zion-Monatsschrift fuer die nationalen
Interessen des juedischen Volkes,* launched by Heinrich
Loewe and the members of *Jung Israel.* For financial reasons
the paper was registered in the name of the firm of Bambus
and Estermann. Difficulties arose when Bambus rejected political Zionism and wanted the paper to publish only news
concerned with colonization.[66] In 1896, therefore, the German Zionists acquired the *Israelitische Rundschau,* which
became the official organ of the ZVfD and was edited by
R. Wohlberg until 1902.[67] When Heinrich Loewe became
editor of the paper in 1902, he did so under the condition
that its name be changed to *Juedische Rundschau(JR).*

In 1919 Robert Weltsch (b. 1891), a former member of
the *Bar Kochba* group of Prague, became editor of the
Juedische Rundschau, a position he retained until 1938.
Under the journalistic skill of Weltsch, who had a socialist-
ethical conception of Zionism, the paper gained its most
widespread influence both within the WZO and the world
Jewish community. Until 1914 the *JR* competed against not
only the established non-Zionist and anti-Zionist German
press, but also against the organ of the WZO, *Die Welt,* which
threatened to make the *JR* superfluous.[68] Indeed there were
discussions about dissolving the *JR* as an unnecessary ex-
pense; an alternative plan was to merge it with *Die Welt.*
After *Die Welt* ceased publication in 1914, the *JR* gained in
importance. In terms of distribution, the *JR* could not com-
pete with the *CVZ* until after 1933.[69] The estimates of *JR*
subscriptions range from five or seven thousand[70] to nine
thousand.[71] The influence of the *JR,* however, like that of
the ZVfD itself, extended farther than the small number of
German Zionist subscriptions would suggest, to include both
Zionists and non-Zionists in many parts of the world.

Although numerically small, the ZVfD was composed of

many groups such as the *Juedische Volkspartei, Mizrachi,* and various youth groups, a fact apparent in the Zionist press. Every interest group within the larger organization published at least one paper or periodical to express its ideological and political definition of Zionism. In addition, a few outstanding individuals published independent journals and periodicals. One of them was Martin Buber (1878–1965), who founded in Berlin the brilliant and intellectually stimulating monthly *Der Jude,* which appeared between 1916 and 1924. Five special issues followed between 1924 and 1928: *Antisemitismus und Juedisches Volkstum, Erziehung, Judentum und Deutschtum, Judentum und Christentum,* and a special issue in honor of Buber's fiftieth birthday. These publications aroused interest in the German Jewish community in general, since they dealt in depth with the dilemma of German Jewish existence. The only periodical comparable in its excellence published by the C.V. was *Der Morgen,* edited by Julius Goldstein and issued by the *Philo Verlag.*[72]

In addition to Buber's *Der Jude* and the ZVfD's official *Juedische Rundschau,* the *Juedisches Lexikon* lists thirty-five Zionist papers and periodicals that appeared in Germany between 1897 and 1938. The *Philo Lexikon* lists an additional publication, the *Palaestina Nachrichten* beginning in 1933. A recent careful study has estimated that the number of Zionist publications in Germany between 1897 and 1938 was thirty-nine.[73] This profusion of literature and propaganda is an indication of the prolific and energetic Zionist activity in Germany. The official publishing house of the ZVfD, the *Juedischer Verlag* in Berlin, was founded in 1902 by members of the "Democratic Fraction" who were opposed to Herzl's rejection of cultural activities. Outstanding intellectuals within the movement contributed to the *Juedischer Verlag,* and it became the cultural center for the German Zionists and the WZO.[74]

The Zionist Perspective on Anti-Semitism

The Zionist papers and periodicals in Germany rarely reported contemporary political events and developments unless they were of direct interest to the Zionist cause. Until the last years of the Weimar Republic editorials and articles in the *Juedische Rundschau* did not deal with defense against anti-Semitism. The Zionists believed that such efforts were doomed to failure because the Jewish Problem was a condition of life in the Diaspora. This problem could not be solved through defense. They vehemently rejected the apologetic and tactical defense strategies of the C.V. that emphasized the German Jews' patriotism *(deutsche Gesinnung);* to them they were useless, undignified, and humiliating. As late as 1932 the *Juedische Rundschau* declared:

> We believe that a Jewish newspaper today has as its most important task the obligation to realize positive and constructive goals and that the discussions with vulgar anti-Semites are to no avail.[75]

The Zionist movement appeared as a reaction to the persecution of Russian and Polish Jews and to the rise of German anti-Semitism.[76] Unlike the C.V., however, whose *raison d'être* was its battle against anti-Semitism, the Zionists in Germany did not include this struggle in their program until the last years of the Weimar Republic. The members of the C.V. and the ZVfD were equally affected by political, social, and economic pressures in Germany, as well as by hostility and inequality within the German civil service and the army.[77] The difference in their reactions stemmed not simply from tactical, but from basic ideological disagreements; their different Weltanschauungen finally led to the schism between the ZVfD and the German Jewish liberal establishment.

As a Jewish national movement, German Zionism was completely opposed to the philosophy of the liberal community. Organizations like the C.V. might claim that the distinguishing feature of the Jews was their religion, but the Zionists maintained that religion was merely one factor and that German Jews had strong cultural and ethnic bonds with Jews throughout the Diaspora. To the German Zionists the Jewish Problem arose from the anomalous situation of a scattered people restrained from any development of their cultural and national heritage. Solutions not directed toward the uniting of the Jewish people in their own homeland were doomed to failure and could constitute only partial and superficial remedies. This "national" question could be solved only by political means, enforced by efforts to raise the Jewish national consciousness.

The Zionists believed that the uniqueness of the Jews, their common group identity, lay at the root of anti-Semitism. The anti-Semites, who were not open to reason, could be opposed only by the emphasizing of Jewish traits and traditions. Begging for acceptance among the Gentiles was to no avail.[78] The Zionists never tired of pointing out that there were two ways to respond to the anti-Semites; the first (the C.V. method) was to deny nationality since the very existence of national traits was a sufficient basis for anti-Semitism. The second (that of the Zionists) was to affirm Jewish nationality, but deny that it was the cause of anti-Semitism. In fact, the Zionists firmly believed that the anti-Semites respected their straightforwardness and honesty as Jews and detested the apologetic arguments of the assimilationists.[79]

The Zionists felt that those Jews who were concerned with defense were wasting their energies; because they did not understand the deep roots of anti-Semitism, they mistakenly considered it a passing phenomenon.[80] The official position of the ZVfD toward defense was most clearly spelled out in 1923 in a confidential report to the representatives of the *Landesverbaende* and *Vertrauensmaenner* of the ZVfD:

> For us anti-Semitism is not a matter of concern as far as the continuation of Jewish life is involved; the fight against it has therefore no Jewish content. Anti-Semitism is the reaction of the non-Jewish world toward the anomalous position of the Jewish nation which, even though it is a nation, has no land; this is a phenomenon that the "normal" nations cannot accept. Anti-Semitism is therefore not a reaction to specific Jewish faults or weaknesses whose disappearance will result in its decline.

Anti-Semitism would not diminish even if all Jews were to be perfect; their perfection would be a sufficient cause for the anti-Semites to attack them. Anti-Semitism would disappear, then, only if the Jewish people were to acquire an equal status among the nations by normalizing their existence, which means the consolidation of the Jewish community through constructive work in Palestine.[81]

Thus anti-Semitism occupied a place of secondary importance in German Zionist ideology, but in certain emergency situations the Zionists did modify their position. Immediately after World War I, Arthur Hantke suggested in a letter to Kurt Blumenfeld that Zionist criticism of other Jewish organizations was not enough; the Zionists should review their stand on anti-Semitism and be prepared to combat its more virulent aspects.[82] The Zionists then made some exceptions to their policy of noninvolvement in matters of defense by cooperating at times with other Jewish organizations. In 1930, the ZVfD worked closely with the C.V. during the Reichstag elections, which were accompanied by particularly violent outbreaks against Jews. In such special circumstances, however, when they did ally themselves with the C.V. and other organizations in matters of defense against anti-Semitism, the Zionists always emphasized that they were doing so merely in an attempt to preserve the honor and dignity of the Jews as members of a distinct ethnic community.[83] They repeatedly said that they, unlike the C.V., were not interested in demonstrating their German loyalty for the benefit of the anti-Semites. Even during the few weeks of their cooperation, they dissociated themselves from the ideology of the C.V.

For the Zionists, philo-Semitism and anti-Semitism were irrelevant; for them the Jewish Question was an internal problem that could be solved only by the Jews themselves. A small Jewish minority could not develop culturally and ethnically within a hostile majority; the only answer, therefore, was the creation of an autonomous national home for the Jewish people. Until that time, the Zionists suggested a temporary expedient for the relaxing of tensions: the German

Jews should abandon their efforts to assimilate into a culture that rejected them and instead, by the assertion of their Jewish consciousness and individuality, contribute to the dominant culture as a valuable minority group.

In accord with this Weltanschauung, the *Juedische Rundschau* published local and international news about Jews, Jewish problems, and Zionism. The official organs of the ZVfD did not report local or national elections, or indeed any news of a political nature. The Zionists saw no need for continual reformulation of their position in response to changing political and economic conditions. Hence the *JR* did not even bother to report the growing anti-Semitic movement in Germany. Instead, it used its pages for two purposes: to inform the public of Zionist ideals and aspirations and to give regular progress reports on economic and political developments in Palestine; and to educate the Jewish public in all matters concerning Judaism and Jewish tradition so as to increase Jewish self-awareness and pride.

Background to German Zionist Ideology

Until World War I, as we have seen, Germany was the intellectual and administrative center of both the ZVfD and the WZO, and it is, therefore, in the context of the intellectual and political trends within the WZO that the development of Zionism there can be understood. From the early days of the movement, the German Zionists were in close touch with Herzl, and some historians have seen them as completely subservient to his ideology.[84] In fact, however, by virtue of its central location between East and West, German Zionism was influenced by a spectrum of ideological positions and developed a special character of its own. Since the central offices and official party organs were located in Germany and were for the most part staffed and directed by Germans, the Zionists there were closely acquainted with all the different ideological and political trends current during the early days of the movement. Perhaps precisely because of the wide range of views, the German Zionists did not adopt any one position, but instead evolved their own branch of Zionism:

Unlike Russian Zionism which was nationalist and messianic, and unlike Western Zionism which was philanthropic, German Zionism was a mixture of both, and at a crucial period [1910] the battlefield of both. German Zionists felt an inner urge to clarify Zionist "theory." They had an independent approach to the problems involved.[85]

The Zionist ideology that emerged in the various countries of Jewish residence was often a coalescence of Zionist aspirations with the particular economic, political, and social factors of its surrounding milieu. Just as Jews in each geocultural area had their own kind of assimilation, so too, Zionism varied with the unique circumstances of each area. Until 1914, the WZO contained representatives of four major ideological Zionist positions: political Zionism as advocated by Herzl; national autonomy as advocated by the Russian Zionists and the Austrian *Volkspartei;* practical Zionism, and cultural Zionism, which were represented by the Democratic Fraction which was formed at the Zionist Congress of 1901.

Herzl's basic tenet was that Palestine should be secured for the Jews by means of an internationally guaranteed charter. Consequently, he opposed any colonization projects ("infiltration") prior to the acquisition by the Jewish people of the legal right to settle in Palestine. Herzl and the Zionists who supported this idea made no long-range cultural or political plans for national Jewish life in the Diaspora and strongly believed that as a people the Jews had no future in that direction; only in Palestine would they be able to develop their cultural and national character. He believed that the "removal of the Jews to Palestine was imminent," and he therefore strongly opposed Zionists' participation and involvement in the political, economic, and cultural affairs of their host countries and even of their Jewish communities.[86]

Herzl did make some exceptions to his policy. In 1898, he issued his call to "conquer the communities" *(Eroberung der Gemeinden),* by which he meant that the Zionists should seize control of Jewish community institutions, but this plan was intended as a tactical move to win the Jewish public over to the Zionist cause. In 1897, Herzl even considered the feasibility of Zionist involvement in government and thought of sending a deputy to the Austrian Parliament.[87] He hoped that this delegate would represent Zionist demands before the Austrian legislature and thus further Herzl's international and political contacts. In this instance, as in the case of the Jewish communities, he conceived of the project not as an end in itself but as a means to advance the goal of settlement in Palestine.

The Austro-Hungarian Empire, composed of many ethnic and linguistic groups, produced a different brand of Zionism that advocated Jewish national-cultural autonomy. The early Zionist student groups in Austria, the *Kadimah, Ivria,* and *Unitas,* led by Nathan Birnbaum (1864–1937), Herzl's secretary, Isidor Schalitt (1871–1954), and Siegmund Werner (1867–1928), the first editor of *Die Welt,* were originally supporters of Herzl's political Zionism. Soon after the creation of the WZO, however, differences of opinion arose between Herzl and those leading Austrian Zionists who wanted to pursue a policy of Jewish autonomy in the empire. In 1898, they founded the *Juedisches Volksverein,* which later developed into the *Juedische Volkspartei.* The first president of the *Volkspartei,* Richard Rappaport, also founded the party's organ, the *Juedische Volkszeitung.*[88]

Unlike Herzlian Zionism, which held that all Jews who would not emigrate to Palestine would be submerged in the cultures of the Diaspora, "autonomists" believed that Palestine and the Diaspora had equivalent importance for Jewish national regeneration.[89] During a lecture in Lemberg in 1899, Nathan Birnbaum, who had turned from political Zionism to Jewish autonomy, declared that Herzl's political solution might well be delayed by unforeseen circumstances. In the meantime Zionists should "not place all their cards on Turkey, but instead try to build up their Jewish national consciousness in Europe." Birnbaum was convinced that a healthy cultural and national Jewish life was possible and desirable outside of Palestine;[90] to him and his fellow autonomists, Zionism was a means of regenerating Jewish pride, a process in which Palestine was an important but not absolutely essential element.

Birnbaum claimed that the essence of Jewish life was

Jewish culture, which had to be legitimized through a political organization that represented Jewish demands.[91] He argued that a Jewish political party was especially feasible in the Austro-Hungarian Empire since the empire's distinctive nature as a collection of nationalities provided the right environment for Jews to claim their own national autonomy. Therefore, he and the leaders of the *Juedische Volkspartei*—Richard Rappaport, Jakob Kohn, Benno Straucher (1854–1940), and others—developed the so-called *Landespolitik* to send Jewish deputies to the Austrian Parliament. They advocated Jewish peoplehood *(Volkstum)* in the Diaspora, large-scale settlement in Palestine, and the formation of an economic and political *"Gegenwart-Program"* in Austria.[92]

Because of Herzl's strong opposition to the Austrian *Landespolitik*, the *Volkspartei* did not advance during his lifetime. Many Austrian Zionists who were in favor of Jewish autonomy in the Diaspora, were too personally committed to Herzl to challenge his authority and policies. The conference of Austrian Zionists, however, which took place in Cracow in 1906, decided in favor of *Landespolitik* and supported Jewish national candidates for the 1907 elections.[93] With the help of the Zionists, four Jews were elected to Parliament.[94] Official support of the Austrian Zionist party was granted, and the direction of Zionism in Austria ensured the continuation and success of the *Juedische Volkspartei*.

From the early days of the movement, the *Volkspartei* reflected the disaffection of a substantial segment of the WZO with Herzl's political Zionism. This segment, particularly the Austrian and Russian Zionist groups, advocated *Gegenwartsarbeit* in the Diaspora as an important element in national Jewish regeneration.[95] At the time of the conference in Cracow, the Russian Zionists had met in Helsingfors in December, 1906, and decided independently that Jewish nationalism should be developed in the Diaspora even though the ultimate aim was to settle Palestine.[96]

Dissatisfaction with Herzl was expressed by another group, the "practical" Zionists, represented by Otto Warburg, Jacob Kohan-Bernstein (1859–1929), Julius Simon (1875–1969), and Menahem Ussischkin (1863–1941). Whereas the

Gabriel Riesser (1806–63).
*Courtesy of the Schwadron
Archives, Jerusalem.*

Moritz Lazarus (1824–1903).
*Courtesy of the Schwadron
Archives, Jerusalem.*

Hermann Cohen (1842–1918).
*Courtesy of the Schwadron
Archives, Jerusalem.*

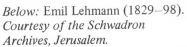
Below: Emil Lehmann (1829–98).
*Courtesy of the Schwadron
Archives, Jerusalem.*

Felix Goldmann (1882–1934).
*Courtesy of the Leo Baeck
Institute Archives, New York.*

Julius Brodnitz (1866–1936).
*Courtesy of the Leo Baeck
Institute Archives, New York.*

Eugen Fuchs (1856–1923).
*Courtesy of the Leo Baeck
Institute Archives, New York.*

Members of the Russisch-Juedisch Wissenschaftlicher Verein in Berlin (1890).
Standing *(left to right):* Simha Rosenbloom, unidentified, Michael Vrosenstein,
Victor Jacobson, Shmarya Levin, Joseph Luria, Nachman Syrkin.
Sitting *(left to right):* Israel Motzkin, Heinrich Loewe, Leo Motzkin.
Courtesy of the Central Zionist Archives, Jerusalem.

Paul Rieger (1870–1939).
*Courtesy of the Leo Baeck
Institute Archives, New York.*

Ludwig Hollaender (1877–1936).
*Courtesy of the Leo Baeck
Institute Archives, New York.*

The founders of the Juedischer Verlag in Berlin (1902). Standing
(left to right): Ephraim Moshe Lilien, Chaim Weizmann, David Trietsch.
Sitting *(left to right):* Berthold Feiwel, Martin Buber.
Courtesy of the Central Zionist Archives, Jerusalem.

Delegation of German Zionists to the grand duke of Baden (1902).
Left to right: Alfred Klee, Julius Moses, Max Bodenheimer,
Rudolf Schauer, Adolf Friedemann, Max Kaufmann.
Courtesy of the Central Zionist Archives, Jerusalem.

The Zionist Student Association Hasmonaea, in Berlin (1905).
Courtesy of the Central Zionist Archives, Jerusalem.

Above left: Max Bodenheimer
(1865–1940). *Courtesy of the
Central Zionist Archives, Jerusalem.*

Above: Max Jungmann (1875–1970).
*Courtesy of the Central Zionist
Archives, Jerusalem.*

Left: David Wolffsohn (1856–1914).
*Courtesy of the Central Zionist
Archives, Jerusalem.*

Emil Bernhard Cohn (1881–1948).
*Courtesy of the Leo Baeck
Institute Archives, New York.*

Adolf Friedemann (1871–1933).
*Courtesy of the Central Zionist
Archives, Jerusalem.*

Franz Oppenheimer (1864–1943).
*Courtesy of the Central Zionist
Archives, Jerusalem.*

Kurt Blumenfeld (1884–1963).
*Courtesy of the Central Zionist
Archives, Jerusalem.*

Felix Rosenblueth (b. 1887).
*Courtesy of the Central Zionist
Archives, Jerusalem.*

Arthur Hantke (1874–1955).
*Courtesy of the Central Zionist
Archives, Jerusalem.*

Richard Lichtheim (1885–1963).
*Courtesy of the Central Zionist
Archives, Jerusalem.*

Sammy Gronemann (1875–1952).
*Courtesy of the Central Zionist
Archives, Jerusalem.*

Right: Moritz Goldstein (b. 1880).
Courtesy of Moritz Goldstein.

Below: Special postcard issued by the ZVfD on the occasion of the Posen Delegiertentag (1912). *Courtesy of the Central Zionist Archives, Jerusalem.*

The first organized trip of students and members of Turnerschaften in Austria and Germany to Palestine (1913). The picture was taken during a visit to the pyramids in Giza (Egypt). *Courtesy of the Central Zionist Archives, Jerusalem.*

political Zionists claimed that large-scale settlement in Palestine could take place only under legal and political guarantees, the practical Zionists asserted that it would be unrealistic to demand political rights before settlement had been undertaken. They argued that *de facto* settlement of Palestine would strengthen the political potential of the movement, and they received most of their support from former *Hovevei Zion* groups.[97] The difference between political and practical Zionism became evident as early as the First Zionist Congress, but it was only after Herzl's East African project, which suggested temporary settlement in Uganda, failed that the practical Zionists began to gain strength within the movement. At the Tenth Zionist Congress (Basel, 1911), Otto Warburg was elected president of the WZO; the Inner Actions Committee formed at that time was composed entirely of practical Zionists. This congress also symbolized the triumph of Chaim Weizmann's "synthetic" Zionism, which hoped to combine the political and practical goals.[98]

Cultural Zionism, another area of opposition to Herzl, originated among the students and academicians from Eastern Europe, and became current mainly in Germany and Switzerland.[99] This group accepted Herzl's political Zionism but opposed his complete neglect of cultural work within the WZO. Under the ideological influence of Ahad Ha'Am (1856–1927), these students considered the education of the Jews in their culture and heritage as important as political Zionism.[100]

During the Fourth Zionist Congress (London, 1900), the debate on cultural matters resulted in a clash between the orthodox Zionists, who rejected cultural activities, and the secularly oriented young Zionists, led by Leo Motzkin and Chaim Weizmann. Discussions were terminated by Herzl before any decisions had been made.[101] The cultural Zionists, who had no intention of leaving the movement but wanted to fight for their ideals within the framework of the WZO, formed the Democratic Fraction in Munich late in 1901. At the Fifth Zionist Congress (Basel, 1901), the Democratic Fraction was represented by thirty-seven delegates who persuaded the Congress to resolve that "the education of the

Jewish people in the national spirit is an essential part of the Zionist program." [102] In addition they strengthened the position of the practical Zionists by declaring that they too demanded the immediate acquisition of land in Palestine for future settlement. [103]

After the Fifth Congress, the Democratic Fraction was never again able to challenge Herzl significantly enough to influence WZO decisions. The Fraction included, however, many individuals such as Chaim Weizmann, Leo Motzkin, Berthold Feiwel (1875–1937), Martin Buber, Leib Jaffe (1876–1948), and others who were to become leaders of the Zionist movement. Its most important achievement was the founding of the publishing house *Juedischer Verlag* by Berthold Feiwel and Martin Buber. [104] Buber, Weizmann, and Feiwel developed a second project, that of founding a Jewish university, after an idea originally proposed by Professor Hermann Schapira. [105] When the Fraction ceased to exist as an independent body and joined the principal faction of practical Zionists, former Fraction members who still retained its ideas exerted their personal influence on the shaping of the Zionist movement. [106]

The theories of political, autonomous, practical, and cultural Zionism influenced German Zionism at various times and to varying degrees. In the period from 1897 to 1912, it was largely Herzl's influence that shaped the ideology of the first generation of German Zionists. Bodenheimer, and others who had been early members of *Hovevei Zion* groups that supported settlement in Palestine, rallied around Herzl's strict opposition to "infiltration," although they did not agree with all his policies. His leadership was sought, because he was regarded as the only man capable of unifying the scattered and ineffective *Hovevei Zion* groups. For the sake of unity the *Hovevei Zion* members were willing to postpone their own projects temporarily. [107] Elias Auerbach (1882–1971), an early German Zionist and one of the first to emigrate to Palestine, said:

Herzl was considered the strong wind which would scatter the fog which hovered over the land. Until his arrival we could see the land only in its outlines; now we were able to clearly see where we were headed. Until then [Herzl's arrival] there were small groups of Jews who discussed ideas and ideals while promoting small-scale settlement. . . . Now a captain had arrived who took firm command of the ship.[108]

This first generation adopted political Zionism for other reasons as well. Political Zionism, based on the legal acquisition of a charter, appealed to this group of loyal German citizens, since the program was directed to the gaining of Germany's formal assent to Jewish colonization of Palestine. Bodenheimer and his collaborators were eager to assist Herzl in his negotiations with the Duke of Baden and the German Kaiser, thus demonstrating their loyalty to both political Zionism and the German fatherland. The autonomous position was inconceivable to these men who, unlike the Austrians and Russians, lived in a nation-state in which German nationality was highly valued, exalted by philosophers and statesmen alike. In this German national environment, separate nationalist aspirations carried with them the connotations of outright treachery.[109]

The particular circumstances of their upbringing and of later local conditions left this first generation of German Zionists relatively immune to cultural and practical Zionism. Unlike the Russians and Austrians who had strong traditional attachments to Judaism, the assimilated German Zionists did not see Jewish culture as a necessary component of their ideology. Again, they were not so close as the Russian Zionists to the plight of Eastern Jewry. This remoteness from the immediacy of persecution may account for their willingness to postpone settlement in Palestine until an opportune moment.

Despite their adherence to Herzl's political ideology, the early German Zionists did not agree with him in all ways about the position of Jews in the Diaspora. They insisted on their status as German citizens and were not willing to dismiss, as did Herzl, the problem of dual loyalty which had emerged for them as Germans and Zionists. They urged their followers to participate in their country's cultural, economic, and political life not only to hasten the acquisition of Palestine, but as an end in itself. They agreed with Herzl that it was futile to establish separate Jewish political parties, but they refused to accept his appraisal that the Zionists' life in the Diaspora was meaningless.

The Ideology of the ZVfD

For a full understanding of the Zionist movement in Germany, three questions must be considered: (1) What were the declared ideologies and goals of the ZVfD when it made its initial impact on German Jewry? (2) How were these aims realized and how did they change between 1897 and 1914? (3) How did the events within the ZVfD between 1910 and 1914 change the nature of the organization and its official ideology?

Shortly after the Basel Congress of 1897, the ZVfD published a pamphlet, *Der Zionismus,* to present its aspirations to the German Jewish community. The pamphlet clearly indicated that Zionism in Germany was a reaction to anti-Semitism. Unlike the liberal Jewish organizations, the Zionists were willing to devise a constructive plan to answer the challenge of anti-Semitism. The pamphlet suggested the following program:

> Zionism strives to find a permanent solution to the Jewish Question through the establishment of a haven, secured through public law, for all those Jews who cannot or will not remain in the countries of their birth. Zionism promotes the return of a great majority of the Jewish people to agriculture in the historic land of Palestine. Zionism aims to: rejuvenate Jewish identity and Jewish ideals; to promote the study of Jewish literature and history; and to educate the Jewish youth to become faithful members of the Jewish nation.[110]

The pamphlet further claimed that emancipation was useless as legislation and that German Jews were, in fact, degraded second-class citizens. Anti-Semitism was a perennial phenomenon threatening not so much the German Jew as his brethren in Russia and Rumania. "The Russian and Rumanian Jews, how do they concern us? Like all other German Jews they too are our brothers. The Zionists view all Jews as brothers who have a common history and a common future." The proposed solution was the creation of a homeland where these people could feel politically, socially, and economically secure: "Jews need a place where they can be free externally as well as internally."[111]

The official publications of the ZVfD usually were not concerned with anti-Semitism. Nevertheless, when confronted with the C.V. argument that anti-Semitism could be defeated by legal and rational means, the ZVfD made occasional public statements to the effect that anti-Semitism was increasing in Germany as Jewish emancipation was weakening. [112] Such public statements were made after new atrocities in Eastern Europe; the Zionists used the occasion of the pogrom of Kishinev (1903) to remind the German Jews that their present comfortable situation could be superseded by the same atrocities. [113] Therefore, they urged them to take advantage of their relative freedom to work for themselves and their Eastern European brothers; this self-help would not conflict with loyalty to the German state—it was the prerogative of a persecuted minority.[114]

The first generation of German Zionists did not reject Jewish life in the Diaspora. They not only continued to live in Germany but felt they were good Germans by virtue of their cultural and social values. Nevertheless, they advocated the conscious emphasis on Jewish ethnic and national traits as important instruments in informing the Jewish youth of its heritage. They considered emancipation a humanitarian and charitable piece of legislation, but without real substance. Contrary to the ideology of the C.V., the German Zionists did not feel that citizenship was synonymous with acceptance into German nationality. They claimed that, since Jews could never become fully integrated into the German nation, they had the right to preserve their own ethnicity and still to remain loyal Germans. "The Jews have a right to their ethnic identity. Patriotism is only one of the duties of a man of honor, and civic loyalty is not impugned by other, compatible loyalties beyond the state." [115]

Although the mainstream of the ZVfD was not religious in terms of ritual observance, but rather was liberal and assimilated like the C.V., the Zionists saw themselves as the true representatives of the continuity of Jewish tradition. In contrast to the liberals they felt a sense of unity with Jews throughout the world. This feeling was intensified during World War I when they actually encountered the *Ostjuden.* Their sense of common responsibility stemmed from their perception of Jews as a scattered, but nevertheless autonomous, people.

Assimilation as the total submergence of the Jewish identity into the German nation was disavowed by the Zionists as impossible, undesirable, and unethical. [116] Anti-Semitism was an unmistakable and definitive declaration of rejection by the Germans of all Jews, including those who wished to assimilate. To counteract assimilation, the Zionists established cultural centers, publishing houses, and special seminars to educate Jews in self-reliance and national pride. [117] As a base and target for these activities the Zionists chose the individual communities (*Gemeinden*), and there they promoted their ideas. Since most *Gemeinden* in Germany espoused the assimilationist ideology, the Zionists entered a few community elections before 1914 and tried in this way to gain influence. [118]

One of the most active and effective instruments in this struggle was the *Juedische Volkspartei* (JVP), led for many years by Max Kollenscher (1875–1937) and Alfred Klee (1875–1943). Its founding stemmed from two sources: Herzl's call during the Second Zionist Congress (Basel, 1898) for the conquest of the communities; [119] and the precedent set by the Austrian *Juedische Volkspartei*. The Zionists of Vienna were among the first to heed Herzl's call and set out to "conquer" the official Jewish Religious Community of Vienna (*Wiener Israelitische Kultusgemeinde*), under the leadership of Jakob Ehrlich, Leopold Plaschkes (1884–1943), Karl Pollak, Robert Stricker (1879–1944), Egon Zweig (1877–1949), and others. Their first success came in 1912 when Ehrlich and Stricker were elected to the board of the community.[120]

Although influenced by both Herzl and the Austrian party, the German *Volkspartei* remained unique. The JVP accepted Herzl's call to conquer the communities, but its purpose was not only to win them over to Zionism. [121] Since the members of the JVP did not reject life in the Diaspora, they believed that their work within the communities would have permanent value for future generations. Their aim was to transform the communities, which had become religious and philanthropic bureaucracies, into institutions that would serve all the needs of the German Jewish community. Although they had adopted their name and aggressive attitude from the Austrian *Juedische Volkspartei,* they had no intention of becoming a political party. Like Bodenheimer, they realized that within the context of the German cultural and political milieu such a party would not find Jewish support.

Until the formation of the *Juedische Volkspartei,* Herzl's call to "conquer the communities" had remained a rhetorical and unfulfilled demand for several years. Among the first to implement it was Max Kollenscher, the author of the pamphlet *Aufgaben Juedischer Gemeindepolitik* (published in 1905) which urged German communities to transform themselves from "religious centers" (*Kultusgemeinden*) into "centers of Jewish nationality" (*Volksgemeinden*). [122] Kollenscher's rationale was that the *Gemeinden* ought to serve the needs of the entire community rather than those of the notables. In his view, the Jewish communities had been the center of Jewish life in the Diaspora before emancipation, later to develop into institutions administered by a few assimilated dignitaries. [123] Although many German Zionists accepted Kollenscher's assessment, only a few were moved to action. The JVP proclaimed the following *Gemeindeprogramm:*

> The nationalization of Jewry is the main function of Zionism in the Diaspora. . . . Participation in community affairs is one of the most important means of achieving this goal, since the communities are the only legally

recognized organizations able to exercise great influence on the Jewish community in the Diaspora. This situation prevails, because the communities control the entire Jewish educational and welfare facilities. In addition they also control most of the rabbis and teachers. . . . There is no doubt that if we are to achieve our goals, this situation has to be changed.[124]

Having recognized the importance of the *Gemeinden,* members of the JVP demanded that the following program be adopted by the ZVfD in its activities within the communities:

1. preservation of Judaism and the Hebrew language;
2. implementation of social work and social welfare programs for all age groups;
3. revision of the rules for community elections and administration to enable all members of the community, including recent immigrants [*Ostjuden*], to participate in the decision-making process of the community; and
4. acquisition of Zionist seats on the boards of the communities through use of the elections machinery.[125]

The leadership of the ZVfD opposed these demands until the fall of 1919 when the JVP received the formal support of many *Ostjuden* and German Zionists who were dissatisfied with the ZVfD leadership. The JVP considered itself an integral part of the ZVfD, but saw as its primary goal the promotion of Zionism and Jewish culture within the communities.[126]

In the 1920s the JVP became increasingly powerful, although its relations with the ZVfD were not always harmonious and were often disrupted by ideological disputes. [127] Both organizations supported the Basel program, but the JVP emphasized the election of Zionists to the community boards, hoping to secure a majority there.[128] Until the mid-1920s, the ZVfD considered that this effort contributed very little to Zionist goals. In the twenties, however, it began to devote some of its energies to *Gemeinde-Politik.*[129]

The official ZVfD opposition to the JVP was maintained by both the first and second generations of German Zionists, represented by Bodenheimer and Blumenfeld respectively. Bodenheimer opposed the JVP on the grounds of his aversion to a radical Zionist program that might appear to compromise the Zionists' German patriotism. Blumenfeld was closer in age and experience to the leaders of the JVP, and they were alike considered "radicals" who broke with the official line of the ZVfD. Blumenfeld's opposition to the JVP, however, was both ideological and practical: he maintained that all efforts must be concentrated on a Jewish commitment to Palestine and that Zionist work within the community framework did not advance the aim of the ZVfD.[130]

Even after the ZVfD decided fully to support the work of the JVP, it divided the tasks between the two organizations by creating a special *Gemeinde Kommission,* directly responsible to the executive of the ZVfD.[131] In 1925, the ZVfD passed the following resolution:

> The Central Committee of the ZVfD is of the opinion that the *Juedische Volkspartei* should be constituted as an organization which is concerned with communal elections. . . . Zionist work in the Diaspora in the field of general politics, education, and national propaganda will remain an integral part of the work of the ZVfD.[132]

Despite the reluctant cooperation of the ZVfD, the JVP managed to make considerable progress within the German Jewish community. In the community elections of Berlin in 1920, four mandates for the JVP were won by Alfred Klee, Heinrich Loewe, Abraham Loeb, and Levitt, all native Germans. Although the JVP had good support among the *Ostjuden,* no *Ostjuden* were submitted as candidates—to forestall accusations of a "foreign" takeover. Through alliances with religious groups and through the support of the majority of the *Ostjuden,* the power of the JVP increased steadily.[133] Its leaders—Georg Kareski (1878–1947), Ahron Sandler (1879–1954), and Max Kollenscher—were untiring in their efforts to win German Jewry to their ideas, and in 1930 they registered their greatest victory when Georg Kareski was elected president of the board of representatives of the Jewish community in Berlin [134] by 30,000 votes.[135]

The program of the Zionist movement in Germany shows that the basic ideologies of the C.V. and the ZVfD were developed within totally different frameworks. The philosophy of the C.V. was developed within the German cultural sphere; it was based on works written by German Jews for the sole consumption of a German Jewish audience that identified itself with German national aspirations. The C.V. was by no means religiously homogeneous; its members included liberal as well as orthodox Jews who belonged to political groups ranging from the Conservative Center party to the Democratic and Socialist parties. The entire membership of the C.V. did adhere, however, to the theories of emancipation and liberalism, firm in the assurance that the Jewish community was progressing toward a more hopeful future. The Weltanschauung of the C.V. was determined only by events of direct concern to the German fatherland and kept it aloof from international matters.

The ZVfD, on the other hand, was open to the influence of political and socioeconomic events outside Germany; the organization was itself, at least initially, a response to the plight of the Eastern European Jews. In addition, its history reflects the disputes within the WZO in respect to world Jewry. The ZVfD then was a politically and ideologically heterogeneous organization which rarely, except for the outbreak of World War I and during the 1930 elections to the Reichstag, concerned itself with German politics.[136]

The C.V. and the ZVfD maintained a peaceful coexistence until 1912. Their relatively harmonious relations prior to this time are surprising, since the tiny Zionist organization was challenging the beliefs and taboos of the German Jewish liberal majority at a time when it was working desperately toward integration into German culture. Despite the Zionist challenge to emancipation and assimilation, the C.V. remained aloof from direct confrontation with the ZVfD. While the *Gemeinde* leaders and rabbis were protesting publicly against the Zionist danger, the C.V. maintained a policy of *Totschweigen*. Its leaders were as opposed to the Zionists as were the *Gemeinden,* but its policy of noninvolvement allowed for continued communication with the Zionist leaders.

A major determinant of coexistence was that, despite their official adherence to Zionist ideology, the first generation of German Zionists, by virtue of their background, age, and upbringing, were very close in their Weltanschauung to the members of the C.V. Both groups had had the same generational experience—they were men of honor who had founded Jewish organizations in defiance of the anti-Semitic insults and threats encountered during their student days. Both sets of leaders came from the same socioeconomic background and entered professions that placed them in the upper middle class. Most Zionists were as completely estranged from the Jewish religion as were most German Jews. They felt rooted in German culture, and their children received the same education as those of other middle-class liberal Jews, an education that in no way emphasized Jewish or Hebrew culture.

Gerhard Holdheim (1892–1967), an early German Zionist, wrote:

> The men who advanced the Zionist idea in Germany were citizens of a land with whose landscape and culture they had very close ties; this land offered them, with few exceptions, all the economic possibilities and opportunities. We came mostly from well-to-do families. Security was one of our most vivid childhood memories.[137]

Elias Auerbach wrote in the *Juedische Rundschau* in 1903:

> How does the Zionist stand vis-à-vis *Deutschtum* and German culture? I deny the assertion that the Zionist Jew has a substantially different attitude toward German culture from the non-Zionist . . . the German Zionist is not less assimilated than any other Jew, although he detests the conscious drive toward assimilation. Is this mode of assimilation [among Zionists] to be condemned? I do not know. Only those who want to embrace Judaism without

modern culture may condemn this assimilation. . . .We must not make the mistake, so common among German Zionists, of glorifying Eastern European Zionism because it is more exclusive. . . .[138]

Adolf Friedemann is typical of the first generation of German Zionists. He came from a cultured family which belonged to the intellectual elite of the Jewish community in Berlin. The members of his family and his circle of friends were highly assimilated Jews; some even took the final step toward assimilation and converted. [139] There was nothing in Friedemann's background to prepare him for Jewish nationalism. His first concern with the Jewish question occurred during his student years when he became acquainted with young men who were dissatisfied with their life in Germany. In October, 1893, Friedemann, Max Oppenheimer, Walter Munk, and Robert Hantke founded the *Juedische Humanitaetsgesellschaft* to "preserve Judaism through the cultivation of its culture and heritage." With Heinrich Loewe, Theodor Zlocisti, and Max Jungmann, Friedemann was also a founder of *Jung Israel* and the *Vereinigung Juedischer Studenten* in Berlin, which had the same goals as the *Juedische Humanitaetsgesellschaft.* [140]

We have seen that Herzl's *Judenstaat,* published in 1896, made its greatest impact among these small clubs. With his student group, Friedemann joined with Max Bodenheimer and David Wolffsohn to establish the *Nationaljuedische Vereinigung fuer Deutschland* and in 1897, he was among the founders of the *Berliner Zionistische Vereinigung.* Friedemann soon occupied an important position within the ZVfD and developed close relations with Herzl, whose cultural and social background was very similar to his own. In 1902 Friedemann accompanied Herzl to Egypt to discuss the feasibility of utilizing El Arish for Jewish settlement, and in 1903 he was elected a member of the *Grosses Aktionskomitee* of the World Zionist Organization, a position he held until 1920. [141] Like his spiritual mentor, Herzl, Friedemann was a staunch believer in political Zionism, a belief he held for the rest of his life.

The first generation of German Zionists—notably Friedemann, Oppenheimer, Bodenheimer, Zwirn—shared Herzl's student background and assimilated upbringing and adhered to his political Zionism. This group that grew up around Bodenheimer in Cologne diverged from Herzl's position on one major issue—they had no intention of moving to Palestine even if a charter were attained. At the same time they separated themselves from the Austrian "autonomists" by striving neither for the creation of a national Jewish culture in the Diaspora nor for a political party in Germany. The position of these early Zionists was defined by Isaak Zwirn:

> We German Zionists came to Zionism out of different motives from those of the *Ostjuden*. Zionism, as we understand it, is the solution from the moral and economic *Judennot*. We did not arrive at Zionism out of love for Palestine; we did not want to solve the problem of the Jewish nation in order to be able to create a Jewish culture. . . . The fate of Judaism in the lands of the Diaspora does not concern us at all.[142]

The Zionism of Zwirn and his generation was addressed to the moral and economic problems of Eastern Jews rather than to the poverty of Jewish and Hebrew culture in Germany.[143]

Adolf Friedemann defined Zionist education in the Diaspora as the "preservation of a sense of community" (*Pflege des Zusammengehoerigkeitsgefuehls*) and "consciousness of a common responsibility" (*Verantwortungsgefuehl*), and this education was designed to cultivate and maintain the honorable history and tradition of the Jews. When explaining the tasks of the Zionists in Germany, Friedemann was faced with a dilemma: he rejected assimilation, but he also rejected the creation of a separate Jewish and Hebrew culture. He rationalized the conflict by claiming that Hebrew culture, although a necessary component of Jewish national consciousness, could find its true environment only in Palestine; a Jewish national culture within Germany would be meaningless.[144] He urged German Zionists to embrace German culture without destroying their Jewish ethnicity:

We live isolated in the midst of a great culture which we imbibed into our inner being with our mother's milk, and we can therefore be only Germans [*Kulturdeutsche*] as far as culture is concerned. Goethe, Schiller, and Kant were our educators. . . . We stand firm on the basis of the Basel program which does not preach Zionist culture in Germany. . . . We shall give our children a good Jewish education with some knowledge of Hebrew, but the bulk of their education will be within German culture. If our children have a sense of their heritage [*Stammesgefuehl*], love for their people, and pride in their history . . . this will be sufficient to make them loyal sons of their nation.[145]

Western Zionists were apt to contrast their form of Zionism with that of the Eastern European Jews.[146] German Zionists described Russian and Austrian Jews as an unassimilated cultural group living among nationalities with cultures alien to their own. In Russia and Galicia, the dominant groups were said not only to have values and occupations different from the Jews, but to have deprived Jews of their political rights. In Germany, on the other hand, the Jews did not constitute a separate nationality: their numbers were small, their economic interests were identical with those of the Christians, their culture was exclusively German, and they had full political equality. Social rejection was not a sufficient cause to abandon Germany nor to create a Hebrew culture within it.[147]

The Zionist view closest to German Jewish liberalism was that of Franz Oppenheimer (1864–1943).[148] Oppenheimer was raised in a highly assimilated middle-class family; at the university he joined a fraternity, in which he distinguished himself as an expert fencer. Like Herzl, he resigned when his fraternity adopted an anti-Semitic stance, for his pride would not permit him to associate with people who rejected his coreligionists as racial and social inferiors.[149] The injury to his pride by anti-Semitism was only one element that brought Oppenheimer to Zionism;[150] his interest in the movement derived above all from his compassion for the Eastern European Jews. Enraged by the atrocities committed against them, he wrote to Herzl on May 25, 1903, "Kishinev makes my blood boil twenty times each day."[151] Nevertheless, the abject conditions of the *Ostjuden* did not alter his image of himself as a man proud both of his Jewishness and his German patriotism:

> I joined the movement without thinking that I myself might one day be a member of its yet to be formed community. . . . I simply followed the dictates of my conscience which urged me to lend a hand to alleviate the immediate problems, without paying too much attention to the future.[152]

Though he considered himself a good Zionist who adhered to the Basel program, Oppenheimer never intended to emigrate to Palestine. He was appalled at the thought of uprooting himself from his beloved fatherland, and the demand that he do so was, in Oppenheimer's estimation, an act of intolerance unacceptable to even the most ardent German Zionist.[153] He denounced extreme forms of Jewish nationalism advocated by men such as Blumenfeld, as the "photographic negative of anti-Semitism."[154] The true aspiration of Zionism was to establish Palestine as a "Levantine Switzerland."[155]

Oppenheimer described his perception of his own identity in a paragraph that bears a striking resemblance to Eugen Fuchs's famous essay "Glaube und Heimat":[156]

> I am not an assimilationist, nevertheless I am assimilated. I am a German and at the same time proud to be a Jew, proud of the heritage of seventy generations of proud men. . . . I am just as proud, however, to have been born and raised in the land of Walter and Wolfram, Goethe, Kant, and Fichte and to have immersed myself in their culture. My *Deutschtum* is holy to me [*Mein Deutschtum ist mir ein Heiligtum*]. I must defend myself against those who deny my Jewish ethnicity [*Stammesbewusstsein*] as against murderers. Germany is my fatherland, my home-

land, the land of all my yearnings, the land in which my forefathers have been buried, the land of my battles and my love, and when I return home from a foreign country I come home . . . to Germany.[157]

We have seen that the program of the first generation of German Zionists was directed only to the suffering Jews of the East; it was not designed to change the lives of its adherents in Germany. Critics of the early Zionists called their philosophy "Zionism out of pity" (*Zionismus aus Mitleid*), Zionism that was nothing but philanthropy on behalf of East European Jews.

German Jews were fully aware of the differences between their kind of Zionism and that of the Jews in the East. Franz Oppenheimer's controversial article, "Stammesbewusstsein und Volksbewusstsein" [158] was accepted as an accurate statement of theory and a reflection of the feelings of most German Zionists, including the conservative members of the younger generation.[159]

Oppenheimer made a distinction between *Stammesbewusstsein,* which referred to a conscious sense of belonging to a great nation and sharing a pride in common descent, blood, and history, and *Volksbewusstsein,* which referred to a consciousness of the present condition of a people with common language, customs, culture, economic and political situation. The intensity of this latter feeling depended on the individual's desire and ability to become part of a collective *Volksbewusstsein;* all individuals with the same *Volksbewusstsein* belonged to the same nation. Oppenheimer then divided *Volksbewusstsein* into *Nationalitaetsbewusstsein* and *Kulturbewusstsein,* and used these categories to clarify distinctions between *Ostjuden* and *Westjuden.*[160] He claimed that *Westjuden* belonged culturally to the host nation (*Wirtsvolk*) and were thus "of a German culture," "of a French culture," and so on. Only in Western European cultures could Western Jews contribute and adapt. These cultures represented the pinnacle of civilization, far superior to the culture of the traditional Jew:

> We cannot be *Kulturjuden,* because Jewish culture as it
> exists in the ghettos of the East . . . stands far below
> modern culture as represented by our nation . . . we are
> composed, culturally speaking, of 95 percent Western
> European culture.[161]

The implication was that the other 5 percent was Jewish
culture.

The second component of *Volksbewusstsein, Nationalitaetsbewusstsein,* or "patriotism," depended on the degree
of equality that each individual had gained within his particular state, social class, or religion. Here again Oppenheimer
perceived a basic difference between the *Ostjuden* and the
Westjuden:

> we are . . . *Nationaldeutsche;* the *Ostjuden*, on the other
> hand, are only rarely *Nationalrussen.* They are *National-
> juden* as much as they are *Kulturjuden.*[162]

Because the *Ostjuden* had been deprived of the rights accorded other citizens, they felt like strangers in the lands of
Eastern Europe and were therefore able to develop their own
language, religious tradition, and culture. On the other hand,
one could rarely find among the *Westjuden,* Zionists included, anyone who truly believed the saying, "Next year in
Jerusalem." Oppenheimer criticized those West European
Jews who called themselves *Nationaljuden* for failing to distinguish between their ethnicity and their patriotic commitment.[163]

Oppenheimer insisted in his essay, as he did later at the
Leipzig *Delegiertentag,* that, though his group's attitude toward Zionism was not that of the *Ostjuden,* its members were
loyal supporters of political Zionism. It was the oppressive,
degrading socio-political systems of Eastern Europe that
made the *Ostjuden* yearn for emigration. Only where Jews
were considered second-rate citizens could they truly believe,
"Next year in Jerusalem"; the *Ostjuden* had turned to Zionism as a last resort, in an attempt to survive as dignified

human beings. Thus for them, Zionism was a practical expedient based on self-preservation, whereas for the *Westjuden,* it was at most "an idealistic movement, a matter of disinterested altruism."[164]

According to Oppenheimer, the Jews of Western Europe had been subjected to so much less pressure and inequality that they would not consider moving to Palestine unless to improve their social situation. Indeed, few of them believed that Palestine would be established in their lifetime, it was not a part of their future. "They think about their 'Stammbrothers' in the East, for whom they labor out of humanitarian feelings . . . to help them achieve self-determination."[165] These Western European Zionists firmly believed that they did not need a land of refuge; they considered themselves, as did all liberal Jews, privileged to be citizens in the lands of their birth. They felt that "they would be thankless indeed" were they to leave them.[166] But Oppenheimer found the Jews more than loyal citizens; they were devoted German patriots:

> We love our fatherland and the German *volk,* its culture and scenic landscape, we serve the cause of our fatherland with all our heart, and will continue to do so in the future . . . we are not guests who intend to leave tomorrow, but citizens who intend to stay forever. . . . Nevertheless, we remain Zionists, because besides our German *Volksbewusstsein* we have a Jewish *Stammesbewusstsein.*[167]

Oppenheimer stressed that the Zionists did not give aid to any needy individual who wanted to rehabilitate himself: "Zionism is a movement aiming at the emigration of the Jewish people as an entity."[168] Unlike other German philanthropic organizatons, such as the C.V. and the *Hilfsverein,* the Zionists were aware of the ethnic and cultural, as well as the economic and political, needs of the Jews of Eastern Europe and were making strenuous efforts to alleviate their sufferings. They insisted that these Jews could find their salvation only in Palestine, where the renaissance of Jewish culture would accompany the renaissance of a Jewish state.[169]

Oppenheimer's essay unleashed tremendous controversy in the pages of *Die Welt* and *Juedische Rundschau,* but most German Zionists and the entire leadership of the ZVfD supported his point of view. [170] Friedemann claimed that it was an unbearable thought that the German Zionists should stoop to a lower (Jewish) culture not only in Palestine but in the Diaspora as well; "as if one could acquire a culture as one acquires a new suit ... one has the right to create this new culture only if one is considering emigration to Palestine in the near future ... and this is a thing of the very distant future in the West." [171] Friedemann finished with a frank admission as to the nature of German Zionism:

> If we do admit to thinking about Zionism in terms of philanthropy, we hope that we will not be turned out of the Zionist movement.[172]
> The Eastern Jews do not have to make great modifications in their thinking to become Zionists... the German Jews become Zionists to be able to strive for a whole personality which will relieve them of their dual existence in the Diaspora.[173]

Oppenheimer's essay reflected the feelings of the majority of older German Zionists before 1914, and it indicates that they did not view their situation in Germany as intolerable. Except for their efforts in respect to Palestine, they shared the same aspirations and Weltanschauung as the rest of the German Jewish middle class, who were represented by such organizations as the C.V., *Verband der deutschen Juden,* the *Deutsch-Israelitischer Gemeindebund,* and others. After a trip to Palestine, even Max Bodenheimer, the most effective figure in the early Zionist movement, wrote:

> Our heart belongs to the land where we first tried to understand the meaning of life. Despite the strong impression which the visit in the Holy Land, the land of our

forefathers, has made on me, it seemed to me that my relationship and feeling toward Palestine, in comparison with my feelings toward my German homeland, was of a dreamlike quality. The period which our forefathers inhabited Palestine seems very remote to us. The stories of the Bible sound to us like fairy tales told to children. Such memories of the past can fill us with pride . . . but they can never replace the first memories of our childhood. After my visit to Palestine, it became clear to me how difficult it must be for a West European Jew to become a Zionist.[174]

The early Zionists thus always affirmed their own German patriotism. [175] This had been their dominant attitude ever since Bodenheimer published his *Wohin mit den Russischen Juden.* [176] In a conversation with Kurt Blumenfeld, Oppenheimer explained: "You must know that Zionism is a process in which we are the directors and the East European Jews must be the actors." [177] Official publications of the ZVfD made the same point, [178] and Richard Lichtheim wrote in 1911 in his *Das Programm des Zionismus* that "the social and political program of Zionism was to direct the East European Jews to Palestine."[179]

It should be stressed, however, that this point of view, which drew such sharp lines between Western and Eastern Zionism, was exclusively that of the ZVfD leadership, and not that of the membership at large. [180] Within the ZVfD there were clearly defined distinctions between the leadership and the membership. The entire leadership of the ZVfD, both before and after World War I, was composed of men born in Germany, usually into well-to-do families; almost all of them were professionals and all were educated in German universities. Most of the rank and file members of the ZVfD, however, were immigrants from Eastern Europe; [181] "they were the great reservoir of German Zionism."[182]

Though little is known about the composition of the ZVfD membership, interviews with the Zionist leaders and activists living today confirm that Eastern European immigrants constituted most of its membership. [183] A more accurate local account estimates that in Kassel 85 percent of all Zionists were from Eastern Europe; but leadership there always remained in the hands of German Jews so as to refute assimilationist accusations that "Zionism in Germany was a movement of foreigners." [184] These figures are of special interest, since Kassel is situated in the center of Germany, unlike Posen or Leipzig where a majority membership of Eastern European Jews could be expected.

In 1907 and 1910, the ZVfD conducted surveys on the membership of the two Zionist student organizations, *Bund Juedischer Corporationen* and *Verein Juedischer Studenten,* which are of interest since they represent 472 Zionist students from thirty-three localities in Germany; thus they give a representative picture of Zionist membership throughout the Reich. The surveys show that at least 295 of the 427 students who were interviewed had come from Eastern Europe (Russia, Rumania, Hungary), or border territories of the German Reich (Pommern, Posen, Sachsen). [185] The surveys also point out that most of those from Eastern Europe were of the lower middle-income class.[186]

The above statistics clearly show that when the official organs and leaders of the German Zionists classified the ZVfD as an example of Western Zionism, they were in fact taking into account only a very tiny fraction of the movement, the German-born Zionists. Even David Wolffsohn, who had helped found the ZVfD and who for all practical purposes had achieved the status of a wealthy German middle-class Jew accepted in such liberal organizations as the *Bnei Briss,* never held an official position within the ZVfD, presumably because of his Eastern European background. It was, therefore, only the small group of German-born Zionists who controlled the leadership; their attitudes toward the Eastern European Jews remained intact until World War I. The ZVfD position did undergo a change during the war. [187] Because the years from 1914 to 1918 saw a huge influx of East European Jews into Germany, [188] many of whom joined the ranks of the ZVfD and the JVP, the ZVfD declared:

We must forge an alliance between the *Ostjuden* and the

Westjuden.... It is important that the *Ostjuden* have
adequate representation in all *Ortsgruppen* and that their
needs be taken seriously.[189]

At the *Delegiertentag* of the ZVfD in Wiesbaden in 1924,
the Zionists in Germany created the *Ostjuedische Kommission,* under the direction of Moses Waldmann, which
aimed to integrate the *Ostjuden* fully into the ZVfD. The
commission cared for the special needs of the *Ostjuden* and
organized lectures on Isaac Leib Perez, Sholem Aleichem, and
Mendele Mocher Seforim. It cooperated in these matters with
the *Verband Ostjuedischer Organisationen* and it supported
the only Yiddish newspaper in Germany, *Unser Leben.*[190]

This new concern of the ZVfD with the needs and demands of the *Ostjuden* was mainly the result of the experiences of German Jewry during World War I. Until about
1912, the German Zionist ideology had come very close to
the assimilationist ideology of the mainstream of German
Jewry. Both the Zionists and the members of the C.V.
struggled to establish a synthesis between their love for
Germany and their loyalty to Judaism. The C.V. found it in
the declaration that its members were loyal German citizens
who held true to the Jewish faith. The Zionist interpretation
was broader; they too considered themselves good German
citizens, but their adherence to Judaism was expressed in
terms of a common national bond with Jews all over the
world. In practice of course, as shown above, these different
Weltanschauungen did not affect the lives of the German
Zionists, and to a large degree, the differences between the
two organizations remained on an abstract level.

Some theoretical discrepancies between the two organizations were simply matters of semantic interpretation. Confusion in terminology extended to members of liberal
organizations as well as to the Zionists. There was no agreement, for example, as to the meaning of the often used terms
of *Nation, Volk, Stamm,* and *Vaterland.*[191] Eugen Fuchs
made a distinction between *Nation*—the individual's adherence to his fatherland irrespective of his religion—and
Stamm—the individual within the historical context of his

ethnic heritage. As discussed above, Oppenheimer constructed an elaborate framework to distinguish between *Volksbewusstsein* and *Stammesbewusstsein.* Bodenheimer, on the
other hand, distinguished between love for the fatherland—
deutsche Vaterlandsliebe and Jewish national feeling—
juedisches Nationalgefuehl. [192] The theoretical and philosophical constructions presented by German Jews to explain
the dilemma of being a German Jew were countless; each
according to his own philosophy ranked the two concepts of
Deutschtum and *Judentum* as equal or subordinate to one
another. The confusion in the terminology reflected the
problem of assimilation. Both this first generation of German
Zionists and the liberals were repeatedly seeking a synthesis
between the two principles. Bodenheimer spoke for the
majority of German Jews, Zionists as well as non-Zionists,
when he wrote that *Deutschtum* and *Judentum* can be joined
"as the love of a child for both his father and mother."[193]

Theoretically and ideologically, Zionism in Germany ran
counter to the hundred-year-old historical process of emancipation and assimilation which had considered the Jews merely a religious community. No conflict occurred during the
pre-1912 period, however, because the Zionists did not
attack the liberals nor did the liberals feel threatened by the
Zionists. Even the *Gemeinden* and the rabbis who had protested most vigorously against Zionism soon came to the
realization that the C.V.'s policy of *Totschweigen* might be a
much more powerful weapon against the Zionists and that
constant protest would only serve to put the Zionists in the
public limelight. By the same token, the first generation of
German Zionists dissociated themselves from such "radicals"
as the members of the JVP, and until after World War I the
Eroberung der Gemeinden remained for the most part an
ideological issue rather than a real threat to the rule of the
notables.

A number of factors helped to postpone the clash between liberals and Zionists: in the pre-1912 period both the
C.V. and the ZVfD had leaders whose personalities were
compatible; Franz Oppenheimer and Adolf Friedemann had
much more in common, culturally and temperamentally and

in the experience of their student days, with Eugen Fuchs and Maximilian Horwitz than with Kurt Blumenfeld or Max Kollenscher. As a result the leaders of the two groups preserved amicable relations, and some of the leaders of the ZVfD, notably Alfred Klee, were members of the C.V. as well.

In addition, the German Zionists before 1912 were not very active and whatever activity there was, was inner-directed—to strengthen the organizational framework and to elaborate Zionist ideology; this lull was characteristic of the WZO as a whole. [194] Herzl's faith that Zionism would solve the problem of the Jews immediately through decisive political action was not borne out. The Zionists did not receive the charter, and the "Young Turks" embarked on a road of nationalism and centralization immediately after seizing control in 1908; this policy made the receipt of a charter unlikely in the near future. [195] Max Nordau warned the Zionists at the Ninth Congress in 1909 to be patient and wait for the political situation to become ripe. Blumenfeld called the Zionist position of the time "the long-winded revolution."

How was Zionism in Germany expressed then? What was the meaning and form of Zionist identity? By declaring themselves to be Zionists, Jews in Germany did not look for personal or immediate consequences for themselves. In essence, they wanted to be Jewish Nationalists by the grace of and for the benefit of the *Ostjuden*. [196] They had no intention of endangering their own German citizenship for Zionism. Many Zionists, however, felt the duality in their situation and tried to come to terms with it. [197] Moses Calvary (1876–1944), a foremost intellectual within the ZVfD, tried to explain:

> There are German Jews who do not believe in the importance of German culture for their own existence; these people will easily be able to ignore the contradiction between *Deutschtum* and *Judentum*. . . . The depth of the problem begins for those Jews who are conscious of the influence of German culture on their entire being. . . . This German world has captured our souls and we Ger-

man Zionists, who are citizens of the German culture, cannot and do not want to give up the ability to work within the German culture. We are not afraid of the accusation that we lead a double life.[198]

Heinrich Stern solved the conflict for himself by declaring that it was possible to be a Jewish nationalist and a loyal citizen of the fatherland at the same time, since the two value systems did not conflict. He claimed that the cultivation of Jewish heritage and values in Germany would serve only to enhance German culture by adding to it the perspective of a cultured minority.[199]

But most German Zionists were less concerned about a double loyalty. Zionists spoke of "living as Jews" or "returning to Judaism" without meaning anything more profound than an adherence to an abstract, and somewhat hazy, Zionist ideology.[200] This secular Judaism that they called "Zionism" found its outlet before World War I mainly in discussions and propaganda.[201] Siegfried Kanowitz, a former member of the Zionist student group, *Maccabaea,* of Koenigsberg, wrote:

The Zionism of our time was based on ideology. Our substance was not changed, we did not become more Jewish, we did not emigrate en masse to Palestine, but we found in ourselves new strength, a new direction for our lives, for the intellectual and social milieu in which we lived . . . in a sense this was a sort of internal rebirth.[202]

Kanowitz makes the value of Zionist ideological controversies clear. Despite their lack of practical consequences in Palestine, Zionist activities in Germany were of immense worth to those Jews who were groping for solutions to their own personal dilemma in the face of the conflict between *Deutschtum* and *Judentum.* Zionism solved the problem for many of them. It generated interest and enthusiasm, especially among young people who discovered in Zionism a meaning for their existence as Jews in a society that had no interest in Judaism.[203] Zionism heightened their feelings of pride and self-respect in their own ethnicity and culture, so that they could confront the influences of their time without being overwhelmed by them. [204]   Blumenfeld, one of those who found self-esteem through the Zionist cause, said, "We are Zionists by the grace of Goethe" (*Zionisten von Goethes Gnaden*), [205]   by which he meant that Zionists were able to assimilate the philosophies of Hoelderlin and Nietzsche without endangering their Zionist ideology.

Herzl coined the phrase that "Zionism is the return to Jewishness before the return to Palestine" (*Der Zionismus ist die Rueckkehr zum Judentum vor der rueckkehr ins Judenland*), [206]   that is, a return to the "Jewish people." The German Zionists adopted another version of this phrase: "Zionism demands [*verlangt*] the return to Judaism before the return to Palestine." Like Herzl, they believed that Zionism, in essence, was the last chance for many Jews to return to the Jewish fold. [207]   Unlike him, they believed that a return to Jewishness could be accomplished in Germany. Gerhard Holdheim, who called this belief "watered-down Zionism" admits its effect on German Jews, and especially on the younger ones, nevertheless: "this Zionism was a therapy for those who felt the conflict between *Deutschtum* and *Judentum*, who realized that Zionism was an idea which could, for the first time, involve the whole of their being."[208]

We have shown that the pre-1912 Zionist demand to "return to Jewishness" was not radical enough to place Zionists in conflict with the German Jewish liberal majority. Zionists' roots in German culture and ideals, coupled with a lack of political initiative, gave them a base in common with the liberals. In fact many leading Zionists of the Weimar period were members of the K.C. and C.V. in the period before 1914. Among them were Max Kollenscher, who later became influential in *Gemeindepolitik;* [209]   Alfred Klee, who was for a short period the president of the ZVfD and who became influential in the JVP; [210]   Isaak Zwirn (1880–1960), and Felix Theilhaber (1884–1956), and many others. [211]   On the occasion of the C.V.'s tenth anniversary in 1903, it was Alfred Klee who gave one of the principal addresses during the ceremonies in Berlin. [212]

The Weltanschauung of the German Zionists is clearly reflected in the figures for German emigration to Palestine. If we use Blumenfeld's term of "postassimilationist Zionism" to describe the German Zionists who were returning to Jewishness, and if we assume that emigration to Palestine (*Aliyah*) was the Zionist ideal, then German Zionism may be described as a stage between postassimilation and *Aliyah*. [213] Even the radical Posen and Leipzig *Delegiertentage,* and the Balfour Declaration, did not induce larger numbers of German Zionists to set out for Palestine.

No accurate statistics are extant, but reports and memoirs of contemporaries show that before 1918 [214] immigration into Palestine was almost nonexistent. [215] There was little increase during the Weimar Republic, and German Jews went to Palestine in substantial numbers only in May 1933, after Hitler had seized final control of the government. [216] It should be pointed out that this does not take into account those German Jewish orthodox groups who had been going to Palestine ever since the midnineteenth century. [217] The number of German Jewish emigrants to Palestine between 1920 and 1933 was 1,282;[218] but in the seven-month period between May and December, 1933, there were 6,602, and another 3,784 Jews came as tourists. [219] The figures include only those who came through the ports of Jaffa and Haifa; those who arrived through other borders were not recorded by the Jewish Agency.[220]

The table on page 142 supplies figures for 1920–32 emigration to Palestine. It should be made clear that the statistics include *all* German Jews, not only those declared Zionists. The data also include large numbers of Eastern European Jews in Germany who were in transit from Eastern Europe to Palestine, but were nevertheless recorded as German Jews by the Jewish Agency. It should also be noted that in the 1920s almost all the pioneers (*Halutzim*) who came through Germany were *Ostjuden.* [221]

Between 1920 and 1933 German Jewish emigration, in comparison with the total Jewish emigration to Palestine, never rose above the 3 percent reached in 1929; only in that year did German Jewish emigration reach that figure. In 1933, however, it comprised 24.8 percent of the total.[222]

Table 3
German Jewish Emigration to Palestine: 1920–32[223]

Year	Number
1920	175
1921	185
1922	38
1923	71
1924	180
1925	262
1926	71
1927	9
1928	6
1929	43
1930	47
1931	42
1932	153
Total	1,282

The above figures show that during years of economic and political crisis—especially between 1920 and 1924, a period of severe economic setback for Germany—there was a sharp rise in emigration. The period after 1933 cannot of course be considered in the context of a Zionist movement to Palestine.

This statistical and biographical information proves our thesis that the majority of German Zionists felt very comfortable in Germany; and that like all other Jews, they had become completely assimilated into the cultural milieu which surrounded them. It has been claimed that the integration and assimilation of the Jews in Germany was an illusion, because most Germans did not respond positively to Jewish demands for equality, and because the anti-Semitic movement rejected all Jews outright. [224] This seems, however, to be true only in retrospect. The German Jews did not find their situation so intolerable, since they had achieved practical and legislative measures of equality which they had never known before; their remaining demands seemed soon to be possible of realization. In the light of their previous history, their economic and political situation seemed, indeed, to be the fulfillment of all their dreams. The following statement by Oppenheimer, regardless of its truth, speaks for most German Jews and many Zionists as well: "I feel that I am composed of 99 percent Kant and Goethe and only one percent Old Testament; and that one percent only through Spinoza's and Luther's translations of the Bible."[225]

IV

Radicalization of the ZVfD

It is clear that the two most decisive influences on ZVfD ideology were the generational experience and the resultant Weltanschauung of its members and the interdependence and overlapping of its organizational structure with the WZO. The ZVfD founders had grown up in the cultural and political milieu of late nineteenth-century Wilhelminian Germany. The organization, as the intellectual and geographical center of the WZO, often adopted trends that were current in the general movement. These factors combined with Herzl's powerful personal influence to shape the early orientation of German Zionists, and, aside from certain changes demanded by particular features of German Zionism, it persisted until 1910–12. The radical changes thereafter can be explained by changes in the WZO and by the new categories of experience encountered by the young German Zionists. How did these generational experiences differ from those of their elders?[1]

The first generation of German Zionists had witnessed, during their formative years as young adults, the rise and wane of political anti-Semitism. Like the rest of the German Jewish community, they still believed in emancipation and the continued improvement of their situation. Again, as ma-

144

ture adults they had seen the rise of post-1871 anti-Semitism; that is, at a time when they could better confront and rationalize the phenomenon. By the same token, they had also personally watched the successful struggle for equal rights.

In contrast to these men, the second generation encountered the most virulent forms of anti-Semitism in the 1890s during their student years in the gymnasia and universities, which were hotbeds of the anti-Semitic movement, at a time in their lives when they were more likely to be deeply hurt by it. They saw the rising *voelkish* movement become progressively more anti-Semitic as it excluded them from the *Wandervogel* and *Turnvereine*. At the same time, the *voelkish* movement provided an example for the young Jews, who were as disenchanted as were the young Christians with the values of the older generation. And finally, unlike their fathers, the young Zionists had not witnessed the successful struggle for civil rights; by the time they began their education in the 1890s they were convinced that anti-Semitism was inevitable and would become progressively more violent. [2] Their experiences with anti-Semitism at an impressionable age and the ideological, cultural, and political transformations that they saw within the WZO and ZVfD accounted for the "radicalism" that found its culmination in the years between 1912 and 1914.

In addition, it is possible—though for lack of sufficient evidence this must remain merely a hypothesis—that certain changes within the anti-Semitic movement in 1912, as it became more vicious and vituperative, contributed to the Weltanschauung of this second generation and may have contributed to the Posen Resolution. Nineteen twelve is the year in which the Social Democrats made important gains in the Reichstag elections, but their victory only strengthened the determination and reactionism of the anti-Semites. As Pulzer indicates, they took the defeat "with deadly seriousness."[3]

A rallying point for them was Heinrich Class, chairman of the Pan-German League, who in 1912 published his famous *If I were the Kaiser: Political Truths and Necessities*. Shaul Esh has pointed out that, "so far as we know, this was the first time that anyone had presented, not just a demand for an 'aliens law' along with a few proposals, but a complete scheme for discriminatory legislation, area by area." Class felt that such legislation should make any self-respecting Jew "brush off from his feet the dust of a Germany so uncongenial to her guests, and seek a homeland elsewhere."[4] Class's book had a tremendous influence in Germany in the period before (and after) 1914, and it was reprinted in many editions. It seems plausible that such publications as this greatly impressed the young Zionists and confirmed their impressions that the Jews had no legitimate place in German society.

The Ideological Background

Whereas Herzl, the first generation of German Zionists, and most other Western Zionists were concerned with the plight of the Jews (*Judennot*), some Eastern European Jews as well as a few Western Zionist intellectuals developed a different conception of the Jewish Problem. Notable among the Eastern Europeans was Ahad Ha'Am who was concerned more with the problem of Judaism than with Herzl's *Judennot*. Ahad Ha'Am and his followers did not oppose the settlement of Jews in Palestine as a political solution, but they did not value colonization as an end in itself. Rather, their objective was to "revive a secular Jewish culture through the medium of the Hebrew language, and to reestablish the consensus of the Jewish people as the prerequisite condition for pursuing their national aims."[5] As early as 1889, seven years before Herzl's *Judenstaat,* Ahad Ha'Am had published his famous essay "*Lo Zeh Haderekh,*" which claimed that colonization or the establishment of a Jewish state were not necessarily the signs of a Jewish national renaissance. His concern was for the internal, personal revival of Jewish education or *Thiyat ha'Levavot,* and of cultural and ethical values, which could then become the foundation for Jewish colonization.[6]

Ahad Ha'Am was deeply disappointed that Herzl's political Zionism rejected such activities within the movement. His skeptical and critical attitude toward the movement's political aims persisted from the first Zionist Congress until his death in 1927.[7] Despite Herzl's personal invitation, Ahad

Ha'Am refused to attend the First Zionist Congress as a delegate and thereby lost his opportunity to influence the proceedings directly. Indirectly, however, he influenced the Democratic Fraction, which urged the congressional delegates to engage in *Gegenwartsarbeit,* amelioration of the cultural and intellectual plight of the Diaspora Jews. This splinter group worked toward Jewish national rebirth in the Diaspora through education in Jewish and national values, practical training in untraditional professions and trades, and general economic improvement. Other practical measures included the dispatch of experts to Palestine to survey the political and economic conditions there and to determine its suitability for Jewish colonization.[8]

Martin Buber, instrumental in the founding and perpetuation of the Democratic Fraction, was undoubtedly the most significant follower of Ahad Ha'Am in Germany.[9] Buber also rejected economic and political interpretations of Zionism in favor of the "cultural renaissance of the nation."[10] In an article written in 1905, he asserted that it was not enough for Zionists to aim at the establishment of a home for the Jewish people. For Buber the pressing questions were the nature of this nation which needed a home and the question as to whether this nation had the energy to continue to exist. Buber believed that the Zionists' first task was to support the existence of a vital Jewish nationality. He criticized as superficial the activities of the Zionist movement that concentrated on collecting the *Shekel* and expanding the membership. He demanded that the movement probe deeper and try to capture the soul and innermost being of the Jew, not only his nominal financial support.[11] As a first step toward regeneration, the Jewish people had to be educated in all the manifestations of their culture:

> Everything . . . belongs to his culture. A folk song, a dance, a wedding custom . . . a tale, a belief, a traditional prejudice, a Sabbath candle . . . a philosophical system . . . all this is culture.[12]

Although convinced that Jewish culture could be fully developed only on its own soil, Buber believed that the work must begin in the Diaspora. He hoped that Jewish youth with their as yet unformed identities, could be challenged to undertake this great task.[13]

Buber's stance received its greatest response among Western European Zionists disillusioned with the "empty formulae" of political Zionism. After a prolonged retirement from public activities, during which he devoted himself to the study of Hasidism,[14] Buber accepted an invitation from the *Bar Kochba* group of Prague, where between 1909 and 1911 he delivered his famous "Reden ueber das Judentum."[15]

In his first lecture Buber asked, "Why do we call ourselves Jewish?" He did not accept the answer that one was a Jew by virtue of his religion or nationality. In the past Jews had undergone unique religious experiences, but in the present they lacked the vital experience of God, or indeed any religious fulfillment or commitment.[16] For Buber, Jewish nationality was as empty a concept as the state of contemporary Jewish religion, for it existed by virtue of the claim of the non-Jewish nations, rather than as an autonomous reality. What then could be done so that the Jew would "feel his nation not only around him, but also within himself?"[17]

Buber analyzed the two realms of every Jew, the realm of external experience and the realm of the inner substance that rested on a descent and blood common to one's forebears and fellow Jews. Most people were aware only of the outer realm of experience, thereby creating an alienated dual existence (*Zwiespaeltigkeit*). Buber's goal was to integrate the two realms. The dilemma of this split, a particular characteristic of the Diaspora, could be resolved by embracing one's heritage (*Abstammung*) and by affirming the special qualities of the Jewish *volk* that Buber identified in his interpretation of Jewish history. Through affirmation (*Bejahung*) the individual Jew would recognize his ties to his people and would come to understand the history of his people as his own:

> The people are now for him a community of men who were, are, and will be—a community of the dead, the living, and the yet unborn who together constitute a unity. It is this unity that, to him, is the ground of his I,

this I which is fitted as a link into the great chain. . . . Whatever all the great men in this chain have created and will create he conceives to be the work of his own unique being; whatever they have experienced and will experience he conceives to be his own destiny. The past of his people is his personal memory, the future of his people his personal task. The way of his people teaches him to understand himself, and to will himself.[18]

The choice before the modern Jew was thus between his external experience in the everyday world and his inner substance as a way of life. The Jewish Question was for Buber the personal question of every Jew. He who chooses the inner substance will become a Jew from within and will live as a Jew "with all the contradictions, all the tragedy and all the future promise of his blood." Buber understood the modern Jew in the Diaspora as a product of his environment and of his own substance, and he therefore did not require total acceptance of one element to the exclusion of the other. Rather, he hoped that in recognizing his own double nature, each Jew would transcend or master it, thus being able to decide which element of the "admixture" he would choose as dominant. Once the Jew has reaffirmed his substance he is united forever with his people and with its future; the future of Judaism will become his personal concern.[19] In a later essay Buber wrote: "Whoever does not remember that God led him out of Egypt, whoever does not personally await the Messiah, is no longer a Jew."[20]

Buber's "Reden" had a strong appeal for the assimilated young Zionists who were searching for meaning in their lives.[21] Cut off from all Jewish traditions, these young men had embraced Zionism for a variety of personal reasons and were uncertain how to combine their newly found Jewishness with the modern *Zeitgeist*. For them Buber seemed to offer a solution:

a renaissance of the total individual or ethnic personality, not a change of one or another aspect of life . . . [a] realization that to be a Jew is to live a life of unconditional commitment, rejecting compromise, that what counts are constructive deeds, not abstract concepts or theories.[22]

Buber led the young generation of German Zionists to the realization that Zionism and Judaism could be fulfilled only through a fully committed life in Palestine. Ignoring the political and economic situation in Palestine, which after 1908 was dominated by the extreme nationalist "Young Turks," they saw in Palestine the opportunity to become wholly Jewish.[23] For them Buber's words were existentially meaningful. For them Zionism ceased to be a political solution and became instead the answer to "our personal problems," the radical renunciation of contemporary bourgeois ideals in all their manifestations, and especially the repudiation of assimilation and emancipation.[24] Gerhard Holdheim described their feelings:

> For us Zionism was the grandiose act of liberation from our unfulfilled existence ... it would be a grave misunderstanding of the psychological and historical makeup of our Zionism, were one to describe it as a mere dissatisfaction with European culture ... it was rather a protest against the form of our existence.[25]

The young generation's dissociation from the old values required a complete renaissance of the individual in terms of ethical and moral standards. They believed that their actions would promote the renaissance of the spirit of the nation and release its latent energies.[26] They renounced Herzl's political Zionist theories, as represented in Germany by Friedemann, Oppenheimer, and Bodenheimer; they called this form of Zionism "vulgar and just as self-satisfied as the usual philanthropy."[27] They considered themselves superior to the rest of the Zionists, more honest in the search for their roots and for "our truly inner and honest being which we thought we had left behind us two thousand years ago."[28]

The Zionist youth of pre-World War I Germany was influenced by ideas that permeated the general thought of

Western European middle-class youth, which was striving to free itself from mechanization and the self-satisfaction of bourgeois ideology. These young men turned instead to nature, simplicity, and comradeship. In the *Wandervogel* movement which reached its apex in 1913 at the *Hohen Meissner,* their ideals found realization.[29] The activities and ideology of the German youth were of great importance to the young Zionists. Soon Jewish *Wanderbuende* groups developed, imitating the German *Wandervogel,* and were later transformed into groups primarily directed toward Jewish fulfillment.[30]

Many statements of the young German Zionists reveal their interest in the conservative *voelkish* movements current in Germany at the turn of the century.[31] In 1911 an article in *Der Juedische Student* included a quotation from Johann Gottlieb Fichte:

> Make a decision which only you, in your own person, will be able to fulfill. It is insufficient to want to do something sometime . . . rather, you should make a decision which will have momentous consequences for your own life.[32]

These words were meant to awaken a new consciousness in the youth. Zionists found exactly what they believed expressed by Goethe: "Man is totally free and happy only when he has the courage to feel his whole being."[33] The similarity between the Zionists and the *voelkish* youth movement was especially evident in the Zionist *Blau-Weiss* youth group, founded in 1912 as a *Wanderbund.*[34] It soon was one of the most active Zionist youth organizations in Germany.

The young Zionists saw the Jewish Question in a completely different light from the "confession-oriented" Jews of the older generation, and an understanding between the two generations became almost impossible. The young Zionists criticized both the older Zionists and members of the C.V. as assimilationists of the worst kind. On the other hand, the young leaders' concept of a "community of blood" (*Gemeinschaft des Blutes*) was alien to the members of the C.V. who, despite occasional references to *Stamm,* firmly believed in a community of religion (*Religionsgemeinschaft*).[35] The "radicals" felt that assimilation into the German *volk* was undesirable and impossible to achieve. Germany, they argued, was not a fertile ground for a German-Jewish synthesis, and should be seen instead only as a temporary stopover on the way to Zion.

Unlike the members of the older generation, these young Zionists intended to act on their theories. Although they had borrowed some of their ideals from the *Wandervogel,* they stressed their dissimilarity from the rest of the German population in custom, habit, and innermost being. Believing that they were strangers on German soil, anti-Semitism was for them the unsurprising, inevitable consequence of German recognition of Jewish "otherness." Accordingly they saw no need to fight the anti-Semites. Another practical consequence was their rejection of obligations that could bind them to Germany, and they fulfilled their obligations to the state only to the extent that was absolutely required.[36] Blumenfeld's suggestion that Zionists should renounce all political positions was readily accepted by many of them.[37]

The Weltanschauung of the young generation within the ZVfD was formulated as a program in the period from 1909 to 1910. On October 1, 1909, the ZVfD appointed Kurt Blumenfeld, a brilliant student of German literature and an excellent speaker, to become first party secretary and official propagandist.[38] Insofar as historical change can be attributed to a single personality, one can say that Blumenfeld altered the ideological course of the German Zionist organization between 1910 and 1914.[39] The young, second-generation German Zionists, rebelling against the political-philanthropic orientation of their elders, recognized in Blumenfeld their most capable spokesman and interpreter of Zionism within the context of German cultural and political conditions.[40] He was an immediate success in winning the Zionist youth movements, such as the *Verein Juedischer Studenten* and the *Bund Juedischer Corporationen,*[41] to his ideas.[42] When he was appointed secretary of the ZVfD, "he was already, in the eyes of many, something like the heir apparent to the leadership of German Zionism."[43] His appointment was innovative, since the organization had very few salaried officials.

In 1910, another change occurred when Max Bodenheimer resigned from the presidency of the ZVfD at the Twelfth *Delegiertentag* in Frankfurt am Main in favor of Arthur Hantke (1874–1955), a young lawyer from Berlin.[44] The new leadership immediately had a substantial impact by moving the central offices of the ZVfD from Bodenheimer's home city of Cologne to Berlin in 1910. This move signaled the demise of Cologne as the power center of the ZVfD. The change of address placed the Zionist movement in the geographical center of Jewish activities in Germany, where it could respond quickly to events within the Jewish community and similarly could no longer be ignored by other leading Jewish organizations in Berlin.

Blumenfeld's and Hantke's appointments, Bodenheimer's resignation, and the move to Berlin reflected the decline of political Zionism within the WZO. At the time when the radical Zionists were challenging the ZVfD establishment, like-minded opponents to political Zionism within the WZO began seriously to oppose David Wolffsohn, the WZO president. Their demand that the offices of the WZO be transferred from Wolffsohn's home city of Cologne to Berlin had been made even before the Ninth Zionist Congress in Hamburg in 1909.[45] In the course of this congress and of the Tenth Congress in Basel in 1911, the young Russian and German Zionists solidified their opposition to Wolffsohn. Among the Germans were Arthur Hantke and Ahron Sandler, supporters of Weizmann's "synthetic" Zionism which gained control of the WZO in these years.[46] As a result of their victory, their demand that the central office be transferred to Berlin was realized by 1911.[47] It is important to emphasize that by 1911 political Zionism, as the major aim of Zionism, had been discredited in the WZO, and practical or synthetic Zionism was seen as a more rational way to achieve Zionist goals. Such trends in the WZO gave moral and ideological support to the young German Zionists.

The Process of Radicalization

In its early years the ZVfD was concerned with expanding its slowly growing membership. The *Delegiertentag* in Hanover in 1900 comprised fifteen delegates; in Berlin in 1901, twenty-nine; and the sixth *Delegiertentag* in Mannheim in 1902, sixty-six delegates representing Zionists throughout Germany. The Frankfurt *Delegiertentag* of 1910 hosted the largest number of delegates up to that time—one hundred, [48] representing the payment of 6,200 *Shekels*. [49] Blumenfeld's major purpose in his extensive and frequent travels was to recruit new members and to disseminate the Zionist ideas in new localities. The more than 50 percent increase in membership between 1910 and 1914 (from 6,200 to 9,800) was primarily the result of his efforts. He and Hantke furthered the work by publishing as many notes and articles concerning the ZVfD as the German and Jewish-German newspapers were willing to accept. The German Zionist press was also revitalized in 1910, the year in which the *Zionistisches Merkblatt, Zionistisches A-B-C Buch, Juedische Gemeindepolitik,* and many other brochures and leaflets were published to awaken general interest in Zionism. [50]

The radicalization of the ZVfD's ideological perspective and the background of the young generation that assumed control of the organization just prior to World War I were well represented by Kurt Blumenfeld (1884–1963), who had become secretary of the ZVfD in 1909. He came from a highly assimilated middle-class family in which "German *Gesinnung* had taken the place of Jewish tradition." [51] Questions of Jewish identity or even of the problems of anti-Semitism were never discussed. For this reason perhaps, instances in which Blumenfeld's Jewish identity was forcibly drawn to his attention were imprinted all the more vividly on his mind. [52] On one occasion a Catholic maid told him that she had confessed to her priest the sin of working for Jews who were the descendants of Christ's crucifiers. [53] On another, while walking with a Christian friend of the family, he met an Eastern European Jew who asked him in Yiddish for some directions. Blumenfeld pretended not to understand, upon which his friend asked if he were embarrassed. The young Blumenfeld showed the man the correct route and ran away.[54] These childhood incidents led Blumenfeld to recognize the fact that Jews were different from all other people and were, indeed, considered a negative element within the German society.

Shortly after beginning his studies at the University of Berlin, Blumenfeld turned to Zionism.[55] His autobiography does not provide an explicit explanation for this. What emerges from the account, however, is that the combined impact of the assimilated Jews of Berlin and of his Christian professors and colleagues led him to confront the Jewish Question. The anti-Semitic movement had confirmed the fact that Jews were essentially different from Germans and therefore undesirable, and Blumenfeld saw in Zionism the key to understanding the Jew in the non-Jewish environment.[56] He did not discover Zionism by rational analysis. Rather, the idea dawned on him suddenly and captured his whole being.[57] Only after he became converted to Zionism did Blumenfeld study the ideology and its roots, and only then did he acknowledge his "Jewishness."

Blumenfeld directed his speeches to the assimilated German Jews who had discarded Judaism and its traditions, yet felt something lacking in their personal lives; he tried to show them that "Zionism was the modern way to Judaism."[58] Blumenfeld's theory was that Zionism was the Judaism of the "postassimilated" German Jews, that it would "enable them to regain their equipoise and to become harmonious personalities who were not time and again thrown off balance by some hidden desire to get rid of their Jewishness."[59] As an authority in German classic literature, Blumenfeld concluded that, since *Deutschtum* as a cultural milieu was alien to the essence of *Judentum,* there could be no synthesis between them. The individual Jew was rootless in Germany; his intellectual, cultural, and emotional destiny could be found only in Zionism and Judaism.[60]

A major difficulty for Blumenfeld was the paradox of the German Zionists' continuing to live and work in a cultural and national milieu that they denied as their own. He tried to reconcile this discrepancy between theory and reality by the concept of "distance" (*Distanz*).[61] That is, the ethnically and nationally conscious Jew had deliberately to keep a certain distance between himself and the German world, a distance necessary to preserve the boundaries (*Grenzueberschreitung*) of his own culture and to preclude adoption of other cultures.[62] Hence Blumenfeld demanded that Jews avoid power positions within the German economy and politics.

Blumenfeld also believed that the Jewish Question in the Diaspora produced a "personality problem" for those who assimilated and repudiated their Jewish nationality. These Jews became insecure and hypocritical in a society that did not accept them as ethnic Jews. The only way to ameliorate this situation was to emigrate to Palestine where a Jew could be himself, totally and unconditionally. Until emigration became possible a temporary measure to alleviate Jewish suffering would be the affirmation of Jewish identity and nationality. His program, therefore, had three stages: reaffirmation of Jewish nationality, heritage, and values; recognition of Jewish rootlessness in German culture and society; and the establishment of a discreet distance from the alien culture.[63] The individual Jew in Diaspora could embark on this program as soon as he recognized Zionism as his road to freedom.[64]

As early as the Frankfurt *Delegiertentag* of 1910, Blumenfeld stressed that the German Zionists must be made aware that Zionism was rooted in Jewish nationalism and not in a vague concept of Judaism. He believed that each Zionist must espouse Jewish nationalism out of a deeply felt personal need. He called on the *Juedische Rundschau* to advance this nationalist consciousness by articles and editorials.[65] He emphasized that those who saw in Zionism a means of returning to their own people needed guidance from firmly rooted, indigenous, ethnic Jews. He suggested that *Ostjuden* might serve as such examples.[66]

Both the first and second generations of German Zionists considered the *Ostjuden* to be "better Jews," in close touch with their tradition and culture. The older generation (for example, Oppenheimer) recognized the differences between German Jews and *Ostjuden,* but without extracting any implications pertinent to their own lives. The younger generation, however, looked to the *Ostjuden* as ideal Jews worthy of emulation.[67] This was largely a romantic idealization, since only a few German Jews had come into close contact with the *Ostjuden* before World War I. The young Zionists assumed that the assimilated Western European Jew must have personality flaws to account for the moral and national decline of Western Jewry. Identification with the *Ostjuden* was one avenue of checking this decline. Love for *Ostjuden* and their Eastern European culture became the answer to their basic and deep personal needs.[68] Blumenfeld warned the German Zionists that they must dedicate themselves more fervently than ever before to Jewish nationalist ideology if they were to be as true to the Zionist idea as their brethren in Eastern Europe. Special effort would be required, because German Zionists lacked the Eastern European Jews' concentrated masses and their traditional ties to their own past. Blumenfeld was the first to exhort German Zionists actually to "return to Palestine" even before the mass emigration of the Eastern Europeans should take place:

Those who see in Zionism a charitable undertaking on behalf of Eastern European Jews are of dubious worth for the achievement of our goals. Only those who are willing to make personal sacrifices can create a free nation in Palestine ... only those who will return to Erez Israel will be true Zionists.[69]

Blumenfeld realized that there would be a period of transition before the Zionists would actually emigrate, and he urged that this time be utilized to strengthen the movement through ideological instruction and growing membership. [70] He proposed a resolution whose broad outlines he deemed necessary for the achievement of these objectives, and the *Delegiertentag* unanimously accepted it:

The *Delegiertentag* believes that the national Jewish

character of our movement should be intensified in the most unambiguous terms; special emphasis should be placed on the basic differences between Zionism as a Jewish national movement and all other Jewish organizations.[71]

The resolution passed almost without being noticed by the delegates; the *Juedische Rundschau* reported it as it did all other resolutions passed by the *Delegiertentag*. No editorials in the Zionist press stressed its importance; Blumenfeld himself in later years called its passage "an accidental victory."[72] The older German Zionists had not thought it worthwhile to oppose a resolution they regarded as mere rhetoric.[73]

It is an indication of Blumenfeld's power as orator and his ability as a leader that within a year after he became an officer of the ZVfD he was one of the best known Zionists in Germany, and he was elected to the central committee of the movement by a large majority.[74] With Blumenfeld other young Zionists were elected into party posts. At the *Delegiertentage* of Posen and Leipzig, they became effective supporters of his struggle to change the orientation of the ZVfD. They included Hugo Schachtel (1876–1949), Max Kollenscher, Richard Lichtheim (1885–1963), Georg Halpern (1878–1962), Hans Gideon Heymann (1882–1918), and Sammy Gronemann, all men born in the late 1870s and 1880s who had just completed their university education. [75] These young Zionists were elected to the executive and central committees of the ZVfD, the two bodies most decisive in forming Zionist policy in Germany.

Between 1910 and 1912, the ZVfD increased its membership by one-third, from 6,200 to 8,400, and collected 20,000 marks in contributions, a substantial sum, which covered most of its expenses.[76] Progress within the ZVfD was measured, however, not only in monetary terms. Hantke's organizational skills centralized its activities and tightened its control over the Zionist offices all over the country.[77] On their constant propaganda tours, Hantke and Blumenfeld founded twenty new Zionist *Ortsgruppen* all over Germany during the same period.[78] The Zionist press continued to publish brochures and pamphlets, the most successful of which was Richard Lichtheim's *Das Programm des Zionismus* (1911), which reached a circulation of more than twenty thousand copies in its first edition.[79] Other important brochures were Max Kollenscher's *Zionismus und Liberales Judentum* and a pamphlet published by the executive of the ZVfD called *Was will der Zionismus?*

Material and organizational progress enabled the Zionists to become increasingly independent of other Jewish organizations and to challenge their ideologies. It is significant that Hantke began his opening address before the *Delegiertentag* in Posen (May 26–28, 1912) by emphasizing the abyss that separated the Zionists from the Jewish liberals and assimilationists; an abyss that he felt could no longer be bridged by empty gestures of good will:

> The Zionists must wait until the rest of German Jewry finds its way to join them in the rejuvenation of Jewish life. . . . We must oppose the contentment [*satte Zufriedenheit*] of the assimilationists time and again and show that Jewish life cannot be cured without a firm national foundation. . . . Our future hopes lie in the creation of a new life in Palestine—a project that should be the focal point of all our thoughts and deeds. . . . Only a radical cure can prevent the total decline of the German Jews [*Untergang der deutschen Juden*].[80]

Hantke's concluding remarks were apparently influenced by the discussion then current in the Jewish press and especially among the young German Zionists about the dissolution of the German Jews because of assimilation, intermarriage, and conversion. In 1911, a few months before Posen, Felix Theilhaber had summed up the discussion in his comprehensive *Der Untergang der deutschen Juden.*

The change in ideological orientation effected at Posen should be viewed in the light of events that took place at the same time within the WZO. The Tenth Zionist Congress (Basel, 1911) saw the triumph of the "synthetic" Zionists who demanded *Gegenwartsarbeit* in addition to political work. During this Congress David Wolffsohn resigned as president. The Congress elected to the *Engeres Aktionskomitee* Otto Warburg (president), Arthur Hantke, Avigdor Jacobsohn, Shmaria Levin, and Nahum Sokolow (1861–1936), all staunch supporters of practical Zionism. As a part of its program, the Congress initiated a variety of cultural and practical programs both in Palestine and the Diaspora.[81]

Certainly the most radical turn of events at Posen was the transformation of the ZVfD orientation from the purely political Zionism of Herzl to practical Zionism, which considered settlement and work in Palestine, at least in theory, to be its most important objective. Hantke had given some intimation of this, but it was left to Blumenfeld to spell out the change in a major speech before the convention.[82] Unlike the unopposed passage of the resolution at Frankfurt, the resolution at Posen was not adopted without opposition. The most outspoken critic was Isaak Zwirn who, true to the tradition of political Zionism, claimed that the Zionists must wait for a charter before settling in Palestine. The pro-Blumenfeld faction, however, which included Zlocisti, Estermann, Biram, and Halpern, proved strong enough to dominate the discussion and to win over the *Delegiertentag*.[83] The result was summed up by Leo Motzkin, who said that, so far as German Zionists were concerned, "Herzlian Zionism was dead."[84]

Historically, the most important expression of the ZVfD's interest in Palestine was its acceptance of two resolutions that were to leave a lasting imprint on the life of German Zionists and the entire German Jewish community. The first was proposed by Zlocisti and Estermann and was based on the ideological changes suggested by Blumenfeld. In his speech Blumenfeld had given careful and detailed exposition of the theories he had held since 1909 on the cultural alienation of the German Jew; he was emphatic in stating that only in Palestine could the Jew be liberated from physical and psychological oppression.[85] The resolution of the *Delegiertentag* followed Blumenfeld's proposals:

Because of the overwhelming importance of the work in Palestine for the liberation of the personality of the individual, and because of the importance of this work as a means to achieve our final goal, the *Delegiertentag* declares that it is the duty of every Zionist—especially those who are economically independent—to incorporate into their life's program a personal emigration to Palestine. Every Zionist should at least establish personal interests in Palestine.[86]

The second resolution, which in view of the importance of the first has been ignored by historians, was proposed by an *Ortsgruppe* from Upper Silesia:

It is the duty of every Zionist who can afford it, to learn about Palestine from first-hand experience. The Central Committee is hereby instructed to take an active initiative in this regard and to plan organized tours to Palestine.[87]

This resolution was in many respects as important as the radical resolution proposed by Zlocisti and Estermann. A few months later, the ZVfD began to organize tours to Palestine; these tours were subsequently greatly expanded with the cooperation of the *Palaestina Reisegesellschaft*. Many German Zionists, despite the Posen Resolution, had no intention of settling in Palestine, yet took advantage of these tours. They returned to Germany with a better knowledge of the needs of Palestine and the ways in which they might be met.

Except for the protest by Zwirn, there was no notable opposition to the first resolution. The old guard—Oppenheimer, Bodenheimer, Friedemann, Struck, and others—did not participate in the discussions that followed Blumenfeld's speech. It is possible that they did not correctly assess the resolution's meaning and importance; they had failed to do so in Frankfurt. But it is more plausible to think that they considered it wise, as Oppenheimer claimed in 1914, to permit the younger generation to "let off steam and

youthful enthusiasm."[88]   Although the older Zionists felt
that the younger men should have more to say in matters of
organization policy, still it is apparent that the resolution
took them by surprise.[89]   Even Hantke, who very often
initiated and promoted important decisions within the ZVfD,
was merely a neutral observer, and he joined the younger
group only after the resolution had been passed.[90]

It seems then that the Posen Resolution had a stronger
impact on German non-Zionists and anti-Zionists than on
Zionists of the older generation.[91]   Those most aware of the
importance of the resolution belonged to the rising young
leadership of the ZVfD; they supported Blumenfeld's "theory of uprooting" (*Entwurzelungstheorie*), whose aim was to
jolt the German Jews out of their comfortable existence by
convincing them that they had no real roots in Germany. [92]
Once the resolution had been passed, the younger men felt
that a danger had been removed: Western Zionism would find
no satisfaction in the empty formula of nationalism.[93]

The Fourteenth Zionist *Delegiertentag,* which took place
in Leipzig on June 14 and 15, 1914, was the most important
event in the history of the ZVfD. It consolidated and confirmed the direction that the ZVfD had begun to take at
Frankfurt and Posen. The fact that in Leipzig the orientation
toward Palestine found its most extreme expression was a
consequence not only of internal evolution in German Zionism, but also of Zionist reaction to the general Jewish community.

The years between 1912 and 1914 were ones of open
strife between Zionists and German Jewish liberals. The
struggle between the two camps began with a series of lectures given by Werner Sombart, who supported Zionist ambitions in Palestine, advised the Jews in Germany to refrain
from occupying positions of power in politics, economics,
the press, and so on; in short to step out of the limelight. He
aroused considerable excitement and controversy between
the Zionists who supported him and the members of the C.V.
and other liberal Jewish organizations who condemned any
limitation of their rights. The hostility between the Zionists
and the liberals was exacerbated by an article by Moritz

Goldstein in the periodical *Kunstwart,* in which he repeated many of Sombart's arguments and like him advised Jews to avoid German public office. In addition, the intervening years between Posen and Leipzig had seen the establishment of an *Antizionistisches Komitee,* and the "language debate" that took place between the Zionists and the *Hilfsverein der deutschen Juden.* Of first importance for the final break between the Zionists and the liberal organizations was the C.V. resolution of 1913, which declared that anyone who did not adhere to *"deutsche Gesinnung"* (i.e., Blumenfeld and the new ZVfD leadership) was no longer a welcome member of the C.V.

The Zionists realized that the *Delegiertentag* in Leipzig would have to take a stand on all these issues; and the forthcoming convention was anticipated with great excitement and some apprehension.[94] The main issues debated at the convention were, as expected, the relation of the ZVfD to the other German Jewish organizations and to the work of German Zionism for and in Palestine. What was unexpected was the sharp split within the ZVfD between the older German Zionists led by Oppenheimer, Bodenheimer, Friedemann, Sandler, and Eli Strauss (1878–1933) and the younger generation consisting for the most part of young intellectuals led by Blumenfeld.[95] Disagreements were not confined to a single issue; on all issues the younger generation preferred more radical and immediate solutions, whereas the older, more established Zionists favored a moderate and gradualist policy both toward other Jewish organizations and within the ZVfD.

The struggle among the factions and individual delegates began immediately after the introductory speech by Hantke, who described the changes that had taken place since Posen both within the ZVfD and within the German Jewish community at large.[96] During this two-year period, the ZVfD had broken off relations with most of the liberal Jewish organizations. As a result of the debates around Sombart's lectures and the *Kunstwart* debate, as well as of the C.V. resolution and the Zionist reply, conflicts had emerged between Zionist and anti-Zionist groups in all the major Jewish

communities in Germany.[97]   His conclusion was that the
ZVfD should reaffirm its position as outlined in Posen and
defend that position against the assimilationists.[98]

Hantke's opening address provoked an immediate retort
by the older Zionists to the "young radicals." Friedemann
led the attack in the name "of all his friends within the
ZVfD":

> We have kept quiet for a long time, since we wanted to
> preserve the unity of the movement. . . . The fact that
> today we can no longer keep silent is truly not our fault.
> It is the fault of our party press organs and official party
> propagandists who constantly preach radicalism among
> us.[99]

Friedemann contended that, since the Basel program was a
compromise resolution between all the factions and shades of
ideology within the Zionist movement, the ZVfD had a moral
obligation not to coerce them into a personal commitment to
Palestine by passing resolutions which were supposed to be
officially binding.

Friedemann also protested against the educating of Zionists in the Hebrew culture, a culture appropriate only in
Palestine or perhaps among the masses of Jews in Eastern
Europe: "Here in Germany the demand for a Jewish national
culture is a bloodless ideal, an empty abstract thought of a
theoretical brain. . . . Even our extreme nationalists have only
a minimal knowledge of Jewish culture and are completely
immersed in that of Germany."[100] He questioned the right
and the ability of the Zionists to require German Jewry to
create a Hebrew culture when the very foundations for such a
culture were lacking. He accused the younger Zionists of hy-
pocrisy and rebellion for its own sake rather than for the
principles involved; they were expounding theories that they
did not intend to put into practice and that served only to
disguise their aggression toward the older generation.

The opponents of the radical Zionist wing saw the call for
Hebrew culture and the Zlocisti-Estermann resolutions, ac-

cepted at Posen and reconfirmed in Leipzig, as demands that artificially tried to uproot the German Jews from their natural surroundings. Friedemann claimed that the Posen Resolution had no practical application within German Zionism:

> All the resolution will accomplish will be to educate the Zionists to become fanatical radicals. The resolution will antagonize other Jewish organizations and we will lose the sympathy of many non-Zionists. . . . In practical terms, on the other hand, we should not expect any constructive accomplishments from this resolution.[101]

He maintained that even if Zionists were to emigrate to Palestine, their economic situation would be impossible: "after all, among two hundred inhabitants in Tel Aviv we have twenty doctors and four dentists; don't we have enough intellectual proletarians in Germany?"[102]

Oppenheimer called Blumenfeld and his supporters "youngsters intoxicated by their own ideas." [103] He understood their radicalism as the product of youthful enthusiasm and rebellion against their elders, a natural phenomenon among the young. [104] He emphasized the accomplishments of the first generation of German Zionists and protested against labeling them "opportunists" or "old-fashioned." [105] Oppenheimer was bewildered by the new demands of the ZVfD:

> Specific actions and obligations are no longer asked of us, but a completely new Weltanschauung. Not even the greatest party has the right to make such a demand upon me. For myself personally I declare herewith, that I have not incorporated migration to Palestine into my life's program. I consider it intolerance to demand that I do so, . . . that I uproot my feelings of *Deutschtum* and live in Germany only until the next moving van comes to pick me up. The new brand of nationalism angers me as a scholar and as a human being. I have devoted a lifetime to destroying the beliefs being put forward at this convention.[106]

A few days before the Leipzig *Delegiertentag* met, Bodenheimer had expressed in a private letter to Friedemann his position on the radicalization of the ZVfD:

> As always I am convinced now too, that I represent a very radical Zionist position. The nonsensical phraseology [*Phrasengewaesche*] of Blumenfeld and his friends is not at all radical. I simply find it silly. These people talk about Jewish national consciousness and Jewish content which they fail to realize in their own personal lives— luckily they are not able to realize these ideas. A political movement must have a realistic program and should not be based on fantasies of the future.[107]

To Bodenheimer, it was not the role of the *Delegiertentag* to direct Zionists to Palestine. He objected to interpreting the Posen Resolution as requiring inner preparation for Palestine by the abandonment of one's *Deutschtum*.[108] For the same reason Jakob Wolff and Hermann Struck (1876–1944) opposed radicalization, claiming that it would destroy the sympathetic attitude of many non-Zionist German Jews toward the movement.[109] They felt that the young generation, which at Frankfurt and Posen had been elected to the top ZVfD posts, were leading the movement in a direction that would not enhance the cause of Zionism, and they proposed a resolution that "all officials of the ZVfD and its recognized press organs henceforth cease from attempts to promote any particular group or direction within the movement."[110] This last-minute attempt to stop the younger generation was, of course, futile; the old-guard Zionists had missed their opportunity at Frankfurt and Posen. The proposal was rejected by a majority of the delegates.

Again it was Blumenfeld who presented the demands of the younger generation. He accused Friedemann and likeminded Zionists of possessing a Weltanschauung indistinguishable from that of the *Kartell Convent,* the C.V., or any other German Jewish assimilationist organization:

> Were we to follow Friedemann's conceptions of Zionism,

we could be certain that a great abyss would be created between Palestine and the German Zionists. If the word Zionism has any meaning at all, it is that we strive toward Zion. As Zionists we have the obligation to say: our task is to get closer to Zion. Today we are Zionists and later we want to live in Zion.[111]

Blumenfeld admitted that the Zionists lacked Jewish education, but he claimed that the merit and intention of the Posen Resolution were to proclaim the will to acquire this knowledge:[112]

For us the word nationalism means an intensification of our Jewishness ... it means that today we are not yet full-fledged Jews and are therefore intent upon a deepening of our nationalist will.[113]

This statement contained the essence of his conviction that Zionism could be equated with Judaism.

Friedemann had voiced his astonishment at the fact that Jews who had grown up within German culture could have Jewish nationalist feelings strong enough to make radicals of them. In response, Blumenfeld asserted that the only radicalism apparent in the young Zionists was their courage to utter the truth about their feelings and to express their emotional turmoil in a world in which they had no real roots. By implication he intimated that the older Zionists were in many ways hypocrites, for they claimed to be Zionists yet did not want to wage the necessary war against the assimilationists. Isaak Strauss, one of Blumenfeld's supporters, put it even more bluntly:

Oppenheimer's position on the relationship of Zionists to *Deutschtum* and *Judentum* is totally alien to the young generation. We cannot sympathize with such old-fashioned views.[114]

The Leipzig *Delegiertentag* represents the end of an era in the history of German Zionism. It was, as Blumenfeld put it, "the decisive battle of German Zionism" (*Entscheidungs-schlacht des deutschen Zionismus*). [115] Theoretically these debates should have taken place at Posen, since there the first clear indication was given of the Palestine-orientation that the ZVfD was to adopt in the coming years. Seemingly, the Posen Resolution was not taken seriously enough by the more established members of the ZVfD. The same delegates who protested against the resolution at Leipzig were present at Posen, yet the proceedings there indicate almost no protest. The founding members of the ZVfD were not overly concerned with statements of personal fulfillment and commitment to Zion; these had been made in the past, but remained empty statements. It was difficult for them to imagine that the younger Zionists, with a liberal assimilated background similar to their own, would actually emigrate. Two years later, at Leipzig, the situation within the German Jewish community had changed radically, largely as a reaction to the Posen Resolution which had after all been taken seriously by the non-Zionists and anti-Zionists. Had the resolution not aroused such furor among the non-Zionists in Germany at a time when external events such as the Sombart lectures and the *Kunstwart* debate had placed it in a continuously prominent position, the chances are that the split within the ZVfD would never have taken place or would at least have been delayed. The strong protest at Leipzig was even more a reaction to the events that had taken place within the general German Jewish community between 1912 and 1914 than to the Posen Resolution.

The *Delegiertentag* at Leipzig had to take a stand on these events. In view of the general community's attacks, the delegates entrenched themselves more resolutely behind the basic postulates of the Posen Resolution. The older generation of German Zionists who had espoused a political-philanthropic version of Zionism could no longer ignore the change within the ZVfD. Like the rest of the German Jewish liberal community, they saw their very existence, their most basic ideological principles, threatened by the radical statements of people identified by all as members of their own organization. When, despite their protests, the Leipzig *Deleg-*

iertentag confirmed their worst fears, most of them resigned from all active positions within the ZVfD.

The new generation of German Zionists conducted themselves on the assumption that they lived in a pluralistic society. Blumenfeld could express his nationalist idealism and his radicalism so long as the German politically liberal *Weltanschauung* permitted such opinions, but the German Jewish liberals feared that such opinions might endanger the Jews as citizens of the state. [116] The liberal versus Zionist controversy remained academic, however, because even the most radical Zionists, deeply concerned with moral and ethical issues, did not accept the practical solution of actual emigration to Palestine. [117] In fact, many Zionist radicals of the pre-World War I period became the Zionist establishment in the 1920s and had in their turn to face the criticism of more radical Zionist groups. [118] Yet the value of the resolutions at the *Delegiertentage* was not diminished by the lack of personal commitment to emigration. They served as a catalyst to bring an awareness of Zionism to German Jewry, and they provided an outlet for the feelings of the younger generation. In addition, the discussions that preceded these resolutions served as a general forum to air intellectual and personal problems weighing upon a generation torn between assimilation and a return to Judaism. [119]

After the 1912–14 period, German Zionists began to realize that civil rights and equality before the law were different matters from the feelings of identification of the individual with his own national group. They felt attracted to German culture, yet they saw their personal fulfillment only through strong ties to their own *volk*. [120] This *Weltanschauung* had appeal mainly for the youth, who had not yet accepted positions of responsibility in society and saw in Zionism a way of return to Judaism. [121] The clearly Palestine-oriented politics of the ZVfD offended an older generation that had viewed Palestine primarily as a haven for *Ostjuden*. Over the years the ZVfD occasionally sharpened its formulations. At the *Delegiertentag* in Jena (December 29–30, 1929) the question of "negation of the Galut" (*Galut-Verneinung*) and "affirmation of the Galut" (*Galutbejahung*) was extensively debated and it became clear that the ZVfD had decisively decided to negate Jewish life in the Diaspora as simply a transient stage in the history of the Jewish people. [122]

With the new generation, Zionism in Germany became an aggressive and belligerent movement; a movement committed to the destruction of bourgeois ideology of the German Jews through constant challenge and to the education of its membership in personal courage, honesty, and pride in belonging to the Jewish nation. [123] Their main objective was the intensification of Jewish life in Germany.[124] The Zionists developed a pronounced feeling of being an elite group; a necessary sentiment for a tiny minority that was trying to combat a long tradition of a majority of Jews who were decidedly German in their outlook. By calling themselves members of a postassimilationist version of Zionism they sought to explain their position in Germany: they were Jews, who by virtue of their education and background belonged to German culture, yet they felt no sense of a legitimate belonging in the German world. Postassimilation was, in fact, the use of assimilation as a springboard for a return to their existence as "true Jews" via the Zionist idea.[125]

V

The C.V. and the ZVfD: 1897-1914

The history of the relationship between the C.V. and the ZVfD before World War I can be divided into two periods: 1897–1912, a period when the two organizations coexisted in an atmosphere of relative harmony; and 1912–14, a period when internal developments in the German Jewish community, as well as events which evolved independently outside it, prepared the ground for the clash between the Zionists and the liberal German Jewish community. During this latter period, and especially through its 1913 resolution, the C.V. became the most representative body of the liberal establishment in its struggle against the Zionists. The chronology outlined above is, of course, not clear-cut and absolute, for even before the official founding of the ZVfD, the C.V. had declared its rejection of any Jewish national or Zionist ideologies.[1] In addition, the open clash between the Zionists and the C.V. can be traced to various events that took place within the community even before 1912. Dividing these years into two distinct periods is intended to show, however, that after 1912 both organizations clearly recognized that their relations had reached a breaking point. This change left its mark on the historical process of German Jewry through 1933.

In a previous chapter we demonstrated that the ideology of the founders of the ZVfD was very similar to that of the founders of the C.V. Given this similarity, the question arises as to why relations between them deteriorated to the degree that after 1912 cooperation was no longer possible. It should also be asked why the C.V., whose purpose was defense, became so involved in the ideological disputes of the community that after 1912 it assumed the role of the principal opponent of the ZVfD. To answer these questions, a short review of the developments within the German Jewish community after 1897 is necessary. This review is important, because the C.V. was so integral a part of the German Jewish liberal establishment that developments within the liberal group at large had an impact on the C.V. Despite the fact that this impact was not always direct and immediate, there was a cumulative effect that was finally expressed in the C.V. resolution of 1913.

Before 1912 Zionism did not greatly concern the liberal community. The widespread, tacit agreement in Jewish establishment circles was that the best way to destroy Zionist influence in Germany was to ignore it completely (*den Zionismus totschweigen*). This method was successfully followed by the liberal press and by the non-Zionist organizations from 1897[2] until 1912.[3] There were, however, two significant exceptions to this policy: first, the reaction of the Munich community and the "Association of Rabbis in Germany" to Herzl's plan to convene the First Zionist Congress in Munich, and second, the dismissal of Emil Cohn, a young rabbi in Berlin, for alleged public propaganda for the Zionist cause.

One cannot claim that until 1912 there was no anti-Zionist mood within the German Jewish community. These feelings, however, found only occasional expression in such periodicals and newspapers as the *Mitteilungsblatt der Juedischen Reformgemeinde zu Berlin,* published by the small but influential radical reform group of Berlin,[4] and *Liberales Judentum,* published by the *Vereinigung fuer das liberale Judentum,*[5] and other publications of limited circulation. Organizations of laymen and religious institutions, both liberal and orthodox, made only occasional anti-Zionist references, and these were usually provoked by specific immediate events.[6] But there was no organized or nationwide effort to fight Zionism in Germany. Conflicts between Zionists and anti-Zionists were confined in each case to a particular locale, and relations between the liberals and the Zionists were determined in each case by the personal compatibility of the leaders of the opposing groups.

The Controversy at Munich

At the end of May, 1897, news reached the German Jewish community that the Zionists intended to convene a congress in Munich on August 25. The reports first appeared in the regular German press, notably in the *Vossische Zeitung, Koelnische Zeitung* and *Muenchener Generalanzeiger.*[7] In reaction to these reports, the executive committee of the Munich Jewish community met in early June. After hearing a detailed report on Zionism, the committee instructed the president of the Munich community, Abraham Ofner, to write to Herzl. In his letter of June 13, Ofner pointed out that:

> there was no sympathy for a Zionist movement in Munich; that to hold the Congress there was considered a grave danger to the welfare of the German Jewish community. The press, quite malevolently, took Zionism as a proof that the Jews were not attached to their fatherland.[8]

Ofner's letter added that there was a possibility that the Jewish community would ask the state to prohibit any foreigner from speaking at the Congress. The community, in short, requested that the Congress not meet in Munich.[9]

This letter crossed in the mail with a letter from Herzl in which he explained that the Jewish community was not requested to attend the Congress, so that its members might be saved the embarrassment of taking a stand against fellow Jews. He asked whether or not the community would protest the meeting of the Congress in Munich,[10] to which the Munich community responded that they had not changed their minds, and that they did protest it.[11] This exchange of letters induced the "Committee for the Preparation of the Zionist Congress" to decide to hold the Congress on August 29 in Basel, where it was hoped the Zionists would be received in a friendlier atmosphere.[12]

References in *Die Welt* and the archives of the Munich Jewish community both indicate that the Zionists' decision to meet in Basel was the result of the formal request by the Munich community. An important added factor in the decision, however, was a protest by two prominent liberal rabbis which carried behind it the weight and prestige of the entire German Jewish liberal establishment, not only that of the Munich community. On June 11, two days before Ofner wrote to Herzl, an article signed by Rabbis Maybaum and Vogelstein and entitled "Against Zionism" appeared in the *Allgemeine Zeitung des Judentums.*[13] They protested against the calling of a congress in Munich, and they claimed furthermore that not a single Jewish community would support the Zionists in Germany. They called Zionism "a movement that tries to reverse the course of Jewish history . . . there are no Jews who do not want to be assimilated into the nations in whose midst they live."[14] They also attacked Zionism as a movement that endangered the position of the Jews in Germany.[15]

It is customarily assumed that the decision to transfer the Zionist Congress from Munich to Basel was the result of the protest by the "Association of Rabbis in Germany" (*Protestrabbiner*), which included members from all the branches of German Jewry. The facts seem to indicate, however, that the decision followed the official request of the Munich Jewish community which had the backing of all the German Jewish organizations with local offices there. Even "neutral" organizations such as the *Bnei Briss* Lodge of Munich published a declaration against the Congress:

> Under the present circumstances, Zionism offers the opponents of Judaism a welcome opportunity to make the unfounded charge that the Jews are a separate national entity and have, therefore, no intention of integrating into the nations in whose midst they live. It is, therefore,

the duty of every Jew who loves his Judaism and his fatherland to take a position against this movement.[16]

The Great Lodge also sent its former president, Dr. Merzbacher, to Vienna, where he met with Herzl and helped to persuade him to change the location of the Congress.[17]

An examination of the available data reveals, then, that the decision by the Zionists to transfer the Congress took place before July 2, 1897,[18] whereas the protest of the Association of Rabbis in Germany was circulated to the press only after July 6.[19] Nevertheless, it was precisely the protest of the prestigious organization of liberal German rabbis that aroused the anger of the Zionists, since it seemed to symbolize the opposition of the entire German Jewish community to Zionism. The publication of the rabbis' declaration even after it had become known that the Zionists would not meet in Munich, was probably intended to demonstrate to the German public that the German Jews were loyal to their fatherland and had no sympathy with Zionist ideology.[20]

The rabbis' protest was preceded on July 2 by that of an anonymous Jewish preacher from Hamburg who said that ever since the days of Mendelssohn and Riesser the German Jews had been *"Nationaldeutsche"* rather than *"Nationaljuden,"* and recommended, in view of the impending Zionist congress, three points to be acted upon by the German Jewish establishment:

1. To persuade all communities in Germany to protest against political Zionism. The entire German Jewish community must protect itself against the accusation that it is not wholly German, but gravitates toward Canaan.

2. To check the agitation of Zionists, who were exploiting the originally philanthropic efforts to colonize Palestine. He proposed the publication of Moritz Guedemann's *Nationaljudentum* to offset Zionist propaganda, and the dispatching of expert speakers throughout Germany to refute Zionist arguments.

3. To demand from the official organizations of rabbis and teachers in Germany a public declaration against political Zionism.[21]

This third suggestion was readily followed.[22] On July 6,

the executive committee of the Association of Rabbis in Germany published their declaration:

> Through the call for a Zionist Congress and through the publication of its agenda, such mistaken notions have been spread about the whole subject of Judaism and about the objectives of its adherents that the undersigned Executive Committee of the Association of Rabbis in Germany regards it as proper to make the following explanations:
>
> 1. The efforts of the so-called Zionists to found a Jewish national state in Palestine contradict the messianic promises of Judaism as contained in the Holy Writ and in later religious sources.
>
> 2. Judaism requires its adherents to serve with devotion the fatherland to which they belong, and to further its national interests with all their heart and with all their strength.
>
> 3. However, those noble aims directed toward the colonization of Palestine by Jewish peasants and farmers are not in contradiction to these obligations, because they have no relation whatsoever to the founding of a national state. Religion and patriotism both lay upon us the duty of asking all who are concerned with the welfare of Judaism to stay away from the above-mentioned Zionist endeavors and most particularly from the congress which is still being planned, despite all the warnings against it.[23]

The declaration aroused the indignation of Zionists both inside and outside Germany, since the attack represented the first strong opposition they had encountered.[24] The *National-Juedische Vereinigung fuer Deutschland* met in Bingen a few days later, and published its response on July 11:

> 1. It is untrue that the Zionist aims contradict the messianic promises. We draw attention to the pamphlet *Drischat Zion* written by one of the greatest rabbinical authorities, Rabbi Kalischer, which clearly disproves this contention. We are not at all concerned with the teach-

ings of Judaism; our only interest is to rectify the anomalous situation of the Jewish nation.

2. We do admit that the "noble aims directed toward the colonization of Palestine by Jewish peasants and farmers," do not coincide with our own aims, however support for Jewish colonization from our ideological point of view does not interfere in any way with the philanthropic aims of other organizations.

There is no justification for anyone, least of all the Association of Rabbis in Germany to warn against the congress in Basel. We hope that the congress will become an impressive declaration of the will of the Jewish people not to abandon their national existence. We want to be a national entity which will work with other nations toward the progress of human culture. In fulfilling this task we are confident that the sympathies of all unprejudiced people will be on our side.[25]

Despite these public pronouncements, the anti-Zionist storm subsided within a few months. The Zionist movement, led by moderate Zionists whose life style and Weltanschauung did not differ substantially from that of the general German Jewish community, ceased to be a target for attack. During the next decade when more radical Zionist groups attempted to make inroads into the liberal establishment through propaganda or community elections, they were successfully checked; Zionism would not again be a major issue of controversy until 1912.[26]

The Cohn Affair

The only exception to this period of comparative calm was the case of Emil Cohn. In February, 1906, Emil Cohn (1881–1948), the son of the well-known Zionist Dr. Bernhard Cohn and himself a member of the Zionist organization, was elected "preacher and teacher of religion" in the Jewish community of Berlin.[27] At the time of his appointment Cohn declared that he was a confirmed Zionist but that he did not intend to use his position to propagate the cause of Zionism.[28] Shortly afterward, however, Cohn was accused by the authorities of the Berlin *Gemeinde* of having propagandized among his students at the *Falk-Realgymnasium*. When in the summer of 1906 he made a memorial speech for Herzl and in addition was reported to have talked about his Zionist beliefs before the Christian director of the *Mommsengymnasium*, the directors of the Berlin community took action.[29] After long deliberations and countless meetings, the *Gemeinde* leaders suspended Rabbi Cohn from his office on April 15, 1907.[30]

The "Cohn affair" infuriated not only the German Zionists, but the world Zionist community as well.[31] During that same year professors Henry Malter, Max L. Margolis, and Max Schloessinger resigned from the Hebrew Union College in Cincinnati, Ohio, because of differences of opinion concerning Zionism with the president of the college, Kaufmann Kohler.[32] Even such small newspapers as the Baltimore, Maryland, *Jewish Comment* discussed Cohn's case in detail.[33] The ZVfD came to his defense and during the controversy that ensued, the liberal Jewish community of Berlin and the German Zionists became the chief antagonists.

The principal issue was whether or not the Jewish community had the right to demand particular beliefs and ideologies of its employees. The president of the community, Julius Jacoby, declared that "since Cohn is employed by us, he must represent our point of view" (*Sie sind bei uns in Lohn und Brot. Sie haben unsere Anschauungen zu vertreten*).[34] The Zionist position, however, stressed freedom of thought and expression and decried the autocratic rule of the Berlin Jewish establishment. The Zionists utilized their press organ, the *Juedische Rundschau*, extensively on behalf of Cohn and held mass meetings in Berlin to support him.[35] In early May, 1907, Emil Cohn summarized his case in a brochure and in early 1908, after it became clear that the community would not reinstate him, he left Berlin.[36] With Cohn's departure the controversy subsided, but the importance attached to his case by the entire Zionist movement was apparent at the Ninth Zionist Congress (Hamburg, 1909), where David Wolffsohn, the president of the Zionist Organization, made a speech praising Emil Cohn for his brave fight against the establishment of the Berlin Jewish community.[37]

C.V.–Zionist Relations: 1897–1912

Apart from the storms aroused by the *Protestrabbiner* and the Cohn affair, there are no indications of any significant conflict between the ZVfD leadership and the Jewish liberal establishment until 1912, although there were occasional disputes between local chapters and the communities, especially on the question of communal elections. Occasionally the *Juedische Rundschau* printed articles calling for "the conquest of the communities" (*Eroberung der Gemeinden*),[38] but in practice little was done to accomplish this goal.[39] The ZVfD maintained peaceful contacts with the major German Jewish organizations such as the *Deutsch-Israelitischer Gemeindebund* and the *Verband der deutschen Juden,* as well as the *Hilfsverein der deutschen Juden.* These organizations took a neutral position toward Zionism, and in return the Zionists did not interfere in their internal affairs and refrained from antagonizing them.[40]

The ZVfD permitted and even encouraged the participation of Zionists in other organizations. In 1906 the Central Committee of the ZVfD issued guidelines "to regulate the relations of German Zionists with other Jewish organizations:"[41]

No Zionist may be a member of an organization which espouses anti-Jewish national ideas. For the rest we recommend that Zionists join organizations which are indifferent to Zionism. Zionists, however, who occupy leadership positions within the ZVfD, should always be careful not to assume leading positions in other organizations which might interfere with their work for the ZVfD. . . . In all cases where a doubt exists whether or not an organization is in fact anti-Zionist or whether the assumption of a position in another organization would interfere with the goals of Zionism, one should consult the president of the ZVfD.[42]

The ZVfD recommended Zionist participation in the *Hilfsverein der deutschen Juden, Verband der deutschen Juden, Bnei Briss, Esra,* C.V., and the *Juedische Turnvereine,* in fact, in all the major Jewish liberal organizations in Germany. The

ZVfD expressed doubt only about participation in the German branch of the *Alliance Israélite Universelle* (*Deutsche Konferenzgemeinschaft der Alliance*), but it explained in the same memorandum that the two organizations might soon come to an understanding.[43]

During the first decade of the century the relations between the ZVfD and the *Hilfsverein der deutschen Juden* were particularly good. The first encounter between the *Hilfsverein* and the Zionists was in a meeting called by the *Hilfsverein* and the *Bnei Briss* in Frankfurt am Main in 1904, in regard to the Eastern European Jewish Question. The *Hilfsverein* was the first large Jewish organization to agree to cooperate with the Zionists, and this at a time when Herzl's death in 1904 had left the Zionists confused and disorganized. This made a great impression on the Zionists, especially since Bodenheimer was accorded the honor of chairing the meetings in Frankfurt. In a report to the Seventh Zionist Congress, Alexander Marmorek (1865–1923) wrote that this was the first time that Zionists and non-Zionists had cooperated and that in return the Zionists would support the *Hilfsverein*.[44]

In 1905, when Wolffsohn issued a call to all German Jewish organizations to help in the work on behalf of the *Ostjuden,* only the *Hilfsverein,* represented by Paul Nathan, responded favorably. Relations between the *Hilfsverein* and the ZVfD became increasingly close, especially since they were working together in Palestine on matters not touching upon the internal affairs of the German Jewish community. The Zionists appreciated the fact that a large German Jewish organization, of twenty thousand members, was willing to establish schools in Palestine where Hebrew was an important part of the curriculum. The *Hilfsverein* was continually praised by the *Juedische Rundschau* as a constructive and efficient organization.[45]

The attitude of the C.V. toward the ZVfD should be examined against this background. The C.V., whose membership comprised mainly Jewish liberals, was of course affected by the attitudes of the liberal organizations; since the liberals and the Zionists found it possible to coexist peacefully, the

C.V. adopted the same position. In addition, it should be kept in mind that the original intent and purpose of the C.V. was to be exclusively a defense organization; thus the C.V. was free to adopt a neutral course in all extra-defense matters that could be dealt with by other organizations.[46] The C.V. leaders did not attack Zionism or the Zionists in Germany unless they felt a strong directive by the general community to do so, or unless their own ideology and purpose seemed to be endangered.

Even though there were no major conflicts until 1912, neither organization compromised its ideology or principles. The basic position of the C.V. was a total rejection of Zionist ideology. As early as October 6, 1895, Eugen Fuchs stated:

> We are not Zionists! As important as pride and self-confidence, which are symbolized by the Zionists, might be; we think that the basic ideology of the Zionists is mistaken. It has in common with the anti-Semites the fact that it tries to denationalize [from German nationality] the Jews, and this is the greatest danger to Judaism. We are Germans and want to remain Germans.[47]

The *National-Juedische Vereinigung* responded to the C.V. statement in kind:

> The *Centralverein deutscher Staatsbuerger juedischen Glaubens* says "we stand firmly on the basis of German nationality, we are not Zionists." This party has in common with the anti-Semites the fact that it tries to denationalize the Jews [from Jewish nationality] and this is the greatest danger to Judaism.[48]

Herzl's *Judenstaat* had been received by the C.V. organ *Im Deutschen Reich* with a mixture of mockery and condescension. The *IDR* dismissed the pamphlet as the work of an Austrian so overcome by feelings of outrage against anti-Semitism that he was willing to forsake the fatherland; "the feelings of the German citizens of the Jewish faith, however, are very different from those of their Austrian brethren

... we say 'no' to his proposals."[49] When shortly afterward the pamphlet by Max Jaffe, *Die Nationale Wiedergeburt der Juden*, appeared, the C.V. denounced both him and Herzl as "Utopian and dangerous dreamers who want to forsake the hard-won emancipation of the Jews and force them back into the ghetto. They deserve thanks and recognition only from the anti-Semites."[50]

Eugen Fuchs was responsible for presenting the C.V.'s ideological position and its stance toward Zionism. His policy statement, made shortly after the Zionist Congress met in Basel in 1897, remained in force for sixteen years:

1. The C.V. has no objections to the colonization of Palestine by people who have not found a haven in their countries of origin. Palestine, however, is not to be preferred over other countries where colonization is also feasible; the only criteria for choosing land for Jews should be its suitability for farming.

2. The C.V. objects to the formation of an international Jewish organization.

3. There is no possibility of strengthening Jewish national feelings, since the Jews are no longer a nation; they constitute merely a community of faith.

4. According to our nationality, which comprises language, education, thinking, and feeling, we are Germans. We are Jews by virtue of our faith alone.

5. The Zionist movement is only a temporary phase in the development of Judaism and affects it as little as does anti-Semitism. Zionism represents an excess of devotion to Judaism [*Glaubenstreue*]; anti-Semitism is an expression of an excess of nationalistic feelings. Both have the virtue of shocking Judaism out of its indifference and of making Jews self-aware and proud of their Judaism. Both phenomena, however, will be overcome. Zionism and anti-Semitism are commiting the same mistakes by not drawing a precise line between nationalism and religion. They do not realize that the modern concepts of statehood and devotion to the fatherland have as little to do with religion as with scholarly, ethical, or aesthetic convictions.[51]

This statement by the foremost ideologue of the C.V. was very mild in comparison with the reactions of the rest of the German Jewish liberal establishment. In essence the C.V. looked on Zionism with condescension as a temporary reaction to anti-Semitism; as such it did not deserve much attention. Fuchs described Zionism as an "excess of *Glaubenstreue*," which, even if it was mistaken in direction, was analyzed as a positive and valid reaction; the C.V. always believed that Zionism had some positive effect, since it restored Jewish pride.

Even though it had no intention of opposing Zionism publicly, the C.V., as an integral part of the liberal establishment, made its opposition to the principles of Zionism known, since the Zionist ideology clearly contradicted everything that liberal German Jews respected and valued. Long before the rest of the liberal establishment, the C.V. concluded that the best way to overcome Zionism was to ignore it completely.[52] The C.V.'s reaction to the Zionist proposal to meet in Munich was typical of its policy until 1912. It merely printed the protest of the Association of Rabbis in Germany in its "correspondence" section without comment.[53] In the same vein, the C.V.'s report on the Congress in Basel was objective and factual. The reporter even complimented the young movement on "the enthusiasm and energy it had generated among Jews."[54] Nevertheless the C.V. considered Zionism a mistaken response:

> The only way to solve the Jewish Question is for the Jews to assimilate as a national entity into the nations in whose midst they reside. It is merely the influence of anti-Semitism that makes serious men chase after the Zionist phantom. In Germany the Zionist goals have found no response or sympathy, and we are certain that this will continue to be the case in the future as well.[55]

The C.V.'s lack of concern was not only the result of its evaluation of Zionism as a passing phenomenon. Added to this was the fact that in its early years the C.V. was seriously trying to be a neutral organization whose platform could include all the members of the German Jewish community.

The C.V., having been established for defense (*Abwehr*) and not for a particular ideology (*Gesinnung*), was unlike such organizations as the ZVfD, the *Verband Nationaldeutscher Juden,* and others. The basic demand of the C.V. was that its members should have "German feelings" (*deutsche Gesinnung*), a vague demand that could be easily fulfilled by the founding members of the ZVfD.[56] On the other hand, the C.V. never demanded any particular Jewish Weltanschauung (*Juedische Gesinnung*) and could welcome into its membership orthodox, liberal, and nonreligious Zionists. As a consequence, paragraph one of the statutes had said:

> The C.V. intends to represent German citizens of the Jewish faith without regard to their religious and political orientation, in order to protect their civil and social equality and to cultivate them in their German *Gesinnung.*[57]

The consensus among the C.V. leadership was that as a neutral organization, they were not required to decide whether or not Zionism had a right to exist (*Die Frage ob der Zionismus berechtigt sei oder nicht, geht den C.V. eigentlich nicht an*).[58] It was left to each member to examine the Zionist ideology and to take a stand consistent with his individual convictions.[59] The C.V. leadership would take no stand against the Zionists provided the Zionists took no stand against the C.V.[60]

The C.V.'s policy of not interfering with its membership's religious and political views so long as they did not violate their loyalty to Germany, and the Zionists' same ideals of *Deutschtum,* made for peaceful and even friendly relations. For their part, the Zionists also maintained their basic positions and stressed the primacy of *Judentum* over *Deutschtum.*[61] In practice, however, these ideological positions led to no difficulties. Until 1912, *Im Deutschen Reich* mentioned German Zionism and its ideology only in passing or when reporting Zionist meetings or *Delegiertentage:* for the most part these notices remained simply factual.[62]

Relations between the C.V. and the ZVfD were indeed so

cordial that, at the tenth anniversary celebration of the C.V.
in 1903, Alfred Klee, a member of both organizations, arrived at the head of a Zionist delegation and said:

> The Zionist movement feels close to the C.V., because it
> too fights indifference among Jews. . . . The ZVfD wants
> to stand shoulder to shoulder with the C.V. in its fight
> for the rights and honor of the German citizens of the
> Jewish faith.[63]

At the eleventh *Delegiertentag* in 1908, the ZVfD broadened
its basis for cooperation with the C.V. and other organizations:

> The eleventh *Delegiertentag* welcomes the work of the
> other large Jewish organizations who try to strengthen
> Jewish self-esteem.[64]

And the C.V. reciprocated these friendly sentiments:

> The Zionist movement has done its share to fight indif-
> ference among Jews. Even though there is a wide abyss
> between the basic Weltanschauungen of the C.V. and the
> ZVfD, we must concede that the ZVfD, like the C.V.,
> tries to promote pride, self-confidence, and loyalty to
> Judaism among the German Jews; the ZVfD tries to
> banish the spirit of assimilation from their ranks.[65]

In view of the C.V.'s attitude, the ZVfD leadership
thought that in time the Zionist members of the C.V. might
swing the C.V. toward Jewish values and perhaps even to
support of Zionist work in Germany.[66]

The ZVfD and the C.V. did cooperate on one project that
required no specific ideological or political commitment; this
was the establishment of the *Arbeitsamt fuer Juedische
Akademiker*. Because of the anti-Semites, Jewish teachers
were gravely hampered in finding suitable posts. In 1909, the
Zionist *Bund Juedischer Corporationen* founded the *Arbeitsamt fuer Juedische Akademiker* to help Jewish academicians

find employment and in fact to fight discrimination against Jews in all matters concerning employment.[67]

The driving force behind the *Arbeitsamt* was Max Berlowitz, an *alter Herr* of the *Bund Juedischer Corporationen*. He enlisted the help of such eminent men of the Jewish community as Landau, the editor in chief of the *Berliner Tageblatt* and Maretzki, a member of the board of governors of the *Bnei Briss* who became chairman of the *Arbeitsamt;* other officers included Ludwig Hollaender of the C.V. and the Zionists Arthur Hantke, Max Ginsberg, Walter Munk, and Siegfried Moses.[68]

During its first decade the ZVfD did not consider the C.V. an ideological opponent; its aims were different but not antagonistic. Whereas the C.V. was a legal-oriented organization for Jewish defense against anti-Semitism, the ZVfD was an ideological-educational movement attempting to define and understand the Judaic tradition and Zionism as countermeasures to assimilation. The ZVfD was not concerned with German anti-Semitism nor other German political activities. This had been made explicit in the resolution of the eleventh *Delegiertentag* of 1908:

> The Zionist organization of Germany rejects, as an organization, any interference in the inner political struggles of Germany and will not support any one political party.[69]

The resolution, however, did not forbid individual political participation. Almost from its inception the ZVfD had been interested in founding a German Jewish central organization that would effectively represent all German Jews.[70] To realize this goal, the ZVfD joined with the German Jewish establishment and especially with the C.V. on two occasions: in 1900–1901 in preparation for the *Judentag* (Jewish Diet),[71] and in 1907 in planning a political umbrella-organization.[72]

The first occasion arose as a result of the anti-Semitic attacks in Western Prussia, Russia, Rumania, and Galicia. In reaction to these pogroms, Martin Philippson, the editor of the *Allegemeine Zeitung des Judentums,* and Bernhard Breslauer, a leader of the Berlin community, attempted to create a Jewish organization strong enough to protect the rights of Jews both in Germany and abroad. The planning committee of the organization (Diet) met in July, 1900, and included the leaders of the C.V., Maximilian Horwitz and Eugen Fuchs.[73] The Zionists supported the plan enthusiastically and declared that it was the duty of every German Jewish citizen to safeguard his constitutional rights by whatever means the law permitted;[74] they emphasized that their aims diminished neither their German loyalty nor their obligation to protect their rights. Within a few weeks, the planners of the Diet invited Zionists to serve on the committee, but it soon became clear that the plan would not be successful. The Jewish liberals attributed the failure of their efforts to Zionist radicalism, while the Zionists blamed the liberals' fear of acting independently of the German liberal political parties. [75] The Zionists then attempted to create an organization of their own with the help of some influential liberals; they failed because they were unable to stir the German Jewish community from its apathy.[76]

In 1906–7, the situation was somewhat different. At this time, the Zionist groups in Posen, in cooperation with the *Juedische Volksvereine,* sought to establish a political umbrella-organization that would represent Jews in the whole German Reich.[77] The undertaking seemed likely to succeed for a number of reasons. First, in recent Posen elections the Jews there had been forced to vote either for Poles or for Germans, and they had inevitably been considered traitors by the losers.[78] Great bitterness was felt by the Posen Jews, and many of them demanded an independent Jewish political party. In addition, during the Reichstag elections of 1907, the German liberal parties had allied themselves with the anti-Semitic parties for the first time since 1893 and had left the German Jews without political recourse.[79] These two dilemmas prepared the German Jews for new political alignments.

In response to this unprecedented situation, the C.V. broadened its support from the liberal *Freisinn* splinter parties, to include negotiations with the Zionists, who proposed

guidelines for a Jewish political party and candidates acceptable to both organizations (Paul Nathan, Eugen Fuchs, and
Alfred Klee). Despite such indications, however, the C.V.
abandoned the plan at the behest of its leading members who
were reluctant to sever connections with the *Freisinn* parties.[80] Again the Zionists tried to proceed alone, but their
plan was doomed to failure for lack of mass backing and
financial support.

The failure of both attempts at political unification cannot be attributed to ideological conflicts among the various
Jewish organizations, but to the liberals who preferred to
abandon the two plans rather than to desert the existing
political parties. Undoubtedly they also feared that independent political action would strengthen anti-Semitic propaganda in respect to Jewish ethnocentrism and disloyalty. In
the context of this study, the importance of both attempts
lies in the fact that Zionists and liberals were able and willing
to cooperate without compromising their respective ideological principles.

It may be asked then how, in the light of so much
common agreement and a basic willingness to cooperate, the
Zionists and the liberal community could become involved in
a conflict that, except for the war years, continued unabated
until 1933. This conflict was due to a constellation of events
that happened to occur simultaneously. Concurrently some
less important incidents between the liberals and the Zionists,
which had their origins in earlier years, had attained by 1912
a cumulative effect of polarization. To understand the historical process and the evolution of the conflict, a review of
these background incidents should be undertaken.

The Emergence of Conflict: 1910–12

In 1910 the central office of the ZVfD was moved from
Cologne to Berlin, where Arthur Hantke replaced Bodenheimer as president and brought new vitality to the organization.[81] The young Zionists who had been elected at the
Frankfurt *Delegiertentag* became active in its leadership and
caused considerable disquiet among the Jewish liberal establishment. They had met in March, 1910, shortly before the

Frankfurt *Delegiertentag* to call Zionists to increased concern with practical work in Palestine. This same group helped to pass the Posen resolution that changed the orientation of the ZVfD toward Palestine, and the resolution demanding more Zionist propaganda among German Jewish youth. When the radical Zionists, therefore, assumed the official leadership of the ZVfD between 1910 and 1912, they were met with hostility by the liberal community. Immediately after 1910, the *JR* began to report conflicts between Zionists and non-Zionists.[82]

The *Juedische Rundschau* was the most sensitive barometer of anti-Zionist attitudes and behavior in Germany and it is therefore significant that the Zionist press organ reports that the first open hostility by the liberal assimilationists against the German Zionists occurred in the winter of 1910–11.[83] This late date for an outbreak of anti-Zionism is related to the Zionists' having delayed until 1910 any active participation in community elections. In these elections their hope was to overthrow the notables of the Jewish community and to change the laws governing community elections. Although the ZVfD leadership had not initiated the unrest in the communities, it did support the local Zionist groups who were taking part in the elections, and it capitalized on gains made by these local groups. The liberals, in turn, were furious, and they denounced the ZVfD as a destructive force within the German Jewish community.

Community tensions became evident in the winter of 1910 during the elections of representatives to the boards of the Jewish communities of Berlin, Munich, and Posen. For the first time the Zionists campaigned for their own candidates.[84] The issue here was not Zionism vs. anti-Zionism, but rather voting procedure: "block lists" of party candidates (*Listenwahl*) as opposed to the election of independent individuals (*Verhaeltniswahl*). The *Listenwahl* method had been common practice and assured the liberals of a majority on the board of the community. It required each party to select a list of candidates; the list receiving the majority of votes would place all its candidates on the board.[85] The Zionists denounced the system as unjust, since it deprived minority groups of representation, and they demanded election by *Verhaeltniswahl* by which an individual would win or lose on the basis of the number of votes he personally received.

Tension was greatest in Berlin where the liberals had gone unchallenged for many years. The weeks before the election were filled with public meetings, electioneering, and programmatic statements by all the parties concerned.[86] On this occasion the newly formed Zionist *Juedische Wahlvereinigung,* the *Verband der Synagogenvereine,* and the orthodox *Verein zur Erhaltung des ueberlieferten Judentums* joined together under Zionist leadership. The result was an expanded set of demands that came to include "preservation of the Sabbath and the Hebrew language, educating the youth in Jewish values, and the establishment of Jewish religious schools."[87] Foremost among the Zionist agitators were Alfred Klee, Heinrich Loewe, Carl Lewin, and Arnold Witkowski.

The liberals, who commanded the resources and press of the Jewish community and who enjoyed the support of the important liberal Jewish-owned papers such as the *Berliner Tageblatt* and the *Vossische Zeitung,* defeated the Zionist lists despite noisy opposition: liberals, 5,400; *Wahlvereinigung,* 3,600. The victory of the liberals was diminished by the relatively large Zionist vote, a tenfold increase over its showing three years before.[88] This relatively strong Zionist vote forced the liberals to recognize for the first time that the Zionists had become a substantial force that could prove threatening if augmented by the orthodox group.[89] The Zionists heightened the tension by declaring after the Berlin elections: "After we have secured for Zionism a position to rival the other parties in the community, we look forward optimistically to our final goal—the conquest of the Berlin Jewish community."[90] Thus the Zionists were eager to utilize the confrontation within the most important Jewish community in Germany as an opportunity to emerge from oblivion. They referred hopefully to the "happy signs . . . which will make a factual discussion about Zionism possible."[91]

The Zionists did not have to wait long for a discussion on Zionism. In the midst of the conflict, an issue appeared that seriously disturbed and angered the entire Berlin community. In 1911, Werner Sombart, who by virtue of his book *Die Juden und das Wirtschaftsleben* had become known as an expert in Jewish affairs, began to lecture throughout Germany on "the future of the Jews."[92] At the end of the year these lectures were collected in a book, *Die Zukunft der Juden.*[93] Sombart's lectures were well attended, especially by Jews, and they received wide publicity in all Jewish and non-Jewish papers.[94] Despite the fact that the Jewish liberal establishment of Berlin decried Sombart as an anti-Semite,[95] his lectures continued to draw a large audience throughout 1911 and 1912.[96]

In raising the Jewish Question, Sombart claimed that he was merely discussing in public what Jew and Gentile were discussing in private.[97] Relying heavily on Ruppin's *Die Juden der Gegenwart,* he spoke of the wretched condition of the Eastern European *Luftmenschen.*[98] Their intolerable situation at home and the fact that many countries were closed to them made it imperative that they find a new land of refuge.[99] He agreed with the Zionist effort toward emigration to Palestine for those deprived of security at home; the Zionist solution to the Jewish Question was uniquely logical and practical.

Sombart was concerned as well with the situation of Western European Jews, who shortly after emancipation had acquired important cultural, political, and economic positions.[100] Their involvement in the affairs of their home countries had led not only to assimilation, but to the negation of a heritage they now saw as an impediment; these Jews had reacted sharply against the Zionist anti-assimilationist position.[101] He argued that assimilation was not feasible, rather than not desirable—much as the Jews might wish to assimilate, most Germans were unwilling to accept them as an integral part of their nation. Jewish involvement in all aspects of German life only intensified the Gentiles' unwillingness to accept them. Daily contacts produced inevitable friction,[102] since Jews and Germans comprised separate and distinct races.[103]

Sombart valued the preservation of national characteristics: "I wish that the Judaizing [*verjudung*] of such large areas of our public and intellectual life could be halted; for the benefit of German culture as well as Jewish culture." [104] Assimilation could only produce unfortunate and unnatural circumstances that could be corrected by Jewish nationalism alone. He denied that Jewish nationalism conflicted with German loyalty and therefore advocated that it be combined with support for the fatherland. Sombart considered the status of Jews inferior to that of the Christians in Germany, yet he suggested that German Jews not press for full access to top posts, such as reserve officer, to which they were by nature ill-suited. [105] He summarized:

> The Western European states should grant their Jewish citizens complete equality, and the Jews should have the intelligence and tact not to make full use of this equality. [106]

Sombart's lectures and his book created considerable excitement among German Jews who reacted each according to his own ideological and philosophical orientation. [107] The first paper to report the lectures, the *Juedische Rundschau,* had been covering them fully and favorably since November, 1911. It is clear that in their inner circles the Zionists were made a bit uneasy by Sombart's conclusions; nevertheless, they recognized the propaganda value of his lectures. They made a sharp distinction between his book *Die Juden und das Wirtschlaftsleben*—with which they disagreed—and his lectures, which to a large extent expressed their own point of view. [108] They gratefully acknowledged that no one since Herzl had been able to bring the Jewish Question and the Zionist ideology to the attention of the Western European public—an achievement beyond Zionist reach for the last fourteen years. [109] They recognized that Sombart's stature and renown had allowed him to triumph where the Zionists had failed: he had forced papers like the *Berliner Tageblatt,* the *Berliner Lokal-Anzeiger,* and the *Vossische Zeitung* to violate their policy of silence on all Zionist issues. With pride and satisfaction, therefore, the Zionist paper reported that the renowned scholar was a concerned supporter of Zionist ideology. [110] In an editorial, the *JR* expressed elation:

> There was a time when our opponents used the weapon of *Totschweigen* against us. After fifteen years, however, the power of our ideas has won over this policy. . . . Our enemies' cowardly retreat [*Ausweichen*] did not hinder our success; it only postponed it. Today our opponents oppose us ever more bitterly and this situation makes us very happy, since it is an additional proof of our increased strength. [111]

The Zionists, however, were virtually alone in their praise. The non-Zionists and anti-Zionists accused Sombart of anti-Semitism under the guise of Zionism; the orthodox and liberals shared their evaluation. [112] The C.V. compared the *Judenpolitik* advertisements of Sombart's lectures to those of the anti-Semite Ahlwardt who announced his lectures as *Judenflinten.* [113] Accusing Sombart of crude anti-Semitism, the C.V. urged its members to avoid his lectures. [114]

By February, 1912, the issue had produced a direct conflict between the ZVfD and the C.V. and had changed from an argument about Sombart's views to a debate about Zionist ideology. Since the C.V. considered Sombart an anti-Semite, steps were taken against him as such. The central office of the C.V. sent a letter to the Munich Jewish community, where Sombart was scheduled to speak, and urged the community to see that its members did not attend. [115] In response, the *Juedische Rundschau* published an "open letter" defending Sombart as a scholar who was expressing opinions on questions relevant to all Germans. [116]

On February 8, 1912, the Munich Zionists passed the following resolution:

> The meeting strongly disapproves of the position which the C.V. leadership has taken against professor Werner Sombart and his lectures on the Jewish Question. It particularly considers the editorial in *Im Deutschen Reich,* which has reported excerpts of Sombart's lectures

in Berlin and has misrepresented them through very un-just criticism, as a strong insult to Sombart and a slight to all his Jewish-conscious listeners.[117]

The Zionists thus adopted Sombart's cause as their own, a cause defined as the right of a man to express his views even if they did not coincide with those of the liberal Jewish establishment.[118]

The most extensive and detailed attack came from Eugen Fuchs, leader of the C.V. His polemic against Sombart received wide attention among the entire German Jewish community and was thought to represent its views.[119] Fuchs's argument was:

1. Sombart is wrong in calling us a different race. We are not foreigners within Germany, although we may have special characteristics by virtue of the religious and social values inherent in the Judaic tradition. The governing factor in our role as Germans is the fact that we want to be Germans.

2. *Deutschtum* and *Judentum* are not basically different and conflicting Weltanschauungen. Both are of great worth to humanity and their synthesis within German Jewry can have only positive results. We cannot reverse the trend of history and try artificially to accentuate our uniqueness by going back to Palestine and speaking Hebrew. We do indeed want to adhere to our Jewish tradition, but only here in Germany.

3. Although theoretically we do not need to become officials of the German bureaucracy nor officers in the army, our moral duty as citizens of Germany demands that we use all the rights granted us by law. Had we had this defeatist attitude a hundred years ago when we began our struggle for emancipation, we would have remained slaves to this very day.

4. We do not need Sombart's advice concerning our conduct within the German state. Our equality is not a matter of tact; it is a question of the rights due to every loyal citizen.

5. The Jews are fully capable of becoming officers in the German army. They have given ample proof of their courage in the German wars of the past century and will do so again when called upon by the fatherland.[120]

Despite his repudiation of Sombart, Fuchs urged peace between the ZVfD and the C.V.:

I do not want Sombart to sow the seeds of controversy among us. We are at one with the Zionists in fostering pride and self-consciousness among the German Jews and in trying to ban the spirit of assimilation which has become so dangerous to Judaism. We are also united with them in the efforts for peaceful cooperation which ultimately aim to improve the cultural and social position of the Jews. We neither use terms such as "volkish," and "nationality," nor see the necessity for a Jewish state which aims to become a home for persecuted Eastern and Western European Jews. But these differences of opinion are trivial in view of our common and basic goals and in view of the long road on which we must travel together toward a renaissance of the Jewish spirit. . . . We want to work together toward Jewish unity, to march together even if in the future our ways must part. I cannot imagine that the Zionists will permit men like Sombart to carry their banner for them. Were I a Zionist I would say: "God protect me from such friends."[121]

Fuchs's hopes for a united front with the Zionists did not materialize. Almost as soon as the Sombart issue died down, another dispute took place that was to have an even more marked and lasting effect on the German Jewish community. In March, 1912, *Der Kunstwart,* a fortnightly devoted to literature, the arts, and music, and which emphasized German national culture, [122] published the essay "*Deutsch Juedischer Parnass*" by the young Jewish editor, Moritz Goldstein.[123] The controversy aroused by the essay was especially intense because the editor of *Der Kunstwart,* Ferdinand Avenarius, had strong nationalistic—if not anti-Semitic—opinions, and its literary critic, Adolf Bartels, was a confirmed, notorious anti-Semite. [124]

Goldstein's essay dealt with the dichotomy between the Jews' hope to serve as administrators of German culture and the attitude of the German people who denied them both right and opportunity to assume this role. [125] He considered it his duty to raise this issue, which had been ignored by all segments of the Jewish community except the Zionists. He attributed to the Jews the control of all the major German papers and hence of their editorial policies, as well as predominance in the theatre and in the field of poetry. [126] Whereas the Jews believed themselves integrated into German culture, the Germans saw them as alien:

> We may produce a Max Reinhardt and bring the stage to new heights of performance, or we may have a Hugo von Hofmansthal who invents a new poetic style to replace the over-used style of Schiller, or we may lead the painters with Max Liebermann—we may call all this German, but the others call it Jewish—and when they do recognize our achievements, they wish that we would achieve a little less. [127]

Goldstein analyzed the dilemma of the German Jews as anti-Semitic persecution on the one hand, and pressure from those Jews who denied the existence of anti-Semitism and tried to negate their Judaism on the other. He agreed with Sombart that these self-deluding Jews endangered the position of those more realistic:

> [The former] have to be removed from all conspicuous positions where they represent Jewry in the worst possible light. We have to silence them and gradually eliminate them so that we, the rest of the German Jews, may once again enjoy our lives under the only condition under which a man can feel free and proud: in an open struggle against an equal adversary [anti-Semitism]. [128]

Goldstein proposed emigration to Palestine as the only reasonable solution. There talent would be appreciated, he argued, regardless of religion. An alternate channel for creative energy for those frustrated by the lie of integration and a schizophrenic existence in Germany was the study of modern Hebrew literature, a virgin territory in which there was no stigma attached to being Jewish. [129] Goldstein's solutions were essentially those of the Zionists; they both saw them as the avenues to an honorable and respectable life for the modern Jew.

Moritz Goldstein was not a member of the Zionist organization in Germany, but as in the case of Sombart, his essay became the basis for a strenuous confrontation between Zionists and anti-Zionists. Sombart's *Die Zukunft der Juden* and Goldstein's *"Deutsch Juedischer Parnass"* overlapped in their assumptions, analysis, and conclusions. During the Sombart controversy, the Goldstein essay received wide publicity. The Goldstein issue was particularly compelling because he was criticizing German Jewry from within their ranks. Whereas some Jews could dismiss Sombart as an anti-Semite, Goldstein demanded serious consideration as a respectable German Jewish liberal. The Zionists were pleased by the publicity their cause was indirectly receiving and thanked Avenarius for giving Zionism an audience in Germany. [130]

Moritz Goldstein's essay had a lasting impact on the community; it became a cause celèbre and was talked about for years. The Zionists were enthusiastic, while the liberals were outraged. The *JR* commented that Herzl's wish for public discussion of the Jewish Question was finally being realized: "It seems to us that through this article a revision of opinion concerning the relationship of the Jews to German culture may come about." [131]

The response of the liberals was not long delayed. In the April issue of *Der Kunstwart,* Ernst Lissauer, an extreme assimilationist, replied at length to Goldstein. [132] He argued that the Jews were not a nation and that they were in the process of evolution from the ghetto to full emancipation. Lissauer saw assimilation as a blissful goal at the end of a slow, difficult process requiring patience and self-control. [133] His solutions to the Jewish Question included emigration or total submission to the German state: those who were seriously dissatisfied should leave Germany quickly; those who wished to remain should demonstrate their loyalty with the utmost vigor regardless of insults by anti-Semites and Zionists.[134]

Immediately after Lissauer's article, a young anonymous Jew was given the opportunity to present his point of view. In an impassioned passage he claimed that thousands of young Jews had become disillusioned with German ideals and wished to live as proud and upright Jews:

> Give us room that we may stretch. You oppress us in your land, therefore give us another one. We want to create a culture the equal of yours . . . we want to be ourselves.[135]

In a succeeding issue, Ludwig Strauss, a member of the ZVfD, supported the cause of a national Jewish culture. [136] Goldstein's essay filled the pages of *Der Kunstwart* for several months, as arguments and counter-arguments by assimilationists, Zionists, and self-proclaimed anti-Semites frankly exposed the sentiments of a large segment of Jews and Germans.

The C.V. responded to the Goldstein essay in October, 1912, [137] almost eight months after its appearance. [138] The response was made by Professor Julius Goldstein, a prominent C.V. member and future editor of *Der Morgen*. He regarded the fact that Goldstein made no distinction between Eastern and Western European Jews as his main fallacy:

> The *Ostjude* may accept Goldstein's remedy that he live only as a Jew both in the cultural and national sense, because he lives in an environment which has no culture; consequently the *Ostjude* may be satisfied with the old and poor Jewish culture of the Middle Ages. We, the Jews of the West, are, and can only be, Germans as far as any culture is concerned . . . not because of our desire to assimilate, but because our whole being is tied to Western cultural tradition with very strong bonds.[139]

In line with the C.V. philosophy, Julius Goldstein stressed

the necessity of total Jewish loyalty to Germany, with insistence on their legitimate rights.[140]

The *Kunstwart* debate occupied German Jewry until World War I. The liberals [141] and the orthodox [142] both considered the essay identical with Zionism and attacked them as common dangers. Each group, from its particular perspective, defined Jews as a religious community; opponents of this view were by definition anti-Semites or Zionists. The arguments became so heated that a 1913 meeting to discuss Goldstein's and Sombart's essays was disrupted by threats of physical violence between members of the ZVfD and the C.V. [143] The C.V. devoted more space and time than any other German Jewish organization to the refutation of Moritz Goldstein;[144] most of the Zionist attacks against the liberal establishment focused therefore on the C.V. For them it had come to represent all liberal Jews.

The anti-Zionist attacks, stimulated by this situation and carried on by virtually the entire German Jewish community, did not intimidate the Zionists, who after all had complained of being ignored by the Jewish community. [145] The controversies focused attention on Zionism and brought the Zionists new members. [146] Instead of crushing the tiny minority, the controversy served to unite the membership of the ZVfD and strengthen its commitment to the organization and its ideology. At the beginning of 1912, the German Zionists were stronger and more confident than ever before:

> Zionism can claim today, after only fifteen years of activity, to have revived Jewish life in Germany and to have reformed German Jewry in the most positive sense .... Zionism is on the march![147]

This self-confidence was bolstered by their victory in the Koenigsberg community elections, where on February 28, 1912, the Zionist *Neuer Juedischer Gemeindeverein* defeated the *Liberale Vereinigung* and won all nine seats on the board of the Jewish community.[148]   Five days later the *Neuer Juedischer Gemeindeverein* in Berlin sent a letter to the Prussian minister of the interior demanding government intervention in changing the community election system from *Listenwahl* to *Verhaeltniswahl*. [149] The Zionist plea for government intervention was unprecedented in community politics, and it represented a direct attack on the German Jewish communities and organizations, all of which supported the *Listenwahl* system.

At the same time, the Zionists focused their attention for the first time on propaganda among German Jewish youth. [150] Zionist youth groups had existed in Germany since the end of the nineteenth century; they were, however, poorly organized and competitive clubs. [151] The liberal establishment, on the other hand, had formed in 1909 a nationwide youth organization, the *Verband der Juedischen Jugendvereine Deutschlands* (VJJD). [152] The main supporters of this youth movement were the *Bnei Briss,* the C.V., and the *Deutsch-Israelitischer Gemeindebund.* The VJJD grew quickly and by 1913 had 14,500 members. [153] The Weltanschauung of the VJJD was in line with the liberal establishment that helped to support it; it believed firmly in the synthesis of *Deutschtum* and *Judentum* and in the necessity of total Jewish integration into German culture, but without negating Judaism.

Like its parent organizations, the *Verband der Juedischen Jugendvereine Deutschlands* was formed as a "neutral" organization; it took no stand on political or religious issues. [154] It was by virtue of this neutral position that many young Zionists joined its ranks and even helped to form new *Ortsgruppen* for the VJJD. An example of joint effort by Zionists and liberals took place in Kattowitz in Upper Silesia, where Kurt Blumenfeld was a founding member of the local chapter of the VJJD. [155] After the Sombart and Kunstwart debates, however, the VJJD and its governing body, which included a member of the C.V., began to take an increasingly hostile posture toward Zionism. Alfred Apfel, the chairman of the organization and an active member of the C.V., declared that "the neutrality of the youth organization is to be interpreted as a shield against Zionist influences."[156]

The VJJD leadership had good reason to suspect that the Zionists were planning to extend their influence among the neutral youth organizations. At the end of 1911, the leadership of the ZVfD realized that its greatest potential for attracting new members lay in the youth groups. Although nominally neutral, most of the groups, such as the K.C. and the VJJD, were strongly influenced by the liberal establishment. In February, 1912, the leadership of the ZVfD met to devise a strategy that would stem this influence and draw German Jewish youth to Zionism. [157] Blumenfeld contended that, since the Sombart and *Kunstwart* debates, Zionist ideology had moved into the center of the Jewish Question and had prepared the ground for Zionist work among the young; he urged that this opportunity not be missed.[158]

The strategy proposed by Blumenfeld was that Zionists should join the neutral liberal youth groups, learn the names and addresses of members, and try to advance the Zionist idea in small discussion groups. He also suggested, in the interest of Jewish education, that each member of the German Zionist youth organizations be given "guidelines for conduct" within the youth groups. [159] Shortly thereafter the ZVfD distributed to all its *Vertrauensmaenner* "Guidelines for the activities and conduct of Zionist *Vertrauensmaenner* in the neutral youth movements." The pamphlet made the following points:

1. Zionism welcomes any organization willing to work constructively in matters concerning Judaism.
2. It is the duty of every Zionist to devote his energies to any organization willing and able to work on behalf of Jewish causes.
3. It is the duty of every Zionist to try to promote any project concerned with Jewish education.
4. It is the duty of every Zionist to prevent the spread of empty clichés [*Phrasenhafte Begriffe*] about the nature of Judaism. Instead Zionists should promote Jewish education, based on positive and constructive guidelines.[160]

The guidelines also recommended that Zionist members of the liberal youth groups should try to initiate discussions about Zionism, advocate the instruction of Jewish history and Hebrew literature, and distribute Zionist propaganda among their fellow members.[161]

Publicly too, the ZVfD emphasized the importance of youth for the future of the movement; the *Juedische Rundschau* printed regular reports on the activities of Zionist youth groups and urged all Zionists to support them to the best of their abilities. At the Posen *Delegiertentag*, Kurt Blumenfeld asked the ZVfD to strengthen its efforts, with the result that Felix Rosenblueth (b. 1887) was elected special secretary for youth work, with Siegfried Moses (1887–1974), as his assistant. In addition, the delegates created a *"Jugendpropaganda Kommission,"* headed by Adalbert Sachs.[162]

Shortly before the Posen *Delegiertentag*, the ZVfD had decided to expand its efforts among the German Jewish youth by turning to the German Jewish sports clubs, which were organized in the *Juedische Turnerschaft*. Almost all the members of the *Vorstand* of the *Turnvereine* were Zionists, and the agreement between the ZVfD and the *Juedische Turnerschaft* was that the Zionists would help the *Turnerschaft* financially while the sports clubs would actively participate in spreading Zionist propaganda.[163] These agreements produced the following resolution at Posen:

> The *Delegiertentag* is of the opinion that systematic physical education is of great importance for the preservation of Judaism and the strengthening of Jewish national consciousness. . . . The *Delegiertentag* recognizes, therefore, the value of the national Jewish *Turn* and *Sportvereine* . . . it sees in them the best means to educate youth to love Judaism and take active part in the Jewish renaissance. . . .
>
> All young Zionists should henceforth take part in the national Jewish *Turnbewegung;* all older Zionists should support them through contributions to the best of their ability.[164]

The *Delegiertentag* also resolved to form its own youth

groups under the guidance and supervision of the ZVfD, [165] and the immediate result was the creation of the *Juedischer Wanderbund Blau-Weiss* in 1912 under the leadership of Dr. Adalbert Sachs. [166]

This deep Zionist interest in German Jewish youth further antagonized the liberals. The C.V. published an aggressive article denouncing Zionist youth groups as detrimental to the position of the Jews in Germany and warning German Jewish youth to "stay away from these chauvinistic groups." [167] The subject was a sensitive one for the liberals, who realized that the Zionists were successfully recruiting primarily within this age range. In a secret memorandum to all its *Ortsgruppen,* the C.V. warned against joining the *Blau-Weiss,* despite its professed neutrality:

> We would like to draw your attention to the propaganda and agitation of the Zionist *Wandervogel 'Blau-Weiss.'* This organization has developed intensive propaganda in order to recruit Jewish students. It is of utmost importance to counteract these attempts. We believe that Jewish *Wandervoegel* should not be formed, unless the Jewish youth is prevented from joining non-Jewish *Wandervoegel.* It is necessary to inform parents about the Zionist orientation of the *Blau-Weiss.* We recommend that Jewish teachers discourage their students from joining this organization. The C.V. will take every opportunity to oppose the *Blau-Weiss.* [168]

Youth work was merely one aspect of the ZVfD reorientation. The Posen *Delegiertentag* determined to a great extent the course of future relationships between the ZVfD and the German Jewish liberals. The militant quality of the *Delegiertentag* and its radical resolutions reveal the dissatisfaction among Zionists with their tenuous peace with the rest of the community. The decisions taken at Posen to require every German Zionist to take an active part in the development of Palestine and the decidedly Palestine orientation of the German Zionists were a direct challenge to the liberal establishment. The *JR* was conscious of this new direction:

People who look back to the *Delegiertentag* in Posen will realize its importance for the history of Zionism [in Germany], because here the battles between two factions in German Zionism were fought. Our utopian epoch has ended. We are now in the epoch of practical-political Zionism. The Posen *Delegiertentag* has pushed the national aspect into the foreground . . . as far as our opponents are concerned, we have decided that all our compromises hitherto have only damaged our cause. Only through the radical propagation of the national-Jewish idea will Zionism be able to win over the youth.

The question of Zionist participation in non-Zionist organizations has not yet been solved, but we may state that Zionists will henceforth limit their participation in such organizations. This will spare us future compromises. We feel strong enough to say: "the strong is strongest when standing alone! . . . " Only radical representation of the national idea will guarantee the Zionists the victory within German Jewry.[169]

The Zionists eagerly awaited confrontation with the liberals. Their radical stand was adopted precisely to evoke a liberal response that would then permit the Zionists to make inroads among German Jewry, especially the youth.[170] To many Zionists this radical phase was a "wonderful and great experience";[171] they bemoaned the fact that occasions for controversy with the liberals were all too rare.[172]

Opportunities for conflicts, however, were not lacking for long. In October of 1912 the *Juedische Rundschau* published an article entitled "The Bankruptcy of the C.V." in which the Zionists described the C.V. as an ineffective and useless organization, incapable of protecting the rights of the Jews.[173] The immediate reason for this accusation was the nomination by the *Fortschrittliche Volkspartei* of the baptized Jew, Otto Mugdan, as a candidate in the Berlin local elections. The C.V.—supporter and ally of the FVP—tried to prevent this nomination, although it did not actively oppose Mugdan during the campaigns that culminated in his victory on October 19, 1912, in a predominantly Jewish district.[174]

This election only reinforced the Zionists' image of the C.V. as powerless and devoid of moral influence.

During a meeting of the central committee of the ZVfD at the beginning of October, the Zionists considered some action of their own to prevent the election of Mugdan. The meeting resolved that Richard Lichtheim would try to induce Theodor Wolff, editor of the *Berliner Tageblatt,* to oppose Mugdan in that paper, although the Zionists realized that their action came too late to influence the course of the election. [175] The leadership of the ZVfD therefore resolved that immediately after the elections, the ZVfD would launch a propaganda campaign against the C.V., attacking its lack of moral courage. [176] It was in line with this resolution that the *JR* published a series of articles against the policies of the C.V., and it represented the first sizable direct attack by the Zionists on the largest and most powerful liberal Jewish organization in Germany.[177]

Both the C.V. and the ZVfD acknowledged the serious deterioration in their relationship. The C.V., which continually proclaimed its neutrality, [178] was not willing to stand by while its ideologies and policies were publicly attacked, and conflicts between members of the C.V. and of the ZVfD became very frequent. [179] The C.V. office in Berlin, for example, wrote to its branch in Koenigsberg to ask that its *Vertrauensmaenner* keep the Zionists from recruiting new members. [180] The C.V. increased its assaults to the degree that, at the beginning of November, Hantke reported to the executive members of the ZVfD that "the C.V. had become the most dangerous enemy of the Zionists." [181] In his opinion the C.V. was able to mobilize against them at this time with great force for the following reasons: the membership of the ZVfD was increasing steadily; the Zionists were receiving more financial support than ever before; their propaganda among youth groups had touched a sensitive nerve in the liberal camp and was stirring unrest in the *Gemeinden;* and the Zionists were interfering in general election campaigns.[182]

The repeated confrontations eventually involved almost all the major Jewish organizations. [183] An important clash between the Zionists and members of the C.V. occurred in Kattowitz at the end of November, 1912, [184] and accordingly the C.V. leadership resolved to convene a special session to discuss relations with the ZVfD. [185] At the Kattowitz meeting, well attended both by Zionists and members of the C.V., Eugen Fuchs spoke on the "future of the Jews," by way of answering Goldstein and Sombart. [186] During the ensuing discussion the Zionists present declared that attacks on Sombart were in essence attacks against Zionists since they agreed fully with Sombart's conclusion that Palestine was German Jewry's only hope. [187] The C.V. members had interpreted Sombart's promotion of Zionism as a technique to maintain the status quo and bar German Jews from restricted professions; they retorted that the Zionists were helping the anti-Semites to oppress the German Jews. [188] Accusations and counter-accusations became so heated that the meeting erupted in physical conflict and was shortly adjourned. [189]

The Founding of the Antizionistisches Komitee

Toward the close of 1912, relations between Zionists and anti-Zionists reached an impasse. The liberal community retaliated openly against the Zionists whom they saw as irritating and powerful. In October, a group of liberals formed the *Reichsverband zur Bekaempfung des Zionismus* under the leadership of Veit Simon. [190] By December the organization had expanded and changed its official title to *Antizionistisches Komitee*. The organizers of the committee, primarily members of the *Vereinigung fuer das liberale Judentum* and other liberal Jewish organizations, issued their program:

> For the last six months the Zionist movement has taken on such forms that we must organize for powerful defense against Zionism. During this period Zionism has turned for support not only to our brethren, but to the conservative and anti-Semitic parties as well. The Zionists have also attempted, through various literary debates, to create a cultural conflict between Jews and Christians. This intolerable situation has reawakened the fear that even those political circles that hitherto have seen the

solution of the Jewish Question in the granting of full emancipation and equality to the Jews, will henceforth, like the Zionists, see the solution of the Jewish Question in the separation of the Jews from other German citizens. To avert this danger we have constituted ourselves a committee and ask you to support us in our struggle against the Zionists.[191]

Without naming specific issues, the program clearly refers to events such as the *Kunstwart* debate and the Sombart affair. The program also indicates that the most notable German Jewish liberal leaders and organizations felt free to try to thwart Zionism.

The *Antizionistisches Komitee* claimed to speak on behalf of the entire German Jewish liberal establishment. In an early leaflet the *Komitee* praised the *Verband der deutschen Juden,* the C.V., and the *Deutsch-Israelitischer Gemeindebund,* for upholding the remaining rights of German Jews, but it criticized the Zionists for jeopardizing this important task. The *Komitee* charged that the Zionists were indirectly assisting the anti-Semites by labeling Jews "rootless strangers" who did not belong in Germany. The *Komitee* regretfully acknowledged that the Zionists had begun to recruit German Jewish youth, and it concluded:

> The national Jewish movement is dangerous to the welfare of the German Jews. To overcome this danger is to overcome Zionism. For us this has become a question of existence and survival.[192]

Like the original letter of the *Komitee,* this leaflet carried the signatures of a cross-section of Jewish notables, including Bernhard Breslauer (1851–1928) (*Vereinigung fuer das liberale Judentum*), Ludwig Geiger (1848–1920) (*Allgemeine Zeitung des Judentums*), Ludwig Haas (C.V. *Vorstand* and a prominent Jewish politician), Rudolf Mosse (1843–1920) (publisher of the *Berliner Tageblatt*), Hermann Veit Simon, and many others.[193]

The creation of the *Antizionistisches Komitee* was facilitated by one of the most influential Jewish liberal organizations in Germany, the *Vereinigung fuer das liberale Judentum*

in Deutschland. From the end of the nineteenth century
German Jewish liberal laymen had been forming groups to
represent their views and interests, such as the *Freisinniger
Verein fuer juedisches Gemeindeleben* (Frankfurt, 1891) and
the *Liberaler Verein fuer die Angelegenheiten der juedischen
Gemeinde* (Berlin, 1895) with its newspaper *Mitteilungen des
liberalen Vereins fuer die Angelegenheiten der juedischen
Gemeinde zu Berlin.* By 1910 these groups controlled the
Jewish communities, and the Zionists were the first to challenge their authority. The liberals had become especially
powerful after May 3, 1908, when they united to form the
Vereinigung fuer das liberale Judentum in Deutschland,
which included most of the liberal German rabbis as well as
all important liberal organizations and lay leaders in Germany. [194] In September of that year this organization began
the publication of its monthly *Liberales Judentum.* [195]

An important founder of the *Vereinigung* was Rabbi
Heinemann Vogelstein (1841–1911) of Stettin, [196] who in
1897, in cooperation with Rabbi Sigmund Maybaum
(1844–1919) of Berlin, had protested against convening the
Zionist congress in Munich; [197] subsequently the new organization adopted an anti-Zionist stand. Its leaders objected to
Zionism on the grounds that it rejected the universal mission
of the Jews and therefore denied a basic tenet of Judaism;
Zionism stated that the Jews had no stake in German culture
and therefore undermined the position of the German Jew
both politically and socially. [198]

In 1912, when the *Antizionistisches Komitee* was
formed, [199] its cochairman was Walter Breslauer, who was
also the cofounder of the *Vereinigung fuer das liberale
Judentum,* and many other leaders of the *Vereinigung* joined
him in the *Komitee.* [200] Until anti-Zionism reached its
full momentum in 1913, the *Vereinigung* was the strongest
supporter of the *Komitee,* and until 1914 both organizations
shared the same offices in Berlin.

Attempts at Reconciliation

We have seen that the ZVfD expected and even welcomed
opposition to its work among the youth groups, to the Posen

Resolution, and so on, yet it is clear that the leadership began to feel apprehensive and even threatened when, within a very short span of time, it found itself attacked by all the major Jewish organizations and by most of the *Gemeinden*. The public organs of the ZVfD continued to attack the C.V. and other liberal organizations, but the meetings of the executive reveal that the leadership felt some trepidation in the face of so much hostility. [201] At the meeting of the central committee on November 3, 1912, Alfred Klee urged the ZVfD leadership to maintain friendly relations with the C.V. Klee explained that it was natural for the C.V. to voice opposition to the Goldstein and Sombart essays and that it would be unwise for the ZVfD to be too sensitive to liberal attack. [202]

In the face of so much opposition, Alfred Klee, Sammy Gronemann, Adolf Friedemann, and even Leo Motzkin and Estermann, called the Posen Resolution "one of the greatest mistakes made by the ZVfD in its entire history." [203] The resolution had antagonized the Jewish liberals unnecessarily; Gronemann contended that in addition, the resolution "had had no positive effect on Zionist work in Germany." [204] Blumenfeld, Hantke, and Heymann disagreed, but a majority of the members of the executive supported Klee's appraisal. Friedemann believed that it was still possible for the Zionists to work with the C.V., and Klee suggested that a joint committee, composed of leaders of the C.V. and of the ZVfD, be formed to try to arrive at a *modus vivendi*. Klee's suggestion was accepted and Michael Heymann was chosen as liaison between the two organizations. [205]

During the first two weeks of November, Heymann corresponded with Maximilian Horwitz about a meeting. [206] and on December 18, 1912, Eugen Fuchs, Maximilian Horwitz, and Ludwig Hollaender of the C.V. met with Arthur Hantke, Michael Heymann, Leo Motzkin, and Kurt Blumenfeld of the ZVfD to discuss the deterioration in relations. [207] Fuchs opened the meeting by complaining of the recent Zionist propaganda in the *Juedische Rundschau* and of the Zionist attacks against the C.V. in respect to the Mugdan case and the meeting in Kattowitz. The Zionists in turn deplored

the articles in *Im Deutschen Reich* that had been systematically attacking the ZVfD since the end of 1911 and criticized
the leaders of the C.V. for their public denunciation of
Zionism.[208]

Toward the end of the meeting the Zionists declared that
they had no objection to C.V. defense work so long as the
Zionists were not attacked. They requested a formal declaration from the C.V. stating that propaganda against the Zionists would cease; in return, the Zionists would not denigrate
the Weltanschauung of the C.V.[209] Although Eugen Fuchs
was ready for such an arrangement, Hollaender and Horwitz
were not; they denied that the C.V. was an anti-Zionist
organization. The meeting ended without finding any constructive solutions.[210] Indeed, the C.V. leadership subsequently decided to give up neutrality and officially
denounce Zionism.

About two weeks before the C.V.'s anti-Zionist stand
became public, Hantke asked Max Bodenheimer, who had
close relations with the leaders of the C.V., to inquire whether
it was still possible to resolve the conflict. On March 20,
1913, Bodenheimer replied that it was too late; his suggestion
was that the Zionists who were active within the C.V. should
try to influence its deliberations. Perhaps they could soften
its resolution so that some *modus vivendi* with the Zionists
could be reached.[211]

The C.V. Resolution

On March 30, 1913, a special session of the C.V. was convened in Berlin to discuss the "relationship between the C.V.
and Zionism."[212] Ludwig Hollaender presented the justification for the meeting: the Zionists had increasingly and systematically sought to disrupt the work of the C.V.; recently
they had declared that they were not members of the German *volk,* but were rootless within Germany. The Zionists
had officially claimed that they were merely German citizens
who fulfilled the obligations required by the law but lacked
German *Gesinnung,* therefore they did not subscribe to paragraph one of the C.V. statutes that required the support of
German *Gesinnung.* Additionally, the meeting had been

called because members of the C.V. were demanding that the C.V. define its own qualifications for membership. The leadership concluded by saying that members must uphold the first paragraph of the statutes if they were to be effective against anti-Semitism; Zionist members of the C.V. who did not adhere to this ideology were eroding the unity and purpose of the organization.[213]

The principal speeches at the C.V. convention, delivered by Professor Falkenheim of Koenigsberg and Eugen Fuchs of Berlin, summarized the position of the C.V. toward Zionism. In the words of Falkenheim:

1. The C.V. does not disapprove of Zionist philanthropic work in Palestine.

2. The C.V. cannot, however, accept the political Weltanschauung of the Zionists which states that they are national Jews whose future lies in Palestine and that in Germany they are simply residents who abide by the laws of the state for the duration of their stay.

3. The C.V. defines its goal as the acquisition of political and social equality for German Jews. The Zionists render this work more difficult because they supply the anti-Semites with arguments against the German Jews.

4. The C.V. wants to strengthen the loyalty of its membership to German *Gesinnung*. By their radical Jewish nationalistic stance, the Zionists obfuscate this goal by contending that they are guests in the host nation waiting for the opportunity to become Turkish citizens of the Jewish faith. This stance is in direct conflict with that of the C.V.[214]

Whereas Falkenheim's speech summarized the general attitude of the C.V., Eugen Fuchs dealt with the reasons for the conflict. He mentioned specific Zionist challenges and attacks against the C.V.,[215] noting that the issues that had prompted the meeting were the controversies over Sombart's *Die Zukunft der Juden*[216] and Goldstein's "Deutsch Juedischer Parnass,"[217] the Posen *Delegiertentag* with its radical resolution, the Mugdan affair, and the recent disruption in

Kattowitz.[218] The proceedings at the C.V. *Hauptversamm-lung* were proof that the controversies between Zionists and non-Zionists after 1910 had frightened and confused the liberal Jewish community. It was under pressure from the liberal community that the C.V. had abandoned its neutral position and taken the lead in the anti-Zionist campaign.

The C.V. leaders were unable to observe with detachment the radicalism of the Zionists and the growing number of Zionist youth movements in Germany. Nevertheless it still made a distinction between "radical" and "philanthropic" Zionists, for the latter were still close to the mainstream of C.V. membership. The C.V.'s favorite example of a Zionist who was also a loyal German was Franz Oppenheimer, and his essay "Stammesbewusstsein und Volksbewusstsein" was repeatedly quoted at C.V. meetings. [219] Those Zionists, how-ever, who insisted that the Jews were different from the Germans were accused by the C.V. of creating semantic confusion for no purpose other than to antagonize the friends of the Jews. Thus, radical Zionists were willfully and knowingly endangering the position of the Jews in Germany and had no place in an organization that was trying to integrate Jews into the cultural and political life of Germany.

The discussion that followed the speeches by Falkenheim and Fuchs was not argumentative, and it culminated in the nearly unanimous approval by delegates and officers of the following resolution:

> The *Centralverein deutscher Staatsbuerger juedischen Glaubens* aims, in accordance with paragraph one of its statutes, to unite all German Jews regardless of their religious and political affiliations under its leadership to strengthen them in their struggle to retain their political and social position and to further cultivate them in Ger-man *Gesinnung*. From this premise comes the position of the C.V. toward the Zionists. We demand from our mem-bers not only the fulfillment of their civic duties, but also German *Gesinnung* and the implementation of this *Gesin-nung,* in their daily life.

We do not want to solve the German Jewish question internationally. We want to participate in German culture as Germans and on the soil of the German fatherland. At the same time we want to remain loyal to our Jewish community which has been sanctified by our religion and history. As long as the German Zionist is striving to find a secure home for the dispossessed Jews of the East or to uphold the pride of the Jews in their history and religion, he is welcome as a member [in the C.V.]. We must remove ourselves, however, from the Zionist who denies German national feeling, who regards himself as a guest within a foreign host-country, and who affirms only Jewish national feeling.[220]

This mild resolution reflects the influence of the moderate wing, led by Eugen Fuchs. The three initial paragraphs contained no new ideological or philosophical statements, but rather reiterated the distance of the C.V. from radical Zionists. The first actual reference to the Zionists does not come until the fourth paragraph, and there the C.V. confirms its support of philanthropic enterprises on behalf of the *Ostjuden* and the fostering of Jewish self-consciousness. It takes exception only to those Zionists who deny German national sentiments and advocate an exclusive and separate Jewish identity.

In short, the resolution appears much milder than the actual debates that impelled it.[221] No objection to Zionism as an ideological Weltanschauung was made, nor to the Basel program, nor even to the ZVfD. The resolution seemed to be directed only against the radical element within the ZVfD which had gained publicity and strength since the Posen *Delegiertentag*. To many members this resolution did not seem adequately to reflect the C.V.'s position. The radical wing, headed by Bruno Weil, demanded that the delegates act on their convictions and condemn Zionism as defined by the Basel program, because the Basel program's call for the "establishment of a home for the Jewish people secured under public law in Palestine" contradicted the position of the C.V.

Since by definition Zionists supported the Basel program, they could not be members of the C.V.[222] Weil, therefore, proposed an addition to the resolution:

> The C.V., therefore, considers Zionism, which is based on the Basel Program, as incompatible with the goals set forth by the statutes of the C.V.[223]

The C.V. rejected this proposal, fearing to offend those Zionists who had been willing to cooperate before Posen.

The resolution, then, was intended less as an attack against the Zionists than as a public statement of loyalty directed to the German Gentiles and the liberal Jewish community. It was in line with the positions of the older generation of German Zionists like Friedemann and Oppenheimer, who agreed with the C.V.'s condemnation of the new radical Zionist wing of Blumenfeld. The resolution clearly distinguished the "good" Zionists who supported philanthropic enterprises in Palestine on behalf of the *Ostjuden,* from the incorrigible radicals who denied a deep attachment to Germany.[224] Its intent was to clarify publicly the C.V.'s position toward *Deutschtum* and *Judentum* without jeopardizing the cooperation of the majority of German Zionists.[225] In fact, the older generation of Zionists who were also members of the C.V. did not hasten to resign; they did not view the resolution as directed against themselves. A month after the resolution only 197 Zionists had resigned from the C.V. in direct protest.[226]

Final Break with the Liberals

Nevertheless, despite its moderate tone, the Zionist leadership regarded the resolution as a direct attack on Zionism in general and the ZVfD in particular. The resolution infuriated the ZVfD, since the alignment of the C.V. with the liberal establishment destroyed the C.V.'s claim to be a neutral organization designed to include all Jewish positions. It severed the last link of the Zionists with the liberals. Within a week after the meeting, the ZVfD published a declaration protesting the C.V.'s slur against the Zionists' German *Gesinnung:*

Jewish nationalism rests on the assumption of the common heritage of all Jews. The denial of the national
character of Judaism, therefore, must result in the gradual dissolution of Judaism. Since we are convinced of the
truth of this statement, we consider it our duty as Jews
to work for the future of the Jewish nation. The achievement of this goal in Palestine serves at the same time to
raise the economic and social conditions of the Jewish
volk, most of whom live in abject poverty in the East.
The Jewish national *Gesinnung* does not in any way
interfere with the interests of the German Reich, nor does
it contradict in any way our civic *Gesinnung* and qualifi-
cation to participate in Germany's public life and institutions. If the C.V. points to such a conflict of interest it
does so out of the mistaken understanding of the national
character of Judaism and the historical relationship between *Judentum* and *Deutschtum.* Our interpretation of
our civic duties does not mean only their formal fulfillment, but also rests upon our recognition of the ethical
significance of the state we serve with loyalty and devotion. This Weltanschauung, however, cannot destroy the
national bond which has united Jews to their brethren for
4,000 years. We therefore decisively reject the public
attempt of the C.V. to cast doubt upon our civic responsibility and to declare that our participation in German
life is not consonant with our Jewish nationalism.

Our ideas have won the approval of many non-Jews.
The protest against Zionism by other Jews will not serve
any German or Jewish interest and will only contribute
to a quicker dissolution of Judaism.[227]

This declaration too was a restatement of the organization's program. The defense against accusations of divided
loyalty implied a reaffirmation of their loyalty to Germany.[228] The Zionists, rejecting their division into "acceptable" and "unacceptable" groups by the C.V., insisted that

any Zionist who accepted the Basel program should not remain a member of the C.V. Since the C.V. was an organization whose declared purpose was the protection of all Jews but was in actuality intolerant toward a segment of its membership,[229] the C.V. had forfeited all claim to neutrality and to its Zionist members.[230]

On May 1, 1913, the ZVfD leaders and *Vertrauensmaenner* held a special meeting in Berlin to deal with the C.V. resolution of the previous month. With the agreement of the *Deutscher Kreis der juedischen Turnerschaft* and the *Kartell Zionistischer Verbindungen*, they passed the following resolution:

> The *Vertrauensmaenner* of the ZVfD who have met in Berlin on May 1, 1913, unanimously reject, as does the central committee of the ZVfD, the attempt by the C.V. to pass judgment on the opinions and beliefs of the German Zionists. We consider this action an affront.
>
> Anti-Semites have already accused all Jewry of lacking in love for its fatherland. Now the C.V. has used the same weapon of denunciation against its own brethren. Only party hatred could have motivated them to misuse the ambiguous concept of "nationalism" to such a dangerous degree and, on the basis of arbitrary definitions, to have played *Judentum* and *Deutschtum* against each other. The national Jewish *Gesinnung* is the consciousness of belonging to the Jewish *volk* and the will to preserve and develop this *volk* in the future through the establishment of a home for the Jewish people secured under public law in Palestine. This *Gesinnung* does not contradict the interests of any state or *volk* and can never hinder the German Zionists from taking active part in the political and cultural life of Germany in accordance with the historic position of the Jews in Germany. Until now, the German Zionists have viewed the C.V. as the representative of the civic interests of the German Jews and have therefore not denied the C.V. their cooperation even though the C.V. has frequently not measured up to its goals and promises. However, after the unheard-of position the C.V. has

taken against the Zionist segment of the German Jews, the German Zionists declare the C.V. as unfit and no longer legitimate to represent the whole of German Jewry.

The *Vertrauensmaenner* of the *Zionistische Vereinigung fuer Deutschland* demand, therefore, that the German Zionists resign their membership in the C.V.

They deem it urgently necessary that an organization be formed which would, under strict observance of neutrality, intervene in all inner Jewish questions which concern the civic rights of the Jews.[231]

This resolution signaled the final and irrevocable break between the Zionists and the liberals. Cooperation was still theoretically possible between C.V. moderates like Eugen Fuchs and Zionist moderates such as Franz Oppenheimer and Carl Lewin. The ZVfD had become more radical, however, under the younger men who in Posen had seized control of its leadership. They saw in the C.V. resolution a declaration of war on Zionism by the liberal establishment. The older generation of Zionists like Friedemann and Oppenheimer had much in common both intellectually and philosophically with the C.V. leadership, but there was a sharp clash of personalities between the young ZVfD leadership (Blumenfeld, Hantke, Rosenblueth) and the young C.V. leadership (Hollaender, Apfel, Weil). These two opposing camps were uncompromising. The ZVfD believed that it must be radical to succeed; the C.V. in return remained entrenched behind its anti-Zionist attitude.

After the C.V. and the ZVfD resolutions, relations between the Zionists and the liberal establishment deteriorated rapidly. An action by one elicited condemnation by the other. The Zionists denounced the liberals as assimilationists, by which they meant renegades who forsook *Judentum* for the sake of *Deutschtum*.[232] The liberals attacked the Zionists as disloyal to Germany and unfit to hold public positions. At the end of 1913, the Zionists founded the *Reichsverein der deutschen Juden* to replace the C.V. The Zionists claimed that this new organization, unlike the C.V., would be a truly representative organization for German Jewry. The *Reichsverein,* however, supported as it was only by the ZVfD, was unsuccessful.

Against this background a new controversy, the "language debate," erupted in Palestine and had widespread repercussions in Germany. This controversy concerned the *Hilfsverein der deutschen Juden,* a twenty-thousand member "neutral" and philanthropic organization with headquarters in Berlin. Among its members the *Hilfsverein* had many anti-Zionists and liberal assimilationists [233] who welcomed any opportunity to attack the Zionists. [234]

The *Hilfsverein* supported educational and philanthropic institutions in Palestine and, until 1913, had cooperated in these tasks with the German Zionists as well as with the *Engere Aktionskomitee* of the WZO. In 1911, a technical high school—a preparatory school for the Technion (Institute of Technology)—was founded in Haifa. [235] Two of the highest officials of the *Hilfsverein,* Paul Nathan and James Simon, who were instrumental in the founding of the school, were members of its governing board. The Zionists demanded that part of the curriculum be taught in Hebrew; the board refused (October 26, 1913), stipulating that German would be the only language of the institution, and the Zionists resigned from the board.

Consequently, the Palestinian *Yishuv* protested the actions of the *Hilfsverein* by means of strikes, protest meetings, and disruption at the *Hilfsverein* institutions. Students and teachers resigned to found Hebrew schools. The strength of the opposition compelled Paul Nathan and James Simon to resign, whereupon the administration submitted to the Zionist demands. [236] The Zionists had gained a victory in Palestine, but the ramifications of the "language debate" in Germany included the shift by formerly neutral members of the *Hilfsverein* to active anti-Zionism. Paul Nathan and James Simon joined the *Antizionistisches Komitee* and signed its statements against the German Zionists; the shift in allegiance of the two *Hilfsverein* leaders was typical of the general reaction against Zionists among German Jews.[237]

By 1914, all the principal Jewish organizations in Germany had joined the anti-Zionist camp. The *Hilfsverein* joined such anti-Zionist organizations as the C.V., the *Vereinigung fuer das liberale Judentum,* the *Antizionistisches Komitee,* and the *Reformgemeinde zu Berlin.* [238] The *Agudat Israel,* founded by the orthodox in 1912, was also militantly anti-Zionist and readily joined in the activities of the liberal organizations. Even such "neutral" organizations as the *Deutsch Israelitischer Gemeindebund,* [239] the *Verband der deutschen Juden,* [240] the *Bnei Briss,* [241] and the *Verband der juedischen Jugendvereine Deutschlands* [242] adopted a decidedly anti-Zionist program.

Until 1914, conflicts between Zionists and anti-Zionists were aired only in the Jewish press. During that year, however, the dispute reached such proportions that the organizations involved in the anti-Zionist campaign brought the issues to the general public. On February 5, 1914, they published a full-page advertisement in all the important German newspapers, including the *Berliner Tageblatt* and the *Vossische Zeitung:*

The large organizations of the German Jews have of late been severely hampered in their humanitarian enterprises as a result of Zionist agitation. Zionists have entered non-Zionist organizations not to cooperate peacefully, but to gain control over them. Consequently, strife and disharmony have been generated. The methods used by these elements have never been practiced in German Jewry before. By presenting facts in a manner suitable to their purposes and through the willful misrepresentation of the opinions of those who oppose them, they seek to strengthen their position. They insult and attack all those who do not support their goals.

The Zionists seek to develop within German Jewry a "national Jewish" chauvinism which would place us in sharp juxtaposition to our Christian fellow citizens from whom in reality nothing separates us except our faith. This is not the place for an analysis of the details of the Zionist program. We are only concerned here with taking a position against such dangerous opinions and pointing out the reprehensible means the Zionists have chosen. Whoever wants to work with us peacefully is welcome. It has become, however, impossible to work with the Zionists even in those areas in which we were able to cooperate on behalf of our spiritual and religious interests. We point to this fact with regret. In the interest of the entire German Jewish community, we can no longer hesitate to draw a definite line between us and them. Those whose unbridled agitation has forced us to make such a declaration, should be accounted responsible. We request our German brethren as a whole to give the world an enlightening example in all matters requiring support of the poor and feeble, social help, and the raising of the mental and ethical standards of humanity. There is a wide and open field for such benevolent activities. We want to practice them as good Jews and good Germans.[243]

This advertisement was signed by some five hundred notables and leaders of the German Jewish community, among them the eminent philosopher Hermann Cohen.[244] It expressed their twofold fear: that Zionism had become powerful enough to attract German Jews and that Christians would identify the entire German Jewish community with the Zionists, thereby adding fuel to the anti-Semitic arguments that Jews were a foreign body within the German nation. Unlike the C.V. resolution of March, 1913, there was no distinction made here between good and bad Zionists; the attack was made against Zionist ideology and all who professed to be Zionists. This declaration's sharpness in comparison with that of the C.V. is to be attributed to participation by the entire Jewish, and especially liberal Jewish, community, for this element opposed Zionism more violently than did the C.V. moderates who had formulated the 1913 resolution.

The Zionists responded in the general press:

Advertisements are not the proper way to conduct battles of ideological warfare or to air internal Jewish differences of opinion. Our work goes on. It can never be hampered by members of our nation who stab in the back those of their brethren who have retained a feeling for the nobility of their community. We will respond to the attacks against us in mass rallies all over Germany, in which the Zionist idea will be the subject of public discussion and elucidation.[245]

The notice was signed by Hantke, Blumenfeld, Heymann, Klee, and Motzkin and gave the places and dates of some seventy-five meetings scheduled for all the major cities in Germany. Clearly the ZVfD was exploiting this last attack for proselytizing purposes. The increasing proportions of the struggle gave the Zionists the opportunity to carry their cause to the most remote parts of Germany. To the leadership of the ZVfD it seemed that a new era of successful Zionist propaganda had begun.

One can only speculate as to what the course of events in the German Jewish community might have been had World War I not intervened. The conflict would probably only have become more bitter and led to further polarization. Certainly the Zionist *Delegiertentag* of June, 1914, made no conciliatory gestures toward the liberal Jewish community. On the contrary, the recent hostility toward them provoked a belligerent response, devoid of remorse.[246] The *Delegiertentag* adamantly rejected the "Old Guard Zionists" whose philosophy of philanthropy for the *Ostjuden* was repugnant to the generation of Blumenfeld. The Posen Resolution of 1912 was reaffirmed; and young, aggressive Zionists who supported the new orientation toward Palestine and the radicalization of the movement were reelected.

The C.V., in turn, viewed the results of the Leipzig *Delegiertentag* as a justification of its resolution of March, 1913:

Our resolution did not cast suspicion on anybody, since we made clear-cut distinctions among the Zionists, it is apparent that we did not denounce all Zionists. . . . That this twofold classification was correct, is proven by the last Zionist *Delegiertentag*.[247]

The Jewish Community and World War I

During the month of August, 1914, the extent to which the Jews, Zionists included, had become integrated and assimilated in Germany became blatantly clear. Regardless of ideological differences, all German Jews responded to the war with a great enthusiasm and a willingness for self-sacrifice. On August 1, the day on which Russia declared war, the C.V. and the *Verband der deutschen Juden* made a joint declaration:

> In this fateful hour the fatherland calls its sons to the banners.
>
> It is self-evident that every German Jew is prepared to sacrifice his property and blood as far as duty demands.
>
> Brethren! We ask you to devote all your energies to the fatherland above and beyond the call of duty. Rush voluntarily to the banners! All of you—men and women—place every personal sacrifice, property, and money at the service of the fatherland![248]

Shortly after, Eugen Fuchs urged all German Jews to forget personal grievances and demands and serve only the interests of the fatherland:

> Now that Germany has been called to arms we must say:
>
> first comes the fatherland and its welfare. . . . *Deutschland! Deutschland ueber alles!*[249]

The Zionists, who only six weeks earlier had proclaimed their alienation from Germany, responded with equal zeal to the war effort. The *Juedische Rundschau* published a joint declaration by the ZVfD and the *Reichsverein der deutschen Juden,* which was supported by the *Kartell juedischer Verbindungen* and the *Ausschuss der juedischen Turnerschaft:*

> German Jews! In this hour we must show again that we, Jews proud of our heritage, belong to the best sons of the fatherland.

The nobility of our four-thousand-year-old history lays upon us this obligation.

We expect our youth to join the banners voluntarily and with happy hearts.

German Jews! We call on you in the tradition of Jewish obligation to place yourself in the service of the fatherland with all your heart, all your soul, and all your fortune![250]

The feverish excitement and the sudden surge of a sense of brotherhood and community gripped almost all German Jews. Ernst Simon wrote that the Jews accepted the war as an "unbelievable experience, an intoxicating happiness which enabled them to forget their complicated egos and to be able to participate in the fate of the fatherland with millions of others."[251] In a letter to the Dutch author Van Eeden, Buber defended Germany's invasion of Belgium by claiming that Belgium had broken its neutrality in allying itself with France and England, and he added: "I protest against the fact . . . that whereas all are guilty, Germany's guilt is singled out."[252] In many other speeches and articles Buber expressed the sentiment of most German Jews by defending Germany's involvement in the war.[253] Even Kurt Blumenfeld, the most radical of the young Zionists, declared that every man saw the war as his personal mission because the future of humanity depended on Germany's victory: "We nationalist Jews are imbued with the recognition that whoever remains loyal to the Jewish nation cannot be disloyal to the German fatherland."[254] The most amazing manifestation of the patriotism of German Zionists is described by Elias Auerbach. In his autobiography he relates that even the few German Zionists who had emigrated to Palestine *before* World War I did not hesitate for a moment to enlist voluntarily and make the long and difficult journey to Germany in order to fight for the fatherland.[255]

The exaggerated sense of patriotism of the German Jews was probably best expressed by Ernst Lissauer, an extreme assimilationist, who composed the "Hassgesang gegen England," soon to become the most popular German war song.[256] Similarly Weyl's "Das Niederlaendische Dankgebet" became the most popular song of the German army, and Richard Linderer's "Stolz weht die Flagge Schwarz, Weiss, Rot," became the favorite song of the German navy.[257]

Many German Jews saw the war as the beginning of a new era in which the last vestiges of anti-Semitic discrimination would disappear with the total fulfillment of emancipation. The C.V.'s goals had miraculously been realized: for the first time Jews were promoted to the rank of reserve officers in the German army and the anti-Semitic press temporarily ceased to attack Jews in view of their manifest and unconditional loyalty to Germany. For the C.V. the ultimate promise of fulfillment came with the words of the Kaiser: "I do not know parties any more, only Germans."[258] The C.V. ideology was confirmed by those Jews who had always claimed Jewish loyalty to the German nation. The general *Burgfrieden* became the symbol of the unity of all Germans in the common struggle.[259]

The war also affected relations within the German Jewish community. In view of the Zionists' patriotism and self-sacrifice, the C.V. and other anti-Zionist organizations halted their attacks against them and acknowledged their contributions to the war effort. The Zionists declared that "despite all hostilities in times of peace, we German Jews have no differences today with other Germans. We stand in this fight together as brothers."[260] For nearly four years all bitterness and strife between Zionists and anti-Zionists came to a halt.[261]

VI

Conclusion

Toward the end of 1913 Ludwig Geiger (1848–1920), a historian and editor of the *Allgemeine Zeitung des Judentums,* said of the status of the Jews in Germany:

> For us, the free-thinking German Jews, the question of assimilation does not exist; we are completely assimilated. . . . By assimilation we mean total integration into *Deutschtum,* into its nationality, language, and culture; without, however, giving up our religious beliefs. We are Germans according to our *Gesinnung* and language, yet we remain Jews. . . . Our assimilation has been completed![1]

Geiger's statement is an accurate reflection of the German Jewish community's position toward *Deutschtum* and *Judentum* prior to World War I. German Jews believed that official emancipation had destroyed the last vestiges of discrimination separating them from the German nation. The unification of Germany in 1871, completing the process of emancipation begun in 1812, not only made Jews equal in the political sense, but it also provided them with their first opportunity to share fully in German culture and civilization.

Logically and legally, Jews could dispense with all particularistic national and ethnic traits and refer to the national culture as their own; emancipation was thus from the start linked with assimilation into German culture; German Jews considered their assimilation into the German nation to be an essential and necessary process for their total integration.[2] They retained their loyalty to the Jewish religion, but only insofar as it did not interfere with adherence to *Deutschtum*.

The rise of organized political anti-Semitism, shortly after the unification of Germany, represented the first serious challenge to German Jewry's belief in emancipation and assimilation. Despite the initial shock, the majority of German Jews reaffirmed their feelings of patriotism and total devotion toward the fatherland. Anti-Semitism served to encourage them to renewed protestations of loyalty to Germany. When the attacks persisted despite their public proclamations, a few German Jewish notables decided to devise new ways of dealing with their persecutors. Professing to be fulfilling their duty as German citizens, they founded the C.V. as a defense organization to protect the honor of the German Jews.

The founders of the C.V. had witnessed the final emancipatory legislation of 1871. They were fervent believers in the slow and steady future progress of the German Jews. Although they had experienced the two waves of anti-Semitism in the 1870s and 1890s, they had also watched the wane of organized anti-Semitism in the mid-1890s, and they tended to consider anti-Semitism an evil which, with time, could be uprooted or at least subdued. In the opinion of the C.V. anti-Semitism could be combated through the dissemination of information, the refutation of anti-Jewish slander, and occasional appeal to the courts to brand the offenders publicly.[3]

The C.V. was founded by and for the German Jewish middle class. The organization was intended as an *Abwehrverein* and its initial activities differed from those of the *Verein zur Abwehr des Antisemitismus* only in the C.V.'s emphasis on public defense and exclusive Jewish membership. Since the propaganda of the C.V. was based on the cultivation of total loyalty to *Deutschtum (unbeirrte Pflege deutscher Gesinnung)*, it soon discovered that the organization had turned into a *Gesinnungsverein*. By virtue of its rapidly increasing membership the C.V. became also a meeting place for those who sought in the organization a means to identify themselves as Jews. In addition, the extensive bureaucratic network of the C.V. and its increasing power within the community gave many Jewish leaders, who had been frustrated by the Gentile public institutions and political parties, a chance to explore their organizational and political talents.[4]

In its role as the largest and most powerful organization of German Jewry, the C.V. developed an ideology that expressed the Weltanschauung of the German Jewish liberal establishment. Paragraph one of the C.V. statutes clearly stated the organization's position toward *Deutschtum*, a position that remained intact until the dissolution of the C.V. in 1938. The C.V.'s definition of Jewish identity was modified under the pressure of changing events, but until 1914 the C.V. maintained that the Jews were essentially a religious community (*Religionsgemeinschaft*). When shortly before the war Eugen Fuchs conceded that Judaism was also a "community of origin" (*Stammesgemeinschaft*),[5] he spoke of a historical fact from which no immediate practical consequences were drawn for those who considered themselves *"deutsche Staatsbuerger juedischen Glaubens."*[6]

For members of the C.V. it was always clear, at least during the period before 1914, that their primary loyalty was to *Deutschtum*, to German *Gesinnung*. Most members of the C.V., like most of the liberal assimilating German Jewish community, were ignorant of the Jewish values they were supposed to defend, but this was not a source of conflict. Ironically, the establishment of an exclusively Jewish organization strengthened their feelings of Jewish identity, even if overt manifestations of loyalty to *Judentum* were lacking. Members of the C.V. achieved a certain sense of pride and honor in their defiance of the temptations of conversion and the onslaught of the anti-Semites.

The ZVfD was the first German Jewish organization to

question the ideology of the liberal establishment. Although its founders accepted political emancipation as an inevitable and even necessary historical stage in the development of Jewish life in the Diaspora, they strongly denounced what they considered the negative consequences of emancipation— the assimilationist ideals of the liberal Jewish establishment. Unlike the liberals, the ZVfD claimed that there was a definite link between *Stamm* and nationality and that German Jews were members not only of a *Religionsgemeinschaft,* but of a *Volksgemeinschaft* as well. As a result, whereas members of the C.V. emphasized their adherence to the German nationality, the Zionists stressed their unique Jewish ethnic and national bonds. It was because these Zionist theories seemed to threaten the position of the German Jews within the German *Volksgemeinschaft* that the Association of German Rabbis reacted so strongly to the proposal of convening a Zionist Congress in Munich. The liberal establishment, which had been aiding Russian Jews for philanthropic and humanitarian reasons, was not willing to be labeled by members of the German Jewish community as having ethnic and national bonds with these Eastern Jews. The declaration by the *Protestrabbiner,* insisting that the German Jews did not honor or even consider national loyalties beyond the German borders, was primarily an explanation to the German Gentile public rather than an attack against the Zionists.

When the first generation of German Zionists declared adherence to a modified program of political Zionism, the attacks of the liberal establishment against the ZVfD ceased. Political Zionism meant that the German Zionists were trying to achieve their goals with legal means and with the consent of the international powers. Germany was one of the first countries that Herzl and the German Zionists approached for these ends. The Kaiser's friendly, although noncommital, attitude toward Zionist aims impressed the liberal Jewish community. In addition the generational experience of the first German Zionists, notably Bodenheimer, Friedemann, and Oppenheimer, had been almost identical to that of the founders of the C.V., and, like them, they believed in the continued social and political progress of the Jews in Germany. Despite adherence to Herzlian Zionism, German Zionists encouraged their ranks to participate fully in Germany's cultural and political life. Their own activity was confined to expanding the membership of the ZVfD and raising funds.

It is true that members of the first generation of German Zionists gave at least equal weight in their Weltanschauung to *Judentum* and *Deutschtum*. Their concern for things Jewish, however, such as Jewish folklore, Hasidism, and the Jewish colonies in Palestine, often remained an individual matter or the subject of interesting articles in the *Juedische Rundschau*. They did not attempt to devise, for example, even a limited cultural program in the Diaspora. Since they did not make any personal or practical application of their theory of Jewish nationalism, they were tolerated by the other Jewish liberal organizations as members of just another philanthropic group. During its first twenty years of existence the C.V., itself an organization opposed to complete Jewish submergence into German culture, viewed Zionists as allies in the common fight against total assimilation. The two organizations, with the exception of a few local disputes, maintained peaceful and even friendly relations. The C.V. leaders commended the Zionists for fostering pride and self-respect among German Jews. As for Zionist plans to colonize Palestine, the C.V. adhered to its policy of *totschweigen* and avoided unduly publicizing such projects. With regard to the *Judennot* in the East, all liberal organizations concurred with the ZVfD that it was the duty of German Jews to alleviate the plight of the *Ostjuden*. In theory the ZVfD proposed to ameliorate this condition by the establishment of a Jewish state. Since the German Zionists, however, supported Herzl's opposition to "infiltration," their policy led to the ironic result that liberal organizations such as the *Hilfsverein der deutschen Juden*, which was adamantly opposed to the creation of a Jewish state, did more to promote Jewish culture and institutions in Palestine during the first decade of the twentieth century than did the ZVfD. Since the first German Zionists also supported Herzl's opposition to cultural work by Zionists in the Diaspora, here again the ZVfD served to minimize an area of possible conflict with the liberals.

For the founding members of the C.V. as for the first generation of German Zionists it was always clear that their personal destinies were in Germany. They might evaluate *Deutschtum* and *Judentum* differently, but the result was the same for both groups—their ideologies provided them with a systematic world-view that anchored them in Germany and enabled them to see their Jewish identity as compatible with German culture. One might say that whereas the members of the C.V. were called "German citizens of the Jewish faith," the older Zionists could equally well have been called "German citizens of Jewish nationality."

The harmonious coexistence between Zionists and liberals was shattered between 1910 and 1914 by the radicalization of the second generation of German Zionists. We have discussed the fact that Kurt Blumenfeld, Richard Lichtheim, Felix Rosenblueth, and many others, were influenced by the general trend within the WZO toward practical and cultural work in Palestine and the Diaspora, by the ideas of the Democratic Fraction within Zionism and its spiritual founders Ahad Ha'Am and Martin Buber, and by the general *voelkish* ideology current in Germany. Their ideological orientation became a composite whose main features were influenced by Herzl's negation of the *Galut* and Buber's admonition to search for their own roots in *Judentum*. The result was that whereas the first generation of German Zionists had believed that they were rooted (*verwurzelt*) in Germany and had therefore the right and even the obligation to participate fully in German culture and politics, these young Zionists adhered to Blumenfeld's "uprooting" theory (*Entwurzelung*) which negated the Diaspora and concentrated all Zionist efforts on Palestine.

Blumenfeld's conflict with the liberal Jewish middle class began with a rebellion against the ideology of the older generation of German Zionists. The young Zionists very often came from the same assimilated background as their elders but their differences of Weltanschauung stemmed from differences in their generational experiences with anti-Semitism, from dissatisfaction with what the older generation had failed to accomplish, and from ideological, practical, and political transformations that had taken place during the first decade of the twentieth century within the ZVfD and the WZO. Buber's exhortations, coupled with the lessons they extracted for their Jewish purposes from the German *voelkish* movement, made the young Zionists reject all that interfered with their Zionist convictions.[7] Whereas the first generation of German Zionists had been content to wait in Germany for a charter for the *Ostjuden,* the young Zionists declared, in fact, that all who did not incorporate Palestine into their life's program were not true Zionists.

Thus the radical Zionists could not accept compromise, either with early Zionism or with the liberal establishment; they viewed *Deutschtum* and *Judentum* as incompatible, rejecting Eugen Fuchs's theory of synthesis, and tried to achieve a modicum of consistency by seeking to put their theories into practice. Their practical achievements before 1914 were threefold: (1) the formulation of a theory to express their existential needs; (2) the break with the liberals; (3) the systematic ideological indoctrination of their members and of the newly created *Turnvereine* and assorted Zionist *Wandervoegel* and clubs to the end that they should maintain a "distance" between themselves and German nationalism.

They struggled with the conflict imposed by the propagation of Zionism within the German cultural sphere. Instead of rationalizing or compartmentalizing their loyalties, the members of the Blumenfeld faction within the ZVfD decided to abandon the fervor of their elders for German nationalism and chauvinism in favor of a total commitment to *Judentum.* To achieve the same commitment from the entire ZVfD membership, a conflict was necessary with those who refused to abandon their double loyalties to *Deutschtum* and *Judentum.* In other words, one might argue that the radicalism of Blumenfeld's faction at the Posen and Leipzig *Delegiertentage* was not only the result of sincere convictions and deeply felt ideology; it was also a political move to dislodge the older generation from the leadership of the ZVfD.

As a tiny minority within a hostile Jewish community, the young Zionists could succeed only through the process of radicalization. Their conflict with the older generation of German Zionists, the C.V., and the rest of the liberal establishment was functional for the achievement of their goals. Once the conflict crystallized and the young Zionists seized positions of power within the ZVfD, the older Zionists receded into the background, and the heightened commitment of the young leadership was adopted by those members who decided to stay with the movement. This reorientation had a homogenizing effect on the eight to ten thousand Zionist members, while it made it difficult for nonradicals to join the ZVfD.[8] The goals of the Blumenfeld group were not realized in respect to emigration to Palestine.[9] Even though the Posen Resolution demanded either emigration or some other personal commitment to Palestine, it was not until the Leipzig *Delegiertentag* of 1914 that the resolution was internalized by members of the ZVfD in such a way that they might feel a conflict in not fulfilling it. The outbreak of World War I, however, suspended all questions of personal commitment to Palestine until the Weimar period. Between 1912 and 1914, the radical theories of the ZVfD served to "purify" the organization of all other positions. Those who remained within the movement were totally committed to the Zionist organization and ideology; external opposition served only to heighten their sense of internal unity.

The radicalization of the ZVfD occurred precisely when the German Jewish community was particularly militant in its loyalty to *Deutschtum*. In 1912 almost every Jewish community in Germany celebrated the one-hundreth anniversary of the edict of emancipation granted by King Friedrich Wilhelm III on March 11, 1812.[10] German Jewry was conscious and proud of its emancipation and successful acculturation. In fact, outwardly all seemed to be going well with the Jewish community: anti-Jewish discrimination seemed to have subsided and Jews became increasingly prominent in the professions—science, art, literature, and the press. The final removal of all anti-Jewish restrictions was expected in the near future and it was therefore with sincere joy and thanksgiving that German Jews professed their continued and unshaken loyalty to the fatherland.[11] These feelings are described by Hans Morgenthau:

German Jewry, being predominantly middle-class in social composition and liberal in political and philosophic outlook, shared to the full the optimistic mood of the liberal middle classes. The world as it existed before the First World War was perhaps not the best of all possible worlds, but it was certainly a good world for the middle classes, and it was bound to get better as time went on. German Jewry appeared to have a particular reason for partaking in this general optimism; for it had progressed farther and faster and against much greater odds than the general middle-class population. Within less than a century, a tiny minority, despised, disenfranchised, and confined to the ghetto, had made a creative contribution of the first order to the intellectual, moral, and economic life of Europe and this in the face of continuing disabilities and discrimination. Why should it not look to the future with optimistic anticipation?[12]

To the members of the German Jewish establishment, the radical Zionists were men who were willfully attempting to destroy all that the Jewish community had struggled to attain and dared to dream of for many decades. For the first time since the beginnings of the emancipation, members of liberal Jewish organizations felt seriously threatened not only by German chauvinism but also by radical Jewish nationalism. In the light of this dual challenge to their integrity as German citizens, they reacted swiftly and with great determination. The liberals declared publicly that for them the claim of *Deutschtum* was stronger than that of *Judentum*. The C.V. served as the main public proponent, explaining that one could form a synthesis of *Deutschtum* and *Judentum* with a decided emphasis on the first component. The vehement reaction against the Zionists by the liberals, climaxed by their formation of the *Antizionistisches Komitee,* was proof that the majority of German Jewry supported the C.V.'s point of view.

By August 1, 1914, the Zionist and anti-Zionist positions in Germany had become well defined. World War I showed, however, that the radicalization of the Zionists had not yet struck deep enough roots and that when called upon the Zionists, like the rest of the German Jewish community, felt committed to aid the fatherland.[13] The *Burgfrieden* between Zionists and anti-Zionists lasted only for the duration of the war; after 1918, the basic positions established before the war were elaborated and vigorously debated. The question of the primacy of *Deutschtum* or *Judentum* dominated the intellectual milieu of the German Jews until the Nazis decided the issue in 1933.

Appendix

Aus dem juedischen Vereinsleben

Sammy Gronemann, a well-known wit, was an important figure within the ZVfD and the WZO. In 1903 he helped found the *Schlemiel,* a satirical Zionist monthly. The following poem is a description of the various ideological and organizational factions in German Jewry as expressed in Gronemann's infamous tongue-in-cheek style.

Wie friedlich lebte man doch und wie stille
In fruehren Zeiten harmlos in der Kille!
An Aufregung war damals kein Gedanke,
Der Frack hang eingekamiert stets im Schranke,
Und nur am Schabbos trug man in der
Synagoge den Zylinder.
Des Chasans Nigen hoerte man mit Schmunzeln,
Die Predigt auch mit krit'schem Stirnenrunzeln,—
Nach Schul ward etwas noch geschmust, geprahlet,—
Dann gings nach Haus zu Kuggel und zu Schalet.
Man nahm zur Hand den Israelit,
Man gaehnte etwas, setzt' sich mued'
Zum Lesen ins gebluemte Sopha rein
Und schlief dann ein.

So hatte man sein Judentum betaetigt,
Und damit war's fuer Jedermann erledigt.

Nun hat das Judentum seit Jahren
Allmaehlich eine ganz ausserordentlich grundlegende und auf
modernen Anschauungen basierende Umwaelzung erfahren:
In allen Gemeinden, selbst den ganz kleinen,
Wimmelt es gradezu von Vereinen,
Von Philanthropen—von Reformatoren,
Und niemand bleibt da ungeschoren.
Wir hoeren von immer neuen Verbaenden,
Und niemand weisst wie das soll enden.
Vor Zeiten kannte man nur die Alliance
Jetzt gibt's gar 'ne juedische Renaissance.
Kurz. so'n lebendiges Leben, wie wir es beginnen,
Dessen koennen sich die aeltesten Leut' nicht entsinnen.

(Notabene: ich habe noch niemals gelesen
Von Leuten, die so vergesslich gewesen
Wie diese aeltesten Leute, die nie sich besinnen,
Man kann, wovon man auch will, zu reden beginnen.
Sie errinern sich niemals,—ich verfolg' es seit Jahren.
Die Zeitungen sollten sich's wirklich ersparen
Sie immer und immer wieder zu fragen.)

Na kurz und gut: in unseren Tagen
Entwickelt sich maechtig das juedische Leben:
Die schlimmsten Leutchen sind die, die "heben."
Sie heben ohne viel Federlesen
Das Kranken—,das Wohnungs—,das Irrenwesen—,
Das juedische Wissen, die Speisehaeuser,—
Den Handwerkerstand,—die juedischen Bauern,
Sie heben,—bleibt ihnen dazu noch Zeit,—
Sehr gern auf dem Lande Die Sittlichkeit
Und alle reden sie laut oder leiser
Und knoepfen Geld ab ohne Bedauern,
Andre machen dafuer in Statistik,—
Andre in Muskeln, andre in Mystik;
Dann gibt's welche, so ferne wie nah,

Die wolln 'ne oeffentlich rechtlich gesicherte Heimstaette in
    Palaestina.
Jeder darum von "unsere Leute"
Ist infolgedessen auch heute
In eins, zwei, drei, vier, fuenf, sechs, sieben Vereinen
Und muss woechentlich ein, zwei, drei, vier, fuenf, sechs
    siebenmal dorten erscheinen.

Denn im ersten Verein ein Jeder ihn kennt
An der Glocke als den leutseligen Praesident,
Im zweiten wieder macht er sich nuetze
Als ebenfalls unentbehrlichen Vice—
Im dritten aber quaelt er sich ohn' Schmollen
Mit hoechst ausfuehrlichen Protokollen,
Wogegen er bei Nummero vier
Hoechst unbeliebt ist als Kassier;
Bei fuenf, sechs und sieben darf er nie sich erfrechen
Zu fehlen, sonst wuerde man schrecklich sich raechen,—
Und bei Nummero eins haett er dann die Ehre
Zu praesidieren bei gaehnender Leere,
Was freilich kein Vergnuegen mehr waere.
So erfuellte er denn hier seine Pflicht in Stille
Und praesidiert dann dort bei gaehnender Fuelle.
Der Aufmerksame leicht gewahrt es:
Ein jeder Verein hat etwas Apartes—
Nehmen wir heute zum Beispiel nur
Den Verein fuer Geschichte und Literatur,
Da herrscht bekanntlich, wo es auch sei,
Immer und ewig ein Einerlei,—
Ein Thema nur weiss man uns zuzumuten,—
Dies Thema lautet: X und die Juden.
Dieses Thema scheint mir hoechst verfaenglich
Das Wort "Juden" hat als hoechst bedenklich
Man seit lange doch schon stets vermieden,
Und man nennt sich deutsche Staatsbuerger juedischen Glau-
    bens oder Israeliten.

Hier jedoch sagt man nur: und die Juden,
Keinen Grund hierzu kann ich vermuten!

Baldigst aendert man es drum gewiss—
Ich empfehle als den mit Recht so sehr beliebten Kom-
    promiss
(Wenn Ihr's tut,—so tut es baldigst nur!)
Den Namen: Verein fuer juedische Geschichte und Israe-
    litische Literatur.

Herr Dr. Y.—Rabbiner zumeist,—
Der seit Jahren auf "X und die Juden" reist,
Zuvoerderst sehr gelehrt uns beweist,
Dass, wer nicht genau ueber X und die Juden berichtet
Auf jeden Anspruch auf Bildung verzichtet.
Drauf hoert man halblaut rechts und links
Zustimmendes Murmeln und "Allerdings!"
Herr X.,—beweist Herr Y. sofort
Lebte von Kindheit an einem Ort,
An dem noch niemals Juden gewesen;
Darueber gibt es verschied'ne Hypothesen,
Doch alle sind falsch,—er beweist es mit Schlaeue,
Und stellt statt dessen auf eine neue.
X ist—man hoert es hoechst beklommen,—
Nie in Beruehrung mit Juden gekommen.
In allen Werken, die X. je geschrieben,
Sind die Juden drum unerwaehnt auch geblieben.
"Die Werke von X. sind drum—Sie verzeihn,
Pueckler wuerde sagen,—ganz judenrein."
Drauf herrscht im Saale weit und breit
Herzerquickende Heiterkeit;
Herr Y. nimmt darauf einen Schluck
Von Wasser zu sich, faehrt fort und—genug!
Er beweist es mit vielen Zitaten,
Dass die Juden mit X. zu tun niemals hatten.
Er schliesst dann mit einem edlen Appell
An Maennlein und Weiblein, die da zur Stell'
Dass edel der Mensch sei, hilfreich und gut,
Das laege besonders im juedischen Blut.
Und besonders schoen sei die Toleranz,
Den Antisemiten fehlte die ganz.
"Sehr richtig!" ruft man von allen Seiten,
Und niemand koenne uns das bestreiten;

Drum seien wir eingedenk unserer Mission.
Die Zeiten bessern allmaehlich sich schon,
Mit dem Antisemitismus auch sei manchmal nix,
Das beweise der Vortrag von den Juden und X.
Drauf spendet alles begeistert Applaus,
Dann geht man ins Café oder nach Haus.
Der Redner bekommt Honorar und Spesen,
Und unter den Hoerern ist Einer gewesen,
Der hat nachtraeglich das Buch gelesen
Von X, der nie Antisemit gewesen.
Gott bewahr' uns vor allem Boesen!!

II

Im zionistischen Verein,
Da wars mal wieder besonders fein.
Diesmal war naemlich wirklich was los,
Denn diesmal sprach der Dr. Moos.
Na,—Sie kennen doch Moos?
Moos aus Berlin?!—Der redet famos!
Kaum betritt er das Katheder,
Ist begeistert schon ein Jeder;—
Kaum sagt er nur: "Meine Damen und Herrn!"
Haben alle kleine Maedchen im Saal ihn so gern!—
Und zittert ihm weiter die Stimme vor Schmerz,
Gewinnt er auch aelterer Jahrgaenge Herz;—
Und spricht er beweglich in Herzens Toenen,
Zerfliesst der ganze Saal in Traenen;—
Und wenn er laechelnd die Zaehne zeigt,
Dann hat er die steinernsten Herzen erweicht;—
Und laesst er anschwellen dann seine Stimme,
In tiefster Empoerung,—in hoechstem Grimme,
Und donnert pathetisch er voller Schwung,—
Dann hat er die Maenner auch, alt und jung!
Und es erdroehnt von maecht'gem Applaus
Der "Harmonie" gefestetes Haus,
    Dem Beifall spendend ohne Ende
    Regen sich fleissig fuenfhundert Haende.

Und nun beginnt die Diskussion:
Das Wort hat Doktor Harald Kohn.

"Meine Herrschaft'n, Sie wissen, ich bin *liberal!*"
Bravo! Bravo! geht's durch den Saal.
"Und der Zionismus ist fin—ster—ste Reaktion,
Darum bin ich sein Gegner—ich, Doktor Kohn!!"
Sehr gut! Vorzueglich! man allseitig rief,
"Sie wissen, Herrschaften, ich bin *Konservativ!*"
Fortfaehrt mit der Begeisterung Ton
Der treffliche Redner der Opposition.
"Der Zionismus, wie ich seh',
Widerspricht der alten Messiasidee!
Und er will nichts wissen von unsrer Mission,—
Darum bin ich sein Gegner, ich Harald Kohn!"
Von stuermischem Jubel unterbrochen,
Hat er nach Kurzem weitergesprochen:
"Meine Herrschaften, Sie wissen, ich bin *Kosmopolit!*
Was zur Evidenz ein jeder schon daraus sieht,
Dass ich meine Kinder hab' taufen lassen.
Der Zionismus; der redet von Rassen,—
Ich weiss nichts von Rassen und nichts von Nation,—
Darum bin ich sein Gegner,—der Doktor Kohn!"
Beifall erscholl drauf aus allen Ecken—
Der Redner begann sich hoeher zu recken:
"Sie wissen, Herrschaften, ich bin *national!*"
Lauter Beifall durchtobt' da den Saal.
"Deutsch—national, damit keiner sich irrt,—
Seit gestern bin ich naturalisiert!
Der Zionismus predigt 'ne internationale Mission,—
Darum bin ich sein Gegner, ich Harald Kohn!"
    Drauf beifallspendend ohne Ende
    Regen sich fleissig fuenfhundert Haende.

Jetzt stand dort oben auf der Tribuene,—
Ein langer, baumstarker Kerl,—ein Huene,
Der zur groessten Verwund'rung von Jedermann
In Fisteltoenen zu pipsen begann:
"Wenn der Zionismus was Gutes wolle,
Sei's noetig, dass man ihm Achtung zolle,—
Dagegen waere das ganz verkehrt,
Falls er etwas Schlimmes begehrt.

Der Doktor Moos haette ihm sehr imponiert,—
Aber Doktor Kohn haette auch manches angefuehrt,—
Und kurz und gut,—so piepst er emphatisch,—
Er staende zu der Sache sympathisch!
    Und beifallspendend ohne Ende
    Regen sich fleissig fuenfhundert Haende.

Darauf erklaert nun auf der Tribuene
Ein Herr mit weisheitsvoller Miene,
Der also seinen Spruch verkuendet,
Dass er die Bewegung sehr annehmbar findet,
Nur muesse sie sich aendern in manchem Stueck.
Der Name schon schrecke viele zurueck
Und viele blieben nur deshalb weg,
Weil ihnen unsympathisch der Zweck;
Man setze sich aus dem Hass und dem Spotte,—
Doch bitter not taete uns eine Flotte!
Kurz,—Deutschland eine Flotte zu schenken,
Da wuerde kein Israelit sich bedenken,
Er hoffe deshalb, man sehe es ein,—
Und aendre den Namen,—die Muehe sei klein,—
In "Deutsch-israelitscher Flottenverein."
Dem wuerde auch er mit Vergnuegen sich weihn,—
So koennte der Zionismus bluehn und gedeihn."
    Drauf beifallspendend ohne Ende
    Regen sich fleissig fuenfhundert Haende.

Nachdem die Debatte so gruendlich erschoepft,
Man Ein'gen den Schekel auch abgeknoepft,
Bekam als besondren Hochgenuss
Herr Dr. Moos das Wort zum Schluss:
Er dankt er allen, die heut' erschienen,
Und der hohen und heiligen Sache dienen,—
Dann nimmt vor mit bitt'rem Hohn
Die Redner aus der Diskussion,—
Vor allem Doktor Harald Kohn.
Mit von edlem Unwillen zitternder Stimme,—
Mit von Wehmut und Mitleid gemildertem Grimme
Stellt den besagten Kohn er dar

Als Idiot, als Dummkopf, als Barbar,—
Als moralisch und geistig verwachsen und schief
(Natuerlich alles nur objektiv!),
Dass man ihn allseitig schon verachtet
Und aus seiner Naehe zu kommen trachtet.
Viel besser geht's dem sympathischen Huenen,
Moos fertigt ihn ab mit laechelnden Mienen,
Zeigt so konziliant sich, so wenig fanatisch,—
Der Huene wird noch etwas mehr sympathisch.
Was betrifft die Flottenvereinsanregung,
Verspricht Dr. Moos ernsthafte Anregung.
Dann wendet er sich zum Schluss an die Damen,
Die ja so ueberaus zahlreich kamen,—
Spricht von juedischer Frau, von Sabbatlichtern,
Von juedischen Muettern, von Bildern und Dichtern,
Von grausigen Aengsten, vom Mene Tekel,—
Kurz, er will auch von ihnen den Schekel.—
Am Ende kann er sich's nicht verkneifen,
Die Versammlung im Ganzen noch anzugreifen.
Es bereite ihm doch einigen Graus
Der ewig fortgesetzte Applaus.
Dass, ob einer rede fuer oder gegen,
Sich alle Haende zum Beifall stets regen,—
Das waere denn doch etwas reichlich naiv,
Das sei ja kindlich, betruebe ihn tief.
Das zeuge von wenig politischer Reife,—
So dass er auf den Applaus jetzt pfeife,
Und darum wuerde viel besser es passen,
Von jetzt an das Klatschen gaenzlich zu lassen.
  Drauf Beifall spendend ohne Ende
  Regen sich fleissig fuenfhundert Haende.

                              S.[ammy] G.[ronemann]

Schlemiel, Illustriertes Juedisches Witzblatt, no. 1 (January 1, 1905), pp. 4—5 and *Schlemiel, Illustriertes Juedisches Witzblatt*, no. 2 (February 1, 1905), pp. 16—17.

Abbreviations

ALBI	Archives of the Leo Baeck Institute, New York
AZdJ	*Allegemeine Zeitung des Judentums*
BLBI	*Bulletin des Leo Baeck Instituts*
CAHJP	Central Archives for the History of the Jewish People, Jerusalem
CVZ	*Centralverein-Zeitung*
CZA	Central Zionist Archives, Jerusalem
HJ	*Historia Judaica*
HYB	*Herzl Year Book*
IDR	*Im Deutschen Reich*
JR	*Juedische Rundschau*
JS	*Der Juedische Student*
JSS	*Jewish Social Studies*
KCB	*K.C. Blaetter*
LBI	Leo Baeck Institute
LBIYB	*Leo Baeck Institute Year Book*
MDIGB	*Mitteilungen des Deutsch-Israelitischen Gemeindebunde*
MDIOME	*Mitteilungsblatt des Irgun Oley Merkaz Europa*

NJM   *Neue Juedische Monatshefte*
PAJHS   *Publications of the American Jewish Historical Society*
ZfDSdJ   *Zeitschrift fuer Demographie und Statistik der Juden*

Notes

Chapter I

1. The term "German Jewish community" will be used throughout in a very general way to include all the *Gemeinden* and organizations of the German Jews. As will become apparent, there was no cohesive "German Jewish community" during the period under discussion.
2. Koppel S. Pinson, *Modern Germany, Its History and Civilization*, p. 83. For a detailed account see Jacob Toury, *Mehuma u'Mevukha b'Mahapekhat 1848*.
3. Toury, *Mehuma*, p. 64.
4. See Nahum N. Glatzer, "Leopold Zunz and the Revolution of 1848," *Leo Baeck Institute Year Book* (hereafter cited as *LBIYB*), vol. 5 (1960), p. 124.
5. Jacob Toury, *Die Politischen Orientierungen der Juden in Deutschland*, pp. 47 ff.
6. Martin Philippson, *Neueste Geschichte des juedischen Volkes*, 1:300.
7. *Allgemeine Zeitung des Judentums* (hereafter cited as *AZdJ*) (March, 1848), p. 204.
8. Glatzer, "Leopold Zunz and the Revolution," p. 126. See also Nahum N. Glatzer, ed., *Leopold and Adelheid Zunz: An Account in Letters 1815–1885*.
9. See Reinhard Ruerup, "Jewish Emancipation and Bourgeois Society," *LBIYB*, vol. 14 (1969), p. 68.
10. See Ismar Elbogen, *A Century of Jewish Life*, p. 4.
11. For a good discussion of the revolution and its aftermath, see Friedrich Meinecke, *1848, Eine Saeckularbetrachtung*.
12. Philippson, *Neueste Geschichte*, 1:300.

13. See Salo W. Baron, "The Impact of the Revolution of 1848 on Jewish Emancipation," *Jewish Social Studies* 11, no. 3 (July, 1949), p. 215.

14. See Moshe Rinott, "Gabriel Riesser—Fighter for Jewish Emancipation," *LBIYB*, vol. 7 (1962), p. 26.

15. *Juedisches Lexikon*, s.v. "Revolutionen im 19. Jhdt."

16. See Veit Valentin, *Geschichte der deutschen Revolution von 1848–1849*.

17. *Juedisches Lexikon*, s.v. "Revolutionen im 19. Jhdt."

18. Pinson, *Modern Germany*, p. 102.

19. See Ernest Hamburger, *Juden im oeffentlichen Leben Deutschlands*, p. 24.

20. Ernest Hamburger, "Jews in Public Service under the German Monarchy," *LBIYB*, vol. 9 (1964), p. 217.

21. For the events leading up to this reaction see Eleonore Sterling, *Er ist wie Du*, p. 192.

22. Hamburger, "Jews in Public Service," p. 217.

23. Wanda Kampmann, *Deutsche und Juden*, pp. 214 ff.

24. See Philippson, *Neueste Geschichte*, 1:329 ff.

25. Elbogen, *A Century of Jewish Life*, p. 13.

26. *Juedisches Lexikon*, s.v. "Deutschland: Rechtsverhaeltnisse der deutschen Juden."

27. Hamburger, "Jews in Public Service," p. 220.

28. Ismar Freund, ed., *Die Emanzipation der Juden in Preussen, Urkundenband*, p. 522.

29. See Ismar Freund, *Die Emanzipation der Juden in Preussen*, pp. 252 ff.

30. See Adolf Kober, "Jewish Communities in Germany from the Age of the Enlightenment to the Destruction by the Nazis," *Jewish Social Studies* 9, no. 3 (July, 1947), p. 198.

31. See Gabriel Riesser, *Gesammelte Schriften*, 4:35.

32. See Ismar Elbogen, *Geschichte der Juden in Deutschland*, p. 267.

33. Ibid., p. 268.

34. Ibid., pp. 268–69. For further details see Felix Theilhaber, *Der Untergang der deutschen Juden*, pp. 53 ff. See also Arthur Ruppin, *The Jews of Today*, pp. 96–97.

35. Jakob Segall, *Die beruflichen und sozialen Verhaeltnisse der Juden in Deutschland*, p. 3.

36. See H. G. Heymann, "Die Lage der Juden in Deutschland," *Juedische Rundschau*, no. 50 (December 13, 1907), pp. 531, 532.

37. For details see Kurt Zielenziger, *Juden in der deutschen Wirtschaft*.

38. For exact figures see Segall, *Die beruflichen*, pp. 26 ff.

39. Ernest Hamburger, "One Hundred Years of Emancipation," *LBIYB*, vol. 14 (1969), p. 14.

40. Hamburger, "Jews in Public Service," pp. 223 ff.

41. It should be pointed out that the various German states devised their own rules concerning positions open to Jews. Thus in Bavaria, a Jew could become an army officer even before 1914; he could also hold positions in the higher courts. One of the means for excluding Jews from the higher courts in Prussia was the provision that any position

from *Landesgerichtspraesident* up was considered administrative, thus open only to Christians.

42. See Eleonore Sterling, "Jewish Reactions to Jew-hatred in the First Half of the Nineteenth Century," *LBIYB*, vol. 3 (1958), p. 121.

43. See Toury, *Mehuma*, pp. 13–14.

44. Theilhaber, *Der Untergang*, p. 116.

45. When applied to the Jewish community, the term "liberal" in this monograph does not refer to a political orientation in the period under discussion unless specifically stipulated or unless it is clear from the context. Rather, the word "liberal" refers to a particular religious segment of the Jewish population in Germany. Liberal Jews comprised the bulk of the German Jewish population and were characterized by a religious orientation which rejected the extremes of religious conservatism (orthodoxy) as well as the extreme reformist group (*Reformgemeinde zu Berlin*).

46. See Toury, *Mehuma*, pp. 65 ff.

47. Quoted by Toury, *Die Politischen Orientierungen*, p. 150.

48. See Manfred Saalheimer, "Ueber eine oeffentlich rechtliche Gesamtorganisation der deutschen Juden" (Ph.D diss., University of Wuerzburg, n.d.).

49. The *Gemeinden* consisted of those registered as Jews whose taxes went to the coffers of the Jewish community. However, those registered did not necessarily consider themselves Jews or even as affiliated with the *Gemeinde*.

50. Kurt Wilhelm, "The Jewish Community in the Post-Emancipation Period," *LBIYB*, vol. 2 (1957), p. 48.

51. See Ahron Sandler, "Die Gesamtorganisation der deutschen Juden," Leo Baeck Institute (hereafter cited as LBI), New York, File C347. Parts of this manuscript have been translated and published. See *LBIYB*, vol. 2 (1957), pp. 76 ff. For the lack of official concern with the organization of German Jewry see also Marjorie Lamberti, "The Prussian Government and the Jews. Official Behaviour and Policy-Making in the Wilhelminian Era," *LBIYB*, vol. 17 (1972), pp. 5–17.

52. Sandler, "Die Gesamtorganisation," p. 15.

53. Philippson, *Neueste Geschichte*, 1:362.

54. Wilhelm, "The Jewish Community," pp. 60–61.

55. See Salo W. Baron, "Aspects of the Jewish Communal Crisis in 1848," *Jewish Social Studies* 14, no. 2 (April 1952), pp. 99–144.

56. Wilhelm, "The Jewish Community," p. 61.

57. See *Die Juedischen Gemeinden und Vereine in Deutschland*, p. 60.

58. *Das Deutsche Judentum, Seine Parteien und Organisationen*, p. 58.

59. See *Zion* 19 (1954): 171–72.

60. Saalheimer, "Ueber eine oeffentlich rechtliche Gesamtorganisation," p. 6.

61. *The Jewish Encyclopedia*, s.v. "Gemeindebund, Deutsch–Israelitischer."

62. See *Mitteilungen des Deutsch-Israelitischen Gemeindebund*, November, 1898.

63. Wilhelm Neumann, "Der Deutsch-Israelitischer Gemeindebund," *Das deutsche Judentum*, p. 59.

64. See *The Jewish Encyclopedia*, s.v. "Gemeindebund, Deutsch—Israelitischer."

65. Philippson, *Neueste Geschichte*, 2: 3.

66. See Pinson, *Modern Germany*, pp. 156 ff.

67. See Sir John H. Clapham, *The Economic Development of France and Germany, 1815–1914.*

68. Philippson, *Neueste Geschichte*, 2: 4 ff.

69. For a detailed analysis of the origin of the term anti-Semitism, see Alex Bein, "Der moderne Antisemitismus und seine Deutung fuer die Judenfrage," *Vierteljahreshefte fuer Zeitgeschichte* (October 1958), pp. 340 ff. Salo Baron in his *Social and Religious History of the Jews* (1937), 2:287, mentions Ernest Renan as a possible originator of this term.

70. The book was first published in 1873. By 1879 it was in its twelfth printing. For a detailed description and analysis of Marr's ideas, see Paul W. Massing, *Rehearsal for Destruction*, pp. 6 ff.

71. Philippson, *Neueste Geschichte*, 2: 11.

72. See Konstantin Frantz, *Der Nationalliberalismus und die Judenherrschaft.*

73. See Rudolf Meyer, *Politische Gruender und die Korruption in Deutschland.*

74. For an analysis of Lagarde, see Fritz Stern, *The Politics of Cultural Despair.*

75. See Kurt Wawrzinek, *Die Entstehung der deutschen Antisemitenparteien (1873–1890).*

76. Massing, *Rehearsal for Destruction*, p. 17.

77. Toury, *Die Politischen Orientierungen*, p. 174.

78. See Walter Frank, *Hofprediger Adolf Stoecker und die Christlichsoziale Bewegung.*

79. See Hans von Gerlach, *Vom deutschen Antisemitismus*, p. 146.

80. See *AZdJ*, no. 41 (October 7, 1879), p. 647.

81. Simon Dubnow, *Weltgeschichte des Juedischen Volkes*, 10:20. The name of the organization was later changed to "Deutscher Reformverein."

82. This warning by the *Frankfurter Zeitung* was reprinted in the *AZdJ*, no. 42 (October 15, 1879), p. 664.

83. *AZdJ*, no. 52 (December 23, 1879), p. 825.

84. Waldemar Gurian, "Antisemitism in Modern Germany," in *Essays on Antisemitism*, p. 230.

85. Hans Liebeschuetz, "Treitschke and Mommsen on Jewry and Judaism," *LBIYB*, vol. 7 (1962), p. 173. See also Heinrich von Treitschke, *Historisch Politische Aufsaetze*, 7th ed., 3: 493 ff.

86. See Walter Boehlich, ed., *Der Berliner Antisemitismusstreit*, p. 242.

87. See Michael Meyer, "Great Debate on Antisemitism," *LBIYB*, vol. 11 (1966), p. 144.

88. Liebeschuetz, "Treitschke," p. 171.

89. Heinrich von Treitschke, "Unsere Aussichten," *Preussische Jahrbuecher* (November, 1879).

90. Boehlich, *Der Berliner*, pp. 9–11.

91. Ibid.

92. Treitschke did not discuss the *History* as a whole and was referring mainly to volume 11 which dealt with the nineteenth century. See Reuwen Michael, "Graetz contra Treitschke," *Bulletin des Leo Baeck Instituts* (hereafter cited as *BLBI*), no. 16 (1961), p. 305.

93. Boehlich, *Der Berliner*, pp. 8–10.

94. Heinrich Treitschke, *Ein Wort ueber unser Judentum.*

95. For a list of replies see Boehlich, *Der Berliner*, p. 244, and Josef Meisel, *Heinrich Graetz*, p. 128, n. 57.

96. See Michael, "Graetz contra Treitschke," pp. 308 ff. See also Zvi Graetz, in *Darkei Ha'Historia Ha'Yehudit*, for an annotated translation of the essay in Hebrew.

97. See Boehlich, *Der Berliner*, pp. 26–28.

98. Ibid., p. 29.

99. The article was entitled "Herr Graetz und sein Judentum."

100. Boehlich, *Der Berliner*, pp. 38 ff.

101. Heinrich Graetz, "Mein letztes Wort an Professor von Treitschke," (December 28, 1879), in Boehlich, *Der Berliner* pp. 45 ff.

102. Boehlich, *Der Berliner*, pp. 50 ff.

103. Meyer, "Great Debate," p. 156.

104. See Reuwen Michael, "Graetz and Hess," *LBIYB*, vol. 9 (1964), pp. 91–121.

105. Ettinger, "Introduction," *Darkei Ha'Historia*, p. 29.

106. Harry Bresslau, "Zur Judenfrage," in Boehlich, *Der Berliner*, pp. 52 ff.

107. Hermann Cohen, "Ein Bekenntnis zur Judenfrage," *Juedische Schriften*, 2: 85–86.

108. See Meisel, *Heinrich Graetz*, p. 115.

109. Meyer, "Great Debate," p. 157.

110. Manuel Joel, "Offener Brief an Heinrich von Treitschke," in Boehlich, *Der Berliner*, pp. 13 ff.

111. See *AZdJ*, no. 3 (January 20, 1880), pp. 36–37.

112. Moritz Lazarus, *Was Heisst National?*

113. See Hermann Cohen, "Ein Bekenntnis" in *Juedische Schriften* 2 as well as *AZdJ*, no. 10 (March 9, 1880), pp. 148–49, and *AZdJ*, no. 11 (March 16, 1880), pp. 161–64. For a detailed analysis see Hans Liebeschuetz, *Das Judentum im deutschen Geschichtsbild von Georg Simmel zu Franz Rosenzweig.*

114. Harry Bresslau, "Zur Judenfrage," in Boehlich, *Der Berliner*, pp. 52 ff.

115. See Toury, *Die Politischen Orientierungen*, "Appendix C," pp. 351 ff. This number includes baptized Jews.

116. See Ludwig Bamberger, *Deutschtum und Judentum.*

117. *AZdJ*, no. 48 (November 30, 1880), pp. 753–57, and *AZdJ*, no. 50 (December 14, 1880), pp. 787–89.

118. See *AZdJ*, no. 44 (October 28, 1879); *AZdJ*, no. 52 (December 23, 1879) and *AZdJ*, no. 46 (November 16, 1880).

119. Toury, *Die Politischen Orientierungen*, pp. 170, 175.

120. Elbogen, *Geschichte*, p. 294.

121. See Uriel Tal, *Yahadut v'Naẓrut ba'Reich ha'Sheni 1870–1914*, pp. 32–33 and p. 33, n. 44.

122. See *AZdJ*, no. 50 (December 9, 1879) and *AZdJ*, no. 1 (January 6, 1880), p. 19.

123. See *AZdJ*, no. 49 (December 2, 1879), pp. 770–71 and *AZdJ*, no. 50 (December 9, 1879), pp. 785–87.

124. Dubnow, *Weltgeschichte*, 10: 25.

125. See Tal, *Yahadut v'Nazrut*, "Appendix," pp. 253–55.

126. Dubnow, *Weltgeschichte*, 10: 25–26.

127. See Moritz Lazarus, "An die deutschen Juden," in *Treu und Frei*, pp. 159–60.

128. Paul Rieger, *Ein Vierteljahrhundert im Kampf um das Recht und die Zukunft der deutschen Juden*, p. 8.

129. Moritz Lazarus, "Unser Standpunkt" in *Treu und Frei*, pp. 117 ff.

130. Ibid., pp. 154–55.

131. Meyer's explanation ("Great Debate," p. 169) that the committee stopped its work because "the year 1881 brought relative quiet" and because the "Jewish question began to recede from public consciousness" seems inconsistent with the facts. In April, 1881, an anti-Semitic petition signed by 250,000 people was presented to Bismarck. It made a great impression on Jews and Gentiles alike. In addition, the year 1881 saw the outbreak of riots against Jews in Berlin.

132. MDIGB, "An unsere Glaubensgenossen," December, 1880.

133. Ibid.

134. Meyer, "Great Debate," p. 164.

135. See Louis Maretzki, *Geschichte des Ordens Bnei Briss in Deutschland 1882–1907*.

136. Ibid.

137. Alfred Goldschmidt, "Der Orden Bnei Briss," *Das Deutsche Judentum*, p. 48.

138. Ibid.

139. Maretzki, *Geschichte des Ordens*, p. 136.

140. Massing, *Rehearsal for Destruction*, p. 39.

141. Ibid., p. 40. Dubnow, *Weltgeschichte*, 10: 37 cites the number of signatures as 300,000; Wawrzinek, *Die Entstehung*, p. 38, n. 24, cites 225,000.

142. Massing, *Rehearsal for Destruction*, p. 44.

143. Hamburger, "One Hundred Years," p. 24.

144. Wawrzinek, *Die Entstehung*, p. 36, n. 15.

145. Quoted in Adolph Asch, *Geschichte des K.C.*, p. 32.

146. Hamburger, "One Hundred Years," p. 24.

147. See Alex Bein, *Theodore Herzl*, p. 40.

148. Elbogen, *Geschichte der Juden*, p. 296.

149. Asch, *Geschichte des K.C.*, p. 36.

150. Kartell Convent, "Zur Errichtung eines K.C. Heimes in Berlin" (1919), Central Archives for the History of the Jewish People (hereafter cited as CAHJP), Freund Archive P2/Me/19.

151. Quoted from Adolph Asch and Johanna Philippson, "Self-Defense at the Turn of the Century: The Emergence of the K.C.," *LBIYB*, vol. 3 (1958), p. 123.

152. Ibid., pp. 124–25.

153. CAHJP, Freund Archive P2/Me/19.

154. Ibid. At the end of World War I the K.C. included approximately twenty local fraternities with a total membership of 1,500, of whom 300 lived in Berlin. Their success was enhanced by the fact that other German youth organizations, notably the *Wandervogel*, were strongly influenced by the anti-Semitic currents. The Jewish youth that had been discriminated against during the years at the gymnasium was more than willing, upon graduation, to turn to the Jewish fraternities at the universities. By 1910 Jewish high school students began to organize their own *Wandervogel* groups which in turn prepared them for the Jewish fraternities. Cf. *K.C.-Blaetter*, nos. 7/8 (July/August 1919). See also Walter Z. Laqueur, "The German Youth Movement and the Jewish Question," *LBIYB*, vol. 6 (1961), pp. 193–205.

155. Robert Weltsch in his introduction to *LBIYB*, vol. 3 (1958), p. xxiii.

156. Asch and Philippson, "Self-Defense at the Turn of the Century," p. 135.

157. See the memoirs of Max Kollenscher and Dr. Spiro, LBI, Jerusalem.

158. Contrary to the exclusive "corps," which admitted only the sons of the aristocracy, the *Burschenschaften* had been much more liberal until the 1870s.

159. Asch and Philippson, "Self-Defense at the Turn of the Century," p. 132.

160. Franz Oppenheimer describes well the expectation and excitement of the young students who had been raised on the stories and anecdotes of their parents. See Franz Oppenheimer, *Erlebtes, Erstrebtes, Erreichtes*, p. 79.

161. See Bein, *Theodore Herzl*, pp. 40–42. Franz Oppenheimer, a first rate fencer, also resigned his membership in his fraternity for the same reasons. See Oppenheimer, *Erlebtes*, p. 81.

162. Asch and Philippson, "Self-Defense at the Turn of the Century," p. 134.

163. The term "assimilation" has been much discussed, yet there is no clear-cut definition of the term. Certainly one must distinguish between the slow and perhaps inevitable process of acculturation and the abandonment of all Jewish identity. In our analysis we do not wish to suggest a specific sociological definition of assimilation. Rather, the word throughout this book is used loosely to point to the complex process of shedding certain Jewish characteristics—primarily national characteristics—while at the same time adopting aspects of German culture. In a certain sense, the whole book is devoted to a portrayal of German Jewry's struggle to find a balance between Jewish identity and German culture and German national values.

164. Georg Herlitz (compiler and editor), "Organisatorische Daten zur Geschichte der Zionistischen Studentenbewegung in Deutschland," Central Zionist Archives (hereafter cited as CZA), Jerusalem.

165. See Bruno Weil, "Speech Held at the American Jewish K.C. Fraternity," November 21, 1957, LBI, New York, file no. 1033.

166. See Walter Gross, "The Zionist Students' Movement," *LBIYB*, vol. 4 (1959), pp. 144–47.

167. This volume was intended as a handbook of refutations of the slanders found in the *Antisemitenkatechismus.*
168. Because of this activity it was often called "Judenschutztruppe."
169. Rieger, *Ein Vierteljahrhundert,* p. 12.

Chapter II

1. Various references spell the name "Zentralverein." The accepted form, however, is that given here.
2. Primary as well as secondary sources on the history, organization, and ideology of the C.V. are sorely lacking. The only contemporary account of its early history is Paul Rieger's fragmentary *Ein Vierteljahrhundert im Kampf um das Recht und die Zukunft der deutschen Juden.* Until recently the secondary sources all dealt with its history and techniques of defense after 1918 without devoting much attention to ideology and organization. The only exceptions are two Ph.D. dissertations which deal with the ideology of the C.V. (as well as other German Jewish organizations) during the Weimar Republic: see Ruth Louise Pierson, "German Jewish Identity during the Weimar Republic" (Department of History, Yale University, 1970), and Sidney M. Bolkosky, "The Distorted Image: German Jewish Perceptions of Germans and Germany, 1918–1935" (Department of History, State University of New York at Binghamton, 1973). For a published account see Eva Reichmann's excellent article "Der Bewusstseinswandel der deutschen Juden," in *Deutsches Judentum in Krieg und Revolution 1916–1923,* Werner E. Mosse and Arnold Paucker, eds, pp. 511–612. The most important study on the history of the C.V. during Weimar is Arnold Paucker, *Der juedische Abwehrkampf,* 2nd ed., 1969. See also Reiner Bernstein, "Zwischen Emanzipation und Antisemitismus–Die Publizistik der deutschen Juden am Beispiel der C.V.-Zeitung ...1924–1933" (Ph.D. diss., Department of History, University of Berlin, 1969) and Brigitte Klein, "Die C.V. Zeitung der Jahrgaenge 1925–1935, zum Problem des Selbstverstaendnisses deutscher Juden" (master's thesis, University of Frankfurt am Main, 1969). The only published account of the early history of the C.V. is Ismar Schorsch's *Jewish Reactions to German Anti-Semitism, 1870–1914,* which deals primarily with its defense tactics. An overlapping analysis is Sanford Ragin's Ph.D. dissertation "Jewish Responses to Anti-Semitism in Germany, 1870–1914" (Department of the History of Ideas, Brandeis University, 1972). This chapter explores the early organizational structure and ideological roots of the C.V.
3. Koppel S. Pinson, *Modern Germany, Its History and Civilization,* p. 285.
4. Peter Pulzer, *The Rise of Political Anti-Semitism in Germany and Austria,* p. 118.
5. Quoted in Paul W. Massing, *Rehearsal for Destruction,* p. 66.
6. Massing, *Rehearsal for Destruction,* p. 66.
7. Pulzer, *The Rise of Political Anti-Semitism,* p. 119. In the Reichstag elections the Conservative party won seventy-two seats.
8. Massing, *Rehearsal for Destruction,* p. 71.

9. Ibid.
10. Ibid., pp. 92 ff.
11. By the end of 1892 it had become obvious that the anti-Semites would gain a large number of seats at the next Reichstag.
12. Rieger, *Ein Vierteljahrhundert*, p. 13.
13. [Raphael Loewenfeld], *Schutzjuden oder Staatsbuerger? Von einem Staatsbuerger.*
14. One of the first public organs to react to the petition of the Berlin community was *Selbst-Emancipation*. See the mocking editorial "Reichs Schutzjuden" in *Selbst-Emancipation*, no. 1 (January 15, 1893), p. 223.
15. Rahel Straus, *Wir lebten in Deutschland*, p. 61.
16. Ibid., pp. 61–62.
17. Shortly after Loewenfeld's brochure, a pamphlet that was published in Berlin was intended as a direct reply. The author, who opposed anti-Semitism, counseled German Jewry to rely less on the Freisinn parties and to support the so-called Mittelparteien and the king. It ended with the warning: "Wenn das Judentum noch weiter geht und sich die verscherzten Sympathien der Mittelparteien wieder zu erobern sucht, wenn es eine reinliche Scheidelinie zwischen sich und die Zeitungen zieht, die man mit dem Collectivnamen 'Judenblaetter' zu bezeichnen gewohnt ist, wenn es sich in allen nationalen Fragen noch nationaler erweist, als die anderen Staatsbuerger, wenn es das berechtigte Nationalgefuehl nicht mit der Lauge von hohn und Spott, die freisinniger Querkoepfigkeit entspringen, uebergiesst, dann wird es wieder dazu beitragen, die staerkste Schranke gegen die reaktionaeren Bestrebungen aufzurichten, die mit dem Antisemitismus hand in hand gehen. Die Juden muessen sich der ueberwiegenden Mehrzahl nach zu den Grundsaetzen eines deutsch-nationalen Programms bekennen, ja was die *berechtigten* Postulate der deutschsozialen partei betrifft, sogar zu dem Programm derjenigen, die auf ihr Verderben ausgehen, sie muessen ihnen sozusagen den Wind aus den Segeln nehmen. Koennen sie dies nicht und folgen sie weiter der Fahne Eugen Richters, den sie ja bis jetzt die 'grossartigsten Erfolge' zu verdanken haben, dann sehen wir sehr schwarz in die Zukunft." See Fr. v. d. Gozel, *Die Juden und die Politischen Parteien. Eine Antwort an den Verfasser der Schrift: "Schutzjuden oder Staatsbuerger?,"* p. 17.
18. [Loewenfeld], *Schutzjuden oder Staatsbuerger?* pp. 3, 11.
19. Ibid., pp. 26 ff.
20. Martin Mendelssohn, "Die Pflicht der Selbstverteidigung," *Jahresbericht des Vorsitzenden in der ersten ordentlichten Generalversammlung des Centralvereins deutscher Staatsbuerger juedischen Glaubens,* p. 12.
21. Rieger, *Ein Vierteljahrhundert*, p. 16.
22. Ibid., p. 17.
23. Ibid.
24. Ibid., p. 18.
25. Ibid., p. 15.
26. For their editorials on the pamphlet in January 1893, see *Die Volkszeitung, Nationalzeitung, Muenchener Neuesten Nachrichten, Leipziger Tageblatt,* and the *Berliner Zeitung*.

27. Quoted by Ernest Hamburger, in "One Hundred Years of Emancipation," *LBIYB*, vol. 14 (1969), p. 24.

28. Marjorie Lamberti points out that "the idea of a Jewish organization like the Center party was suggested by Dr. Isidor Kastan, a journalist, in January, 1893." See her "The Attempt to Form a Jewish Bloc: Jewish Notables and Politics in Wilhelminian Germany," *Central European History* 3:1/2 (March/June, 1970). See also Jacob Toury, "Attempts at the Establishment of a Central Organization of German Jews (1893–1920)," *LBIYB*, vol. 13 (1968), pp. 57 ff.

29. The *Comité* was founded at the end of January, 1893, with the approval of the *Verein zur Abwehr des Antisemitismus*. Its purpose was to fight anti-Semitism through every feasible legal means. See Schorsch, *Jewish Reactions to German Anti-Semitism*, p. 113, as well as p. 241, n. 37.

30. Rieger, *Ein Vierteljahrhundert*, p. 18.

31. Mendelssohn, *Die Pflicht*, p. 7.

32. See CAHJP, 124/la/1.

33. *C.V. Kalender fuer das Jahr 1929*, p. 34.

34. Centralverein deutscher Staatsbuerger juedischen Glaubens, "Ein Aufruf" (May, 1893) CAHJP, TD/24.

35. See *Vossische Zeitung* (November 19, 1893), p. 2.

36. See *Juedische Wochenschrift* (October 20, 1893).

37. Rieger, *Ein Vierteljahrhundert*, p. 25.

38. See Maximilian Horwitz, "Ehrenpflichten," *Vortrag gehalten im Centralverein deutscher Staatsbuerger juedischen Glaubens am 20. Januar, 1898*. Archives of the Leo Baeck Institute, New York, pp. 4–5.

39. C.V., *Satzung des Centralvereins deutscher Staatsbuerger juedischen Glaubens E.V., 1893*. CAHJP, TD/24.

40. Horwitz, "Ehrenpflichten," p. 16.

41. Ibid.

42. See Eugen Fuchs, "Referat ueber die Stellung des Centralvereins zum Zionismus," in *Um Deutschtum und Judentum*, p. 236.

43. Such as Eugen Fuchs's employment of *Stamm* as a component of *Judentum*. See my subsequent analysis.

44. *K.C. Blaetter*, no. 3 (August 5, 1927), p. 49.

45. Cf. *K.C. Blaetter* nos. 7/8 (July/August, 1919).

46. See Horwitz, "Ehrenpflichten," pp. 1–16.

47. Ibid., p. 2. For a similar evaluation of Jewish alternatives in the face of anti-Semitism see Gustav Levinstein, *Zur Ehre des Judentums* (1911). Archives of the Leo Baeck Institute, New York. On the tenth anniversary of the Centralverein, Levinstein composed the following poem which echoes Horwitz's speech:

> Zehn Jahre sind es an dem heutigen Tage [1903]
> Da sich die Ueberzeugung laut brach Bahn,
> Dass nicht mit Schweigen, nicht mit leerer Klage
> Der Kampf zu fuehren gegen Trug und Wahn,
> Dass wir vereinet nicht mit Furcht und Bangen
> Den Nacken beugen, dass der Blick nicht fleht,
> Dass wir nicht bitten, nein, dass wir verlangen,
> Dass man uns wahr' des Rechtes Majestaet.

48. Ludwig Foerder, *Die Stellung des Centralvereins zu den innerjue-dischen Fragen in den Jahren 1919–1926*, p. 8. Until 1908 only men could join the C.V.; after that date, women were accepted.

49. CAHJP, A 33 (173, 192, 212).

50. Rieger, *Ein Vierteljahrhundert*, p. 24.

51. See *Die Welt*, no. 46 (November 14, 1902).

52. See Eugen Fuchs, "Juedische Organisationen in Deutschland" in *Sueddeutsche Monatshefte*, 1916, p. 843. Bernstein, p. 73, cites for the same year only 35,597 individual members.

53. Arnold Paucker, "Der juedische Abwehrkampf," *Entscheidungs-jahr 1932*, p. 412.

54. These are round figures. For a detailed demographic analysis of German Jewry during the Weimar Republic see Abraham Margaliot's dissertation: "Ha'Tguva ha'Politit shel ha'Mosadot v'Hairgunim ha'Yehudiyim b'Germania l'Nokhaḥ ha'Mediniyut ha'Anti-Yehudit shel ha'Nazionalsozialistim ba'Shanim 1932–1935" (The Hebrew University, 1971).

55. R. Bernstein, "Zwischen Emanzipation und Antisemitismus," p. 73.

56. Bruno Weil, "Zum Gedenken an Ludwig Hollaender," Leo Baeck Institute Archives, file no. 1033.

57. R. Bernstein, "Zwischen Emanzipation und Antisemitismus," p. 73.

58. Heinemann Stern, *Angriff und Abwehr, Ein Handbuch ueber die Judenfrage*, p. 30.

59. R. Bernstein, "Zwischen Emanzipation und Antisemitismus," p. 73. This is the upper limit of possible Zionist membership. Bernstein bases his figures on the number of German Jews who contributed a *Shekel* to the "Zionistische Vereinigung fuer Deutschland," which is a highly unreliable source for estimating actual membership. A much more accurate estimate is probably that of Ludwig Pinner who esti-mates the number of Zionists as two percent of the total German Jewish population. This means that, at most, the Zionists in Germany numbered somewhere between 11,000 and 12,000. See Pinner, "Vermoegenstransfer nach Palaestina 1933–1939," *In Zwei Welten*, pp. 133–66.

60. There are no figures available for corporate membership. The only indication is contained in a speech of Eugen Fuchs in 1907 in which he claimed that the C.V. had 120 corporate memberships. See Fuchs, *Um Deutschtum*, p. 100. One might safely assume that these included all members of the "Hilfsverein der deutschen Juden" and "Verband der deutschen Juden" as well as most liberal German *Gemeinden*. In the 1920s most members of the "Reichsbund juedischer Frontsoldaten" were members of the C.V.

61. There seems to be some doubt whether or not Paul Nathan was an official member of the C.V. Reiner Bernstein claims (p. 69) that Nathan served as a deputy to the president of the C.V., Julius Brodnitz. The *Juedisches Lexikon*, s.v. "Nathan, Paul," states clearly that Paul Nathan was "Vorstandsmitglieder des C.V." Nathan's biographer, how-ever, only implies that Nathan was a member of the executive commit-

tee of the C.V. See Ernst Feder, "Paul Nathan, the Man and His Work," *LBIYB*, vol. 3 (1958), p. 79.

62. Documentation of support from all major Jewish organizations in Germany is abundant: cf. CAHJP, TD/23.

63. The earliest list which I was able to find is in the CAHJP and is dated 1899. It gives the following picture of professions held by members of the C.V. Vorstand: Maximilian Horwitz (law), Eugen Fuchs (law), Leopold Dom (law), Julius Schneider (education), Raphael Loewenfeld (theater), Isidor Ginsberg (industry), Gustav Josephtal (law), L. Kallisch (publishing), Eugen Landau (public service), S. Blaschke (higher education), Julius Blumenthal (board of health), Julius Martin Friedlaender (industry) Joseph Lewy (medicine), Martin Loevinson (law), Alfred Loewenberg (banking), Emanuel Mendel (higher education), Martin Mendelssohn (higher education), Moritz Moszkowski (academy of arts), Curt Pariser (medicine), Adolf Pinner (higher education), Fedor Pringsheim (city administration), R. Rosenthal (business), Hermann Senator (higher education), Otto Wiesenthal (medicine), Julius Wolff (higher education). CAHJP, TD/24.

64. See Sigbert Feuchtwanger, *Die Judenfrage*, p. 44.

65. Rieger, *Ein Vierteljahrhundert*, pp. 73–81. R. Bernstein, "Zwischen Emanzipation und Antisemitismus," p. 72, lists some of the leading rabbis of the C.V.

66. See *C.V. Kalender fuer das Jahr 1929*, pp. 59 ff.

67. The extant membership lists as well as descriptions in the *Im Deutschen Reich* (hereafter cited as *IDR*) and *Centralverein Zeitung* (hereafter cited as *CVZ*) which sometimes include economic and social data substantiate this assertion. For a complete list of the C.V. administration for the year 1922, see Jonas Kreppel, *Juden und Judentum von Heute*, pp. 627–28.

68. See Institute of Social Research, "Analysis of Central Verein Policy in Germany," "Appendix."

69. See Bruno Weil, "Zum Gedenken Ludwig Hollaender," Leo Baeck Institute Archives, New York, file 1033.

70. *K.C. Blaetter*, no. 2 (November 1, 1913), pp. 32–33. It is obvious that one cannot equate the composition of the K.C. with that of the C.V. since membership of the K.C. was, due to the very nature of the association, made up mostly by students and academicians. One could say, however, that the K.C. furnished the professional component of the C.V., though it did not necessarily represent the membership structure of the C.V.

71. Many *Ostjuden* were not eligible since they lacked German citizenship. See Foerder, p. 8. Curiously, many members of the C.V., including its leadership, came from the eastern provinces; e.g., Eugen Fuchs came from Upper Silesia and Julius Brodnitz from Posen.

72. Loewenfeld claimed in his pamphlet that most German Jews were dissociated from Talmudic Judaism and the "obscurantist orthodox community," which had refused to accommodate itself to the changing social and political conditions of the German Jews. See Loewenfeld, *Schutzjuden oder Staatsbuerger*, pp. 9–10.

73. For criticism of the C.V.'s position on religion see Franz Rosenzweig, *Briefe*, p. 590.

74. Rieger, *Ein Vierteljahrhundert*, p. 53.

75. Bernstein, p. 66, cites two revisions in 1928 and in 1935. Schorsch, *Jewish Reactions to German Anti-Semitism*, p. 120, cites an additional revision, of 1909, which permitted the formation of local chapters and regional associations. The first discussions about decentralization took place as early as 1905. See *166. Vorstandssitzung des C.V.*, May 1, 1905. Leo Baeck Institute Archives, New York, Alfred Hirschberg Collection, Catalogue no. AR-A. 1185.3965.

76. Centralverein, *Satzung des Centralvereins*, p. 3.

77. For an interesting comparison of a similar arrangement by the American Jewish Committee see Ben Halpern, "The American Jewish Committee," *Jewish Frontier* (December 1943): 14.

78. Schorsch, *Jewish Reactions to German Anti-Semitism*, p. 120.

79. Ismar Elbogen and Eleonore Sterling, *Die Geschichte der Juden in Deutschland*, p. 275; Rieger, *Ein Vierteljahrhundert*, pp. 75–81.

80. Stern, *Angriff*, p. 30.

81. *Juedisches Lexikon*, s.v. "Central-Verein Deutscher Staatsbuerger juedischen Glaubens."

82. R. Bernstein, "Zwischen Emanzipation und Antisemitismus," p. 68.

83. Institute of Social Research, "Analysis."

84. R. Berstein, "Zwischen Emanzipation und Antisemitismus," p. 67.

85. For distribution of K.C. members in the German Reich see *K.C. Blaetter*, no. 2 (November 1, 1913), p. 33.

86. Among the "honorary members" were the author and editor Julius Bab, Rabbi Leo Baeck, and the lawyer and Reichstag deputy Ludwig Haas.

87. R. Bernstein, "Zwischen Emanzipation und Antisemitismus," p. 67.

88. In 1908 Ludwig Hollaender began as a *syndicus* for the C.V. and became its executive director after World War I. See Alfred Hirschberg, "Ludwig Hollaender, Director of the C.V.," *LBIYB*, vol. 7 (1962), pp. 39–44.

89. In 1894, Mendelssohn, a physician, resigned his post because of professional obligations.

90. Fuchs was born in Upper Silesia in 1856 and studied law. His efforts to enter the academic field were doomed, because the anti-Semitic movement of the 1880s made it virtually impossible for a Jew to enter the field. He became a successful lawyer and official in the highest courts of Prussia and published learned articles on legal matters, cf. *C.V. Kalender fuer das Jahr 1929*, p. 38.

91. R. Bernstein, "Zwischen Emanzipation und Antisemitismus," p. 29.

92. Rieger, *Ein Vierteljahrhundert*, pp. 48 ff.

93. After May 4, 1922, a weekly paper, *Central-Verein Zeitung* was published by the C.V. with the subtitle "Blaetter fuer Deutschtum und Judentum: Allgemeine Zeitung des Judentums." The reference to the old and respected liberal *Allgemeine Zeitung des Judentums* which had ceased publication by then is obvious. The subtitle meant to indicate that the *CVZ* intended to be a worthy substitute to the *AZdJ* as the representative of all liberal Jews in Germany.

94. See "Die Bedeutung des Kampfes gegen den Antisemitismus," *K.C. Blaetter,* no. 6 (March 1, 1914), pp. 125–28.
95. Fuchs, *Um Deutschtum,* p. 65.
96. The Zionists were in the habit of ridiculing the C.V. by calling it not a "Gesinnungsverein," but a "Geselligkeitsverein."
97. Ismar Freund, "Centralverein," CAHJP, P2/Me/19. Franz Rosenzweig made a similar observation in a letter to Benno Jacob of May 17, 1927: "Denn es stimmt noch viel mehr fuer C.Ver, dass ihnen der C.V. das Judentum ersetze . . . unter zehn Juden waren da gewiss neun, denen der C.V. an der Stelle der Religion stand." *Briefe,* p. 590.
98. One can, of course, find exceptions to the statement that most C.V. members were religiously liberal Jews. In general, however, this statement holds true for the period before 1914 as well as after World War I.
99. See Ismar Freund's analysis of the C.V.'s attitude toward Judaism, CAHJP, P2/Me/19.
100. Ernst Feder, "Paul Nathan, the Man and His Work," *LBIYB,* vol. 3 (1958), p. 64.
101. Fuchs, *Um Deutschtum,* pp. 56–57.
102. Quoted in Abraham Margaliot, "Ha'Tguva ha'Politit," p. 30.
103. See Massing, *Rehearsal for Destruction,* pp. 113 ff.
104. Institute of Social Research, "Analysis" (microfilm).
105. Ibid.
106. CAHJP, INV/751/3 (1907).
107. Fuchs, *Um Deutschtum,* pp. 56–57.
108. Horwitz, "Ehrenpflichten," p. 12. Many scholars and even former C.V. members erroneously attribute this saying to Ludwig Hollaender, who, in fact, adopted it from Horwitz. See Eugen Strauss, Adolf Asch, and Alfred Hirschberg.
109. Toury, *Die Politischen Orientierungen,* p. 203.
110. Fuchs, *Um Deutschtum,* pp. 66 ff.
111. Ibid., p. 69.
112. Toury, *Die Politischen Orientierungen,* p. 205. In 1893 the "Deutsch Freisinnige Partei" split into the "Freisinnige Volkspartei" (FVP), and "Freisinnige Vereinigung" (FVg); hence the use of the plural form when referring to the "Freisinnige."
113. See Toury, *Die Politischen Orientierungen,* p. 206.
114. Fuchs, *Um Deutschtum,* pp. 68 ff.
115. Toury, *Die Politischen Orientierungen,* p. 207.
116. Ibid., p. 209.
117. Fuchs, *Um Deutschtum,* p. 72.
118. Ibid., p. 82.
119. The reference was to a Jewish lawyer by the name of Friedemann who was elected with the help of the C.V. in 1898.
120. Fuchs, *Um Deutschtum,* p. 74.
121. Ibid., p. 78.
122. For an analysis of events 1916–23, see Eva Reichmann, "Der Bewusstseinswandel der deutschen Juden," in *Deutsches Judentum in Krieg und Revolution 1916–1923,* pp. 511–612.
123. CAHJP, TD/24.
124. This remained the *official* position of the C.V. until its final

dissolution in 1938. Nevertheless, *Judentum* gained an ever-increasing prominence among many members of the C.V. (especially the younger generation) who even cooperated actively with the Jewish Agency, *Keren Hayessod*, etc.

125. Evidence for this statement is abundant. For Lazarus: Eugen Fuchs, *Um Deutschtum und Judentum*, p. 90; Ludwig Hollaender, *K.C. Blaetter* (April 1, 1914), pp. 146 ff.; for Riesser: Fuchs, *Um Deutschtum*, pp. 106, 109, 116, 133, 257, 269, 346 ff, 351, 355; for Cohen: *IDR* (1907), pp. 611 ff; Felix Goldmann, *Der Jude im deutschen Kulturkreise*, pp. 9, 12, 106, 172; *IDR* (April, 1917), pp. 164 ff. In an article in memory of Eugen Fuchs, Ludwig Hollaender went so far as to say: "Der Vorstand unseres Central-Vereins hat in dem Nachrufe auf Eugen Fuchs unseren heimgegangenen Fuehrer einen *Vollender des Werkes von Gabriel Riesser genannt.*" Hollaender, "Unserem Eugen Fuchs zum Gedenken," *CVZ*, nos. 1–2 (January 10, 1924), p. 1.

126. Gabriel Riesser, *Gesammelte Schriften*, 2: 91 ff.

127. Ibid., p. 364.

128. Cf. Moshe Rinott, "Gabriel Riesser, Fighter for Jewish Emancipation," *LBIYB*, vol. 7 (1962), p. 18.

129. Riesser, "Besorgnisse und Hoffnungen fuer die kuenftige Stellung der Juden in Preussen," *Gesammelte Schriften*, 3: 417 ff.

130. Rinott, "Gabriel Riesser," p. 18.

131. Ibid., pp. 31–32.

132. Riesser, *Gesammelte Schriften*, 2:92.

133. An exception to this statement is Lazarus's polemical brochure *Die Sittliche Berechtigung Preussen's in Deutschland.*

134. Lazarus, *Was Heisst National?* See also Lazarus, "Unser Standpunkt," and "An die deutsche Juden," in *Treu und Frei, Gesammelte Reden und Vortraege.*

135. For details see *Zeitschrift fuer Voelkerpsychologie und Sprachwissenschaft*, 4 :265 ff. and 1 :41 ff.

136. Lazarus, *Was Heisst National?*, p. 28.

137. Ibid., p. 29.

138. Ibid., p. 30.

139. Ibid., p. 52.

140. Hermann Cohen, "Ein Bekenntnis in der Judenfrage," *Juedische Schriften*, 2:87.

141. See, for example, *IDR*, no. 3 (September, 1895); *IDR*, no. 1 (January, 1897); *IDR*, no. 11 (November, 1907).

142. Cohen, "Deutschtum und Judentum," in *Juedische Schriften*, 2:300. This statement was made in 1915. Despite the fact, as Schorsch points out (p. 140), that Cohen retreated from his "early [1880] equivocal stand on the issue of Jewish survival," and had in 1890 begun to advocate the retainment of Jewish identity ["Der Religionswechsel in der neuen Aera des Antisemitismus," 2 :342–45] he continued for the rest of his life to minimize any contradictions between *Deutschtum* and *Judentum*.

143. Cohen, "Deutschtum und Judentum," 2 :93; "das kraeftigste, das wirksamste Bindemittel fuer eine innige nationale Verschmelzung."

144. Ernst Simon, "Martin Buber und das deutsche Judentum,"

Deutsches Judentum, Aufstieg und Krise, pp. 64 ff. For a short analysis of Hermann Cohen see Egmont Zechlin, *Die deutsche Politik und die Juden im Ersten Weltkrieg*, p. 11.

145. Cohen, "Deutschtum und Judentum," 2 :84–85.

146. Ibid. Cohen's opposition to Jewish nationalism never changed. See his well-known debate with Martin Buber in 1916, "Deutschtum und Judentum," 2 :319–40.

147. Ibid., 2 :92.

148. Cohen, "Deutschtum und Judentum," 2 :316–17.

149. Emil Lehmann, *Gesammelte Schriften*, p. 2.

150. Ibid., p. 4.

151. Ibid., p. 386.

152. Ibid., p. 297.

153. Lehmann, "Der Deutsche juedischen Bekenntnisses," speech held at the C.V. meeting of September 27, 1893. Cf. Lehmann, *Gesammelte Schriften*, p. 387.

154. See C.V., *Satzung des Centralvereins*, CAHJP, TD/24.

155. CAHJP, INV/751/3; Fuchs, *Um Deutschtum*, p. 54.

156. According to Alfred Hirschberg the change was due mainly to the efforts of Ludwig Hollaender; cf. *LBIYB*, vol. 7 (1962), p. 44. All evidence, however, points to the fact that this change came much earlier than 1908, the year when Hollaender was summoned to Berlin by the C.V. leadership.

157. Fuchs, *Um Deutschtum*, pp. 51 ff.; Martin Mendelssohn, *Die Pflicht der Selbstverteidigung*, pp. 5 ff.; Rieger, *Ein Vierteljahrhundert*, p. 50.

158. *IDR*, nos. 5/6 (May/June, 1913), pp. 224–25.

159. See *K.C. Blaetter*, no. 9 (June 1, 1913), p. 186; *K.C. Blaetter*, no. 6 (March 1, 1914), p. 127; and *K.C. Blaetter*, no. 5 (February 1, 1914), p. 109.

160. *K.C. Blaetter*, no. 7 (April 1, 1914), pp. 148 ff.

161. Ibid. These thoughts were elaborated often and in great detail throughout the history of the C.V. See, for example, *CVZ*, no. 8 (February 12, 1930), p. 89; *CVZ*, no. 17 (April 24, 1924), p. 229; *CVZ*, no. 1 (January 2, 1925), p. 2; *CVZ*, no. 29 (July 17, 1925), p. 504; *CVZ*, no. 1 (January 2, 1931), p. 1.

162. On the Zionist position prior to World War I see Jehuda Reinharz, "Ideology and Practice in German Zionism 1897–1914," in *Conference on Intellectual Policies in American Jewry* (1972), pp. 51–61.

163. See Alfred Hirschberg, "Ludwig Hollaender," p. 42. In fact, the C.V. devoted a great deal of its energy to the battle against apostasy.

164. Ludwig Hollaender, "Vaterlandsrede," *K.C. Blaetter*, no. 7 (April 1, 1914), p. 149.

165. Felix Goldmann, *Zionismus oder Liberalismus, Atheismus oder Religion*, p. 17.

166. Ibid., 17 ff. For a detailed refutation of Goldmann's point of view, see the pamphlet by Max Kollenscher, *Zionismus oder Liberales Judentum*.

167. Max Hirsch, "Judentum und Juedisches Volksbewusstsein," *CVZ*, no. 38 (September 23, 1927), p. 537; Ludwig Hollaender, "Inner-

juedische Befriedung," *CVZ*, no. 27 (July, 1928), p. 384; Hermann Vogelstein, *Um Wahrheit Recht und Frieden*, p. 9.

168. Goldmann, *Zionismus oder Liberalismus*, p. 17.

169. See R. Bernstein, "Zwischen Emanzipation und Antisemitismus," pp. 56–58; Hirschberg, "Ludwig Hollaender," p. 62. Schorsch mentions the more positive attitude of the C.V. before World War I (p. 148), but does not discuss it further and seems to support the opinions of these scholars. Sanford Ragins points in his dissertation (p. 146) to a usage of *Abstammung* by the C.V. in 1902. However, the term was not elaborated in the C.V. publications at the time and did not have any impact on the ideology of the C.V.; see *IDR*, no. 2 (February 21, 1902), pp. 85 ff.

170. See *Haolam* (September 3, 1928); *Haolam* (October 2, 1928); Ludwig Hollaender, Kurt Cohn, and Ludwig Tietz, *Der Central-Verein der Zukunft. Eine Denkschrift zur Hauptversammlung 1928 des Central-Vereins deutscher Staatsbuerger juedischen Glaubens E.V.* See also Ludwig Hollaender, *Deutsch-Juedische Probleme der Gegenwart*.

171. Ludwig Hollaender, "Unserem Eugen Fuchs zum Gedenken," *CVZ*, nos. 1–2 (January 10, 1924). In fact, Fuchs used the term *Stamm* and *Stammesgeschichte* in describing *Judentum* already as early as 1912; see Fuchs, *Um Deutschtum*, p. 118. It is curious that Hollaender did not mention his own employment of the term *Stamm* (in 1914) as a component of *Judentum*. Hollaender said at the time, "damit erfuellen wir die Forderung, welche heute als Forderung der Einheit des Judentums mit umfasst wird. Und darum das Gefuehl der Treue zum Judentum als einer uns angestammtem Notwendigkeit. . . ." *K.C. Blaetter*, no. 7 (April 1, 1914), p. 148.

172. Fuchs, *Um Deutschtum*, pp. 252–53.

173. Ibid., p. 253. A similar view, making a distinction between *Stamm* and "nationality" was expressed in 1913 by another member of the C.V.: "Wir leugnen keineswegs die starken Momente, die uns mit den Juden ausserhalb Deutschlands verbinden. Wir haben auf Grund der Gemeinsamkeit der Religion, der Stammesgemeinschaft und infolge gemeinsamer Leiden durch antisemitische Verfolgungen ein warmes Mitgefuehl mit unseren osteuropaeischen Glaubensgenossen . . . Aber diese Gefuehle sind nicht nationaler Natur. Es besteht kein gemeinsames nationales Zusammenleben zwischen den deutschen und den ostjuedischen Juden." See Karl Loewenstein, "Nationaljudentum," *K.C. Blaetter*, no. 9 (June 1, 1913), p. 184. By 1914 Fuchs's assertions about *Stamm* and "nationality" were accepted as commonplace by the C.V. Thus, in a detailed article Julius Guttmann wrote the following: "Dass die Juden durch gemeinsame Abstammung, durch Geschichte und religioese Ueberlieferung verbunden sind, wird ebenso allegemein anerkannt, wie die politische und kulturelle Gemeinschaft, die sie mit ihrer Umgebung vereint." See Julius Guttmann, "Der Begriff der Nation in seiner Anwendung auf die Juden," *K. C. Blaetter*, no. 4 (January 1, 1914), p. 69.

174. See the analysis of Ruth Louise Pierson, "German Jewish Identity in the Weimar Republic," pp. 62–63. I am indebted to Pierson for having drawn my attention to some sources which have been used for

my analysis. I accept her conclusions, but do not agree with all the details of her argument.

175. See Eugen Fuchs, "Was Nun," *Neue Juedische Monatshefte*, nos. 7/8 (January 10, 1919), p. 140.

176. Fuchs, *Um Deutschtum*, pp. 236–37.

177. The C.V. often admitted that its emphasis, even before 1914, on Jewish identity, was the result of the constant challenge by the Zionists. See CAHJP, INV/124/2; Fuchs, *Um Deutschtum*, pp. 236 ff.

178. In his review of Schorschs's book, Michael Meyer suggests a third reason for the strengthening of Jewish identity in the ideology of the C.V.: "It seems, rather, that the 'expanded concept of Judaism' which the Centralverein achieved in the last years before the War was linked to a general resurgence of Jewish identification marked by the creation of numerous new Jewish organizations. . . . It should be noted that the contemporary Jews felt this to be a period of resurgent religious idealism in Germany in which religion . . . seemed again to matter. . . . The brief resurgence of Jewish self-assertion must, in addition, be understood in relation to a temporary more conducive cultural atmosphere and a political climate which—as the results of the 1912 elections would indicate—was for a short period becoming more liberal." See *Conservative Judaism*, vol. 27, no. 2, winter, 1973.

However, one must note that though the anti-Semites suffered great losses during the elections of 1912, this year also saw a strong anti-Semitic backlash, the strengthening of the Pan-Germans, and the publication and immense circulation of the anti-Semitic book by Daniel Frymann [Heinrich Class] of *Wenn ich der Kaiser waer'—Politische Wahrheiten und Notwendigkeiten*. In 1912 the "Reichskammerbund," one of the most active anti-Semitic organizations in pre-war Germany was also founded. See Werner Jochmann, "Die Ausbreitung des Antisemitismus," *Deutsches Judentum in Krieg und Revolution*, pp. 409–511.

179. *IDR*, no. 2 (February, 1907), p. 120.

180. On the element of "apologetics" in the ideology of the C.V., see the article by Zeev Levi "Mekomah shel ha'Apologtika ba' "Agudah ha'Merkazit" shel Yehudei Germania ba'shanim ha'rishonot l'kiyumah," in *Yalkut Moreshet*, 1969. Although Levi makes some astute observations concerning the element of apologetics in the C.V. theory, he seems to me wrong in his wholesale condemnation of the C.V.; his article tends to generalize from quotations taken out of context. I do wish to acknowledge my indebtedness to Levi's article, which drew my attention to a number of important passages in *IDR* which are used here; place references are quoted here in full.

181. See Felix Theilhaber, *Der Untergang der deutschen Juden*, and *IDR*, no. 4 (April, 1907), pp. 201–7.

182. *IDR*, no. 1 (January, 1903), p. 20.

183. See, for example, *JR* (May 8, 1914), p. 197.

184. Felix Goldmann, "Assimilation," *IDR*, nos. 7/8 (July/August, 1914), p. 317. See also pp. 318–19.

185. *IDR*, no. 4 (October, 1895), pp. 148–49.

186. Herbert A. Strauss, "Jewish Reactions to the Rise of Anti-

semitism in Germany," *Conference on Antisemitism: Papers Delivered at the American Federation of Jews from Central Europe*, p. 15.

187. Felix Goldmann, "Deutschtum und Judentum," *IDR*, no. 4 (April, 1917), pp. 164–68.

188. *IDR*, no. 11 (November, 1907), pp. 611–12.

189. The most notable difference was that Cohen described Judaism as a spiritual, rational religion which was destined to merge with Protestantism, whereas the C.V., noting the spiritual and ethical relationships between Judaism and Protestantism, still maintained the eternal individuality and uniqueness of Judaism which made its disappearance into a higher form of monotheism unlikely.

190. Cf. *IDR*, no. 3 (September, 1895), pp. 121–22.

191. *IDR*, no. 1 (January, 1897), p. 9.

192. Ibid., pp. 14–15.

193. Goldmann, "Deutschtum und Judentum," p. 165.

194. See Levi, "Mekomah shel ha'Apologetika," p. 72.

195. Cf. *IDR*, no. 6 (December, 1895), pp. 280–81.

196. *IDR*, no. 1 (January, 1903), pp. 45–46.

197. *IDR*, no. 1 (January, 1896), p. 6.

198. Centralverein deutscher Staatsbuerger juedischen Glaubens, *An die deutschen Staatsbuerger juedischen Glaubens.*

199. See Levi, "Mekomah shel ha'Apologetika," p. 65. See also *IDR*, no. 1 (January, 1908), p. 60.

200. Riesser, *Gesammelte Schriften*, 4 :320.

201. Cf. *IDR*, no. 12 (December, 1907), p. 671; *IDR*, no. 4 (April, 1908), p. 210.

202. *IDR*, nos. 7/8 (July/August, 1897), p. 366.

203. *IDR*, no. 5 (May, 1904), p. 279.

204. *IDR*, no. 4 (April, 1901), pp. 204–5.

205. Cf. *IDR* (February, 1903), p. 187.

206. *IDR*, no. 1 (January, 1896), pp. 36–46.

207. *IDR*, nos. 7/8 (July/August, 1906), pp. 407–25; *IDR*, no. 9 (September, 1906), pp. 512–25.

208. *IDR*, no. 4 (April, 1901), pp. 185–91.

209. *IDR*, no. 8 (August, 1902), p. 462.

210. See *K.C. Blaetter*, no. 9 (June 1, 1913), pp. 181 ff.

211. Ludwig Hollaender, *Die Kongresspolitik der Zionisten und ihre Gefahren*, p. 14.

212. *IDR*, no. 4 (April, 1896), p. 190.

213. Ibid., p. 193.

214. These changes in anti-Zionist attacks before and after 1912 hold true not only for the C.V., but for all other liberal Jewish organizations in Germany as well.

215. *IDR*, nos. 5/6 (May, 1913), p. 246.

Chapter III

1. For the purpose of our analysis we will identify the *Zionistische Vereinigung fuer Deutschland* as the representative institution of Zion-

ism in Germany. The standard abbreviation for this organization is ZVfD.

2. In Zionist terminology the term "assimilation" meant turning one's back on Judaism and submerging oneself totally in German culture to the exclusion of all that was Jewish; in their opinion, this process led to conversion. Although, as will become apparent, they themselves were assimilated, the Zionists considered their assimilation a form of acculturation, which at the same time gave them freedom to accentuate their *Judentum.*

3. Adolf Boehm, "Die Anfaenge des Zionismus und die moderne Judenheit," *Juedische Rundschau* (hereafter cited as *JR*), nos. 31/32 (April 17, 1935).

4. Walter Laqueur, "The Jewish Question Today," *Encounter* 37 (August, 1971) :46.

5. For example, Theodor Herzl subtitled his *Judenstaat, Moderne Loesung der Judenfrage.*

6. See Simon Dubnow, *History of the Jews in Russia and Poland,* 2:243 ff.

7. Ibid., p. 350.

8. Ibid., pp. 401 ff.

9. See Shalom Adler-Rudel, *Ostjuden in Deutschland 1880—1940,* p. 6.

10. See Arthur Ruppin, *The Jews of Today,* pp. 92—93 and Schriften des Arbeitsfuersorgeamtes der juedischen Organisationen Deutschlands, *Die Einwanderung der Ostjuden,* p. 6.

11. See Klara Eschelbacher, "Die ostjuedische Einwanderungsbevoelkerung der Stadt Berlin," *Zeitschrift fuer Demographie und Statistik der Juden,* vols. 1—6 (January—June, 1920), p. 2.

12. See Shmarya Levin, *Youth in Revolt,* p. 227.

13. See Adler-Rudel, *Ostjuden,* "Appendix II," p. 163.

14. Ibid., p. 14.

15. Levin, *Youth in Revolt,* pp. 234 ff.

16. Richard Lichtheim, *Toldot Ha'Zionut b'Germania,* pp. 63 ff.

17. See Jehuda Louis Weinberg, *Aus der Fruehzeit des Zionismus,* pp. 71 ff.

18. See Levin, *Youth in Revolt,* pp. 252 ff. For further details concerning the aims and activities of the *Russisch-Juedisch Wissenschaftlicher Verein* see Shmarya Levin, *Iggrot Shmarya Levin;* Chaim Weizmann, *Trial and Error;* and *The Letters and Papers of Chaim Weizmann,* vol. 1.

19. See Mordechai Ehrenpreis, *Beyn Mizrah l'Maarav,* p. 48.

20. Ibid., pp. 48—49; and Israel Klausner, *Opposizia l'Herzl,* pp. 10—12.

21. See Adolf Boehm, *Die Zionistische Bewegung,* 1 :136.

22. Ibid., p. 185.

23. See Getzel Kressel, "Selbst-Emancipation," *Shivat Zion,* 4 :92.

24. Lichtheim, *Toldot Ha'Zionut b'Germania,* p. 74.

25. Ibid., p. 75.

26. See Mordechai Eliav, *Ahavat Zion v'Anshei Hod, Yehudei Germania ba'Meah ha'19,* pp. 308—10.

27. Ibid., p. 315.

28. See *Encyclopedia of Zionism and Israel,* s.v. "Esra."

29. "Petition der in Berlin befindlichen juedischen Studenten aus Russ-

land an das Centralcomité zur Unterstuetzung russischer Juden in Berlin," in *Selbst-Emancipation*, no. 13 (July 2, 1891).

30. Eliav, *Ahavat Zion*, p. 365.

31. See Ben Halpern, *The Idea of the Jewish State*, p. 149.

32. Quoted by Halpern, ibid., p. 151.

33. See Max Bodenheimer, *So Wurde Israel*, p. 34.

34. Ibid., pp. 43–44.

35. Ibid., p. 61.

36. See M. Bodenheimer's letter to Schapira on June 23, 1897, in Henriette Hannah Bodenheimer, *Toldot Tokhnit Basel*, p. 58.

37. M. Bodenheimer, *So Wurde Israel*, p. 54. For a review of Bodenheimer's brochure, see *Selbst-Emancipation* (August 18, 1891).

38. M. Bodenheimer, *So Wurde Israel*, p. 55.

39. Hans Martin Klinkenberg, "Zwischen Liberalismus und Nationalismus in zweiten Kaiserreich 1870–1918," in *Monumenta Judaica, 2000 Jahre Geschichte und Kultur der Juden am Rhein*, pp. 343 ff.

40. See H. Bodenheimer, ed., *Im Anfang der Zionistischen Bewegung*, p. 19, n. 2.

41. See letter of M. Bodenheimer to Colonel Goldsmid and the latter's reply to Bodenheimer, *So Wurde Israel*, p. 309.

42. Ibid., p. 311.

43. H. Bodenheimer, *Im Anfang*, pp. 19–21.

44. See, for example, M. Bodenheimer, *So Wurde Israel*, p. 65; Ehrenpreis, *Beyn Mizraḥ*, p. 49; Chaim Weizmann, *Trial and Error*, p. 43; Elias Auerbach, *Pionier der Verwirklichung*, p. 79.

45. See Halpern, *The Idea*, p. 84

46. See Sammy Gronemann, *Zikhronot shel Yekke*, p. 121.

47. Halpern, *The Idea*, pp. 136–40.

48. See H. Bodenheimer, *Toldot Tokhnit Basel*, 2; translation adopted from Halpern, *The Idea*, p. 139.

49. Halpern, *The Idea*, p. 139.

50. See H. Bodenheimer, "The Three Delegates' Conferences of German Zionists (1897)," *Herzl Year Book*, 7 :176.

51. H. Bodenheimer, *Toldot Tokhnit Basel*, p. 34.

52. H. Bodenheimer, "The Three Delegates'," p. 180.

53. Lichtheim, *Toldot Ha'Zionut b'Germania*, p. 90; see also H. Bodenheimer, *Im Anfang*, p. 58, n. 27.

54. *Juedisches Lexikon*, s.v. "Zionistische Vereinigung fuer Deutschland."

55. For a short while Alfred Klee served with Rosenblueth as copresident.

56. "Report of the 14th Delegiertentag of the ZVfD," *JR*, no. 19 (1914), p. 264.

57. See *Sefer Warburg*, p. 5.

58. Lichtheim, *Toldot Ha'Zionut b'Germania*, p. 124.

59. Editor of the *JR* 1908–13.

60. The *Juedische Rundschau*, the official organ of the ZVfD, was also located here.

61. *Juedisches Lexikon*, s.v. "Zionistische Vereinigung fuer Deutschland."

62. The value of the *Shekel* changed between 1897 and 1914 from one German mark to about twelve.

63. See ZVfD, *Zionistisches A-B-C Buch,* pp. 289—90.

64. Ibid., p. 287. For details on the organization of the ZVfD, see ZVfD, *Statut der ZVfD,* and Gerhard Holdheim and Walter Preuss, *Die Theoretischen Grundlagen des Zionismus,* pp. 71—72.

65. This freedom was conditional, of course, on the approval of the C.V. office in Berlin and *Vertrauensmaenner* were careful to act in accord with official policies.

66. H. Bodenheimer, *Im Anfang,* p. 58, n. 27.

67. R. Bernstein, "Zwischen Emanzipation und Antisemitismus," p. 25.

68. "Protokoll der XIII Sitzung des Geschaeftsfuehrenden Ausschusses vom 27. April 1912," p. 5. CZA, A15/VII/25.

69. In 1935, the *JR* had a circulation, for a short period of time, of 40,000 which matched that of the *CVZ.* In general, the circulation gap was considerably narrowed after 1933. See Margaret Edelheim-Muehsam, "The Jewish Press in Germany," *LBIYB,* vol. 1 (1956), p. 173.

70. This is the estimate of Robert Weltsch. See also Hans Lamm, "Die Innere und Aeussere Entwicklung des deutschen Judentums im Dritten Reich," p. 175, n. 1.

71. Fritz Loewenstein, "Zionismus," *Das Deutsche Judentum, seine Parteien und Organisationen,* p. 31.

72. R. Bernstein, "Zwischen Emanzipation und Antisemitismus," p. 25.

73. Ibid.

74. For details see Klausner, *Opposizia,* pp. 170—71.

75. *JR,* no. 2 (January 8, 1932), p. 2.

76. Lichtheim, *Toldot Ha'Zionut b'Germania,* p. 63. See also Laqueur, "The Jewish Question," p. 48.

77. Until World War I Jews could not be commissioned officers.

78. See Richard Lichtheim, *Das Programm des Zionismus,* pp. 11—12.

79. Felix Rosenblueth, "Nationaljudentum und Antisemitismus," *JR,* no. 13 (March 28, 1913), pp. 126—28.

80. Lichtheim, *Das Programm des Zionismus,* pp. 13—14.

81. ZVfD, "An die Mitglieder des Landesvorstandes und des Zentralkomitees; an die Zionistischen Ortsgruppen und Vertrauensleute (Streng Vertraulich)," January 15, 1923. Schocken Archives, Jerusalem, file 53/32.

82. Arthur Hantke to Kurt Blumenfeld, September 20, 1913. CZA, Z3/729.

83. ZVfD, "An die Mitglieder."

84. See Lichtheim, *Toldot Ha'Zionut b'Germania,* p. 94.

85. Robert Weltsch, Review of Richard Lichtheim's *Toldot Ha'Zionut b'Germania* in *Jewish Social Studies,* no. 1 (January, 1955).

86. Halpern, *The Idea,* p. 141.

87. See Theodor Herzl, *Tagebuecher,* 1 :586.

88. See Arthur Freund, "Um Gemeinde und Organisation," *BLBI,* no. 10 (1960), pp. 95—98.

89. See Simon Dubnow, *Die neueste Geschichte des juedischen Volkes,* 10 :345 ff.

90. See Mordechai Salipoy, *Ha'Oleh ha'Gadol,* p. 30.

91. See Nathan Birnbaum, "Juedische Autonomie," in *Ost und West,* no. 1 (January, 1906), and Mattias Acher (Nathan Birnbaum) "Die Autonomiebestrebungen der Juden in Oesterreich," in *The Jews of Austria,* pp. 140–43.

92. See Werner J. Cahnman, "Adolf Fischhof and His Jewish Followers," *LBIYB,* vol. 4 (1959), pp. 133–34.

93. See *Die Welt,* no. 28 (1906), pp. 7 ff.

94. Dubnow, *Neueste Geschichte,* 10 :417 ff.

95. See *Stenographisches Protokoll der Verhandlungen des 5. Zionistenkongresses,* p. 176.

96. See *Die Welt,* no. 52 (1906), p. 5.

97. See *Encyclopedia of Zionism and Israel,* s.v. "Practical Zionism."

98. See N. M. Gelber, *Ha'Kongressim ha'Zionim,* pp. 38–39.

99. See *Iggrot Shmarya Levin,* pp. 14–15; and also Weizmann, *Trial and Error.*

100. See Weizmann's letter to Ahad Ha'Am, October 31, 1901, in *The Letters and Papers of Chaim Weizmann,* 1 :194–96.

101. See Klausner, *Opposizia,* pp. 40–42.

102. Ibid., pp. 147–48.

103. See Chaim Weizmann, *Reden und Aufsaetze 1901–1936,* pp. 2–16.

104. See Zalman Shazar in *Berthold Feiwel,* p. 14.

105. See Martin Buber, Berthold Feiwel, and Chaim Weizmann, *Eine Juedische Hochschule.*

106. Klausner, *Opposizia,* pp. 248–49.

107. See M. Bodenheimer, *So Wurde Israel,* p. 69, and H. Bodenheimer, *Im Anfang,* p. 26.

108. Auerbach, *Pionier der Verwirklichung,* p. 80.

109. See letter of Max Bodenheimer to Franz Oppenheimer, May 13, 1914. CZA, A15/18e.

110. ZVfD, Flugblatt, no. 1, "Der Zionismus." CZA, collection of printed manuscripts.

111. Ibid.

112. ZVfD, "Aufruf." CZA, collection of printed manuscripts.

113. ZVfD, Flugblatt, no. 6, "Deutsche Juden." CZA, collection of printed manuscripts.

114. Ibid.

115. Halpern, *The Idea,* p. 143. The following passage is a typical expression of this attitude: "Der Zionismus kann niemals und nirgends in einen Gegensatz zum Patriotismus gebracht werden. Der Zionist ist ein treuer Buerger, ein guter Patriot in seinem Heimatlande. Er wird ihm stets gute Dienste leisten. Seine Liebe zur alten Heimat der Vaeter, zum juedischen Volke, dem er angehoert, und fuer dessen Wohl und wuerdige Zukunft er unablaessig sorgt, steht er damit in keinem Widerspruch. Im Gegenteil. Die Treue, die er seinem Volke und dessen alter Heimat weiht, rechtfertigt ueberall und in allen Laendern das Vertrauen zu ihm." Max Kollenscher, *Zionismus und Staatsbuergertum,* p. 12.

116. ZVfD, *Zionistisches A-B-C Buch,* pp. 15—16.

117. One of the most effective methods for raising Jewish national pride was the celebration by the Zionists of Jewish holidays such as *Ḥanukkah* and *Pessaḥ* as national holidays. See, for example, the speech given by Franz Oppenheimer on the occasion of *Ḥanukkah.* Franz Oppenheimer, *Alte und neue Makkabaeer, Gedenkrede gehalten auf der juedischen Gedenkfeier zu Berlin am 22. Januar 1906.*

118. See Max Kollenscher, *Aufgaben Juedischer Gemeindepolitik.*

119. See N. M. Gelber, *Ha'Kongressim,* p. 26.

120. See *Encyclopedia of Zionism and Israel,* s.v. "Austria, Zionism In."

121. Herzl saw the "conquest of the communities," both in his *Judenstaat* and during the Second Zionist Congress, as an instrument for realizing immigration to Palestine. The German Zionists changed the concept and scope of his aim.

122. See Kollenscher, *Aufgaben,* p. 4.

123. Ibid., p. 4. For a comprehensive program of the JVP before World War I, see Gustav Witkowsky, Max Kollenscher, Heinrich Loewe, Victor-Wandsbek, Joseph-Stolp, Leo Mamsu, Ernst Kalmus, Elias Straus, Felix Theilhaber, Hans Goslar, and others in *Juedisches Gemeinde-Jahrbuch 1913/1914.*

124. CZA. A15/VII/25.

125. See Gustav Witkowsky, "Ein Gemeindeprogramm," *Juedisches Gemeinde-Jahrbuch,* pp. 7—11.

126. See Emil Simonsohn, *Die Juedische Volksgemeinde.*

127. Interview by Dr. Ball Khadouri with Hans Klee (son of Alfred Klee). Yad Vashem Archives, Jerusalem, 01/217.

128. See Simonsohn, *Die Juedische Volksgemeinde.*

129. Interview with Dr. Pinhas Rosen (Rosenblueth), September 22, 1970; and with Dr. Siegfried Moses, September 15, 1970. Both support this assertion. This is not to say that from the middle of the 1920s the ZVfD gave full support to the JVP. Quite the contrary. From the time Blumenfeld assumed official leadership of the ZVfD in 1924, the opposition to the JVP became, if anything, more determined. Whatever help the ZVfD granted the JVP was given reluctantly and only because of pressure from within the movement.

130. After the Leipzig Delegiertentag of 1914, Blumenfeld went so far as to say: "Gemeindepolitik ist anti-Zionismus. Wir machen Zionismus Palaestinozentrischen Zionismus." See interview with Kurt Blumenfeld, oral history section, Institute of Contemporary Jewry, Jerusalem. Catalogue no. 990; file 26/4.

131. "Protokoll der IV sitzung des Geschaeftsfuehrenden Ausschusses vom Dienstag den 15 Oktober, 1912." CZA, A15/VII/25.

132. "Protokoll der V Sitzung des Landesvorstandes vom 20 Mai, 1925." Schocken Archives, Jerusalem, file 53/32.

133. Khadouri, interview with Hans Klee, Yad Vashem Archives, 01/217.

134. Ibid.

135. Alfred Klee, "Zionismus und Gemeinde." CZA, 142/246.

136. See speech by Arthur Hantke at the XIII Delegiertentag, *JR*, no. 22 (May 31, 1912), p. 196.

137. Gerhard Holdheim, "Die Deutsche Alijah—Ihre Physiognomie—Ihre Reaktionen—Ihr Zionismus," CZA, G/1293.

138. Elias Auerbach, "Deutsche Kultur im Zionismus," *JR*, no. 7 (February 13, 1903), p. 50.

139. Georg Herlitz, "Adolf Friedemann," *JR*, nos. 103/104 (December 30, 1932), p. 506.

140. The "Verbindungen Juedischer Studenten" became the forerunner of the Zionist "Kartell Juedischer Verbindungen."

141. Herlitz, "Adolf Friedemann," p. 506.

142. *JR*, no. 22 (May 31, 1912), p. 206.

143. See *JR*, no. 6 (February 9, 1912), p. 43.

144. *JR*, no. 25 (June 19, 1914), p. 267.

145. Ibid.

146. See, for example, Franz Oppenheimer's essay in *Judentaufen*, Werner Sombart, ed., pp. 115–17.

147. Adolf Friedemann, "Ist eine Nationaljuedische Partei in Deutschland moeglich?" *Die Welt* (October 26, 1906), pp. 6–7.

148. *JR*, no. 25 (June 19, 1914), p. 267.

149. See Franz Oppenheimer, *Erlebtes, Erstrebtes, Erreichtes*, p. 81.

150. See Alex Bein, "Franz Oppenheimer als Mensch und Zionist," *BLBI* no. 25 (1964), pp. 8 ff. For an English translation of Bein's article, see *Herzl Year Book*, 7:71–127.

151. Quoted by Bein in *Herzl Year Book*, p. 95.

152. Oppenheimer, *Erlebtes*, p. 212.

153. Ibid.

154. Quoted by Adolph Loewe, "In Memoriam Franz Oppenheimer," *LBIYB*, vol. 10 (1965), p. 139.

155. Ibid.

156. Eugen Fuchs, "Glaube und Heimat," *Um Deutschtum und Judentum*, pp. 247–62.

157. *JR*, no. 25 (June 19, 1914), p. 267.

158. *Die Welt*, no. 7 (February 18, 1910).

159. Interview with Rosen, September 22, 1970.

160. Oppenheimer in *Die Welt*, no. 7 (February 18, 1910), pp. 139–40.

161. Ibid.

162. Ibid.

163. Ibid., p. 141.

164. Ibid.

165. Ibid., p. 142.

166. Ibid.

167. Ibid.

168. Quoted by Bein, *Herzl Year Book*, p. 76.

169. Ibid., p. 143.

170. The main critic of Oppenheimer's point of view was Jacob Klatzkin. See *Die Welt*, no. 12 (March 25, 1910), pp. 257–60, and *Die Welt*, no. 15 (April 15, 1910), pp. 329–31.

171. See *JR*, no. 13 (April 1, 1910), p. 148, and *Die Welt*, no. 14 (April 8, 1910), pp. 304–5.

172. Ibid.

173. Adolf Friedemann, "Westlicher Zionismus," *Die Welt*, no. 14 (April 8, 1910), p. 305.

174. M. Bodenheimer, *So Wurde Israel*, p. 108. See also his *Der Zionismus in Deutschland und der Judentag*, p. 12.

175. See Walter Gross, "The Zionist Students' Movement," *LBIYB*, vol. 4 (1959), p. 148.

176. See, for example, Franz Oppenheimer, "Alte und neue Makkabaeer," p. 12. See also Max Kollenscher, *Zionismus und Staatsbuergertum*, pp. 9–10.

177. Kurt Blumenfeld, *Erlebte Judenfrage*, p. 52. See also Franz Oppenheimer's article in *Judentaufen*, pp. 115–17.

178. ZVfD, *Was Will der Zionismus?* p. 14.

179. Richard Lichtheim, *Das Programm des Zionismus*, p. 11. Curiously this statement was not changed when the pamphlet appeared in a second edition in 1913, *after* the Posen Resolution.

180. Sigbert Feuchtwanger, *Die Judenfrage*, p. 44.

181. Kurt Blumenfeld, "Drei Zeitabschnitte," *JR*, no. 48 (June 18, 1937), p. 4.

182. ZVfD, "Informationen der Zionistischen Vereinigung fuer Deutschland," nos. 1/2 (February, 1925). To date there is no exact knowledge about the composition of the ZVfD membership; this is the first attempt to make a classification.

183. Interview with Dr. Walter Katz, May 27, 1971. Also interviews with Dr. Siegfried Moses, September 15, 1970; with Dr. Pinhas Rosen, September 22, 1970; and with Dr. Adler-Rudel, November 10, 1970.

184. Interview with Dr. Katz, May 27, 1971.

185. See *Der Juedische Student* 7 (August 24, 1910): 130–32.

186. Ibid. See also interview with Dr. Katz.

187. See Eva Reichmann, "Der Bewusstseinswandel der deutschen Juden," *Deutsches Judentum in Krieg und Revolution 1916–1923*, pp. 511–613.

188. For details see Adler-Rudel, *Ostjuden*.

189. ZVfD, "Informationen der ZVfD," nos. 1/2 (February, 1925).

190. Ibid.

191. Egmont Zechlin, *Die Deutsche Politik und die Juden im Ersten Weltkrieg*, p. 70.

192. Ibid.

193. M. Bodenheimer, *So Wurde Israel*, p. 52.

194. Robert Weltsch, "Leo Hermann u'Zmano," *Prag v'Yerushalayim*, p. 135. Weltsch is referring to German Zionism, not to the Zionists of Prague.

195. Ibid.

196. Kurt Blumenfeld analyzed the situation: "Es gab in Deutschland Zionisten, eine zionistische Bewegung gab es nicht. Da gab es einzelne Zionisten von ganz verschiedener Art, die einen politische, die anderen praktische. Die politischen unter Fuehrung von Friedemann, Hans Gideon Heymann waren Leute die den Zionismus als eine charitative Bewegung auffassten; sie waren Zionisten fuer das Ostjudentum d.h. fuer

die Juden die den Zionismus brauchten." See interview with Kurt Blumenfeld, oral history section, catalogue no. 990, file 26/4.

197. The most outspoken critic of this period of German Zionism is Gerhard Holdheim; see "Die deutsche Alijah."

198. Moses Calvary, *Die Aufgabe des deutschen Zionismus,* p. 7. See also *Die Welt,* no. 1 (January 6, 1911), pp. 5–8.

199. Heinrich Stern, "Zentralverein, Zionismus, Kongress," CZA, Z3/739.

200. Kurt Blumenfeld described these Zionists in his characteristically cynical manner; "Die eine Quelle des Zionismus in Deutschland war das Gewohnheitsjudentum.... Diese Zionisten waren daher antiliberal, nicht orthodoxe, aber Traditions-Gewohnheitsjuden. Der Zionismus war charakterisiert durch Posener Muerbekuchen oder Oberschlesische Ganseleber, d.h. Sitte, Essen, die Gemuetlichkeit des juedischen Lebens dargestellt, in eine andere Zeit versetzt, in 'Jettchen Gebert.' Das Ziel dieser Zionisten war, in Deutschland als Juden zu leben. Die Vorstellung des Nach-Palaestina-Gehens war kaum vorhanden." See interview with Kurt Blumenfeld, oral history section, catalogue no. 990, file 26/4.

201. Holdheim, "Die deutsche Alijah."

202. Siegfried Kanowitz, "Vom Post-assimilatorischem Zionismus zur Post-Zionistischen Assimilation," *Rueckkehr und Besinnung,* p. 22.

203. See Robert Weltsch, "Deutscher Zionismus in der Rueckschau," *In Zwei Welten, Siegfried Moses Festschrift,* pp. 29–30. See also Kurt Blumenfeld's essay in *JR* (September 2, 1910), reprinted in *Zionistische Betrachtungen.*

204. Weltsch, "Deutscher Zionismus," pp. 29–30.

205. See interview with Kurt Blumenfeld, oral history section, catalogue no. 990, file 26/4.

206. Quoted by Kurt Blumenfeld, "Verein Juedischer Studenten Koenigsberg," *Rueckkehr und Besinnung,* p. 5.

207. Kanowitz, "Vom Post-assimilatorischem Zionismus," pp. 21–22.

208. Holdheim, "Die deutsche Alijah." See also Ahron Sandler, "Memoirs," CZA, A69/2.

209. Max Kollenscher, "Memoirs," Leo Baeck Archives, Jerusalem.

210. See Adolf Asch, "Memoirs," Leo Baeck Archives, Jerusalem.

211. Ibid.

212. Paul Rieger, *Ein Vierteljahrhundert,* p. 54.

213. Siegfried Kanowitz, "Vom Post-assimilatorischem Zionismus," p. 20.

214. Lichtheim names about thirty German Zionists who settled in Palestine before 1914; this is the highest estimate. See *Toldot Ha'Zionut b'Germania,* pp. 93–94, n. 1. See also Elias Auerbach, *Pionier der Verwirklichung.*

215. Holdheim estimates that only about ten German Zionists emigrated to Palestine before 1914. See "Die deutsche Alijah."

216. Siegmund Kaznelson, ed., *Juden im deutschen Kulturbereich,* p. 995. Kaznelson asserts that the number of German Zionists who emigrated to Palestine before 1933 was minimal, but does not quote figures.

217. For details see Eliav, *Ahavat Zion.*
218. These figures were collected by the Jewish Agency. See the Jewish Agency, Department of Immigration and Works, *Haaliyah,* 1:32. Gustav Landauer cites the total emigration of German Jews before 1933 as 2,000. See *Der Zionismus im Wandel Dreier Jahrzehnte,* p. 83. This figure is probably the upper limit of German Jewish emigration for that time period.
219. Jewish Agency, *Haaliyah.* Many who came as tourists remained without permission from the Mandate authorities.
220. Jewish Agency, *Haaliyah.*
221. The study does not quote figures for German Jews who left Palestine. For detailed statistics on *Ostjuden* in Germany, especially Berlin, see Eschelbacher, "Die ostjuedische Einwanderungsbevoelkerung."
222. Jewish Agency, *Haaliyah.*
223. Jewish Agency, *Haaliyah.* Unfortunately we do not have accurate figures before World War I. Although this book deals with the Wilhelminian period, it is important to include this table of the Weimar period, since it indicates the lack of consistency between ideology and practice of both the first generation of German Zionists and the "radical" generation which grew around Kurt Blumenfeld. See chapters 4 and 5.
224. See, for example, "Wider den Mythos vom deutsch-juedischen Gespraech," *Fuer Margarete Sussman,* p. 231.
225. Oppenheimer, *Erlebtes,* p. 212.

Chapter IV

1. Ismar Schorsch has suggested, "Many of these early Zionists were firmly rooted in knowledge of Judaism. Childhood experience, synagogue affiliation, study, and practice had prepared them for a nationalistic reaffirmation of Judaism. Zionism had not represented as great a personal transformation for them as it did for the totally alienated second generation. Thus the concern for Eastern Jewry and the familiarity with Judaism, sometimes one alone, destined the Zionism of men like Bodenheimer, Wolffsohn . . . to be a form of moderate protest." On the other hand Schorsch argues that "the turn to Zionism of the second generation of middle-class university students and young professionals represented an intensely personal reaction to the circumstances of Jewish life in the Second Reich. Men like Blumenfeld and Lichtheim came from completely and successfully assimilated homes." Schorsch, *Jewish Reactions to German Anti-Semitism,* p. 192.
   It seems to me that Schorsch's lines are too rigid. The two generations were by no means clearly defined. There were first-generation Zionists who came from totally assimilated homes (Friedemann, Oppenheimer) and second-generation Zionists who came from strictly orthodox backgrounds (Martin and Felix Rosenblueth, Sammy Gronemann, Moses Calvary).
2. Another historian has put it succinctly: "The Jewish youth who

entered the universities after 1890 encountered a generation of young Germans who were more likely to be antisemitic, and more profoundly antisemitic, than those met by their fathers and uncles two or three decades earlier. Moreover, the quality of the antisemitism which confronted the Jewish youth in the universities of the 1890's was different from that which their elders had known in their own student years; antisemitism was now 'modern,' expressed in *avant garde* vocabulary of racial or *voelkisch* theories." See Sanford Ragins, "Jewish Responses to Antisemitism in Germany 1870–1914," p. 233. Ragins deals at length with the influence of the *voelkisch* ideology.

3. Pulzer, *The Rise of Political Anti-Semitism*, p. 291.
4. See Shaul Esh, "Designs for Anti-Jewish Policy in Germany up to the Nazi Rule," *Yad Vashem Studies* 4 (1967):96–99.
5. Halpern, *The Idea*, p. 25.
6. See Ahad Ha'Am, "Lo Zeh Ha'Derekh," in *Kol Kitvei Ahad Ha'Am*, pp. 11–16.
7. See Leon Simon, *Ahad Ha'Am*, pp. 169 ff.
8. Klausner, *Opposizia*, pp. 175–81.
9. See, for example, Martin Buber, "Ein geistiges Zentrum" (1902); "Renaissance und Bewegung" (1903). Both articles were reprinted in *Die Juedische Bewegung*, pp. 78–108. See also Buber's "Achad Ha'Am, Gedenkreden gehalten von Nahum Sokolow und Martin Buber in der Eroeffnungssitzung des XV Zionistenkonkresses in Basel am 30. August 1927" (London: Zentralbureau der Zionistischen Organisation).
10. See Hans Kohn, *Martin Buber*, pp. 49 ff.
11. See Martin Buber, "Das Juedische Kulturproblem und der Zionismus," in *Die Stimme der Wahrheit*, pp. 210–11.
12. Ibid., p. 216.
13. Ibid., p. 215.
14. See Kohn, *Martin Buber*, pp. 68 ff.
15. Concerning Buber's impact on the Prague group see *Vom Judentum*, "Herausgegeben vom Verein Juedischer Hochschueler Bar Kochba in Prag"; also Hans Kohn, *Buerger vieler Welten*, p. 93, and interview with Dr. Robert Weltsch, August 25, 1969.
16. See Martin Buber, "Das Judentum und die Juden," *Der Jude und Sein Judentum*, pp. 9 ff. For the present exposition, the translation of Eva Jospe has been used and page numbers refer to *On Judaism*.
17. Ibid., p. 13.
18. Ibid., p. 16.
19. Ibid., pp. 19–20.
20. Martin Buber, "Der Preis," *Der Jude* (1917/1918), p. 507.
21. See Hans Kohn, "Rueckblick auf eine gemeinsame Jugend" in *Robert Weltsch zum 70. Geburtstag*, p. 115.
22. Nahum N. Glatzer, "Postscript" in *On Judaism*, p. 239.
23. See Robert Weltsch, "Nachwort" in Gustav Landauer, *Der Zionismus im Wandel Dreier Jahrhunderte*, p. 458.
24. Kurt Blumenfeld, "Urspruenge und Art einer Zionistischen Bewegung," *BLBI* (1957/1959), p. 129.
25. *JR*, no. 13 (February 15, 1927), p. 92.
26. Blumenfeld, "Urspruenge," p. 132.

27. Martin Buber, "Wege zum Zionismus," *Die Juedische Bewegung*, 1:39 ff.

28. Quoted by Zechlin, *Die deutsche Politik*, p. 73.

29. See Walter Laqueur, *Young Germany*, pp. 32 ff.

30. See Robert Weltsch in *Der Zionismus im Wandel*, p. 458.

31. See George Mosse, *Germans and Jews*, pp. 102 ff.

32. See *Der Juedische Student*, no. 12 (March, 1911), p. 336.

33. *Der Juedische Student*, no. 1 (January, 1911), p. 24.

34. Ibid., p. 100. See also Hans Tramer, "Juedischer Wanderbund Blau-Weiss," *BLBI*, no. 17 (1962), pp. 23 ff.

35. Moritz Bileski, "Die deutschen Juden in der deutschen Politik," *Der Jude* (1917/1918), 2:230.

36. Although the young Zionists considered themselves German citizens, they clearly emphasized their *Judentum* over their *Deutschtum*. Thus, in his "Lebenslauf" (curriculum vitae) required at the end of all dissertations, Felix Rosenblueth described himself as follows: "Ich bin Jude und preussischer Staatsangehoeriger." This was a conscious repudiation of the "Deutscher Staatsbuerger juedischen Glaubens." The theme of his dissertation, written in 1910, is also noteworthy: "Zur Begriffsbestimmung von Volk und Nation."

37. There were, of course, exceptions; a notable one was Hans Goslar, who occupied a high government post. Another example was Hermann Badt. After World War I the controversy as to whether Zionists should participate in government erupted around an article by Erich Cohn in the *JR*. The ZVfD never formulated an official position on this question.

   A point of view opposed to Blumenfeld's was expressed by Max Kollenscher, an active member of the JVP; see his *Zionismus und Staatsbuergertum*, pp. 9–10.

38. Kurt Blumenfled, *Erlebte Judenfrage*, p. 52.

39. Interviews with Pinhas Rosen and Siegfried Moses. Both Rosen and Moses make the same causal estimate; see also Richard Lichtheim, *Rueckkehr*, p. 127.

40. *JR*, no. 32 (August 12, 1910), p. 377.

41. Walter Gross, "The Zionist Students' Movement," p. 148.

42. Interviews with Pinhas Rosen and Siegfried Moses.

43. Ibid., and Gross, "The Zionist Students' Movement," p. 149.

44. *JR*, no. 37 (September 16, 1910), p. 437. On Hantke see also Zalman Shazar, *Or Ishim*, pp. 108–17.

45. For details on the conflict between Wolffsohn and the opposition see Julius Berger, "Bitkufat Koeln" in *Sefer Sokolow*, pp. 346 ff.

46. The Ninth Congress elected Arthur Hantke and Ahron Sandler to the Engere Aktionskomitee; both men subsequently declined.

47. N. M. Gelber, *Hakongressim*, pp. 36–39; Georg Herlitz and Michael Heymann in their "Introductory Notes" to *The Central Zionist Office, Berlin*, CZA, Jerusalem.

48. *JR*, no. 36 (September 9, 1910), p. 425; *JR*, no. 21 (May 25, 1912), p. 183.

49. See *JR*, no. 37 (September 16, 1910), p. 437.

50. In addition, the ZVfD began publication in October 1910 of the

bi-monthly periodical *Jung Israel* which was designed to attract the German Jewish youth. This periodical had to be discontinued in 1912 for lack of funds.

51. See Kurt Blumenfeld, "Wetterleuchten," *BLBI*, no. 8 (1959), p. 206.
52. See Pierson, "German Jewish Identity," p. 154.
53. Blumenfeld, "Wetterleuchten," p. 206.
54. Ibid.
55. Blumenfeld, *Erlebte*, pp. 36 ff.
56. Ibid., p. 63.
57. Ibid., p. 39. Shaul Esh has summarized Blumenfeld's conversion to Zionism by stating that "The problem of Jewish personality had brought Blumenfeld to Zionism." See Esh's "Kurt Blumenfeld on the Modern Jew and Zionism," *Jewish Journal of Sociology*, no. 2 (December, 1964), 6:240. For an incisive analysis of Blumenfeld's theories and the position of Jew and Zionist in the Diaspora, consult the entire article.
58. Blumenfeld, *Erlebte*, p. 39.
59. Gross, "The Zionist Students' Movement," p. 147.
60. Blumenfeld, *Erlebte*, p. 70.
61. See Robert Weltsch, "Deutscher Zionismus in der Rueckschau," *In Zwei Welten*, p. 34.
62. Blumenfeld, "Urspruenge," p. 137. See also Pierson, "German Jewish Identity," pp. 161–62.
63. Blumenfeld obviously knew that German Jews were rooted in German culture; he himself was the example par excellence of one who came to Zionism through study and observation of German culture. He was rather referring to the *Kulturkonflikt* which emerged when Jews "suddenly realize that their cultural ambience is not quite the same as that of their friends, acquaintances, and colleagues. . . . They find it a terrible tragedy to have to think in a language which is not adequate to their creative abilities. *Kulturkonflikt* has become a problem of the Jewish personality." See Esh, "Kurt Blumenfeld," p. 234.
64. Blumenfeld, "Urspruenge," p. 137. See also Pierson's analysis which examines in great detail Blumenfeld's concept of "Distanz," "rootlessness" and "Grenzueberschreitung." Pierson, "German Jewish Identity," pp. 168–70. In my description of Blumenfeld's theories I have used Pierson's perceptive analysis, which is modified by Esh's incisive observations.
65. *JR*, no. 37 (September 16, 1910), p. 444.
66. Ibid.
67. See *JR* (September 2, 1910).
68. See Ruth Gladstein-Kerstenberg, "Athalat Bar Kochba" in *Prag V'Yerushalayim*, p. 97, and Sammy Gronemann, *Zikhronot shel Yekke*.
69. Kurt Blumenfeld, "Deutscher Zionismus," *Zionistische Betrachtungen*, p. 13.
70. Ibid., p. 14. Blumenfeld's choice of words is telling since it is a prelude to similar formulations presented in Posen: "Da wir aber gezwungen sind, noch eine Zeit des Uebergangs hier zu ertragen, so gilt es, in dieser Zeit uns stark zu machen und neue Kraefte fuer uns zu

gewinnen, die Juden bleiben wollen und die Kraft des Erkennens haben, dass nur im eigenen Lande die dauernde Erhaltung unseres Volkes moeglich sein wird, und die Kraft des Wollens haben, diese Erhaltung fuer sich als persoenliche Notwendigkeit zu empfinden."

71. *JR*, no. 37 (September 16, 1910), p. 444.

72. Kurt Blumenfeld in an interview with Shaul Esh, oral history section, Institute of Contemporary History, Hebrew University, catalogue no. 990, file 26/4.

73. Ibid.

74. *JR*, no. 37 (September 16, 1910), p. 443.

75. Ibid.

76. *JR*, no. 22 (May 31, 1912), p. 196. See also "Protokoll der ersten Plenarsitzung des Zentralkomitees vom 3. November, 1912."

77. See *Bericht des Actions Comites der Zionistischen Organisation an den XI Zionisten Kongress*, Wien, September 2–9, 1913.

78. *JR*, no. 22 (May 31, 1912), p. 196.

79. See "Protokoll der 6 Sitzung des Geschaeftsfuehrenden Ausschusses vom Dienstag den 17 Dezember, 1912." CZA, A15/VII/25. A second edition of 5,000 copies was issued by the ZVfD in 1913.

80. *JR*, no. 22 (May 31, 1912), p. 197.

81. See Adolf Boehm, *Die Zionistische Bewegung*, 1:381 ff.

82. Blumenfeld's speech was not printed by the *JR*. The editor indicated that because of its length, it would be printed separately at a later date; this, however, never came about. Information about the speech comes mainly from the discussion at the convention and from eyewitness reports. See *JR*, no. 23 (June 7, 1912), pp. 206–7, and interview with Pinhas Rosen. See also "XIII Delegiertentag der Zionistischen Vereinigung fuer Deutschland," *Die Welt*, no. 22 (May 31, 1912), pp. 641–58. *Die Welt* did not print the speech, but did editorialize on it.

83. *JR*, no. 23 (June 7, 1912), pp. 206–7.

84. *JR*, no. 24 (June 14, 1912), p. 217.

85. Hence it is usually, erroneously, assumed that the resolution was proposed by Blumenfeld.

86. *JR*, no. 24 (June 14, 1912), p. 222.

87. Ibid.

88. *JR*, no. 25 (June 19, 1914), p. 264.

89. The opposition to the resolution developed after it had passed, during internal meetings of the leadership of the ZVfD. At these meetings even Klee and Gronemann, not only Oppenheimer and Friedemann, considered the resolution a mistake and a senseless provocation of the major German Jewish organizations. See "Protokoll der ersten Plenarsitzung des Zentralkomitees vom 3 November, 1912." CZA, A15/VII/25.

90. See Blumenfeld, *Erlebte*, p. 69. He states that at Posen he considered Hantke an opponent of the resolution.

91. Interview with Pinhas Rosen.

92. Blumenfeld, *Erlebte*, p. 90. See also oral history section, Institute of Contemporary Jewry, catalogue no. 990, file 26/4.

93. Hans Tramer in his "Foreword" to *Erlebte Judenfrage*, p. 17.

94. See, for example, *JR*, no. 18 (May 8, 1914); *JR*, no. 19 (May 11,

1914); *JR*, no. 20 (May 15, 1914), and *JR*, no. 21 (May 21, 1914). See also private correspondence among Zionists. CZA, A15/18e.

95. Blumenfeld, *Erlebte*, p. 113.

96. *JR*, no. 25 (June 19, 1914), p. 264.

97. Ibid., p. 262.

98. Ibid. For more details see also *Bericht des Actions Comites der ZVfD an den XI Zionisten Kongress.*

99. *JR*, no. 25 (June 19, 1914), p. 264.

100. Ibid., p. 267.

101. Ibid.

102. Ibid., p. 268.

103. Ibid.

104. Ibid., p. 269.

105. Ibid., p. 270.

106. Ibid.

107. Letter of Bodenheimer to Friedemann, May 29, 1914. CZA, A15/18e.

108. *JR*, no. 25 (June 19, 1914), p. 264.

109. Ibid., p. 271.

110. Ibid.

111. Ibid., p. 268.

112. Blumenfeld was probably referring to himself, since he was often accused of propagating the use of Hebrew language, while he himself was not able to speak it. Interview with Professor Gershom Scholem, December 15, 1970.

113. *JR*, no. 25 (June 19, 1914), p. 269.

114. Ibid., p. 270.

115. See Keren Hayessod, *Hantke l'Gvurot*, p. 8; Blumenfeld, *Erlebte*, p. 113.

116. Lichtheim, *Toldot Ha'Zionut b'Germania*, p. 108.

117. Gerhard Holdheim comments cynically: "Auf dem Posener Delegiertentag wurde 'Palaestina in das Lebensprogramm aufgenommen.' Das Ergebnis waren zwei 'Wanderfahrten' die als sensationelle Tat empfunden wurden. Was die Menschen, die wie man sich scherzhaft erzaehlte, mit dem Liede 'Wohlan, lasst das Sinnen und Sorgen' in Tel Aviv einzogen, empfunden haben mochten, war Romantik, die so fernab jeder Wirklichkeit lag, dass sie den Willen zu einer persoenlichen Uebersiedlung nicht aufloesen konnte. Die Zahl unserer Vorkriegs-Palaestinenser erreichte kaum zehn, und die—oder ist das ein Irrtum— gingen *vor* 1912 und waren meist Gegner der Richtung, die die Posener Beschluesse durchsetzte." Gerhard Holdheim, "Die deutsche Alijah." CZA, G1293.

118. Interview with Professor Jacob Toury (May, 1971) and with Professor Gershom Scholem (December, 1970). Scholem is particularly critical of Blumenfeld whose radicalism, he claims, "was watered down to radical verbiage" throughout the Weimar period. See also Siegfried Moses, "Kurt Blumenfeld zum 5 Todestage," *Mitteilungsblatt des Irgun Oley Merkaz Europea*, no. 20 (May 17, 1968), p. 35.

119. Lichtheim, *Toldot Ha'Zionut b'Germania*, p. 109.

120. See, for example, *JR*, no. 15 (April 11, 1913), p. 147.

121. Blumenfeld, "Urspruenge," p. 137.
122. *JR*, no. 1 (January 3, 1930), and *JR*, no. 2 (January 7, 1930).
123. Blumenfeld, "Urspruenge," p. 138.
124. Ahron Sandler, "Memoirs," CZA, A69/2.
125. Blumenfeld, "Urspruenge," p. 131.

Chapter V

1. Fuchs, *Um Deutschtum*, p. 58; Rieger, *Ein Vierteljahrhundert*, p. 54.
2. See *Die Welt*, no. 13 (August 27, 1897).
3. See *JR*, no. 28 (July 12, 1912), p. 259.
4. Interview with Klaus Hermann (June, 1969), who claims that the 2,000 members included the richest and most powerful men of the German Jewish community. It should be pointed out that from a legal point of view the "Reformgemeinde zu Berlin" was not really a *Gemeinde* but rather a *Privatverein* of reform Jews. It was not a *Separatgemeinde* like that of the orthodox. The confusion stems from the fact that they called themselves *Gemeinde* rather than *Verein*.
5. The *Liberales Judentum* began publication in September, 1908, and was edited by Rabbi Caesar Seligmann.
6. See, for example, Elias Auerbach, *Pionier der Verwirklichung*, p. 140, where he reports one such conflict.
7. For a detailed analysis, see Werner J. Cahnmann, "Munich and the First Zionist Congress," *Historia Judaica* 3 (1941):7-23.
8. Ibid., p. 15.
9. Ibid. See also the "Appendix," p. 21.
10. See *Die Welt*, no. 5 (July 2, 1897), pp. 1-2.
11. Ibid., p. 2.
12. Ibid.
13. *Allgemeine Zeitung des Judentums*, no. 24 (June 11, 1897), p. 277. The article was written on June 8, 1897.
14. Ibid.
15. Ibid. See also *Die Welt*, no. 3 (June 18, 1897), p. 5.
16. See *JR*, no. 20 (May 17, 1907), pp. 203-4. Also Louis Maretzki, *Geschichte des Ordens Bnei Briss in Deutschland*, pp. 138 ff.
17. Ibid.
18. See *Die Welt*, no. 5 (July 2, 1897).
19. See *Allgemeine Zeitung des Judentums*, no. 29 (July 16, 1897), p. 338.
20. See paragraph 2 of the protest in *AZdJ*, no. 29 (July 16, 1897), p. 338 and *AZdJ*, no. 24 (June 11, 1897), p. 277.
21. *AZdJ*, no. 27 (July 2, 1897), p. 339.
22. Although we have no proof that the association took this article into consideration, its publication in the most prestigious German Jewish newspaper indicates that the protest by the Rabbis was a reflection of the mood of the Jewish community.
23. For the original declaration see CZA, F4/34. It was reprinted in all major Jewish newspapers and periodicals. See, for example, *IDR*, nos.

7/8 (July 7, 1897) and *A Zd J*, no. 29 (July 16, 1897). The translation is adapted, with slight changes, from Ben Halpern, *The Idea*, p. 144. See also pp. 144—47.

It is interesting to note that, according to the by-laws of the Association of Rabbis in Germany, decisions concerning basic issues had to be approved by the entire national membership. However, since time was short and the dangers of Zionism imminent, the executive of the association apparently decided to take the responsibility for issuing the declaration. Only in June, 1898, with a delay of almost one year and after the First Zionist Congress had taken place (in August, 1897) was the national membership consulted. Rabbi Maybaum chaired the meeting and allowed only a very limited discussion. The result was that the national assembly of the association confirmed the original declaration. See *Verhandlungen und Beschluesse der Generalversammlung des Rabbiner Verbandes in Deutschland* (1898), p. 31. See also *IDR*, nos. 6/7 (June/July, 1898), p. 335.

24. See especially Herzl's famous "Protestrabbiner," *Die Welt*, no. 7 (July 16, 1897) and Alex Bein, *Theodore Herzl*, pp. 221—25. See also the little known but very detailed brochure by Heinrich Sachse [Loewe], *Zionisitenkongress und Zionismus... eine Gefahr?*, and H. Salomonsohn's *Widerspricht der Zionismus unsere Religion?*

25. See *Koelnische Zeitung* (August, 1897). Also CZA, F4/34.

26. For example the young rabbis at the "Lehranstalt fuer die Wissenschaft des Judentums" who founded a "National—juedischer Verein" in 1901, were forced to disband it. For details see Kurt Wilhelm, "Der Zionistische Rabbiner," *In Zwei Welten*, pp. 66—67. See also Rahel Halpern, *Dr. Biram u'Veit ha'Sefer ha'Reali b'Haifa*, p. 55.

27. For the controversy around Cohn see Hans Tramer, "Bernhard und Emil Cohn, Zwei Streiter fuer den Zionistischen Gedanken," *BLBI*, no. 32 (1965).

28. See *JR*, no. 20 (May 17, 1907), p. 197.

29. See Emil Cohn's "Erklaerung," *JR*, no. 19 (May 10, 1907), p. 189.

30. Emil Cohn, "Die Geschichte meiner Suspension" reprinted in *JR*, no. 17 (April 26, 1907), p. 171. See also Emil Cohn, "Memorandum an die Vorsteher und Vertreter der Juedischen Gemeinde zu Berlin" (February, 1907), CZA, collection of printed manuscripts.

31. So-called by the German Zionists. See *JR*, no. 17 (April 26, 1907), p. 167.

32. See Naomi Wiener Cohen, "The Reaction of Reform Judaism in America to Political Zionism 1897—1922," *Publications of the American Jewish Historical Society*, no. 40 (1950/1951), pp. 361—94.

33. See Tramer, "Bernhard und Emil Cohn," p. 342, n. 13.

34. *JR*, no. 17 (April 26, 1907), p. 169.

35. See *JR*, no. 23 (June 7, 1907), pp. 230—32.

36. Emil Cohn, "Mein Kampf ums Recht" (1907). Reprinted in *JR*, no. 20 (May 17, 1907).

37. See Tramer, "Bernhard und Emil Cohn," p. 342.

38. See, for example, Gideon Heymann, "Der Zionismus und die Juedischen Gemeinden," *JR*, no. 27 (July 15, 1907).

39. This analysis does not include the situation in Posen which was not

within the mainstream of Jewish life in Germany. See Berthold Haas, "Memoirs," Leo Baeck Institute, Jerusalem.

40. During the first decade of the century the ZVfD did all it could to avoid conflicts, even when under direct attack. See the confidential letter of the "Berliner Zionistische Vereinigung" of September 26, 1906, addressed to the "Liberales Verein fuer die Angelegenheiten der juedischen Gemeinde zu Berlin," in which the BZV explains that even though it had been attacked by the "Verein" it was willing to forego a counter-attack "for the sake of peace and unity within Jewry," CAHJP, KGE/64.

41. ZVfD, "Protokoll der Sitzung des Centralcomités in Coeln vom 27, August 1906; *Streng Vertraulich.*" CZA, A11/16/3/2.

42. Ibid.

43. Ibid.

44. See Moshe Rinott, "Peulatah shel 'Hevrat ha'Ezra l'Yehudei Germania' ba'Hinukh b'Erez-Israel (1901–1918)," Ph.D. diss., Hebrew University, Jerusalem, 1969, p. 203. Published as *Hevrat ha'Ezra l'Yehudei Germania* (1971). References here are to the dissertation.

45. Rinott, "Hevrat ha'Ezra," pp. 205, 208. The only ZVfD criticism of the Hilfsverein was of its anti-Zionist representative in Palestine, Ephraim Cohn.

46. In the case of Emil Cohn, for example, the C.V. did not interfere, since it considered the case the exclusive concern of the Berlin Jewish community.

47. Fuchs, *Um Deutschtum*, p. 58.

48. ZVfD, "Flugblatt no. 2," August, 1897. CZA, W/147/1.

49. *IDR*, no. 4 (April, 1896), p. 193.

50. Ibid., p. 195. See also *IDR*, no. 3 (March, 1897).

51. See Fuchs's article in the *Berliner Vereinsboten*, December 24, 1897.

52. In fact, this policy was quite effective and despite numerous attempts, the Zionists could not break the "conspiracy of silence" within the German Jewish community. See Martin Rosenblueth, *Go Forth and Serve*, p. 152.

53. *IDR*, nos. 7/8 (July/August, 1897).

54. *IDR*, no. 10 (October, 1897), p. 484.

55. Ibid.

56. See *Satzung des Centralvereins deutscher Staatsbuerger juedischen Glaubens*, paragraph 1.

57. Ibid., p. 1.

58. See the proceedings of the "147. Vorstandssitzung, am Montag den 2. November, 1903." CAHJP, INV 124/lb.

59. "Vorstandssitzung no. 147 des C.V., November 2, 1903." CAHJP, INV 124/1a–16.

60. "C.V. Vorstandssitzung, March 14, 1900." CAHJP, INV 124/1a–16. See also "125. Vorstandssitzung, December 2, 1901; 135 (ausserordentliche) Vorstandssitzung, October 20, 1902." CAHJP, INV 124/lb.

61. See, for example, Elias Auerbach, "Deutsche Kultur im Zionismus," *JR*, no. 7 (February 13, 1903), p. 50.

62. See, for example, *IDR*, no. 9 (September, 1903), p. 550; *IDR*, no. 10 (October, 1906), p. 607; *IDR*, no. 2 (February, 1910).
63. *IDR*, no. 2 (February, 1903), p. 187. Also Rieger, *Ein Vierteljahrhundert*, p. 54.
64. *IDR*, nos. 7/8 (July/August, 1908), p. 450.
65. *IDR*, no. 11 (November, 1905), p. 700.
66. See letter of Hugo Schachtel (Breslau) to Arthur Hantke, August 20, 1906. CZA, A15/VII/46.
67. See *Der Juedische Student*, no. 9 (December 21, 1909), p. 210.
68. *Der Juedische Student*, nos. 11/12 (March 24, 1910), p. 249.
69. *IDR*, nos. 7/8 (July/August, 1908), p. 452.
70. Ibid.
71. See Jacob Toury, "Plans for a Jewish Diet and the Zionists in Germany," *Zionism* (1970), pp. 9–57.
72. Jacob Toury, "Plans for a Jewish Political Organization in Germany (1893–1918)" *Zion*, no. 28 (1963).
73. Toury, "Plans for a Jewish Diet," p. 12.
74. Ibid., p. 17.
75. Ibid., pp. 20–21.
76. The only result was the creation of the *Verband der deutschen Juden* on April 29, 1904, in which the ZVfD was not represented.
77. Toury, "Plans for a Jewish Political Organization," p. 178.
78. See Berthold Haas's and Max Kollenscher's "Memoirs," both in the Leo Baeck Institute, Jerusalem, for the Jewish situation in Posen.
79. Toury, "Plans for a Jewish Political Organization," p. 187.
80. Ibid., pp. 191–94.
81. See *JR*, no. 37 (September 16, 1910), p. 437.
82. *JR*, no. 21 (May 27, 1910), pp. 245–46.
83. *JR*, no. 14 (April 7, 1911), p. 157.
84. Previous Zionist attempts to "conquer the communities," notably in 1907, were half-hearted and did not arouse much attention. See *JR*, no. 27 (July 5, 1907).
85. The voters could strike names off the list but could not enter other names. If a certain percentage of the voters struck a name off a list, the candidate had to be removed, but the party had the right to substitute another candidate of its own choice.
86. See, for example, *JR*, no. 46 (November 18, 1910), p. 525.
87. Ibid.
88. See *JR*, no. 48 (December 2, 1910), p. 549.
89. During elections the orthodox usually shifted to the group which promised to meet most of their demands.
90. *JR*, no. 48 (December 2, 1910), p. 549.
91. *JR*, no. 14 (April 7, 1911), p. 157.
92. See Werner Sombart, *Die Juden und das Wirtschaftsleben* (1911).
93. See Werner Sombart, *Die Zukunft der Juden* (1912).
94. In Berlin almost 2,000 people came to hear Sombart's lectures, despite the high entrance fee. See *JR*, no. 46 (November 17, 1911), p. 541.
95. The C.V., for example, asked members of the *Ortsgruppe* of

Hamburg to stay away from Sombart's lectures since he was an anti-Semite. See "Protokoll der 1. Plenarsitzung des Zentralkomitees im Jahre 1912, am 4. Februar 1912." CZA, A15/VII/25.

96. *JR*, no. 23 (June 7, 1912), p. 209; *Der Israelit*, no. 21 (June, 1912).

97. Sombart, *Die Zukunft*, p. 6.

98. See Arthur Ruppin, *Die Juden der Gegenwart* (2d ed., 1911).

99. Sombart, *Die Zukunft*, p. 27.

100. Ibid., pp. 31–36.

101. Ibid., p. 39.

102. Ibid., p. 48.

103. Ibid., p. 52.

104. Ibid., p. 58

105. Ibid., p. 85.

106. Ibid., p. 87.

107. See Kurt Blumenfeld, *Erlebte Judenfrage*, p. 58.

108. See "Protokoll der 1. Plenarsitzung des Zentralkomitees im Jahre 1912, am 4. Februar 1912." CZA, A15/VII/25.

109. Ibid. See also *JR*, no. 46 (November 17, 1911), p. 541.

110. *JR*, no. 50 (December 15, 1911), p. 589.

111. *JR*, no. 5 (February 2, 1912), p. 34. See also *JR*, no. 28 (July 12, 1912), p. 259.

112. See, for example, "Sombart als Zionistischer Apostel," *Der Israelit*, no. 18 (May 2, 1912), pp. 1–3.

113. *IDR*, no. 2 (February, 1912), p. 105.

114. Ibid., p. 106.

115. *JR*, no. 7 (February 16, 1912), p. 51.

116. Ibid., pp. 51–52.

117. Ibid.

118. "Sombart Hetze und kein Ende," *JR*, no. 23 (June 7, 1912), p. 209.

119. Eugen Fuchs, "Sombart und die Zukunft der Juden," *IDR*, no. 6 (June, 1912), pp. 257–75.

120. Ibid.

121. Fuchs, *Um Deutschtum*, p. 139.

122. The subtitle of the *Kunstwart* was "Halbmonatschau fuer Ausdruckskultur auf allen Lebensgebieten."

123. See *Der Kunstwart*, vol. 25, no. 11 (March, 1912).

124. See Moritz Goldstein, "German Jewry's Dilemma before 1914," *LBIYB*, vol. 2 (1957), p. 246.

125. *Der Kunstwart* (March, 1912), p. 283.

126. Ibid.

127. Ibid., p. 286.

128. Ibid., p. 294.

129. Ibid., p. 290.

130. *JR*, no. 33 (August 16, 1912), p. 309.

131. *JR*, no. 11 (March 15, 1912), p. 97.

132. Ernst Lissauer became famous in 1914 because of his nationalistic song, "Hassgesang gegen England."

133. *Der Kunstwart* (April, 1912), p. 6.

134. Ibid., p. 12.
135. Ibid., p. 13.
136. *Der Kunstwart* (August, 1912), pp. 238–44.
137. *IDR*, no. 10 (October, 1912).
138. The C.V. was not the only German Jewish paper to delay its response. The major liberal papers such as the *Berliner Tageblatt* did not respond at all. See letter of Walter Benjamin to Ludwig Strauss, September 11, 1912. Ludwig Strauss Collection, Buber Archives, Jerusalem.
139. *IDR*, no. 10 (October, 1912), p. 448.
140. Ibid., p. 450.
141. See *AZdJ*, no. 46 (November 15, 1912), and *AZdJ*, no. 47 (November 22, 1912).
142. See *Der Israelit*, no. 37 (September 11, 1912).
143. *IDR*, no. 1 (January, 1913), pp. 22–27.
144. See, for example, *IDR*, no. 3 (March, 1913), pp. 97–117.
145. *JR*, no. 42 (October 18, 1912), p. 399.
146. *JR*, no. 22 (May 31, 1912), p. 196.
147. *JR*, no. 5 (February 2, 1912), p. 33.
148. *JR*, no. 11 (March 8, 1912), p. 81.
149. Ibid.
150. See "Protokoll der 1. Plenarsitzung des Zentralkomitees im Jahre 1912, am 4. Februar 1912," CZA, A15/VII/25.
151. See Walter Gross, "The Zionist Students' Movement," *LBIYB*, vol. 4 (1959), pp. 143–64.
152. See Herbert Strauss, "The Jugendverband, a Social and Intellectual History," *LBIYB*, vol. 6 (1961).
153. See Chaim Schatzker, "Tnuat ha'Noar ha'Yehudit b'Germania beyn ha'Shanim 1900–1933," Ph.D. diss., Hebrew University, Jerusalem, 1969, p. 60.
154. Ibid., p. 78.
155. See Heinemann Stern, "Memoirs," Leo Baeck Institute Archives, New York, file C395.
156. Schatzker, "Tnuat ha'Noar," p. 66.
157. See "Protokoll der 1. Plenarsitzung des Zentralkomitees im Jahre 1912, am 4. Februar 1912," CZA, A15/VII/25.
158. Ibid.
159. Ibid.
160. CZA, collection of printed manuscripts, 2/7/10/2.
161. Ibid.
162. "Protokoll der ersten Sitzung des Geschaeftsfuehrenden Ausschusses am Dienstag den 20 Juni, 1912," CZA, A15/VII/25.
163. On February 4, 1912, Scholem presented the problems of the "Bar Kochba Turnverein" before the executive of the ZVfD and declared that the *Turnvereine* were ready to cooperate with the ZVfD. See "Protokoll der 1. Plenarsitzung des Zentralkomitees im Jahre 1912, am 4. Februar 1912." See also "Protokoll der XIII Sitzung des Geschaeftsfuehrenden Ausschusses vom 27 April, 1912." CZA, A15/V11/25.
164. *JR*, no. 22 (May 31, 1912), p. 199.

165. Ibid.

166. There is some doubt as to whether or not the *Blau-Weiss* was founded by the ZVfD. Pinhas Rosen (Rosenblueth) and Siegfried Moses claim that the group was a creation of the German Zionist movement. (See interviews of September 22, 1970, and September 15, 1970.) Schatzker, "Tnuat ha'Noar" (pp. 83 ff), and Gross, "The Zionist Students' Movement" (p. 151), claim that it grew independently. The internal protocol of the ZVfD confirms Moses and Rosen.

167. *IDR*, nos. 7/8 (July/August, 1912), pp. 373–74.

168. CAHJP, INV/1968/1–3.

169. *JR*, no. 23 (June 7, 1912), pp. 207–8. See also "Protokoll der 1. Plenarsitzung des Zentralkomitees vom 3. November 1912." CZA, A15/VII/25.

170. *JR*, no. 28 (July 12, 1912), p. 259.

171. *JR*, no. 37 (September 11, 1912), p. 349.

172. Ibid. In an interview with the author, Pinhas Rosen (Felix Rosenblueth) admitted: "One of our major problems was the lack of strong, wholesome anti-Zionists. We needed them desperately in order to develop our own ideology and we sought every opportunity to do battle with them." See interview of September 22, 1970.

173. *JR*, no. 41 (October 11, 1912), p. 390. See also *Die Welt*, no. 41 (October 11, 1912).

174. *JR*, no. 44 (November 1, 1912), p. 419.

175. CZA, Z3/796.

176. Ibid.

177. *JR*, no. 44 (November 1, 1912), p. 419. The ZVfD deliberately used the Mugdan Affair to attack the C.V. Arthur Hantke suggested to the executive of the ZVfD "Dagegen sollten wir den Zentralverein stark angreifen und zwar bietet uns hierzu die Affaere Mugdan ein gutes Angriffsobjekt." See "Protokoll der ersten Plenarsitzung des Zentralkomitees vom 3. November 1912." CZA, A15/VII/25.

178. As late as June, 1911, the C.V. declared its neutrality in inner-Jewish affairs. See *IDR* (June, 1911) and *JR*, no. 1 (January 1, 1914).

179. See CZA, Z3/796.

180. "Protokoll der 3. Sitzung des Geschaeftsfuehrenden Ausschusses, October, 1912." CZA, A15/VII/25.

181. "Protokoll der ersten Plenarsitzung des Zentralkomitees vom 3. November, 1912." CZA, A15/VII/25.

182. Ibid.

183. See *Koelner Israelitischer Gemeindeblatt*, October, 1912; *Strassburger Israelitischer Familienblatt*, November, 1912; and *Hamburger Israelitischer Familienblatt*, December, 1912.

184. See *IDR*, no. 1 (January, 1913), p. 22.

185. *IDR*, nos. 5/6 (May, 1913), p. 217.

186. *IDR*, no. 1 (January, 1913), pp. 23–24.

187. Ibid., p. 24.

188. Ibid., p. 25.

189. Ibid., p. 27. See also "Memoirs" of Heinemann Stern who was present at the meeting. Archives of the Leo Baeck Institute, New York, file C395.

190. *JR*, no. 42 (October 18, 1912), p. 399. See also CZA, Z3/796.

191. *JR*., no. 50 (December 13, 1912), p. 483.

192. CAHJP, KGE/64.

193. Ibid.

194. See Walter Breslauer, "Die Vereinigung fuer das liberale Judentum in Deutschland und die Richtlinien zu einem Programm fuer das liberale Judentum. Errinerungen aus den Jahren 1908–1914," *BLBI* (1966), p. 305.

195. See Michael Meyer, "Caesar Seligmann and the Development of Liberal Judaism in Germany at the Beginning of the Twentieth Century," *Hebrew Union College Annual*, vols. 40–41 (1969–70), p. 537.

196. Ibid., p. 535.

197. See *AZdJ*, no. 24 (June 11, 1897).

198. Meyer, "Caesar Seligmann," pp. 551–52.

199. Michael Meyer, Egmont Zechlin, and others erroneously give the founding date of the "Komitee" as 1913.

200. Meyer, "Caesar Seligmann," p. 552.

201. See ZVfD, *Jahresbericht ueber die Taetigkeit der Zionistischen Organisation fuer Deutschland* (1912).

202. "Protokoll der ersten Plenarsitzung des Zentralkomitees vom 3. November 1912," CZA, A15/VII/25.

203. Ibid. Klee even suggested that the ZVfD publicly restate the Posen Resolution as follows: "Die immer steigende Bedeutung der Palaestinaarbeit erfordert eine straffe Organisierung dieser Arbeit in Palaestina. Es werden deshalb unsere Gesinnungsgenossen, die die Moeglichkeit haben, gebeten, sich dieser Arbeit in Palaestina persoenlich zur Verfuegung zu stellen."

204. Ibid. See also Hantke's assessment of the resolution and of the misgivings of the ZVfD executive. CZA, A2/7/10/2.

205. "Protokoll der ersten Plenarsitzung . . . vom 3. November, 1912," CZA, A15/VII/25.

206. "Protokoll der V. Sitzung des Geschaeftsfuehrenden Ausschusses vom Mittwoch, den 13 November, 1913." CZA, A15/VII/25.

207. See CZA, collection of printed manuscripts, A102/49.

208. Ibid.

209. Ibid.

210. Ibid.

211. Letter of Max Bodenheimer to Arthur Hantke, March 20, 1913. CZA, A15/18e.

212. *IDR*, nos. 5/6 (May/June, 1913), p. 194.

213. Ibid., pp. 195–98.

214. Ibid., p. 213.

215. Ibid., pp. 215–16.

216. Ibid., p. 217.

217. Ibid., pp. 222, 231.

218. Ibid., p. 217.

219. Ibid., p. 220.
220. Ibid., pp. 246–47. The K.C. fully supported the C.V. resolution. See "Zentralverein und K.C.," *K.C. Blaetter*, no. 8 (May 1, 1913).
221. An example of the intensity of recriminations and abuse exchanged between the C.V. and the ZVfD just prior to the C.V. resolution is a speech given by Justizrat Auerbach before the C.V. in which he accused the ZVfD of endangering the civil rights of the German Jews and which ended with the words: "Einst wird man den Tag verfluchen, an dem der Zionismus geboren wurde." See *JR*, no. 10 (March 7, 1913), p. 93.
222. *IDR*, nos. 5/6 (May/June, 1913), pp. 236–38.
223. Ibid. See also Rieger, *Ein Vierteljahrhundert*, p. 56.
224. Nevertheless, the older Zionists still felt committed to the ZVfD and almost all of them refused to cooperate with the C.V. See letter of Max Bodenheimer to the C.V. of December 29, 1913. CZA, A15/18e.
225. See Ludwig Foerder, *Die Stellung des C.V. zu den innerjuedischen Fragen in den Jahren 1919–1926*, p. 9.
226. Rieger, *Ein Vierteljahrhundert*, p. 56. Rieger, however, does not give the total number of Zionists in the C.V.
227. CZA, collection of printed manuscripts, A102/H9.
228. The Zionists defended themselves against accusations of double loyalty in a number of articles. The following is typical: "Das Gefuehl des Staatsbuergers fuer den Staat das sich in Patriotismus, in der Liebe zum Land und zum Herrscher auessert, basiert auf der Gleichheit der Interessen, auf der Einsicht dass alle wirtschaftlichen und kulturellen Wohltaten die Existenz des Staates zur Voraussetzung haben. Darum wird der gute Staatsbuerger ganz selbstverstaendlich den Staat foerdern, ihn schuetzen und mit Gut und Blut fuer ihn eintreten . . . Nationalgefuehl und staatsbuergerliches Gefuehl sind ganz verschiedene Dinge. Wichtiger fuer den Staat ist das letztere. . . ." See Ludwig Wassermann, "Deutsches Nationalgefuehl," *JR*, no. 15 (April 11, 1913), p. 147.
229. Julius Moses, "Post Festum," *JR*, no. 14 (April 4, 1913).
230. Ibid., p. 136.
231. *JR*, no. 18 (May 2, 1913), p. 178. See also "Protokoll der internen Tagung der Zionistischen Vertrauensmaenner in Berlin am 1. Mai, 1913." CZA, Z3/796.
232. The Zionists, for example, called the C.V. "Zentralverein der Germanen monistischen Glaubens," or "Zentralverein deutscher Staatsbuerger juedischen Unglaubens." See *JR*, no. 29 (July 18, 1913), p. 297.
233. See Rinott, "Hevrat ha'Ezra," p. 219.
234. The details of the dispute are well known. They are recapitulated here briefly to complete the description of anti-Zionism. For details see: Zionistisches Actions Comite, *Im Kampf um die Hebraeische Sprache;* Paul Nathan, *Palaestina und palaestinensischer Zionismus; JR*, no. 44 (October 31, 1913); *JR*, no. 45 (November 7, 1913), pp. 479–80; *JR*, no. 47 (November 21, 1913), pp. 502–3; see also Rinott, "Hevrat ha'Ezra," pp. 272–75 and Adolf Boehm, *Die Zionistische Bewegung*, 1:470–76.
235. Boehm, *Die Zionistische*, p. 471.

236. Ibid., pp. 472–75.

237. ZVfD, *Im Kampf*, p. 3.

238. The Hilfsverein and the C.V. cooperated in anti-Zionist attacks. See *Berliner Tageblatt*, February 5, 1914.

239. See *JR*, no. 25 (June 19, 1914), p. 263.

240. Ibid., p. 266.

241. *JR*, no. 8 (February 20, 1914), p. 80.

242. See the proceedings of the "Verband der juedischen Jugendvereine Deutschlands" of May 11–12, 1913. *IDR*, no. 7 (June, 1913).

243. See *Handels-Zeitung des Berliner Tageblattes*, no. 64 (February 5, 1914), p. 23, and *Vossische Zeitung* (February 5, 1914), p. 15.

244. See *JR*, no. 7 (February 13, 1914). See also Salman Schocken, "Philosophie und Politik; Hermann Cohen und der Zionismus," *JR*, no. 12 (March 20, 1914), p. 123.

245. See *Drittes Morgenblatt der Frankfurter Zeitung*, no. 46 (February 15, 1914), p. 6.

246. See *JR*, no. 25 (June 19, 1914), pp. 263–65, 273.

247. *IDR*, nos. 7/8 (July/August, 1914), p. 302.

248. *IDR*, no. 9 (September, 1914), p. 339. See also the speech delivered by Horwitz on November 23, 1914, in which he urged again that German Jews serve the fatherland *beyond* the call of duty. *Im Deutschen Reich, Feldbuecherei des Centralvereins deutscher Staatsbuerger juedischen Glaubens*, p. 5.

249. *Im Deutschen Reich, Feldbuecherei*, p. 20.

250. *JR*, no. 32 (August 7, 1914), p. 343.

251. Ernst Simon, *Bruecken*, p. 19. See also "Wie ich Zionist Wurde," *Meilensteine, Vom Wege des Kartells Juedischer Verbindungen (K.J.V.) in der Zionistischen Bewegung*, Eli Rothschild, ed., p. 44.

252. Letter to Van Eeden, September, 1914. Buber Archives, Hebrew University, Jerusalem, file 184. Also reprinted in *Der Neue Merkur, Monatsschrift fuer geistiges Leben*, nos. 10/11 (January/February, 1915), pp. 489–92.

253. See, for example, Martin Buber, "Die Loesung," *Der Jude* (1916/1917). Also Hans Kohn, *Martin Buber*, pp. 162 ff. Buber's position was so pro-German that he was reprimanded by his friend Gustav Landauer. See Buber Archives, MS Varia 350, file 61.

254. Kurt Blumenfeld, "Nationale Lehren des Weltkrieges," *JR*, no. 8 (February 19, 1915), p. 65. A recent article has tried to prove that the German Jewish youths who went to war did so not only out of patriotism for the German fatherland, but also to "fight for Jewish aims." See Chaim Schatzker, "Emdato ha'Yehudit-Germanit shel ha'Noar ha'Yehudi b'Germania b'Et Milhemet ha'Olam ha'Rishonah v'Hashpaatah shel ha'Milhamah al Emdah zo," *Mehkarim b'Toldot Am Israel v'Erez Israel*, vol. 2. Edited by B. Oded, U. Rappaport, A. Shochat, and Y. Schatzmiller (1972), pp. 187–215.

255. Auerbach, *Pionier der Verwirklichung*, pp. 352 ff.

256. See Egmont Zechlin, *Die deutsche Politik*, p. 97.

257. Sigbert Feuchtwanger, *Die Judenfrage*, p. 11, n. 4.

258. *IDR*, no. 9 (September, 1914), p. 342.

259. *IDR*, nos. 10/12 (October/December, 1914), p. 377.

260. *JR*, no. 32 (August 7, 1914), p. 343 and *JR*, nos. 41/42 (October 16, 1914), p. 387. Similar statements were made by the C.V. Thus on November 23, 1914, Eugen Fuchs declared: "Der Krieg hat uns recht geeint. Der Krieg ist, so paradox es klingt, der grosse Friedenstifter. Er, der furchtbarste Spalter der Voelker, ist der groesste Einiger der Volksgenossen. Der Krieg nach aussen ist der Friede im Innern, die staerkste Kraft der Einigung." See *IDR, Feldbuecherei des C.V.*, p. 6.

261. There were of course exceptions to this idyllic *Burgfrieden*, notably the famous debate on Zionism between Martin Buber and Hermann Cohen. See Cohen, "Religion und Zionismus; Ein Wort an meine Kommilitonen juedischen Glaubens," Sonderabdruck aus der 11. Kriegsausgabe der K.C. Blaetter. Reprinted in *Juedische Schriften*, 2:319–27. See Buber's "Begriffe und Wirklichkeit, Brief an Herrn Geh. Regierungsrat Prof. Dr. Hermann Cohen," *Der Jude*, no. 5, August 1916. See also the rejoinder by Cohen "Antwort auf das offene Schreiben des Herrn Dr. Martin Buber an Hermann Cohen," *Juedische Schriften*, 2:328–40.

Chapter VI

1. See *AZdJ* (October, 1913), p. 484. For Geiger's views on the role of the Jews in Germany, see also his article in *Judentaufen*, Werner Sombart, ed., pp. 44–48.

2. See Jacob Toury, "Emanzipazia v'Assimilazia, Musagim u'Tnaim," *Yalkut Moreshet*, 1964.

3. Institute of Social Research, "Analysis of C.V. Policy in Germany."

4. See Ismar Freund's analysis of the C.V. in the Freund Archives, CAHJP, P2/Me/19.

5. See Eugen Fuchs, "Referat ueber die Stellung des Centralvereins zum Zionismus," *Um Deutschtum*, p. 241.

6. As was shown in the analysis of the C.V., Fuchs's ideas about *Stamm* were not typical or representative of the C.V.'s ideology at this time. They are significant for the understanding of Fuchs's Jewish identity which was more positive than that of most of the C.V.'s leadership.

7. The entire question of Buber's influence on German Zionism is still open to debate and has not yet been sufficiently examined. It seems that his lectures and articles did make an impact on the young German Zionists. At the same time one ought to keep in mind that precisely in the period before World War I, Blumenfeld often dissociated himself from Buber's ideas.

8. This statement is true at least for the period before 1914.

9. The few German Zionists who did emigrate went to Palestine before 1912 and not as a response to the Posen Resolution.

10. See Eugen Fuchs, "Zur Jahrhundertwende des Emanzipationsedikts," *Um Deutschtum*, pp. 102 ff.

11. Note the statement by the Jewish historian Kayserling: "Wir erblicken unser ideal darin, als Deutsche dem deutschen Staat mit Gut und Blut zu dienen und als Juden den Ewigen unserem Gott zu lieben."

Moritz Kayserling, *Juedische Geschichte und Literatur,* p. 201. For an assessment of Jewish emancipation during the empire see Hamburger, "One Hundred Years of Emancipation," p. 25.

12. See Hans Morgenthau, "The Tragedy of German-Jewish Liberalism," Leo Baeck Memorial Lecture, no. 4 (1961), p. 7.

13. It is true that everywhere Zionists joined the armies of their host countries and there are almost no instances of disloyalty to the fatherland by Zionists. The enthusiasm of the German Zionists—including the radical generation—for the German war effort, however, was matched only by that of the liberal German Jewish community.

Bibliography

Archives

Martin Buber Archives, Hebrew University, Jerusalem

MS Varia 350, file 61. Correspondence between Martin Buber and Gustav Landauer.
File 184. Letter of Martin Buber to Van Eeden, September 1914.

The Central Archives for the History of the Jewish People, Jerusalem

INV/124/1 Protokolle des Centralvereins 1895–1905, vol. 1.
INV/124/2 Protokolle des Centralvereins 1894–1905, vol. 2.
INV/751/3 Aufrufe des Centralvereins 1907.
INV/1698/1–3 C.V. pamphlets.
KGE/64 Antizionistisches Komitee.
P2/Me/19 Archive of Ismar Freund.
TD/24 Aufruf des Centralvereins, membership lists, 1893.
TD/23 Collaboration of major German Jewish organizations with the C.V.

Rabbinerverband in Deutschland
M 4/1 Protokolle 1896–99.

Koenigsberg
Kn II/AII 3 Verein zur Abwehr des Antisemitismus 1891–1922.
Kn II/AII 4 Gesamtorganisationen der deutschen Juden 1901–7.

Regensburg
A/33 Emancipation und Abwehr des Antisemitismus 1813–1900.

The Central Zionist Archives, Jerusalem

Z2 Central Zionist Office, Cologne, 1905–11.
Z3 Central Zionist Office, Berlin, 1911–20.
F4 Zionist Organization in Germany, 1897–1938.
A231 "K.J.V."—Kartell Juedischer Verbindungen (and its predecessors), 1892–1955.

CZA Private Archives

A28 Willy Bambus.
A206 Julius Berger.
A222 Kurt Blumenfeld.
A15 Max I. Bodenheimer.
A141 Adolf Boehm.
A8 Adolf Friedemann.
A135 Sammy Gronemann.
A55 Georg Halpern.
A11 Arthur Hantke.
A142 Alfred Klee.
A56 Richard Lichtheim.
A146 Heinrich Loewe.
A161 Franz Oppenheimer.
A69 Ahron Sandler.
A102 Hugo Schachtel.
A124 Hermann Struck.
A12 Otto Warburg.
A48 Theodor Zlocisti.

G/1293 Gerhard Holdheim, "Die Deutsche Alijah—Ihre Physiognomie—Ihre Reaktionen ihr Zionismus."

W/147/1 Collection of printed manuscripts.

Leo Baeck Institute, Jerusalem

Haas, Berthold. "Memoirs." (Typewritten MS.)
Kollenscher, Max. "Memoirs." (Typewritten MS.)

Archives of the Leo Baeck Institute, New York

Asch, Adolph. "Posener und Berliner Errinerungen 1881–1931."
Breslauer, Walter. "Errinerungen."
Calvary, Moses. "Errinerungen."
File of Emil Cohn.
Goldstein, Moritz. "Ein Mensch wie ich."
Gronemann, Sammy. "Errinerungen."
Haas, Ludwig. [Schrag Haas, Judith]. "Errinerungen an meinem Vater Ludwig Hass."
Herzfeld, Ernst. "Lebenserrinerungen."

Hollaender, Ludwig [Strauss, Eugen]. "Gedaechtnisrede fuer Ludwig Hollaender gehalten am 28. Februar, 1957."
Lichtheim, Richard. "Memoiren. Band I: Ein Rest ist zurueckgekehrt (1904–1921)."
Sandler, Aron. "Errinerungen."
Seligmann, Caesar. "Mein Leben. Errinerungen eines Grossvaters."
Stern, Heinemann. "Lebenserrinerungen eines deutschen Juden und Paedagogen."
Translateur, Salo. "Errinerungen aus meiner ersten zionistischen Taetigkeit: Breslau, Schlesien von 1898–1904."
Weil, Bruno. "Im Dienste des deutschen Judentums. Errinerungen."

Institute of Contemporary Jewry (oral history section), Hebrew University, Jerusalem

Catalogue no. 990, file 26/4. Interview of Kurt Blumenfeld by Dr. Shaul Esh.

Schocken Archives, Jerusalem

File 53/32, Protokoll der V. Sitzung des Landesvorstandes vom 20. Mai, 1925.

Wiener Library, London

Institute of Social Research, "Analysis of Centralverein Policy in Germany" [New York, 1945]. (Microfilm)
See also the replies: [Alfred Wiener]. "The Centralverein deutscher Staatsbuerger juedischen Glaubens—Its Meaning and Attitudes." [John F. Oppenheimer]. "Some Remarks on the Study 'Analysis of Central—Verein Policy in Germany . . . ' " [New York, 1945].
See also Eva Reichmann: "Zur Kritik von 'Analysis of Central—Verein Policy in Germany," Cambridge, 1945.

Yad Vashem Archives, Jerusalem

01/217. Interview by Dr. Ball Khadourie of Hans Klee.

Newspapers and Periodicals

The following newspapers and periodicals were a valuable source in the research of this book.

Allgemeine Zeitung des Judentums, Leipzig/Berlin.
Berliner Tageblatt, Berlin.
Blau-Weiss Blaetter, Berlin.
Central European History, Atlanta, Georgia.
Centralverein-Zeitung, Blaetter fuer Deutschtum und Judentum, Organ des Central-Verein deutscher Staatsbuerger juedischen Glaubens, E.V. -Allgemeine Zeitung des Judentums, Berlin.
Encounter, London, England.

Frankfurter Zeitung, Frankfurt am Main.
General-Anzeiger fuer die gesamten Interessen des Judentums, Berlin.
Hamburger Israelitischer Familienblatt, Hamburg.
Historia Judaica: A Journal of Studies in Jewish History, Especially in the Legal and Economic History of the Jews, New York.
Im Deutschen Reich, Zeitschrift des Central-Verein deutscher Staatsbuerger juedischen Glaubens, Berlin.
Informationen der Zionistischen Vereinigung fuer Deutschland fuer die Vorstandsmitglieder der Ortsgruppen und die Vertrauensleute, Berlin.
Israelitische Rundschau, Berlin.
Israelitische Wochenschrift, Breslau and Magdeburg.
Israelitische Wochenschrift, Kassel.
Jewish Social Studies, New York.
Der Jude. Eine Monatsschrift. Begruendet von Martin Buber, Berlin.
    Sonderheft [1]:*Antisemitismus und Juedisches Volkstum.* Berlin, 1925.
    Sonderheft [2]: *Erziehung.* Berlin, 1926.
    Sonderheft [3]: *Judentum und Deutschtum.* Berlin, 1926.
    Sonderheft [4]: *Judentum und Christentum.* Berlin, 1926.
    Sonderheft [5]: *Sonderheft zu Martin Bubers 50. Geburtstag.* Berlin, 1928.
Die Juedische Presse, Berlin.
Juedische Rundschau, Berlin.
Der Juedische Student, Monatsschrift des Bundes Juedischer Corporationen, Berlin.
Die Juedische Turnzeitung, Berlin.
Juedische Wochenschrift, Berlin.
Der Israelit, Centralorgan fuer das orthodoxe Judentum, Mainz/ Frankfurt am Main.
K. C. Blaetter, Monatsschrift der im Kartell-Convent vereinigten Korporationen, Berlin.
K.C. Mitteilungen: Mitteilungsblatt der im Kartell-Convent der Verbindungen deutscher Studenten juedischen Glaubens vereinigten Korporationen, Berlin.
Koelner Israelitischer Gemeindeblatt.
Der Kunstwart: Halbmonatschau fuer Ausdruckskultur auf allen Lebensgebieten, Muenchen.
Liberales Judentum: Monatsschrift fuer die religioesen Interessen des Judentums, Frankfurt am Main.
Midstream, New York.
Mitteilungen aus dem Verein zur Abwehr des Antisemitismus, Berlin.
Mitteilungen der Juedischen Reformgemeinde zu Berlin, Berlin.
Mitteilungen des Deutsch-Israelitischen Gemeindebund, Berlin.
Mitteilungen des Liberalen Vereins fuer die Angelegenheiten der juedischen Gemeinde zu Berlin, Berlin.
Mitteilungen des Syndikus des Centralvereins deutscher Staatsbuerger juedischen Glaubens, Berlin.
Mitteilungen des Verbandes der juedischen Jugendvereine Deutschlands, Berlin.
Mitteilungsblatt des Irgun Oley Merkaz Europa, Tel Aviv.
Der Morgen. (Zweimonatsschrift), Berlin.

Neue Juedische Monatshefte: Zeitschrift fuer Politik, Wirtschaft und Literatur in Ost und West, Berlin.
Ost und West. Monatsscrift fuer modernes Judentum, Berlin.
Preussische Jahrbuecher, Berlin.
Publications of the American Jewish Historical Society, New York/ Waltham.
Schlemiel, Illustriertes juedisches Witzblatt, Berlin.
Selbst-Emancipation, Organ der Juedisch-Nationalen, Vienna and Berlin.
Strassburger Israelitischer Familienblatt.
Vierteljahreshefte fuer Zeitgeschichte, Berlin.
Vossische Zeitung, Berlin.
Die Welt, Wien/Berlin.
Yalkut Moreshet, Tel Aviv.
Zeitschrfit fuer Demographie und Statistik der Juden, Berlin.
Zion, A Quarterly for Research in Jewish History, Jerusalem.

Reference Works

Baron, Salo W. *A Social and Religious History of the Jews.* 3 vols. New York: Columbia University Press, 1937.
Bureau fuer Statistik der Juden. *Zeitschrift fuer Demographie und Statistik der Juden.* Berlin: Bureau fuer Statistik der Juden, 1905–14.
Das Deutsche Judentum: Seine Parteien und Organisationen. Eine Sammelschrift. Berlin/Muenchen: Verlag der Neuen Juedischen Monatshefte, 1919.
Department of Immigration and Public Works of the Jewish Agency for Israel. *Haaliya, Studies Concerning Matters of Immigration.* Vols. A–C. Jerusalem: Department of Immigration and Public Works of the Jewish Agency for Israel, 1934–36.
Dubnow, Simon. *History of the Jews in Russia and Poland from the Earliest Times Until the Present Day.* Translated by I. Friedlaender. 3 vols. Philadelphia: The Jewish Publication Society of America, 1916–20.
––––. *Die Neueste Geschichte des juedischen Volkes 1789–1914.* 3 vols. Berlin: Juedischer Verlag, 1920–23.
––––. *Weltgeschichte des juedischen Volkes von seinen Uranfaengen bis zur Gegenwart.* 10 vols. Berlin: Juedischer Verlag, 1925–29.
Elbogen, Ismar. *A Century of Jewish Life,* 6th ed. Philadelphia: The Jewish Publication Society of America, 1966.
Encyclopaedia Judaica. Das Judentum in Geschichte und Gegenwart. Edited by Jakob Klatzkin and Ismar Elbogen. Vols. 1–10, A–L. Berlin: Verlag Eschkol A.G., 1928–34.
Encyclopaedia Judaica. Vols. 1–16. Edited by Cecil Roth and Geoffrey Wigoder. Jerusalem: Keter Publishing House, 1971.
Encyclopedia of Zionism and Israel. Edited by Raphael Patai. 2 vols. New York: Herzl Press/McGraw Hill, 1971.
Enzyklopaedia le'Haluzei ha'Yishuv u'Vonav. Vols. 1–10. Edited by David Tidhar. Tel Aviv: Sefarim Rishonim, 1949–71.

From Weimar to Hitler Germany, 1918–1933. Edited by Ilse R. Wolff. 2d ed., rev. The Wiener Library, catalogue series no. 2. London: Vallentine, Mitchell, 1964.

German Jewry: Its History, Life and Culture. Edited by Ilse R. Wolff. The Wiener Library, catalogue series no. 3. London: Vallentine, Mitchell, 1958.

Graetz, Heinrich, *Geschichte der Juden von den aeltesten Zeiten bis auf die Gegenwart.* 11 vols. Leipzig: O. Leiner, 1853–76.

Grosse Juedische National-Biographie. Ein Nachschlagwerk fuer das juedische Volk und dessen Freunde. Edited by Salomon Wininger. Vols. 1–7. Czernowitz, 1925–36.

Handbuch der Juedischen Gemeindeverwaltung und Wohlfahrtspflege 1924–1925. Herausgegeben von dem Deutsch-Israelitischen Gemeindebund und von der Zentralwohlfahrtsstelle der deutschen Juden. Berlin: Bearbeitet von dem Bureau fuer Statistik der Juden. 1925.

Herzl Year Book. Edited by Raphael Patai. Vols. 1–7. New York: Herzl Press, 1958–1970.

The Jewish Encyclopedia. Edited by Isidore Singer. Vols. 1–12. New York/London: Funk and Wagnalls Co., 1916.

Das Juedische A.B.C.: Ein Fuehrer durch das Juedische Wissen. Edited by Emil Bernhard Cohn. Berlin: Verlag Erwin Loewe, 1935.

Juedisches Lexikon, Ein Enzyklopaedisches Handbuch des Juedischen Wissens. Edited by Georg Herlitz and Bruno Kirschner. Vols. 1–4. Berlin: Juedischer Verlag, 1927–30.

Kaznelson, Siegmund., ed. *Juden im deutschen Kulturbereich.* 3d ed. Berlin: Juedischer Verlag, 1962.

Kreppel, Jonas. *Juden und Judentum von heute.* Zuerich/Wien/Leipzig: Amalthea Verlag, 1925.

Leo Baeck Institute Year Books I–XVIII. Edited by Robert Weltsch. London: East and West Library, 1956–73.

Mahler, Raphael. *Divrei Yemey Israel ba'Dorot ha'Ahronim.* 5 vols. Merhavya: Sifriat Poalim, 1956.

Philippson, Martin. *Neueste Geschichte des juedischen Volkes.* 2d ed. 3 vols. Frankfurt am Main: Kauffmann Verlag, 1922.

Philo-Lexikon, Handbuch des juedischen Wissens. Edited by Emanuel bin Gorion, Alfred Loewenberg, Otto Neuburger and Hans Oppenheimer. Berlin: Philo Verlag, 1936.

Segall, Jakob. *Die beruflichen und sozialen Verhaeltnisse der Juden in Deutschland.* Veroeffentlichungen des Bureaus fuer Statistik der Juden, vol. 9. Berlin: Verlag von Max Schildberger, 1912.

Shivat Zion. Edited by B. Dinur. 4 vols. Jerusalem: Hasifria Hazionit, 1950–56.

Sigilla Veri. Edited by P. Stauff. Vols. 1–4. U. Bodung Verlag, 1929.

Silbergleit, Heinrich. *Die Bevoelkerungs und Berufsverhaeltnisse der Juden im Deutschen Reich.* Berlin: Akademic Verlag, 1930.

Sokolow, Nahum. *History of Zionism, 1600–1918.* 2 vols. London: Longmans, Green, 1919.

Sperlings Zeitschriften und Zeitungs-Addressbuch: Handbuch der deutschen Presse. Leipzig: Verlag des Boersenvereins der Deutschen Buchhaendler zu Leipzig, 1926–31, 1933.

The Universal Jewish Encyclopaedia in Ten Volumes. Edited by Isaac Landman. New York: Universal Jewish Encyclopaedia, Inc., 1939–43.

Principal Sources

Adler, S. *Assimilation oder Nationaljudentum.* Berlin: Verlag Emil Apolant, 1894.

[Ahad Ha'Am]. *Kol Kitvei Ahad Ha'Am.* Jerusalem: The Jewish Publishing House, 1947.

Antizionistisches Komitee. *Der Zionismus, seine Theorien, Aussichten und Wirkungen.* Schriften zur Aufklaerung ueber den Zionismus, Berlin, n.d.

_____. *Zionistische Taktik.* Schriften zur Aufklaerung ueber den Zionismus. Berlin, n.d.

Arbeitsfuersorgeamt der juedischen Organisationen Deutschlands. *Die Einwanderung der Ostjuden: Eine Gefahr oder ein Sozialpolitisches Problem.* Berlin: Welt Verlag, 1920.

_____. *Ostjuden in Deutschland.* Berlin: Philo Verlag, 1921.

Auerbach, Elias. *Palaestina als Judenland.* Berlin: Juedischer Verlag, 1912.

_____. *Pionier der Verwirklichung.* Veroeffentlichung des Leo Baeck Instituts. Stuttgart: Deutsche Verlags-Anstalt, 1969.

Auerbach, Leopold. *Das Judentum und seine Bekenner in Preussen und in den anderen deutschen Bundesstaaten.* Berlin, 1890.

Bach, Albert. "Die Loesung der Judenfrage und die Aufgaben des Centralvereins deutscher Staatsbuerger juedischen Glaubens." *Nord und Sued* (November, 1912).

Baeck, Leo. *Mahut ha'Yahadut.* Jerusalem: Mossad Bialik and Leo Baeck Institute, 1968.

Bamberger, Ludwig. *Gesammelte Schriften.* 5 vols. Berlin: Rosenbaum und Hart, 1894–98.

Barth, Aron. *Orthodoxie und Zionismus.* Berlin: Welt Verlag, 1920.

Bernstein, Simon Gerson. *Der Zionismus: sein Wesen und seine Organisation.* Berlin: Juedischer Verlag, 1919.

Birnbaum, Nathan. *Ausgewaehlte Schriften zur juedischen Frage.* Czernowitz: Verlag der Buchhandlung Birnbaum und Kohut, 1910.

Blankenfeld, Fritz, Kimchi, Ernst, and Pinner, Ludwig. *Los vom Zionismus.* Frankfurt am Main: J. Kauffmann Verlag, 1928.

Blumenfeld, Kurt. *Erlebte Judenfrage: Ein Vierteljahrhundert Deutscher Zionismus.* Stuttgart: Deutsche Verlags-Anstalt, 1962.

_____. *Im Kampf um den Zionismus.* Berlin: Zionistische Vereinigung fuer Deutschland, n.d.

_____. "Urspruenge und Art einer zionistischen Bewegung." *Bulletin des Leo Baeck Instituts,* no. 4 (July, 1958), pp. 129–40.

_____. "Wetterleuchten: Aus Errinerungen eines deutschen Zionisten." *Bulletin des Leo Baeck Instituts,* no. 8 (August, 1959), pp. 206–11.

_____. "Der Zionismus; eine Frage der deutschen Orientpolitik." *Preussische Jahrbuecher* 161 (1915): 1–32.

_____. *Zionistische Betrachtungen.* Berlin: Broschueren-Bibliothek des K.J.V., 1916.

Bodenheimer, Henriette Hannah. *Im Anfang der Zionistischen Bewegung.* Frankfurt am Main: Europaeische Verlagsanstalt, 1965.

_____. *Toldot Tokhnit Basel.* Jerusalem, 1947.

Bodenheimer, Max I. *So Wurde Israel.* Herausgegeben von Henriette Hannah Bodenheimer. Frankfurt am Main: Europaeische Verlagsanstalt, 1958.

_____. *Wohin mit den russischen Juden?* Hamburg: Verlag des Deutsch Israelitischen Familienblattes, 1891.

_____. *Zionismus und Judentag.* Koeln: Verlag der Zionistischen Vereinigung fuer Deutschland, n.d.

Boehlich, Walter, ed. *Der Berliner Antisemitismusstreit.* Frankfurt am Main: Insel Verlag, 1965.

Boehm, Max Hildebert. "Vom Juedischdeutschen Geist." *Preussische Jahrbuecher,* vol. 162, no. 3 (1915), pp. 404–20.

Braun-Vogelstein, Julie. *Was niemals stirbt: Gestalten und Errinerungen.* Stuttgart: Deutsche Verlags-Anstalt, 1966.

Breuer, Isaac. *Das Juedische Nationalheim.* Frankfurt am Main: J. Kauffmann, 1925.

Brodnitz, Julius. "Zum Ostjudenproblem." *Mitteilungen der Juedischen Reformgemeinde zu Berlin,* no. 1 (January, 1926).

Brunner, Constantin. *Der Judenhass und die Juden.* Berlin: Oesterheld und Co., 1918.

Buber, Martin. *Der Jude und sein Judentum: Gesammelte Aufsaetze und Reden.* Koeln: J. Melzer Verlag, 1963.

_____. *Die Juedische Bewegung. Gesammelte Aufsaetze und Ansprachen 1900–1915.* Berlin: Juedischer Verlag, 1916.

_____. Feiwel, Berthold, and Weizmann, Chaim. *Eine Juedische Hochschule.* Berlin: Juedischer Verlag, 1902.

_____. Nahum Sokolow, and Achad Ha'am. *Gedenkreden gehalten von Nahum Sokolow und Martin Buber in der Eroeffnungssitzung des XV Zionistenkongresses in Basel am 30. August, 1927.* London: Zentralbureau der Zionistischen Organisation, 1928.

Calvary, Moses. *Beyn Zerah l'Kazir.* Tel Aviv: Am Oved, 1947.

_____. *Die Aufgabe des deutschen Zionismus.* Berlin: Buchdruckerei Wilhelma R. Saling and Co., 1911.

_____. *Das Neue Judentum.* Berlin: Schocken Verlag, 1936.

Centralverein [Zentralverein] deutscher Staatsbuerger juedischen Glaubens. *An die deutschen Staatsbuerger juedischen Glaubens., Ein Aufruf.* Berlin, 1893.

_____. *Generalversammlung des Centralvereins deutscher Staatsbuerger juedischen Glaubens.* Berlin, 1893.

_____. *Die Kongresspolitik der Zionisten und ihre Gefahren.* Berlin: Gabriel Riesser Verlag, 1919.

_____. *Die Loesung der Judenfrage und die Aufgaben des C.V.* Neustadt, 1913.

_____. *Luxus und Not: Zeit und Streitfragen.* Berlin: Philo Verlag, 1922.

_____. *Satzung des Centralvereins deutscher Staatsbuerger juedischen Glaubens E.V., 1893.* Berlin, 1893.

_____. *Taetigkeitsbericht fuer die Jahre 1924–1925.* Berlin, 1925.

Cohen, Hermann. *Juedische Schriften.* 3 vols. Berlin: C.A. Schwetschke und Sohn, 1924.

Cohn, Emil. *Die Geschichte meiner Suspension.* Berlin, 1907.

_____. *Juedisch-Politische Zeitfragen.* Berlin: Kommissions-Verlag Leonhard Simion, 1899.

_____. *Mein Kampf ums Recht.* Berlin, 1908.

Demokratische Zionistische Fraktion. *Programm und Organisations Statut der Demokratisch Zionistischen Fraktion.* Heidelberg, 1902.

Dienemann, M. *Galuth.* Berlin: Philo Verlag, 1929.

Ernst, Ludwig. *Kein Judenstaat sondern Gewissensfreiheit.* Leipzig/Wien: Literarische Anstalt, 1896.

Feuchtwanger, Sigbert. *Die Judenfrage als wissenschaftliches und politisches Problem.* Berlin: Carl Heymanns Verlag, 1916.

Foerder, Ludwig. *Die Stellung des Centralvereins zu den innerjuedischen Fragen in den Jahren 1919–1926.* Breslau, 1927.

Freund, Ismar. *Die Emanzipation der Juden in Preussen unter besonderer Beruecksichtigung des Gesetzes vom 11, Maerz 1812.* Ein Beitrag zur Rechtsgeschichte der Juden in Preussen. 2 vols. Berlin, 1912.

Friedemann, Adolf. *Wir und die Ostjuden.* Berlin/Muenchen: Verlag der Neuen juedischen Monatshefte, 1916.

Frymann, Daniel [Heinrich Class]. *Wenn ich der Kaiser waer'. Politische Wahrheiten und Notwendigkeiten.* Leipzig: Verlag von Theodor Weicher, 1912.

Fuchs, Eugen,. *Um Deutschtum und Judentum: Gesammelte Reden und Aufsaetze.* Edited by Leo Hirschfeld. Frankfurt am Main: Verlag von J. Kauffmann, 1919.

_____. *Glaube und Heimat.* Berlin: Philo Verlag, 1928.

_____. *Rueckblick auf die Zehnjaehrige Taetigkeit des Centralvereins.* Berlin: Verlag Haasenstein und Vogler, 1904.

_____. *Die Zukunft der Juden.* Leipzig: Verlag von Duncken und Humboldt, 1912.

Glatzer, Nahum N., ed. *Leopold and Adelheid Zunz: An Account in Letters 1815–1885.* London: East and West Library, 1958.

_____., ed. *On Judaism.* New York: Schocken Books, 1967.

Goldmann, Felix. *Der Jude im deutschen Kulturkreise.* Berlin: Philo Verlag, 1930.

_____. *Taufjudentum und Antisemitismus.* Frankfurt am Main: Verlag von J. Kauffmann, 1914.

_____. *Das Wesen des Antisemitismus.* Berlin: Philo Verlag, 1924.

_____. *Zionismus oder Liberalismus; Atheismus oder Religion.* Frankfurt am Main: Voigt und Gleiber, 1911.

Goldstein, Moritz. *Begriff und Programm einer juedischen Nationalliteratur.* Berlin: Juedischer Verlag, n.d.

_____. "Deutsch-juedischer Parnass." *Der Kunstwart,* vol. 25, no. 11 (March, 1912), pp. 281–94.

_____. "German Jewry's Dilemma: The Story of a Provocative Essay." *Leo Baeck Institute Year Book,* vol. 2 (1957), pp. 236–54.

_____. "Der 'Kunstwart'—Aufsatz zur Judenfrage." In *Von Juden in Muenchen.* Edited by Hans Lamm. Muenchen: Ner Tamid Verlag, 1959, pp. 130–34.

Gozel, Fr. v.d. *Die Juden und die politischen Parteien. Eine Antwort an den Verfasser der Schrift "Schutzjuden oder Staatsbuerger?"* Berlin: Verlag Richard Wilhelmi, 1893.

Graetz, Zvi. *Darkei ha'Historia ha'Yehudit.* Edited by Samuel Ettinger. Jerusalem: Mossad Bialik, 1969.

Gronemann, Sammy. *Zikhronot shel Yekke.* Tel Aviv: Am Oved, 1945.

Heckt, Georg. *Der Neue Jude.* Leipzig. Gustav Engel Verlag, 1911.

Herlitz, Georg. "Die Lehranstalt fuer die Wissenschaft des Judentums in Berlin; Errinerungen eines Hoerers aus den Jahren 1904–1910." *Bulletin des Leo Baeck Instituts,* no. 35 (1966), pp. 197–212.

Herold, U. *Die Suenden des Berliner Tageblattes.* Hanover: Verlag von Otto Weber, 1920.

Herzl, Theodor. *Tagebuecher.* 3 vols. Berlin: Juedischer Verlag, 1934.

Hirschberg, Alfred. "Der Centralverein deutscher Staatsbuerger juedischen Glaubens." *Wille und Weg des deutschen Judentums.* Berlin: Vortrupp Verlag, 1935.

Holdheim, Gerhard. *Palaestina: Idee, Probleme, Tatsachen.* Berlin: Schwetschke und Sohn, 1929.

_____. "Ueber die Voraussetzungen und das politische Ziel des Zionismus." *Preussische Jahrbuecher,* vol. 162, no. 3 (1915).

_____. "Der Zionismus in Deutschland." *Sueddeutsche Monatshefte/Die Judenfrage,* vol. 27, no. 12 (September 1930), pp. 814–17.

Holdheim, Gerhard, and Preuss, Walter. *Die Theoretischen Grundlagen des Zionismus.* Berlin: Welt-Verlag, 1919.

Hollaender, Ludwig. *Deutsch-Juedische Probleme der Gegenwart.* Berlin: Philo Verlag, 1929.

Juedische Rundschau. *Ja-Sagen zum Judentum.* Eine Aufsatzreihe der "Juedischen Rundschau" zur Lage der deutschen Juden. Berlin: Verlag der Juedischen Rundschau, 1933.

Jungmann, Max. *Errinerungen eines Zionisten.* Jerusalem: Rubin Mass, 1959.

Kanowitz, Siegfried. "Vom Post-Assimilatorischen Zionismus zur Post-Zionistischen Assimilation." *Rueckblick und Besinnung, Aufsaetze Gesammelt aus Anlass des 50. Jahrestages der Gruendung der Verbindung Juedischer Studenten "Maccabaea."* Tel Aviv, 1954.

Kartell-Convent. *Protokoll ueber die Verhandlungen des XII ordentlichen K.C. Tages in Muenchen vom 20 und 21 Juli, 1907.*

_____. *Unser Ludwig Hollaender.* Berlin: Philo Verlag, 1936.

Kaulla, Rudolf, *Der Liberalismus und die deutschen Juden.* Muenchen/Leipzig: Verlag von Duncker und Humboldt, 1928.

Klaerung, 12 Autoren ueber die Judenfrage, Berlin: Verlag Tradition Wilhelm Kolk, 1932.

Klein, Ludwig. *Marxismus und Zionismus.* Prague, 1932.

Kobler, Franz., ed. *Juden und Judenthum in deutschen Briefe aus drei Jahrhunderten.* Vienna: Saturn Verlag, 1935.

Kohn, Hans. *Die Politische Idee des Judentums.* Muenchen: Meyer und Jessen, 1924.

Kohn, Hans, and Weltsch, Robert. *Zionistische Politik.* Maehrisch-Ostrau: Verlag Dr. R. Faerber, 1927.

Kollenscher, Max. *Aktive und Passive Judenpolitik.* Berlin: Rubin Mass, n.d.

———. *Aufgaben juedischer Gemeindepolitik.* Posen: Philipp'sche Buchhandlung, 1905.

———. *Rechtsverhaeltnisse der Juden in Preussen.* Berlin, 1910.

———. *Zionismus oder Liberales Judentum.* Berlin: Zionistische Vereinigung fuer Deutschland, 1912.

———. *Zionismus und Staatsbuergertum.* Berlin: Verlag Zionistisches Zentralbureau, 1910.

Krojanker, Gustav. *Zum Problem des neuen deutschen Nationalismus.* Berlin: Verlag der Juedischen Rundschau, 1932.

Landau, Jacob. *Unsere Einstellung zu Eretz Israel.* Frankfurt am Main: Verlag Palaestina Centrale der Agudas Israel, 1928.

Landauer, Karl, and Weil, Herbert. *Die Zionistische Utopie.* Muenchen: Hugo Schmidt, 1914.

Lazarus, Moritz. *Treu und Frei: Gesammelte Reden und Vortraege.* Leipzig: E. F. Winter'sche Verlagshandlung, 1887.

Lehmann, Emil. *Gesammelte Schriften.* Herausgegeben im verein mit seinen Kindern von einem Kreis seiner Freunde. Berlin: Hermann Verlag, 1899.

Lelewer, Hermann. *Was will der Zionismus?* Berlin: Zionistische Vereinigung fuer Deutschland, 1920.

Levin, Shmaryahu. *Iggrot Shmaryahu Levin.* Tel Aviv: Devir, 1966.

———. *Youth in Revolt.* Translated by Maurice Samuel. New York: Harcourt, Brace and Co., 1930.

Levinstein, Gustav. *Zur Ehre des Judentums.* Berlin: Centralverein Deutscher Staatsbuerger Juedischen Glaubens, 1911.

Lichtheim, Richard. *Kritische Reise durch Palaestina.* Eine Antwort an Dr. Alfred Wiener, Syndikus des Zentralvereins. Berlin: Zionistische Vereinigung fuer Deutschland, n.d.

———. *Das Programm des Zionismus.* 2d ed. Berlin: Zionistische Vereinigung fuer Deutschland, 1913.

———. *Revision der Zionistischen Politik.* Berlin: Ewer Verlag, 1930.

———. *Rueckkehr: Lebenserinnerungen aus der Fruehzeit des deutschen Zionismus.* Veroeffentlichung des Leo Baeck Instituts. Stuttgart: Deutsche Verlags-Anstalt, 1970.

[Loewenfeld, Raphael]. *Schutzjuden oder Staatsbuerger? Von Einem Staatsbuerger.* Berlin: Verlag von Schweitzer und Mohr, 1893.

Marx, Jakob. *Das Deutsche Judentum und seine juedischen Gegner.* Berlin: Philo Verlag, 1925.

Mayer, Gustav. *Errinerungen.* Zurich and Vienna: Europa Verlag, 1949.

Mecklenburg, Georg. *Zionismus und Centralverein.* Chemnitz, 1926.

Mendelsohn, Martin. *Die Pflicht der Selbstverteidigung.* Berlin: Verlag von Imberg und Lefson, 1894.

Minden, Georg. "Unsere Stellung im Judentum und Deutschtum." *Mitteilungen der Juedischen Reformgemeinde zu Berlin,* no. 2 (April 1, 1930), pp. 6–7.

Mueller, Eugen. *Judentum und Zionismus.* Koeln: Verlag J. A. Bachem, n.d.

Nathan, Paul. *Palaestina und palaestinensischer Zionismus.* Berlin: H. S. Hermann, 1914.

Nordau, Max. *Der Zionismus und seine Gegner.* Berlin, 1905.

_____. *Zionistische Schriften.* Berlin: Juedischer Verlag, 1923.

Norden, Joseph. *Grundlagen und Ziele des religioes-liberalen Judentums.* Frankfurt am Main: Druck von Voigt und Gleider, 1918.

Oppenheimer, Franz. *Alte und neue Makkabaeer.* Berlin: Verlag Juedische Rundschau, 1906.

_____. *Erlebtes, Erstrebtes, Erreichtes.* Duesseldorf: Joseph Melzer Verlag, 1964.

Rabbinerverband in Deutschland. *Verhandlungen und Beschluesse der Generalversammlung des Rabbiner Verbandes in Deutschland.* Berlin: Verlag M. Poppelauers, 1898.

Raf, Hans. *Schicksalswende: Ein Wort an die deutschen Juden.* Berlin: Verlag Juedischer Rundschau, 1920.

_____. "Der Centralverein deutscher Staatsbuerger juedischen Glaubens." *Sueddeutsche Monatshefte* (September, 1930).

Rawidowicz, Simon., ed. *Sefer Sokolow.* Jerusalem: The World Zionist Organization and Mossad Bialik, 1943.

Rieger, Paul. *Ein Vierteljahrhundert im Kampf um das Recht und die Zukunft der deutschen Juden.* Berlin: Verlag des Centralvereins deutscher Staatsbuerger juedischen Glaubens, 1918.

_____. *Vom Heimatrecht der deutschen Juden.* Berlin: Philo Verlag, 1921.

Riesser, Gabriel. *Gesammelte Schriften.* 4 vols. Herausgegeben im Auftrag des Comite der Riesser-Stiftung von M. Isler. Frankfurt am Main: Verlag der Riesser Stiftung, 1867–68.

Rosenblueth, Martin. *Go Forth and Serve.* New York: Herzl Press, 1961.

Rosenzweig, Franz. *Briefe.* Unter Mitwirkung von Ernst Simon, Ausgewaehlt und herausgegeben von Edith Rosenzweig. Berlin: Schocken Verlag, 1935.

Rothschild, Eli., ed. *Meilensteine.* Vom Wege des Kartells Juedischer Verbindungen (K.J.V.) in der Zionistischen Bewegung. Eine Sammelschrift im Auftrage des Praesidiums des K.J.V. Tel Aviv, 1972.

Sachse, Heinrich [Loewe]. *Antisemitismus und Zionismus.* Berlin: Verlag von Hugo Schildberger, 1895.

_____. *Der Liberalismus macht Selig und der Sonntagsgottesdienst macht Liberal.* Berlin: Verlag G. Hermann, 1901.

_____. *Dr. Vogelsteins Propaganda fuer den Zionismus.* Berlin: Verlag Juedischer Rundschau, 1906.

_____. *Zionistenkongress und Zionismus . . . eine Gefahr?* Berlin: Verlag von Hugo Schildberger, 1897.

Salomonsohn, H. *Widerspricht der Zionismus unserer Religion?* Berlin: H. Itzkowski, 1898.

Schoen, Lazar., ed. *Die Stimme der Wahrheit.* Wuerzburg: Verlag N. Philippi, 1905.

Schoeps, Hans Joachim. *Wir Deutsche Juden.* Berlin: Vortrupp Verlag, 1934.

Segal, Benjamin. *Der Weltkrieg und das Schicksal der Juden.* Berlin: Verlag von Georg Stilke, 1915.

Simon, Ernst. *Bruecken: Gesammelte Aufsaetze.* Heidelberg: L. Schneider, 1965.

Simon, F. *Wehrt Euch, Ein Mahnruf an die Juden.* Berlin, 1893.

Sombart, Werner., ed. *Judentaufen.* Muenchen: Georg Mueller Verlag, 1912.

_____. *Die Zukunft der Juden.* Leipzig: Verlag von Duncker und Humboldt, 1912.

Steinhardt, Meier. *Juedische Zeit und Streitfragen.* Frankfurt am Main: J. Kauffmann, 1930.

Stern, Ernst. *Ernst Machen: Ein Wort an die Religions-Liberalen Juden.* Berlin, 1935.

Stern, H. *Warum sind wir Deutsche?* Berlin: Philo Verlag, 1926.

Straus, Rahel. *Wir Lebten in Deutschland: Errinerungen einer deutschen Juedin, 1880–1933.* Stuttgart: Deutsche Verlags-Anstalt, 1962.

Strauss, Eduard. *Judentum und Zionismus.* Frankfurt am Main: J. Kauffmann, 1919.

Sueddeutsche Monatshefte/Die Judenfrage. vol. 28, no. 12, September 1930.

Susman, Margarete. *Ich habe vicle Leben gelebt.* Stuttgart, 1964.

Theilhaber, Felix A. *Der Untergang der deutschen Juden.* 2d ed., rev. Berlin: Juedischer Verlag, 1921.

Thon, Jacob., ed. *Sefer Warburg.* Tel Aviv: Massada, 1948.

Trietsch, Davis. *Juden und Deutsche.* Wien: R. Loewit Verlag, 1915.

Treitschke, Heinrich von. *Historische und Politische Aufsaetze.* 3 vols. 5th ed. Leipzig: S. Hirzel, 1886.

_____. "Unsere Aussichten." *Preussische Jahrbuecher,* vol. 44 (November, 1879), pp. 559–76.

Verband der Juedischen Jugendvereine Deutschlands. *Die Juedische Jugend und der Antisemitismus.* Berlin: Philo Verlag, 1919.

Vogelstein, H. *Der Zionismus, Eine Gefahr fuer die gedeihliche Entwicklung des Judentums.* Berlin, 1906.

Vom Judentum. Ein Sammelbuch. Herausgegeben vom Verein juedischer Hochschueler Bar-Kochba in Prag. Leipzig: Kurt Wolff Verlag, 1913.

Wassermann, Jakob. *Mein Weg als Deutscher und Jude.* Berlin: S. Fischer Verlag, 1921.

Weil, Bruno. *Die juedische Internationale.* Berlin: Verlag fuer Politik und Wirtschaft, 1924.

_____. *Der Weg der deutschen Juden.* Berlin: Centralverein deutscher Staatsbuerger juedischen Glaubens, 1934.

_____., ed. *K.C. Jahrbuch 1908.* Strassburg: Verlag von Josef Singer, 1908.

Weil, Bruno, and Cohn, D. *Palaestina, Reiseberichte.* Berlin: Philo Verlag, 1927.

Weizmann, Chaim. *The Letters and Papers of Chaim Weizmann.* 6 vols. Jerusalem: Mossad Bialik, Oxford University Press, and Israel University Press, 1969–74.

_____. *Reden und Aufsaetze,1901–1936.* Edited by Gustav Krojanker. Berlin: Juedischer Buchverlag Erwin Loewe, 1937.

_____. *Trial and Error.* New York: Schocken Books, 1966.
Weltsch, Felix. *Judenfrage und Zionismus.* London: Herausgegeben von dem Zentralbuero der Zionistischen Organisation, 1929.
_____. *Judentum und Nationalismus.* Berlin: Welt Verlag, 1920.
Wiener, Alfred. *Juden und Araber in Palaestina.* Berlin: Philo Verlag, 1930.
_____. *Kritische Reise durch Palaestina.* Berlin: Philo Verlag, 1927.
Wille und Weg des deutschen Judentums. Deutschjuedischer Weg/Eine Schriftenreihe, no. 2. Berlin: Vortrupp Verlag, 1935.
World Zionist Organization. *Bericht des Actions Comites der Zionistischen Organisation an den XI Zionisten Kongress,* Wien, 1913.
_____. *Juedisches Gemeinde-Jahrbuch, 1913/1914-5674.* Berlin: Zionistische Vereinigung fuer Deutschland, 1913.
_____. *Protokoll des XV Delegiertentages der Zionistischen Vereinigung fuer Deutschland.* Berlin: Juedischer Verlag, 1919.
Zionistisches Handbuch. Edited by Gerhard Holdheim. Berlin: Berliner Buero der Zionistischen Organisation, 1923.
Zionistisches Actions-Comité. *Im Kampf um die Hebraeische Sprache.* Berlin: Siegfried Scholem, 1913.
Zionistische Vereinigung fuer Deutschland. *Ausgewaehlte Kongressreden.* Berlin: Verlag des Berliner Bueros der Zionistischen Organisation, n.d.
_____. *Deutsches Staatsbuergertum und juedisches Volkstum.* Berlin: Zionistische Vereinigung fuer Deutschland, 1918.
_____. *Jahresbericht (1911) ueber die Taetigkeit der Zionistischen Vereinigung fuer Deutschland.* Berlin: Zionistische Vereinigung fuer Deutschland, 1912.
_____. *Jahresbericht (1912) ueber die Taetigkeit der Zionistischen Vereinigung fuer Deutschland.* Berlin: Zionistische Vereinigung fuer Deutschland, 1913.
_____. *Statut der Zionistischen Vereinigung fuer Deutschland beschlossen auf dem XIII Delegiertentag.* Posen: Zionistische Vereinigung fuer Deutschland, 1912.

Secondary Sources

Adler, H.G. *Die Juden in Deutschland.* Muenchen: Koesel Verlag, 1960.
Adler-Rudel, Shalom. "East-European Jewish Workers in Germany," *Leo Baeck Institute Year Book,* vol. 2 (1957), pp. 136–61.
_____. *Ostjuden in Deutschland. 1880–1940.* Schriftenreihe wissenschaftlicher Abhandlungen des Leo Baeck Instituts of Jews from Germany, vol. 1. Tuebingen: J.C.B. Mohr, 1959.
Asch, Adolph. *Geschichte des K.C.* London: Selbstvertrag, 1964.
Asch, Adolph, and Philippson, Johanna. "Self-Defense at the Turn of the Century: The Emergence of the K.C." *Leo Baeck Institute Year Book,* vol. 3 (1958), pp. 122–39.
Baron, Salo W. "Aspects of the Jewish Communal Crisis in 1848'." *Jewish Social Studies,* vol. 14 (April, 1952), pp. 99–144.
_____. "The Impact of the Revolution of 1848 on Jewish Emancipa-

tion." *Jewish Social Studies*, vol. 11, no. 3 (July, 1949), pp. 195–248.

_____. "Jews and Germans: A Millenial Heritage." *Midstream*, vol. 13, no. 1 (January, 1967), pp. 3–13.

Bein, Alex. "Franz Oppenheimer als Mensch und Zionist." *Bulletin des Leo Baeck Instituts*, no. 25 (1964), pp. 1–21.

_____. "Der moderne Antisemitismus und seine Deutung fuer die Judenfrage." *Vierteljahreshefte fuer Zeitgeschichte* (October, 1958).

_____. *Theodore Herzl*. Translated by Maurice Samuel. Philadelphia: Jewish Publication Society, 1940.

Ben Horin, Shalom. *Ḥamishim Shnot Ẓionut*. Jerusalem: Rubin Mass, 1946.

Bennathan, Esra. "Die demographische und wirtschaftliche Struktur der Juden." In *Entscheidungsjahr 1932: Zur Judenfrage in der Endphase der Weimarer Republik*. Edited by Werner E. Mosse and Arnold Paucker (1965), pp. 87–131.

Bernstein, F. *Der Antisemitismus als Gruppenerscheinung*. Berlin: Juedischer Verlag, 1926.

Bernstein, Reiner. "Zwischen Emanzipation und Antisemitismus—Die Publizistik der deutschen Juden am Beispiel der 'C.V.-Zeitung' Organ des Centralvereins deutscher Staatsbuerger juedischen Glaubens, 1924–1933." Ph.D. dissertation, Free University of Berlin, 1969.

Bienenfeld, F. R. *The Germans and the Jews*. London: Secker and Warburg, 1939.

Black, Friedrich. *Die Juden in Deutschland*. Berlin: Verlag von Karl Curtius, 1911.

Bloch, Jochanan. *Judentum in der Krise: Emanzipation, Sozialismus und Zionismus*. Goettingen: Vandenhoeck und Ruprecht, 1966.

Boehm, Adolf. *Die Zionistische Bewegung*. 2d ed., rev. 2 vols. Tel Aviv: Hozaah Ivrith Co. Ltd., 1935.

Broszart, Martin. "Die antisemitische Bewegung im Wilhelminischen Deutschland." Ph.D. dissertation, University of Koeln, 1953.

Cahnman, Werner J. "Adolf Fischhof and His Jewish Followers." *Leo Baeck Institute Year Book*, vol. 4 (1959), pp. 111–39.

_____. "Munich and the First Zionist Congress." *Historia Judaica*, vol. 3 (1941), pp. 7–23.

Clapham, John Harold. *The Economic Development of France and Germany, 1815–1914*. 2d ed. Cambridge: At the University Press, 1923.

Cohn, Emil Bernhard. *David Wolffsohn, Herzl's Successor*. New York: The Zionist Organization of America, 1944.

Das deutsche Judentum. Seine Parteien und Organisationen. Eine Sammelschrift. Berlin: Verlag der Neuen Juedischen Monatshefte, 1919.

Deutsche und Juden. Beitraege von Nahum Goldmann, Gershom Scholem, Golo Mann, Salo W. Baron, Eugen Gerstenmaier und Karl Jaspers. Frankfurt am Main: Edition Suhrkamp, 1967.

Deutsches Judentum: Aufstieg und Krise: Gestalten, Ideen, Werke. Edited by Robert Weltsch. Veroeffentlichung des Leo Baeck Instituts. Stuttgart: Deutsche Verlags-Anstalt, 1963.

Deutsches Judentum in Krieg und Revolution 1916–1923. Edited by Werner E. Mosse and Arnold Paucker. Schriftenreihe Wissenschaftlicher Abhandlungen des Leo Baeck Instituts, 25. Tuebingen: J.C.B. Mohr, 1971.

Edelheim-Muehsam, Margaret T. "The Jewish Press in Germany." *Leo Baeck Institute Year Book*, vol. 1, London: East and West Library, 1956, pp. 163–76.

Elbogen, Ismar. *Geschichte der Juden in Deutschland*. Berlin: Erich Lichtenstein Verlag, 1935.

Elbogen, Ismar, and Sterling, Eleonore. *Die Geschichte der Juden in Deutschland*. Frankfurt am Main: Europaeische Verlagsanstalt, 1966.

Eliav, Mordechai. *Ahavat Zion v'Anshei Hod, Yehudei Germania ba'Meah ha'19*. Tel Aviv University, the Institute of Zionist Research. Tel Aviv: Hakibbutz Hameuchad, 1970.

Engelman, Uriah Z. "Intermarriage among Jews in Germany." *Sociology and Social Research*, vol. 20, no. 1 (September–October, 1935) pp. 34–39.

———. *The Rise of the Jew in the Western World*. New York: Behrman's Jewish Book House, 1944.

Entscheidungsjahr 1932: Zur Judenfrage in der Endphase der Weimarer Republik. Edited by Werner E. Mosse and Arnold Paucker. Schriftenreihe Wissenschaftlicher Abhandlungen des Leo Baeck Instituts, 13. Tuebingen: J.C.B. Mohr, 1966.

Esh, Shaul. "Designs for Anti-Jewish Policy in Germany up to the Nazi Rule." *Yad Vashem Studies*, vol. 6. Jerusalem: Yad Vashem, 1967, pp. 83–120.

———. "Kurt Blumenfeld on the Modern Jew and Zionism." *Jewish Journal of Sociology*, vol. 6, no. 2 (December, 1964), pp. 232–42.

———. *Iyunim b'Heker ha'Shoa v'Yahadut Zmanenu.* Jerusalem: Institute of Contemporary Jewry, The Hebrew University of Jerusalem, Yad Vashem, Leo Baeck Institute, 1973.

Feder, Ernst. "Paul Nathan and His Work for East European and Palestinian Jewry." *Historia Judaica* 14 (1952), pp. 3–26.

———. "Paul Nathan, the Man and His Work." *Leo Baeck Institute Year Book*, vol. 3 (1958), pp. 60–80.

Festschrift zum 80. Geburtstag von Rabbiner Dr. Leo Baeck am 23. Mai, 1953. Edited by Eva Reichmann. Published by the Council for the Protection of the Rights and Interests of the Jews from Germany. London: Graphis Press Ltd., 1953.

Flohr, Paul. "From Kulturgeschichte to Dialogue: An Inquiry into the Formation of Martin Buber's Philosophy of I and Thou." Ph.D. dissertation, Brandeis University, Department of Near Eastern and Judaic Studies, 1973.

Freund, Arthur. "Um Gemeinde und Organisation: Zur Haltung der Juden in Oesterreich." *Bulletin des Leo Baeck Instituts*, no. 10 (July, 1960), pp. 80–101.

Friedlaender, Fritz. *Das Leben Gabriel Riessers*. Berlin: Philo Verlag, 1926.

Gladstein-Kestenberg, Ruth. "Athalat Bar Kochba." *Prag v'Yerushalayim*. Edited by Felix Weltsch. Jerusalem: Keren Hayessod, 1954.

Glatzer, Nahum. "Leopold Zunz and the Revolution of 1848." *Leo Baeck Institute Year Book*, vol. 5 (1960), pp. 122–39.

———. *Leopold Zunz–Jude, Deutscher, Europaer*. Schriftenreihe Wissenschaflichter Abhandlungen des Leo Baeck Instituts, 11. Tuebingen: J.C.B. Mohr, 1964.

Goldring, P. *Zur Vorgeschichte des Zionismus.* Frankfurt am Main: J. Kauffmann Verlag, 1925.

Goldschmidt, Hermann L. *Hermann Cohen und Martin Buber.* Geneve: Collection Migdal, 1946.

Graupe, Heinz Mosche. *Die Entstehung des modernen Judentums: Geistesgeschichte der deutschen Juden 1650–1942.* Hamburger Beitraege zur Geschichte der deutschen Juden, vol. 1. Hamburg: Leibniz Verlag, 1969.

Gross, Walter. "The Zionist Students' Movement." *Leo Baeck Institute Year Book*, vol. 4 (1959), pp. 143–64.

Gurian, Waldemar. "Antisemitism in Modern Germany." In *Essays on Antisemitism.* Edited by Koppel Pinson, New York, 1946, pp. 218–67.

Halpern, Ben. "The American Jewish Committee." *Jewish Frontier* 10 (December, 1943), pp. 13–16.

_____. *The Idea of the Jewish State.* 2d ed. Cambridge: Harvard University Press, 1969.

Hamburger, Ernest. "Jews in Public Service under the German Monarchy," *Leo Baeck Institute Year Book*, vol. 9 (1964), pp. 206–38.

_____. *Juden im oeffentlichen Leben Deutschlands: Regierungsmitglieder, Beamte und Parlamentarier in der monarchischen Zeit 1848–1918.* Schriftenreihe wissenschaftlicher Abhandlungen des Leo Baeck Instituts, 19. Tuebingen: J.C.B. Mohr, 1968.

_____. "One Hundred Years of Emancipation." *Leo Baeck Institute Year Book*, vol. 14 (1969), pp. 3–66.

Herlitz, Georg. *Der Zionismus und sein Werk.* Berlin: Verlag Juedische Rundschau, 1933.

Hermann, Leo. *Nathan Birnbaum: Sein Werk und Seine Wandlung.* Berlin: Juedischer Verlag, 1914.

Hirschberg, Alfred. "Ludwig Hollaender, Director of the C.V." *Leo Baeck Institute Year Book*, vol. 7 (1962), pp. 39–74.

Holdheim, Gerhard. *Der Politische Zionismus: Werden-Wesen-Entwicklung.* Schriftenreihe der Niedersaechsischen Landeszentrale fuer Politische Bildung, 1964.

In Zwei Welten: Siegfried Moses zum 75. Geburtstag. Edited by Hans Tramer, Tel Aviv: Bitaon Verlag, 1962.

Isaak, Bernhard. "Der Religionsliberalismus im deutschen Judentum." Ph.D. dissertation, University of Leipzig, 1933.

Die Juedischen Gemeinden und Vereine in Deutschland. Gedruckt mit Unterstuetzung der Gesellschaft zur Foerderung der Wissenschaft des Judentums. Veroeffentlichungen des Bureaus fuer Statistik der Juden, 3. Berlin/Halensee, 1906.

Kahler, Erich. *The Jews Among the Nations.* New York: Frederick Ungar Publishing Co., 1967.

_____. "The Jews and the Germans." *Studies of the Leo Baeck Institute.* Edited by Max Kreutzberger. New York: Frederick Ungar Publishing Co., 1967, pp. 17–43.

Kampmann, Wanda. *Deutsche und Juden.* Studien zur Geschichte des deutschen Judentums. Heidelberg: Verlag Lambert Schneider, 1963.

Katz, Jacob [Jakob] . "Die Entstehung der Judenassimilation in Deutschland und deren Ideologie." Ph.D. dissertation, University of Frankfurt, 1935.

―――. "The German-Jewish Utopia of Social Emancipation." Studies of the Leo Baeck Institute. Edited by Max Kreutzberger, 1967, pp. 59–80.

Kayserling, Moritz. *Juedische Geschichte und Literatur.* 9th ed. Leipzig: Gustav Engel, 1914.

Kaznelson, Siegmund., ed. *Juden im deutschen Kulturbereich.* 3d ed. Berlin: Juedischer Verlag, 1962.

Keren, Hayessod. *Arthur Hantke l'Gvurot.* Jerusalem: Keren Hayessod, 1944.

Klein, Brigitte. "Die C.V.-Zeitung der Jahrgaenge 1925–1935. Zum Problem des Selbstverstaendnisses deutscher Juden." Master's dissertation, Johann Wolfgang Goethe-Universitaet, 1969.

Klinkenberg, Hans Martin. "Zwischen Liberalismus und Nationalismus im zweiten Kaiserreich 1870–1918." *Monumenta Judaica, 2000 Jahre Geschichte und Kultur der Juden am Rhein.* Koeln: Handbuch, 1963.

Kober, Adolf. "Germany." *The Universal Jewish Encyclopaedia.* Edited by Isaac Landmann. Vol. 4 (1969), pp. 541–84.

―――. "Jewish Communities in Germany from the Age of the Enlightenment to Their Destruction by the Nazis." *Jewish Social Studies,* vol. 9, no. 3 (July, 1947), pp. 195–238.

Kohn, Hans. *Martin Buber, sein Werk und seine Zeit: Ein Beitrag zur Geistesgeschichte Mitteleuropas 1880–1930.* 2d ed. Koeln: J. Melzer, 1961.

Krupnick, Baruch. *Die Juedischen Parteien.* Berlin: Juedischer Verlag, 1919.

Lamberti, Marjorie. "The Attempt to Form a Jewish Bloc: Jewish Notables and Politics in Wilhelminian Germany." *Central European History,* vol. 3, nos. 1/2 (March/June, 1970), pp. 73–93.

―――. "The Prussian Government and the Jews. Official Behaviour and Policy-Making in the Wilhelminian Era." *Leo Baeck Institute Year Book,* vol. 17 (1972), pp. 5–17.

Lamm, Hans. "Die Innere und auessere Entwicklung des deutschen Judentums im Dritten Reich." Ph.D. dissertation, Univeristy of Erlangen, 1951.

Laqueur, Walter Z. "The German Youth Movement and the 'Jewish Question.' " *Leo Baeck Institute Year Book,* vol. 6 (1961), pp. 193–205.

―――. *A History of Zionism.* New York: Holt, Rinehart and Winston, 1972.

―――. "The Jewish Question Today: Between Old Zionism and New Antisemitism." *Encounter,* vol. 37, no. 2 (August, 1971), pp. 43–52.

―――. "The Tucholski Complaint." *Encounter,* vol. 33, no. 4 (October, 1969), pp. 76–80.

―――. *Young Germany.* New York: Basic Books, 1962.

Lemm, Alfred. *Der Weg der Deutschjuden.* Leipzig: Der Neue Geist, 1919.

Leschnitzer, Adolf. *The Magic Background of Modern Anti-Semitism.* New York: International Universities Press, 1956.

_____. *Saul and David.* Heidelberg: Verlag Lambert Schneider, 1954.

Levi, Zeev. "Ha'Apologetika ba'Aguda ha'Merkazit shel Yehudei Germania," *Yalkut Moreshet,* no. 12 (July, 1970), pp. 63–83.

Lichtheim, Richard. *Der Aufbau des Juedischen Palaestina.* Berlin: Juedischer Verlag, 1919.

_____. *Die Geschichte des Deutschen Zionismus.* Jerusalem: Verlag Rubin Mass, 1954.

_____. *Toldot ha'Zionut b'Germania.* Jerusalem: ha'Sifria ha'Zionit, 1951.

Liebeschuetz, Hans. *Von Georg Simmel zu Franz Rosenzweig. Studien zum Juedischen Denken im deutschen Kulturbereich.* Schriftenreihe Wissenschaftlicher Abhandlungen des Leo Baeck Instituts, 23. Tuebingen: J. C. B. Mohr, 1970.

_____. "Treitschke and Mommsen on Jewry and Judaism." *Leo Baeck Institute Year Book,* vol. 7 (1962), pp. 153–83.

Lowe, Adolph, "In Memoriam Franz Oppenheimer." *Leo Baeck Institute Year Book,* vol. 10 (1965), pp. 137–49.

Maretzki, Louis. *Geschichte des Ordens Bnei Briss in Deutschland, 1882–1907.* Berlin: M. Cohn [1907].

Margaliot, Abraham. "The Political Reaction of German Jewish Organizations and Institutions to the Anti-Jewish Policy of the National-socialists 1932–1935 (Until the publication of the Nuremberg Laws)." Ph.D. dissertation, Hebrew University, Jerusalem, 1971.

Massing, Paul. *Rehearsal for Destruction: A Study of Political Anti-Semitism in Imperial Germany.* New York: Harper and Brothers, 1949.

Mayer, Max. "A German Jew goes East." *Leo Baeck Institute Year Book,* vol. 3 (1958), pp. 344–57.

Meinecke, Friedrich. *1848. Eine Saekularbetrachtung.* Berlin: Blanvalet [1948].

Meyer, Michael. "Caesar Seligmann and the Development of Liberal Judaism in Germany at the Beginning of the 20th Century." *Hebrew Union College Annual,* vols. 50–51 (1969–1970), pp. 529–55.

_____. "Great Debate on Antisemitism-Jewish Reaction to New Hostility in Germany 1879–1881." *Leo Baeck Institute Year Book,* vol. 11 (1966), pp. 137–70.

_____. *The Origins of the Modern Jew.* Detroit: Wayne State University Press, 1967.

_____. Review of Ismar Schorsch's *Jewish Reactions to German Anti-Semitism. Conservative Judaism,* vol. 27, no. 2, Winter, 1973, pp. 84–87.

Michael, Reuwen. "Graetz and Hess." *Leo Baeck Institute Year Book,* vol. 9 (1964), pp. 91–121.

_____. "Graetz contra Treitschke." *Bulletin des Leo Baeck Instituts,* no. 16 (December, 1961), pp. 301–23.

Morgenthau, Hans J. "The Tragedy of German-Jewish Liberalism." *The Leo Baeck Memorial Lecture,* no. 4. New York: Leo Baeck Institute, 1961.

Mosse, George L. *Germans and Jews.* New York: Howard Fortig, 1970.

_____. "The Influence of the Voelkisch Idea on German Jewry." *Studies of the Leo Baeck Institute.* New York: Frederick Ungar Co., 1967, pp. 83—114.

Mosse, Werner E. "The Conflict of Liberalism and Nationalism and its Effect on German Jewry." *Leo Baeck Institute Year Book,* vol. 15 (1970), pp. 125—39.

Offenburg, Benno. "Das Erwachen des deutschen Nationalbewusstseins in der preussischen Judenheit." Ph.D. dissertation, University of Hamburg, 1933.

Paucker, Arnold. *Der juedische Abwehrkampf.* 2d ed. Hamburg: Leibniz Verlag, 1969.

————. "Der juedische Abwehrkampf." In *Entscheidungsjahr 1932.* Edited by Werner E. Mosse and Arnold Paucker. Tuebingen: J. C. B. Mohr, 1965, pp. 405—99.

Philippson, Martin. *Neueste Geschichte des juedischen Volkes,* vols. 1—3. Leipzig: Gustav Fock, 1910.

Pierson, Ruth Louise. "German Jewish Identity in the Weimar Republic." Ph.D. dissertation, Yale University, 1970.

Pinner, Ludwig. "Vermoegenstransfer nach Palaestina 1933—1939." *In Zwei Welten.* Edited by Hans Tramer. Tel Aviv: Verlag Bitaon, 1962, pp. 133—66.

Pinson, Koppel S. *Modern Germany, Its History and Civilization.* 2d ed. New York: The Macmillan Company, 1966.

————, ed. *Essays on Antisemitism. Jewish Social Studies,* no. 2. New York: Conference on Jewish Relations, 1946.

Pollak, Adolf. *Zionismus: Eine historische Darstellung.* Berlin: Verlag der Juedischen Rundschau, 1934.

Pulzer, Peter G. J. *The Rise of Political Anti-Semitism in Germany and Austria.* New York/London/Sydney: John Wiley and Sons, Inc., 1964.

Ragins, Sanford. "Jewish Responses to Anti-Semitism in Germany, 1870—1914." Ph.D. dissertation, Department of the History of Ideas, Brandeis University, 1972.

Reichmann, Hans. "Der Centralverein deutscher Staatsbuerger juedischen Glaubens." *Festschrift zum 80. Geburtstag von Leo Baeck.* London: Council for the Protection of the Rights and Interests of Jews from Germany, 1953.

Reichmann-Jungmann, Eva. "Der Bewusstseinswandel der deutschen Juden." *Deutsches Judentum in Krieg und Revolution 1916—1923.* Edited by Werner E. Mosse and Arnold Paucker. Tuebingen: J. C. B. Mohr, 1971, pp. 511—613.

Reinharz, Jehuda. "Consensus and Conflict between Zionists and Liberals in Germany before World War I." *Texts and Responses: Studies Presented to Nahum N. Glatzer.* Edited by Michael A. Fishbane and Paul R. Flohr. Leiden: E. J. Brill, 1975, pp. 226—38.

————. "Deutschtum and Judentum in the Ideology of the Centralverein deutscher Staatsbuerger juedischen Glaubens, 1893—1914." *Jewish Social Studies,* vol. 36, no. 1 (January, 1974), pp. 19—39.

————. "Ideology and Practice in German Zionism, 1897—1914." *Conference on Intellectual Policies in American Jewry.* Edited by Herbert

Strauss. New York: American Federation of Jews from Central Europe, 1972, pp. 51–64.

_____. Review of Ismar Schorsch's *Jewish Reactions to German Anti-Semitism, 1870–1914*. *Jewish Social Studies,* vol. 35, nos. 3–4 (July–October, 1973), pp. 297–99.

Rinott, Moshe. "Peulatah shel 'Hevrat ha'Ezra l'Yehudei Germania' ha'Ḥinukh b'Erez-Israel (1901–1918)." Ph.D. dissertation, Hebrew University, Jerusalem, 1969. Published as *Hevrat ha'Ezra l'Yehudei Germania.* Jerusalem: School of Education, Haifa University and Leo Baeck Institute, 1971.

_____. "Gabriel Riesser—Fighter for Jewish Emancipation." *Leo Baeck Institute Year Book,* vol. 7 (1962), pp. 11–38.

Rosenblueth, Felix. *Begriffsbestimmung von Volk und Nation.* Berlin: Verlag Emil Ebering, 1910.

Ruerup, Reinhard. "Jewish Emancipation and Bourgeois Society." *Leo Baeck Institute Year Book,* vol. 14 (1969), pp. 67–91.

Ruppin, Arthur. *The Jews of Today.* London: Bell and Sons, 1913.

Saalheimer, Manfred. "Ueber eine oeffentlich rechtliche Gesamtorganisation der deutschen Juden." Ph.D. dissertation, University of Wuerzburg, (n.d.).

Sandler, Ahron. "The Struggle for Unification." *Leo Baeck Institute Year Book,* vol. 2 (1957), pp. 76–84.

Schatzker, Chaim. "Emdato ha'Yehudit-Germanit shel ha'Noar ha'Yehudi b'Germania b'Et Milḥemet ha'Olam ha'Rishonah v'Hashpaatah shel ha'Milḥamah al Emdah zo." *Meḥkarim b'Toldot Am Israel v'Erez Israel,* vol. 2. Edited by B. Oded, U. Rappaport, A. Shochat and Y. Shatzmiller. Haifa: University of Haifa, 1972.

_____. "Tnuat ha'Noar ha'Yehudit b'Germania beyn ha'Shanim 1900–1933." Ph.D. dissertation, Hebrew University, Jerusalem, 1969.

Schilling, Konrad, ed. *Monumenta Judaica: 2,000 Jahre Geschichte und Kultur der Juden am Rhein.* Koeln: Handbuch, 1963.

Schloesser, Manfred, ed. *Fuer Margarete Sussman: Auf gespaltenem Pfad.* Darmstadt: Erato Presse, 1964.

Scholem, Gershom. "Jews and Germans." *Commentary,* vol. 42, no. 5 (November, 1966), pp. 31–38.

Schorsch, Ismar. *Jewish Reactions to German Anti-Semitism 1870–1914.* New York and Philadelphia: Columbia University Press and Jewish Publication Society of America, 1972.

Schwab, Georg D. "German Jewish Thoughts on Vital Problems During the Years 1920–1933." B.A. thesis, College of the City of New York, 1954.

Segall, Jacob. *Die deutsche Juden als Soldaten im Kriege 1914–1918.* Mit einem Vorwort von Heinrich Silbergleit. Berlin: Philo Verlag, 1922.

Shazar, Zalman. *Or Ishim.* 3 vols. Jerusalem: Hasifria Ha'Zionit, 1964.

Simon, Ernst, "Martin Buber and German Jewry." *Leo Baeck Institute Year Book,* vol. 3 (1958), pp. 3–39.

Simon, Leon. *Ahad Ha'Am.* Philadelphia: Jewish Publication Society, 1960.

Slipoi, Mordechai. *Haoleh Hagadol.* Jerusalem: Pninim, 1963.

Steinman, Ulrich. "Some Notes on James Simon." *Leo Baeck Institute Year Book*, vol. 13 (1968), pp. 277–82.

Sterling, Eleonore. *Er ist wie Du: Aus der Fruehgeschichte des Antisemitismus in Deutschland, 1815–1850*. Muenchen: Kaiser Verlag, 1956.

_____. "Jewish Reaction to Jew-Hatred in the First Half of the 19th Century." *Leo Baeck Institute Year Book*, vol. 3 (1958), pp. 103–21.

Stern, Fritz. *The Politics of Cultural Despair: A Study in the Rise of the Germanic Ideology*. New York: Doubleday and Co., 1965.

Strauss, Herbert A. "Jewish Reactions to the Rise of Antisemitism." *Conference on Antisemitism: Papers delivered at the American Federation of Jews from Central Europe*, 1969.

_____. "The Jugendverband." *Leo Baeck Institute Year Book*. vol. 6 (1961), pp. 206–35.

Studies of the Leo Baeck Institute. Edited by Max Kreutzberger. New York: Fredrick Ungar Publishing Co., 1967.

Tal, Uriel. *Yahadut v'Nazrat ba'Reich ha'Sheni 1870–1914*. Jerusalem: the Magnes Press and Yad Vashem, 1969.

_____. "Milhemet ha'Tarbut v'Maamadam shel ha'Yehudim b'Germania." *Zion*, vol. 29, nos. 3–4, 1964.

_____. "Liberal Protestantism and the Jews in the Second Reich 1870–1914." *Jewish Social Studies* 26 (1964), pp. 23–41.

Theilhaber, Felix A. *Die Juden im Weltkriege*. Berlin: Welt Verlag, 1916.

Toury, Jacob. "Emanzipazia v'Assimilazia-Mussagim u'Tnaim." *Yalkut Moreshet*, no. 2 (April, 1964).

_____. "Organizational Problems of German Jewry—Steps Towards the Establishment of a Central Organization (1893–1920)." *Leo Baeck Institute Year Book*, vol. 13 (1968), pp. 57–90.

_____. "Ostjuedische Handarbeiter in Deutschland vor 1914." *Bulletin des Leo Baeck Instituts*, no. 21 (1963), pp. 81–92.

_____. "Tokhnit Yom ha'Kahal v'Ziyoney Germania." *Zionism*. Studies in the History of the Zionist Movement and of the Jews in Palestine, vol. 1. Edited by Daniel Karpi. Tel Aviv: Hakkibutz ha'Meuchad, 1970, pp. 9–56.

_____. "Nisionot l'Nihul Mediniut Yehudit Azmait b'Germania (1893–1918)." *Zion*, vol 28, nos. 3–4 (1963), pp. 165–205.

_____. *Die politischen Orientierungen der Juden in Deutschland: Von Jena bis Weimar*. Schriftenreihe wissenschaftlicher Abhandlungen des Leo Baeck Instituts, 15. Tuebingen: J. C. B. Mohr, 1966.

_____. *Mehumah u'Mevukha b'Mahapekhat 1848*. Tel Aviv: Moreshet and Tel Aviv University, 1968.

Tramer, Hans. "Bernhard und Emil Cohn." *Bulletin des Leo Baeck Instituts*, no. 8 (1965), pp. 326–45.

_____. "Juedischer Wanderbund Blau-Weiss: Ein Beitrag zu seiner aeusseren Geschichte." *Bulletin des Leo Baeck Instituts*, no. 17 (June, 1962), pp. 23–44.

Valentin, Veit. *Geschichte der deutschen Revolution von 1848–1849*. 2 vols. Berlin: Verlag Ullstein, 1930–31.

Walter, Frank. *Hofprediger Adolf Stoecker und die christlich-soziale Bewegung*. Berlin: R. Hobbing, 1928.

Wawrzinek, Kurt. *Die Entstehung der deutschen Antisemitenparteien (1873–1890).* Berlin: Verlag von Emil Ebering, 1927.

Weinberg, Jehuda Louis. *Heinrich Loewe: Aus der Fruehzeit des Zionismus.* Jerusalem: Verlag Rubin Mass, 1946.

Weltsch, Felix, ed. *Prag v'Yerushalayim: Sefer lezekher Leo Hermann.* Jerusalem: Keren Hayessod Publications, (n.d.).

Wiener, Alfred. *Das Deutsche Judentum in Politischer, Wirtschaftlicher und Kultureller Hinsicht.* Berlin: Philo Verlag, 1924.

Wilhelm, Kurt. "The Jewish Community in the Post-Emancipation Period." *Leo Baeck Institute Year Book,* vol. 2 (1957), pp. 47–75.

Zechlin, Egmont. *Die deutsche Politik und die Juden im Ersten Weltkrieg.* Goettingen: Vandenhoeck und Ruprecht, 1969.

Zielenziger, Kurt. *Juden in der deutschen Wirtschaft.* Berlin: Welt-Verlag, 1930.

Index